Crime and Justice

Crime and Justice

An Annual Review of Research

Edited by Michael Tonry and Norval Morris

VOLUME 3

The University of Chicago Press, Chicago and London

The University of Chicago Press, Chicago 60637
The University of Chicago Press, Ltd., London

ISSN: 0192-3234
ISBN: (cloth) 0-226-80795-9
        (paper) 0-226-80796-7

This volume was prepared under Grant Number #80-IF-CX-0022
awarded to the University of Maryland by the National Institute
of Justice, U.S. Department of Justice, under the Omnibus
Crime Control and Safe Streets Act of 1968 as amended. Points
of view or opinions expressed in this volume are those of the editors
or authors and do not necessarily represent the official position
or policies of the U.S. Department of Justice.

Contents

Introduction

With the publication of this third volume of *Crime and Justice: An Annual Review of Resarch* we have the sense of a series launched. The first volume was a tentative event; the second, a hopeful repetition; but with the third, it may not be foolish optimism to believe that the series will continue and make a growing and lasting contribution to knowledge about crime and its treatment. If a burst of puffing is permitted we believe the series has achieved the unusual combination of high scholarly standards and readability.

In the introduction to volume 1 we told of the initiative of senior officials in the National Institute of Law Enforcement and Criminal Justice (later the National Institute of Justice) in starting this series, and we added the affectedly smart comment that the bureaucracy is not always regarded as a setting congenial to the production of obviously useful plans. Editing these volumes has taught us a good deal, not the least that that was a silly sentence. As one looks back over the diversity of topics discussed in the first three volumes it becomes clear that much of the knowledge presented in these essays is a product of studies supported by the National Institute and that many of our authors have pursued substantial parts of their recent scholarly work under its aegis. It is fashionable but silly in academic circles to minimize the important encouragement received from federal sources; and this series is another example, in our view, of the value of that support to the acquisition and dissemination of knowledge about crime and its treatment.

As to the menu in this volume. The intellectual net is cast wide as a glance at the table of contents will reveal.

Speaking of fashions, you would be unwise not to give close attention to Martin Orne's essay on the use and misuse of hypnosis in court; much sensational rubbish is written on that topic; an originally skeptical Board shifted to confident acceptance of this essay.

The essays by Richard Sparks on surveys of victimization, by Elizabeth Loftus on psychological research on eyewitness testimony, by Shearing and Stenning on modern private security, and by Ted Robert Gurr on historical trends in violent crime are state-of-the-art surveys on topics falling within the accepted core of research on crime and justice. The other two essays do not and merit further introductory comment.

Michael Ignatieff's critique of recent social histories of punishment is refreshing in that it presents the work of the three best-known historians of that topic, Michel Foucault in France, David Rothman in America, and Michael Ignatieff in England, and with fine impartiality offers vigorous revisionist criticism of the views of all three, himself included.

David Richards discusses the important emerging philosophies of human rights and their implications for criminal justice theory, in particular the work of H. L. A. Hart and John Rawls and the movement away from utilitarianism as a sufficient guide to criminal law and punishment policies. These philosophical developments, it must be admitted, are not yet seen as in the mainstream of criminal justice research and discussion; but we have no doubt of their central importance.

To repeat: with this third volume we have a series launched. We hope you find it of value; we hope it attracts your support.

Michael Tonry

Norval Morris

Richard F. Sparks

Surveys of Victimization— An Optimistic Assessment

ABSTRACT

Surveys of victimization—in which members of the public are asked directly about crimes which may have been committed against them—have been carried out in the United States and other countries since 1966. The National Crime Surveys, currently being conducted by the U.S. Census Bureau for the Law Enforcement Assistance Administration, are the largest program of surveys of this kind and may represent the largest and most expensive data collection effort ever undertaken in criminology. Though the victimization survey has great potential where the measurement of crime is concerned, the method still has many problems; it almost certainly undercounts victimizations, and there is some evidence of bias associated with class-linked variables such as education. The NCS surveys, moreover, now make no use of the longitudinal design which could throw much light on both causes and consequences of victimization. Despite their limitations, the surveys done to date show crime to be relatively rare, and far from uniformly or randomly distributed in the population; other important findings may emerge as the NCS data are better and more fully analyzed. Moreover, the surveys have a great potential impact on police statistics of crime, and may in time constitute an extremely valuable social indicator.

The first modern-day surveys of criminal victimization were carried out fifteen years ago, for the President's Commission on

Richard F. Sparks is Professor of Criminal Justice in the School of Criminal Justice, Rutgers University.

I

Law Enforcement and Administration of Justice.[1] This research technique—which typically involves asking samples of the general public about crimes which may have been committed against them in some preceding period, such as a year—is thus no longer in its infancy. The method's accomplishments to date, however, seem to have been mostly inadvertent or accidental, and as often harmful as beneficial. Should such surveys be discarded as a technique? I think not; but I shall try to show that the victimization survey is still in need of much development before it can become fully useful to society. The question is what kind of development that is to be.

Different constituencies—policy-makers, administrators, academic researchers—want different things from victimization surveys; and it is by no means clear that these different demands are compatible, or that victimization surveying can fully satisfy any of them. For example, federal legislators and administrators may wish to know whether the crime rate is increasing in the country as a whole; state and local law enforcement planners, by contrast, may want data for their own jurisdictions (or, if they cannot have that, then for small areas like their own), and may be more interested in cross-sectional data than in changes in crime rates over time. Researchers who are skeptical about police statistics may want victimization data to test hypotheses about the *causes* of crime, whereas those wanting to provide compensation or other services to victims are naturally more interested in the *consequences* of crime. It is by no means clear that the technique of asking samples of the public about their experiences of criminal victimization is the best way of obtaining each of these kinds of information; and it is even less clear that a single program of surveys can provide all of them.

[1] Ennis 1967; Biderman et al. 1967; Reiss 1967. According to Wolf and Hauge (1975) a similar survey was carried out in Aarhus, Denmark, in 1730; in addition, I once read an account of a nineteenth-century police constable in the West Midlands in England who went door-to-door asking villagers about crimes that had been committed against them, and I should be grateful to have a reference to this account, as I can no longer find it. In modern times the use of survey methods to measure victimization appears to have been advocated at about the same time by Inkere Anttila, Albert Biderman, and Peter Rossi (see Antilla 1964; Ennis 1967, p. v).

The plan of this essay is as follows. I begin by reviewing briefly the victimization surveys which have been carried out, in the United States and elsewhere, since 1966; I then describe what is by far the largest and most important program of surveys of this kind, namely the National Crime Surveys (NCS) which have been carried out by the U.S. Census Bureau on behalf of the Law Enforcement Assistance Administration (LEAA) since 1972. Next, I attempt to summarize the main findings of victimization surveys to date in which one may have some confidence. This section of the essay may seem rather thin; the fact is, however, that there are not yet many findings in which much confidence *can* be had. I then review, at some length, the major methodological problems raised by victimization surveys in general, and by the NCS in particular. One object of this discussion is to estimate the amounts and kinds of methodological research which need to be done in the future; another is to emphasize the extreme caution with which data from victimization surveys done to date must be interpreted. Finally, I attempt to assess the future prospects of this method of studying crime, on the assumption—perhaps rash—that the methodological problems listed earlier can be overcome. I argue that future victimization surveys need to take a number of different forms, in order to provide the several different kinds of data about crime that are wanted by the different constituencies using them.

I. The President's Commission Surveys and Their Impact

Three separate surveys were carried out on behalf of the 1967 President's Commission. The first, avowedly a pilot study, was conducted in Washington, D.C., by the Bureau of Social Science Research (BSSR) under the direction of Albert D. Biderman. A random sample of 511 adults living in three police precincts interviewed in the first part of this study were asked about offenses which might have been committed against them in the preceding fourteen to eighteen months; after some modification of the questionnaire and interviewing procedures, a further 283 adults were interviewed in a fourth precinct (see Biderman et al. 1967). A second survey, also primarily method-ological in character, was conducted by the Institute for Social Research (ISR) of the University of Michigan, under the direc-tion of Albert J. Reiss, Jr. This study included a sample of 595 adults residing in two precincts in Boston and two in Chicago; in addition, interviews were conducted with the owners or managers of a total of 768 businesses and other organizations in those precincts and the four used in the BSSR Washington sur-vey (Reiss 1967). The third of the President's Commission sur-veys was carried out by the National Opinion Research Center (NORC), under the direction of Philip H. Ennis. The design of this survey was by far the most ambitious of the three: it in-volved interviews with the members (again all of them adults) of a national probability sample of 9,644 households (Ennis 1967). The interviewing procedures used in the three surveys were similar.

Respondents were asked questions of the general form, "Since ———, did anyone do X to you?"—where X was an ordinary-language paraphrase of the legal definition of an of-fense, such as "break into your house/flat." Those who gave affirmative answers to these "screening" questions were asked further questions designed to elicit details of the incidents, e.g. the amount of property stolen or damaged or injury inflicted, and whether the incident had been reported to the police; in all three surveys, respondents were also asked a variety of ques-tions on their attitudes to crime, the criminal justice system, the safety of their neighborhoods, etc. (These last data were only cursorily analyzed, and few were ever published; but see McIntyre 1967.)

These three surveys—planned and carried out at remarkable speed—were without doubt landmarks in the study of crime. As I have suggested elsewhere (Sparks 1980a), the three be-tween them uncovered almost all of the methodological issues (discussed in detail later in this essay) which have since been found to be inherent in the victimization survey technique. For example, to what extent can respondents remember crimes that were committed against them, and mention them to interviewers? Will they remember *when* those incidents took place? The major substantive findings of the President's Commission surveys were to be confirmed by most of the surveys carried out in later years. The BSSR, ISR, and NORC surveys had a substantial impact on academic criminology, and stimulated at least three dozen similar surveys (reviewed briefly in the next section of this essay) which were carried out in the decade or so after the three commission surveys appeared. (Paradoxically, the NORC survey, which suffered from a number of serious methodological defects, had the greatest impact of the three, in the sense of being the most widely cited and copied.)[2] The surveys' impact on the commission's own findings is far less clear. The commission actually based most of its conclusions about crime in the United States on data from the *Uniform Crime Reports* (UCR); its two main recommendations concerning the measurement of crime were for centralized and more effective procedures for collecting these statistics, and for a separation, in the UCR "crime index," of violent and property crimes. The commission added, however, that "the survey technique has a great untapped potential as a method of providing additional information about the nature and extent of our crime problem and the relative effectiveness of different programs to control crime" (U.S. President's Commission 1967a, p. 22).

Moreover, in a separate report, one of the commission's task forces pointed out that "further development of the survey procedure is needed to improve the reliability and accuracy of the findings. However, the Commission found these initial experiments produced useful results that justify more intensive efforts to gather such data on a regular basis" (U.S. President's Com-

---

[2] In addition to using questions which were often worded in a very cumbersome way, the NORC study set an arbitrary upper limit of three incident forms per respondent (or possibly per household—the report is not clear on this); "household" offenses such as burglary were arbitrarily imputed to the head of the household; and mentioned incidents were excluded if in the opinion of the research staff they were so trivial that the police probably would have done nothing about them.

mission 1967b, p. 40). The vehicle by which these "intensive efforts" came about was the result of another of the commission's recommendations, namely a National Criminal Justice Statistics Center.[3] This center—first known as the Statistics Division of LEAA, later known as the National Criminal Justice Information and Statistics Service, now a part of the Bureau of Justice Statistics created by the reorganization of LEAA which took place in 1980—began in 1969 to meet with various divisions of the U.S. Census Bureau, to plan a national program of victimization surveying.[4]

This program—which became known as the National Crime Surveys (NCS)—will be described in detail below. At this point, however, two things should be noted. The first is that the NCS surveys were designed and implemented with what can only be described as indecent haste. A full-scale program of national and city-level surveys began in mid-1972; thus little more than two years was allowed for pretesting a new (and very expensive) research technique, in order to try to overcome the problems concerning the "reliability and accuracy" of survey findings which the President's Commission had uncovered. Even the little time that was allowed for pretesting was badly used. Three small-scale pilot studies and a larger field trial were carried out by the Census Bureau in 1970 and 1971; and some supplemental questions on criminal victimization were tacked onto the Quarterly Household Surveys carried out by the Census Bureau in 1971 and 1972. But in my opinion these efforts were both puny and inept; they answered none of the questions raised by the BSSR, ISR, and NORC studies but did raise a

[3] The commission held that such a center "would serve as a central focus for . . . statistics relating to the crime problem, [including] victim surveys" (U.S. President's Commission 1967a, p. 269). Yet at no time so far has it been politically possible to give LEAA's statistical division control over the *Uniform Crime Reports*, which remain firmly in the clutch of the Federal Bureau of Investigation and are likely to continue to do so.

[4] For a detailed account of the inception of the NCS by one of its midwives, see Turner 1975. Turner, a Census Bureau statistician, was at the time temporarily assigned to LEAA; I have relied heavily on his account of the early years of the NCS, though he is not of course responsible for my views on the NCS pretest program and may well not agree with them.

variety of further questions of their own.[5] (For a discussion of these pretests, see Penick and Owens 1976, chap. 3; Sparks, Genn, and Dodd 1977, chap. 3). It is not clear just what bureaucratic imperatives were responsible for this state of affairs.[6] Whatever they may have been, the effect was like launching a battleship after having floated a couple of small and leaky toy boats. As we shall see, the NCS in its present form suffers from a number of defects and limitations; and it is clear, in my opinion, that many of these stem directly from the program's over-hasty implementation.

The second point concerns the motivation behind the President's Commission surveys and most of the others done since that time. Survey methods were first proposed as a way of *measuring* crime; this was done because of dissatisfaction with the *Uniform Crime Reports* and other police statistics, which were widely (and correctly) believed to be not only incomplete but also biased indicators of the incidence of criminal behavior. The "dark figure" of crimes not recorded in police statistics had haunted criminologists for over a century;[7] surveys of victimization were seen as a way of retrieving those "hidden" crimes, and thus of "calibrating" police statistics so as to make them more accurate (see, for example, Anttila 1964, p. 413; Biderman et al. 1967, p. 26; Reiss 1967, pp. 2–3, 143–44; Ennis 1967, pp. 2–3). Little or no attention was given to the problem of *explaining* crime and victimization, or to studying the *consequences* of crime and its impact on society. It can be argued, however, that it is these objectives—and not the mere tallying of numbers of

[5] It is also not clear how much impact the findings (such as they were) of these studies had on the design of the NCS itself. Thus, the San Jose pretest concluded that for certain purposes a twelve-month recall period was not worse than a six-month one; yet, as the report on that pretest makes clear, the decision to use a six-month period in the NCS had already been made—apparently because "timely" data were wanted. Cf. Penick and Owens 1976.

[6] If one were to speculate, a reasonable culprit would be the infamous "high impact" crime reduction program funded by LEAA, which began in 1972; it may have seemed sensible to somebody to evaluate this nonsensical package of dubious crime-prevention tricks by using victimization surveys. But this may be unfair; too often, bureaucrats are forced to seize the day, when it comes to spending such large sums of public money.

[7] For some recent discussions of the problem, see McClintock 1971; Kitsuse and Cicourel 1963; Wheeler 1967.

incidents[8]—with which victimization surveys should be concerned; and that accuracy of measurement, though of course important, is just a preliminary to these ends and not an end in itself. If this point be accepted, it has important implications for the design of victimization surveys which may be done in the future—and for the redesign of the NCS.[9]

II. Surveys in the United States and Other Countries

Because the survey of victimization seemed to promise a solution to the long-standing "dark figure" problem, it is not surprising that in the years after 1967 criminologists were quick to try out the new research technique, not only in the United States but in other countries (in particular the Nordic ones) in which there was a well-established tradition of empirical research on crime and the criminal justice system. Among the earliest surveys done in this country were ones carried out in Phoenix (Institute for Local Self Government 1969) and Minneapolis (Reynolds et al. 1973); according to Turner and Dodge (1972) similar ad hoc surveys were also done in Boston, Washington, D.C., Toledo, Dallas, Brooklyn, and Detroit in the years between 1969 and 1972. Most of these surveys used the NORC questionnaire and procedures (as did the Australian survey carried out by Congalton and Najman 1974).

It is unnecessary here to review the findings of these early studies in any detail. Most seem to have been inspired primarily by the novelty of the method and to have had no further pur-

[8] As used here, and in NCS publications, an *incident* is a specific criminal act involving one or more victims and offenders; a *victimization*, by contrast, is a criminal act against a single victim (whether a person, a household, or a commercial establishment). Thus a single incident may involve several victimizations.

[9] Research in preparation for the redesign of the NCS is currently being carried out by a consortium headed by the Bureau of Social Science Research, Inc., under the direction of Dr. Albert Biderman, and funded by LEAA (contract no. J-LEAA-015-79). At the time of this writing I am associated with this consortium, and many of the views expressed in this paper have no doubt been influenced by discussions which I have had with colleagues involved in this project. I should like, in particular, to acknowledge my indebtedness to Albert Biderman, Robert Groves, Robert Lehner, James Lynch, Albert Reiss, and Howard Wainer. However, none of these persons is responsible for my views (with which they may well disagree); nor do the views in this essay represent the views of the redesign consortium or the Bureau of Justice Statistics.

pose than to show—what the President's Commission studies had already shown—that one could produce evidence of much more crime than could be found in police statistics. Their methodologies were mostly fairly primitive, even by the standards of what was known in 1967; and where (as occasionally happens) there are differences in their findings on some substantive point of importance, it is impossible to tell how far this reflects real differences in crime rates between the areas surveyed, rather than being an artifact of different procedures and associated methodological defects. In most of these surveys, for example, respondents were asked about things which might have happened to them within the twelve months preceding the interview; in others, however, respondents were asked to report on things which might have happened two or even three years previously (e.g. Waller and Okihiro 1977). For a variety of reasons, most of which relate to the fallibility of human memory, it is perilous to compare victimization rates from surveys which differ in this respect. This is so, not only because of possible differences in the rate of falling-off of recall and mentioning of incidents, but also because of the possible existence of a "reporting load effect" (Neter and Waksberg 1965) which may cause people to remember less efficiently when they have *more* things to recall, whether or not those things are *more distant* in time (see Sparks 1980c for a more detailed discussion).

Of more interest are those surveys carried out to try to evaluate crime-prevention programs of various kinds. One of the uses of the victimization survey suggested by the President's Commission, this remains, in principle, an important one. Even if a preventive program should lead to a decrease in the numbers of crimes actually committed, it could also lead to an increase in the reporting of offenses to the police; to the extent that this happens, the impact of the program may be masked in police statistics of crime. But surveys of victimization may furnish an independent measure of crime before and after the program; and by asking those who mention crime incidents whether the police were notified, the surveys can be used to estimate changes that may have occurred in citizens' reporting behavior.

One of the first victimization surveys to be used in this way was the one carried out by Kelling et al. (1974) in connection with the Kansas City Preventive Patrol Experiment; a similar effort at evaluating a team policing program was made by the Urban Institute in Cincinnati in 1973–74 (Clarren and Schwartz 1976). In 1974, Anne Schneider conducted a survey in Portland, Oregon, in an effort to evaluate a number of crime-prevention programs in that city; on comparing her findings with those of an LEAA-funded survey done in Portland in 1972, Schneider found that survey-estimated burglaries had declined but that the percentage of burglaries reported to the police had increased, so that there had been an increase in police-recorded crimes (Schneider 1976).

A few surveys have been explicitly aimed at comparisons of victimization rates, either between different areas of the same city or metropolitan region (Sparks, Genn, and Dodd 1977; Reynolds et al. 1973) or between different cities (Clinard 1978; Stephan 1974; Schwind 1975). By far the most ambitious comparative program of this kind has been carried out in the Nordic countries under the sponsorship of the Scandinavian Research Council for Criminology; this has involved surveys on violent crime and on certain property offenses in Finland, Denmark, Sweden, and Norway (Aromaa 1971, 1974a, 1974b; Wolf and Hauge 1975; Aromaa and Leppa 1973). In part as a consequence of this and other European research, the Organization for Economic Cooperation and Development has recommended that victimization surveys be used to supplement police statistics in OECD countries, though as yet no results from the program have been published (see OECD 1976 for discussion).

In addition, a few studies were expressly designed to investigate the methodology of victimization surveys (Sparks, Genn, and Dodd 1977; Fiselier 1974; Catlin and Murray 1979), and a few others have devoted some attention to methodological issues (e.g. Schneider 1978; Tuchfarber and Klecka 1976). A variety of methodological analyses has also been carried out by Census Bureau staff (see n. 40 below).

There has been something of a falling-off in the numbers of victimization surveys carried out by university-based or other individual researchers since the flurry of activity which characterized the early 1970s. This may be an indication that the novelty of the technique has to some extent worn off and that there is no longer much status within the criminological community to be gained from doing such a survey unless it serves a further important purpose.[10] But it also seems likely that—at least in the United States—the decline in recent years in the number of ad hoc, small-scale victimization surveys is due in part to the existence of a large-scale continuing series of victimization surveys, namely the NCS. Since 1973, the NCS program has produced more data on criminal victimization in the United States than could be adequately analyzed by the entire criminological community within the next decade; no doubt that has had some bearing on researchers' apparent disinclination to collect any more data of their own. In one sense this is unfortunate, since—as we shall see in a later section—the data collected by the NCS to date have a number of serious flaws, and it could well be that smaller-scale studies would have produced data of higher quality and more utility than the mountain produced by the NCS. (It is also unfortunate that almost all of the resources expended on the NCS to date has been spent on *collecting* the data; very little has been spent on data *analysis*, and, at least until recently, virtually nothing was spent on methodological development. For a discussion of this see Penick and Owens 1976.) At any rate, the NCS program seems likely to continue, in something like its present form for at least the next few years; despite its many defects, it is clearly the most important source of data on criminal victimization in this country or anywhere else in the world. Before discussing the findings of victimization surveys and the methodological prob-

---

[10] It is unfortunately impossible to discount completely the problem of "trendiness" here, which has its parallels in the mindless and often inappropriate use of new statistical techniques (path analysis, log-linear models, LISREL) in the *American Sociological Review* and less prestigious journals. Genuinely useful research techniques usually survive this, however; self-report studies, for example, have done so.

lems of the NCS and other surveys, therefore, I shall give a brief description of the NCS and of the data which it has produced.

III. The National Crime Surveys

When it began in July 1972, the NCS program had four components: (1) a *national household* survey; (2) a number of *city-level household* surveys; (3) a *national commercial* survey; and (4) some *city-level commercial* surveys. Of these four, the first is by far the most important and is the only one still in existence; data from the other three components have formed the basis of a number of publications (e.g. Hindelang 1976; Hindelang, Gottfredson, and Garofalo 1978), however, and are available for secondary analysis by other researchers. (These three now-defunct components are briefly described in the Bibliographic Note at the end of this essay.)

The national household survey is based on a sample of about 72,000 dwelling units. Deducting those units found to be vacant, demolished, converted to nonresidential use, etc., interviews are typically conducted at about 60,000 of these dwelling units, with households containing about 136,000 persons aged 12 and over. The sample of addresses or dwelling units is selected according to an extremely complicated multistage design, so as to represent the homes of the population of the United States (for descriptions of the sample design, see Penick and Owens 1976; Fienberg 1977). The total sample is divided into subsamples of about 10,000 (occupied) dwelling units each; interviews at one such subsample are conducted each month, so that the entire sample gets interviewed every six months, or twice a year. Once selected, a dwelling unit remains in the sample for a total of three years, or for seven interviews in all; the subsamples themselves are organized in such a way that one group of 10,000 (occupied) dwelling units is rotated out of the sample at the end of each six-month period, to be replaced by a new group of about equal size. (In the earlier years a few households remained in the sample, for technical reasons, for more than seven interviews; this no longer happens.) The net effect of this design is that the subsample of addresses at which interviews are conducted in any given month will consist in about equal parts of addresses where interviews have been done 1, 2, . . . 7 times. Population estimates of victimization for any particular month are based on data collected from a large number of subsamples which have been in the sample for different periods of time and were interviewed a different number of months after the month in question. (Thus, for instance, population estimates for the month of June 1980 were based on incidents mentioned by persons interviewed during the months of July through December 1980; each of these groups, in turn, was composed about equally of persons at addresses where there had been two, three, etc., interviews.)

At each interview, persons residing in the selected dwelling units are asked about incidents involving victimization which might have happened to them in the preceding six months.[11] Data from the first interviews conducted at each address are not used for making population estimates of victimization, however. Instead, they are used to "bound" the second interviews, which are conducted six months later; that is, they are used to establish a reference point which will prevent duplicate reporting in the second interviews of incidents that in fact happened before the first interviews. In a similar fashion, the second interview—from which data *are* used—"bounds" the third; and so on, until seven interviews have been completed. The purpose of "bounding" (and, to some extent, of the complicated sample design) is to minimize certain biases to which such surveys are prone—about which more later.

Interviewers in the NCS make a personal visit to each included dwelling unit in the first instance, to obtain basic demo-

---

[11] This is not *quite* true, since the questionnaire contains a "forward bound"; respondents are asked about "the last six months—between ———— 1, 19— and ———— 1, 19—." Most households are interviewed in the first week or two of the second of these two months; yet respondents are instructed *not* to mention experiences which may have occurred in that period (until their next interview, if there is one). This mnemonic nuisance is long overdue for demolition.

graphic data for the household living there, and to obtain information from one adult respondent[12] about victimizations involving such things as burglary and car theft which may have been regarded as having been committed against the whole household rather than its individual members. A further set of questions is then asked of that respondent, and of others who are present, about individual victimization (assault, robbery, personal theft, etc.). Persons who answer "Yes" when asked if they have experienced any of these things are then asked a further series of detailed questions about the incidents they have mentioned—the circumstances in which they took place, whether the police were notified, the value of property stolen, and so on. Household members who are not available when the interviewer first calls are contacted later, either in person or by telephone. Proxy respondents are used for 12- and 13-year-old members of the household, as well as for persons who are temporarily hospitalized or otherwise absent, or are incompetent to be interviewed in person.

From the incidents mentioned in these interviews, estimates of victimization in the population[13] are made. Typically, these are estimates of the *numbers of victimizations* which have taken place in, for example, a calendar year, or of the *victimization rate* (per 1,000 households, or per 1,000 persons aged 12 and over, as the case may be) per year. Victimizations are classified by type of crime, using definitions which correspond approximately to those used in the *Uniform Crime Reports;* the offenses covered by the NCS include robbery, burglary, assault, rape, and various types of household and personal theft (including theft of motor vehicles). Where appropriate, these data are further disaggregated to show victimization rates among different subgroups of the population (e.g. by age, sex, race, income), though these breakdowns are seldom by more than one

[12] Who is known as the "household respondent." Until 1975, any competent member of the household aged 14 or over could serve as household respondent. Since then, that person is required to be at least 18, unless the head or wife is under that age.
[13] The "population" in question is the civilian noninstitutionalized population; that is, it excludes persons in mental hospitals or penal institutions, and members of the armed forces (and their families) who are living on military bases.

or two variables at a time for reasons of statistical reliability. Estimates are also made concerning the characteristics of reported incidents (for example, the proportions in which the police were said to have been notified, the amounts of injury or property loss involved, the place in which the incident took place).

This brief account of the NCS is obviously intended to be no more than a snapshot. Anyone seriously interested in the history, structure, and defects of this series of surveys should begin by consulting the final report of the Panel for the Evaluation of Crime Surveys of the National Academy of Sciences, whose evaluation of the NCS was published in 1976 (Penick and Owens 1976; other detailed accounts are contained in Sparks 1980a; Hindelang 1976; Hindelang and Garofalo 1977; U.S. House of Representatives 1978). This account of the NCS has attained its present length for two reasons. The first is that, by any reasonable standards, the NCS constitutes one of the most important (and expensive) attempts to collect data on crime and criminal victimization ever undertaken by anyone, anytime, in any place. I am reasonably certain that—even with government support, much less without it—no criminological research on the scale of the NCS has *ever* been done.[14] Between 1972 and 1977, according to official estimates, the NCS cost about $10 million a year;[15] whether or not those funds were in some sense "wisely" spent, the fact remains that the investment in this research technique is unprecedented and that the potential returns from the NCS surveys are—in comparison to the yield from pretty well everything that took place in the field during the preceding century or more—virtually limitless.

My second reason for focusing here on the NCS is that this

[14] Possible exceptions include the work done on behalf of the Wickersham Commission and the 1967 President's Commission, and by a few of the British Royal Commissions of the nineteenth century. None of these, however, did anything like so much original data collection.

[15] See U.S. House of Representatives 1977b, p. 49, where a figure of $53 million between 1972 and 1977 was given by Mr. James Gregg, then acting administrator of LEAA; Mr. Gregg also stated that data collection costs alone were then (i.e. in 1977) running at about $6 to $7 million per year. The exact basis of these cost figures is unclear.

series of surveys illustrates, more clearly and convincingly than any other set of surveys now available, the problems now confronting this method of research. In a later section of this paper I list a small portion of the methodological defects of the NCS surveys in their present form and show how these defects place distinct limitations on the interpretation and application of the vast amounts of NCS data so far collected. But at least some of those defects, and their associated limitations, are in no way peculiar to the NCS; on the contrary, they are intrinsic to the method of victimization surveying itself and are if anything more clearly exemplified in the ad hoc surveys listed earlier. If, therefore, I use the NCS as a sort of stalking-horse, it is in part for reasons of convenience of exposition, but also in part from a feeling that it is unfair to shoot small fish in a barrel. The NCS has been scrutinized, from a methodological point of view, far more closely in its brief life than most (if not all) of the large-scale surveys conducted by the U.S. Census Bureau. But that merely makes its defects more *obvious* than those of, say, the Current Population Surveys or the decennial census itself; it does not necessarily make them any more *serious*. (Many criticisms of the NCS—in particular, those relating to its sample design and analysis plan—apply with exactly equal force to the Current Population Survey, since the two surveys are very similar in these respects (see Fienberg 1977.) With so much by way of a disclaimer of malevolent intention, let us turn to the findings which have emerged from the NCS and other victimization surveys done to date.

IV. Substantive Findings from Victimization Surveys

The past decade and a half has produced an enormous amount of data on the victims of crime and what befell them. Unfortunately, for methodological reasons to be discussed in the next section of this essay, the amount of information that can be gleaned from these data is limited; most findings to date must be qualified—and many must be qualified right out of existence—because of the limitations of the survey technique in its present form. A few generalizations can, however, be made, on the basis of research to date, which seem to me to be both substantively important and well founded.

1. To begin with, at least if we confine ourselves to a restricted subset of all crimes—roughly, those which make up the UCR "crime index," excluding homicide—it is clear that, for the populations of the United States and other western countries in which surveys have been done, criminal victimization is an extremely rare event. In particular, crimes of interpersonal violence are extremely uncommon. In 1977, for example, NCS data show that crimes of violence including robbery occurred at a rate of 33.9 victimizations per 1,000 persons aged 12 and over; about three-quarters of these incidents involved attempts only and did not result in any physical injury. To take into account the undercounting of such incidents in the NCS, let us arbitrarily double the published rate, being reasonably confident that most of the nonmentioned incidents will be of the less serious kind; such crimes are still rare. A rate per 1,000 persons per year, after all, reflects 365,000 person-days of exposure to risk; double the published NCS rate is roughly equivalent to one incident of "violent" victimization per 5,400 such days, with cases involving actual injury probably occurring about once per 25,000 person-days. The symbolic meaning of criminal injuries is of course quite different from that of accidental injury. But as a cause of *injury*, crimes of violence are much less important than motor vehicle accidents, industrial injuries, falls in the home, and the other natural shocks that flesh is heir to in western industrial societies. The relative rarity of the kinds of crime included in most surveys leads to some formidable methodological problems, but that rarity is also of substantive importance, and, as I have argued elsewhere (Sparks 1980a), it should be kept constantly in mind when we are Thinking About Crime.

2. There is abundant evidence that criminal victimization is not uniformly or randomly distributed among individuals within the population as a whole; and there is some evidence that it is not randomly distributed among any easily definable

subgroup of the population. Most people interviewed in victimization surveys (in the NCS, about 90 percent) report no incidents at all as having happened to them. A small proportion will report one such incident; successively smaller proportions will report two, three, four, etc., incidents as having befallen them; at the extreme end of this frequency distribution, a small number of respondents will have suffered so many incidents that they cannot remember details of discrete occasions and can only recount that a "series" of things took place.[16] In statistical jargon, the distribution of victimization is extremely "skewed"; all surveys done to date have found more "multiple victims" than would be expected purely by chance (see Sparks 1980c; Sparks, Genn, and Dodd 1977, chap. 4; Aromaa 1971, 1974a; Hindelang, Gottfredson, and Garofalo 1978; Nelson 1980). This skewness is also a source of methodological problems for victimization surveys.[17] But it is also substantively important for at least two reasons. The first is that multiple victimization makes the victimization rate (so many victimizations per 1,000 persons or households) highly misleading as an indicator of the *risk* of victimization. Since all of a multiple victim's incidents are counted in the numerator of such a rate, but he or she is counted only once in the denominator, the resulting rate grossly overstates the risk of victimization for the population; at the same time, of course, it grossly understates the risk confronting the unfortunate minority (see Penick and Owens 1976, pp. 126–30; Sparks 1980d, for a more detailed discussion). Despite this, the victimization rate is virtually the only statistic used in

[16] These "series" incidents are not included in the rates published in routine reports on the NCS; numbers of such reports (though not of the incidents involved in them) are separately tabulated. An estimate can be made of the approximate numbers of incidents involved in "series" reports; if these numbers are added to nonseries incidents, the rate of assault in the NCS would be increased by about 75 percent. It is not clear, however, that this is the most appropriate way to treat such cases: some of them may better be regarded as a continuing condition. For a further discussion see Penick and Owens 1976; Sparks 1980a.

[17] One such problem is that the skewness of the distribution greatly increases standard errors; another is that a comparatively small proportion of respondents produces a disproportionate amount of information on all incidents of victimization. For a further discussion see Sparks 1980a.

published NCS reports. These reports, and those of almost all other surveys done to date, perpetuate a confusion between two measures which it is crucially important to distinguish. The first is the *incidence* of victimization; this is what is measured by the victimization rate. The second is the *prevalence* of victimization, that is, the proportions of the population experiencing one, two, etc., acts of criminal victimization in a given period of time. Both of these measures are important; each answers a different kind of question. Measures of incidence might be important, for example, in estimating demands for police services or aid to victims; prevalence measures are needed for the estimation of risk. At the moment, the latter are rarely reported; which is rather like counting up the number of measle-spots in a given year, rather than the number of persons who have had the measles.

The second reason for the importance of the distribution of victimization lies in the almost certain difference in the *impact* of crime upon those who are frequently or chronically victimized, in comparison to those for whom crime is only an occasional mishap. A general finding of surveys since those done for the President's Commission is that direct experience as a victim has remarkably little effect on people's perceptions of the incidence or prevalence of crime, their expressed fear of crime, or their attitudes to the police. In part this is because most people have only minimal direct experience as victims.[18] But the small minority who display an apparently high "proneness" to suffering from crime may well be different. At the moment, we have only scarcely begun even to try to understand *why* some people are multiple victims and others are not (see Sparks 1980b; Hindelang, Gottfredson, and Garofalo 1978). Still less do we understand the consequences of multiple victimization, its impact on the lives of those thus affected, their demand for

[18] Where then do people's perceptions of "the crime problem" come from? To a certain extent, no doubt, from the mass media—especially for those who, like myself, live in areas polluted by the newspapers of Mr. Rupert Murdoch. But there may also be an important effect of what might be called *vicarious* victimization—e.g. of one's friends, family, workmates, or neighbors. This subject has not yet been investigated.

social services, etc. Investigation of the phenomenon of multiple victimization is one of the highest priorities for future research in this area.

3. We have a fair amount of information from surveys about the spatial, social, and temporal distribution of criminal victimization: as a result, a number of well-founded generalizations can by now be made about when and where criminal victimization takes place, at least in western industrial societies. To give a few examples: for most if not all kinds of personal crime, the incidence of crime (like the incidence of crime-committing) is highest among adolescents and young adults, declining monotonically thereafter with age—with those aged 65 and over being the least likely to be victims (see U.S. House of Representatives 1977a, 1978). Again, in general, urban rates of crime are higher than suburban rates, which in turn are higher than rural rates; in this respect, and many others, the patterns of crime which emerge from most surveys are broadly similar to those which emerge from police statistics (see e.g. U.S. Department of Justice 1980a; Gibbs 1977; and compare Wilks 1967). It is also clear that males have higher rates of violent victimization than do females; that blacks (in the United States) have higher rates of violent victimization than do whites; that most personal crime is intraracial; and that in interracial crimes (of the kinds covered by most surveys) blacks victimize whites more than whites victimize blacks. (See, for evidence from the NCS city-level surveys and a discussion, Hindelang 1976; Hindelang, Gottfredson, and Garofalo 1978.)

4. The vast majority of all crimes against individuals are "absorbed" by the victims themselves, without ever being reported to the police. The proportions of cases in which the police are notified vary according to the type of crime involved, of course; commercial burglary and robbery, and car theft, are well reported. But even fairly serious personal crimes—such as household burglary and personal robbery—are said in most surveys to be reported to the police less than one time in two; and when it is recalled that the bulk of crimes not mentioned to survey interviewers are probably not reported to the police either, the

proportion of cases in which the police *are* notified becomes
even lower. It is of interest to note that the available NCS data
show very little variation, either over time or across areas, in
the proportions of mentioned incidents in which the police were
said to have been notified. Some differences do emerge, here
and there; but so far these have not been either marked or consistent (see table 1; and for further data and discussion, see
U.S. Department of Justice 1979, 1980a; Hindelang, Gottfredson, and Garofalo 1978). There are insufficient data, as yet, to
permit us either to confirm or to deny Quetelet's speculation as
to the constancy over time of the "dark figure" of unrecorded
crime. What the survey data now available do show is that
those who argued that the "dark figure" was enormous—and
that police statistics need accordingly to be treated with great
caution, if not ignored altogether—were undoubtedly right.

Table 1 shows victimization rates (per 1,000 persons or
households) for offenses classified as robbery, personal larceny
without contact, burglary and household larceny, in the NCS
in the years 1973–79; it also shows the percentages of incidents
of each type in which, according to survey respondents, the
police were notified. Evidently there are some slight year-to-
year changes in both rates and percentages in this table; some of

TABLE 1

Victimization Rates, and Percentages of Incidents in
Which the Police Were Said to Have Been Notified,
for Selected Offenses in the NCS, 1973–79

Year	Burglary Reported	Rate*	Household Larceny Reported	Rate*	Robbery Reported	Rate†	Personal Larceny withoutContact Reported	Rate†
1973	46.0%	93.0	25.0%	109.0	51.0%	7.0	21.0%	90.0
1974	47.8	92.6	25.3	123.4	53.6	7.1	24.2	91.8
1975	48.6	91.5	27.1	125.2	53.3	6.7	26.0	92.7
1976	48.2	88.9	27.1	124.1	53.3	6.5	26.3	93.2
1977	48.8	88.5	25.4	123.3	55.5	6.2	24.5	94.6
1978	47.1	86.0	24.5	119.9	50.5	5.9	24.3	93.6
1979	47.6	84.1	25.1	133.7	55.5	6.3	23.6	89.0

*per 1,000 households.
†per 1,000 persons aged 12 and older.

these actually attain statistical significance, in the sense that they are unlikely to be due merely to sampling variability. Some more marked fluctuations appear in the figures for various subgroups of the population. Yet it is plain that the general picture which emerges from the table is one of relative stability over time; the same picture emerges from a comparison of percentages of incidents in which the police were said to have been notified, in the thirty-nine city-level NCS surveys carried out between 1972 and 1975. For a variety of reasons, direct comparison of NCS data with the *Uniform Crime Reports* is perilous. But it is clear that the UCR crime index is much more volatile than the data in table 1 would lead one to expect. In 1974, for example, the total number of index crimes known to the police jumped by no less than 16 percent compared with 1973; victimization rates as measured by the NCS were virtually the same in both years. Over the entire period 1973–79, UCR index crime rates increased by 34 percent; personal and household victimization rates for all offenses included in the NCS rose by only 3 and 8 percent respectively, and the percentage of all reported victimizations in which the police were said to have been notified was virtually unchanged.

The available evidence is consistent with the view that victims' decisions to call the police are based mainly on a fairly rational assessment of the costs and benefits of doing this rather than on general attitudes to the police or the machinery of criminal justice. As Skogan (1976) has put it, "the simplest interpretation of [the data] is that people do not report [to the police] when they think that nothing will happen as a result, and that often they are right." Every survey done to date has found that notification of the police is related to the "seriousness," in common-sense terms, of the incident in question. Thus, for example, the police are more likely to have been notified about completed crimes than about attempts; about violent crimes involving a weapon than about those in which no weapon was used; about crimes involving a violation of secure personal space (e.g. burglary) than about those which did not; about crimes involving higher values of property stolen or damaged, or greater degrees of injury. There are of course many qualifications which need to be made to this agreeably rationalistic account. For one thing, some account must be taken of people's perceptions of "seriousness," as well as objective factors like those just mentioned (for an example in which this was done, see Sparks, Genn, and Dodd 1977, pp. 121–24). Some account must also be taken of the influence of victim-offender relationships; this is not easy to do, given the evidence that many crimes by spouses, family members, etc., are not mentioned to survey interviewers. Nonetheless, the general picture is fairly clear.

What are the prospects that victimization surveys may contribute to comparative criminology, and more generally to the cross-cultural study of crime and social control? Clinard (1977) has argued that surveys can provide a basis for cross-national studies of victimization, and in his *Cities with Little Crime* (1978) he has attempted a number of such comparisons, between Switzerland (which by several indicators has a low crime rate) and Sweden (which appears to have a much higher, and increasing, crime rate). A number of illuminating comparisons also emerge from the program of surveys done in the Nordic countries in the early 1970s (Wolf and Hauge 1975), though for methodological reasons the results of these surveys cannot be compared with the NCS or indeed with anything except themselves.[19] Clinard (1977) has also noted that victimization surveys may be especially useful in developing countries, in which police statistics of crime are typically nonexistent. For the moment, however, such comparisons would seem premature. To be well founded, they would need to be based on surveys using identical questionnaires and procedures, which do not now exist; they would also have to deal with variations between countries in both legal and cultural definitions of criminal and deviant behavior. For the moment, victimization surveys seem

---

[19] The Nordic surveys did not use a questionnaire like the NORC or NCS ones. Instead, they used relatively short questionnaires (on average, interviews lasted about fifteen minutes), dealing only with a few crimes or types of crime (e.g. interpersonal violence). These were translated into the different languages involved and administered by a commercial survey firm (in Finland, it was the Gallup organization).

to me to add little if anything to cross-national comparisons of crime rates based on police statistics.

If this list of findings seems depressingly short, remember that it is deliberately so. I have not sought to summarize all of the findings—even the believable ones—from every victimization survey done during the past fifteen years; in particular, I have eschewed a summary of the ever-increasing mountain of "facts" to be found in the more recent reports on the NCS, to which the passionate lover of numbers is referred. Perusal of those reports will show, in fact, what a tremendous *potential* source of information that series of surveys is. A wealth of data is now routinely collected, processed, and published on a range of crime-related topics on which almost nothing at all was known even a decade ago—on where and when crimes take place, on what those crimes cost in terms of injury and property loss, on what the victims did about their victimization, on their compensation or insurance against loss, on who (some of) the assailants were, and a variety of other topics. The data are in important respects incomplete and are thus less informative than they might be; and they are necessarily tentative, for the methodological reasons outlined in the following section. But it should be borne in mind that future methodological research may show that at least some of the data from surveys which have so far been done are correct; to the extent that this is so, it is better to suspend judgment than to condemn outright. Methodological defects in this field may make findings uncertain, without necessarily making them invalid.

V. Methodological Problems of Victimization Surveys

In this section I discuss six sets of problems which may affect the data from victimization surveys and review such empirical evidence on those problems as is available. The first set concerns the failure of some respondents to mention to survey interviewers some incidents which in fact happened to them and the effects which this underreporting may have on population estimates of victimization. The second concerns biases in

survey data caused by differential reporting by various subgroups in the samples or populations surveyed. Third, in surveys (like the NCS) in which respondents are interviewed at
more than one point in time, there is a tendency for fewer incidents to be mentioned in the second and subsequent interviews than were mentioned in the first ones. Fourth, there is
some evidence that the reporting of incidents involving victimization may be affected by the method of interview (e.g. over
the telephone versus face to face). Fifth, and again peculiar to
the NCS at the present time, there are problems of sample at-
trition in a longitudinal or repeated-interview design. Sixth,
some things important for an understanding of observed rates
and patterns of victimization have not been measured at all by
the questionnaires used in the NCS and most other victimization surveys.

A. Under-reporting to Interviewers

All victimization surveys to date have found evidence of far
more crime than appeared in the relevant police statistics; in
some cases, survey estimates were as much as ten times as large
as police-recorded totals. Despite this, there is a variety of evidence that the surveys, in particular the NCS, have substantially underestimated the volume of crime which takes
place. In part, this is because most surveys have only asked
about a subset of crimes; most have focused on the traditional
offenses of interpersonal violence and individual property crime
and have not aimed to measure fraud, "white-collar" crime, or
other categories of misbehavior which the middle classes find
most congenial.[20] But it is also clear that even those crimes
which victimization surveys have tried to measure have been
undercounted, in some cases substantially.

---

[20] It must be added that fraud and many other types of "white-collar" crime are
exceedingly difficult to measure using survey methods, not least because establishing
that such crimes have been committed requires an imputation of intention which may
well be incorrect or unfounded; while this is also true for "ordinary" crimes like assault
or burglary, the problem seems less difficult in those cases. It is moreover true that
victimization surveys to date have focused almost exclusively on crimes that have individuals (rather than organizations) as victims; this too leads to the systematic exclusion
of many crimes committed by the well-to-do.

There are several reasons for this. Perhaps the most important is that the great majority of incidents involving criminal victimization are simply not very salient to the people to whom they occur and are consequently not easy to remember. Evidence on this question comes from a number of studies of survey methodology dealing not only with crime but with illness, medical treatment, and purchases of durable consumer goods (see Sudman and Bradburn 1974, 1977 for an extended discussion). In these studies (known for some reason as "reverse record checks") survey responses are compared with independent validating data; in the case of criminal victimization, for example, persons who have reported crimes to the police are selected (from police or other records) and are then interviewed to see if they mention the incidents in question.[21] The three pretests conducted by the Census Bureau before the NCS program began were of this type (U.S. Bureau of the Census 1970; Yost and Dodge 1970; NILECJ 1972); similar studies have been carried out in England (Sparks, Genn, and Dodd 1977) and in Edmonton and Hamilton, Canada (Catlin and Murray 1979). Without exception, these studies found that considerable numbers of known incidents simply were not mentioned by the victims during the interviews. The proportions not mentioned varied in the six studies, and also varied by type of crime: incidents classified as burglary or robbery were generally the most likely to be mentioned, with about 90 percent being captured by the interviewers; less serious forms of theft, vandalism, and some assaults, however, were not so likely to be recounted to interviewers. In the Census Bureau's pretest in Baltimore (Yost and Dodge 1970), only a third of the victims of incidents involving assaults recalled those incidents and mentioned them to the interviewers.

In all of the studies just cited—and in others involving recall of such things as medical treatment—there was evidence that incidents of any kind were less likely to be remembered and

[21] Strictly speaking, perhaps, one ought not to regard police crime reports as validating survey responses; even if the two accounts of a particular incident are in agreement, both may be incorrect.

reported to interviewers as the time between the incident and the interview increased.[22] Thus, incidents which had happened a year previously were less likely to be captured by the survey interviews than ones which had happened only a month or two previously. This finding, though perhaps unsurprising, has important implications for the design of victimization surveys. To get the most complete and accurate count of crime incidents, respondents should ideally be asked to report on a relatively short period—perhaps just a week, or a month; if this is done, however, very large samples will be needed to produce enough incidents to permit reasonably stable population estimates of victimization. The optimum period about which survey respondents can be asked to report still remains to be determined; it may be that, with proper interviewing techniques, sufficient information can be obtained by asking about a period as long as a year preceding the interview. But that is probably the maximum; the few surveys in which respondents have been asked to report on longer periods (e.g. Waller and Okihiro 1977; Reynolds et al. 1973) almost certainly failed to capture substantial proportions of the "older" incidents which had in fact befallen their respondents. A recent study of crime and victimization in American schools produced evidence of as much victimization among students by asking about *one month*, as the NCS, in which respondents are asked about the preceding six months, estimated to have occurred in a full year. See U.S. National Institute of Education 1978.

It is a truism of social survey practice that the validity of survey data depends primarily on questionnaire design and interviewing techniques. Unfortunately, there is good reason to believe that the questions asked in the NCS and other victimization surveys done to date are very far from being as good as they might be. In most cases, the series of "screening" questions (of the general form, "In the past six months, did anyone X?") has been almost perfunctory. Interviews in the NCS, for

[22] See Sparks 1980c for a more detailed discussion. Sudman and Bradburn (1974) have suggested that such mnemonic losses increase exponentially with time; analysis of available data (e.g. from Catlin and Murray 1979) show, however, that a linear model gives a perfectly good fit.

instance, average only half an hour; those in the Nordic surveys (Aromaa 1971, 1973, 1974a; Wolf and Hauge 1975) took only about fifteen minutes. There is, moreover, good reason to believe that the wording of questions about victimization, in the NCS and other surveys, has been extremely inefficient, so far as prompting respondents' memories and inducing them to report on their experiences is concerned (for a detailed criticism of current NCS questionnaires, see Penick and Owens 1976, chap. 4).[23] At the time of writing, research on this subject is at last getting underway.[24] The fact remains that the data on victimization so far collected, in the NCS and other surveys, have undoubtedly understated the incidence and prevalence of crime in the populations surveyed. Virtually nothing is known about the distribution of that understatement, i.e. the extent to which a failure to mention victimizations occurs disproportionately among particular groups (such as blacks or the elderly).[25]

There is some reason to think that one very important group may be especially underrepresented in surveys done to date. This is the probably small group of "multiple victims" to whom two or more incidents happened in the six months (or other period) preceding their interviews on which they are asked to report. In part this is because such persons obviously have more to remember than one-time victims or nonvictims (and hence may do less well at remembering any of it).[26] In part, however, it is because of a singularly inept feature of the screening questions used in almost all surveys done to date: respondents who answer yes to a question like "Were you assaulted at any time in the past six months?" are asked "How many times?"—with

[23] In particular, the panel argued that the NCS "screen" questions were worded in ways that reflected UCR crime categories, rather than being designed to stimulate respondents' memories. The classification of mentioned incidents (e.g. robbery or burglary) is done on the basis of information contained in the incident forms and not from responses to screening questions; the function of the questions themselves is, or should be, to facilitate recall of incidents.

[24] As part of the redesign consortium mentioned in n. 9 above.

[25] In one study (Sparks, Genn, and Dodd 1977) it was found that failure to mention incidents appeared to be a more or less random phenomenon; but see the discussion of "education effects" in section VB below.

[26] This is another instance of the "reporting load effect" mentioned above; to my knowledge, no methodological research done to date has systematically investigated this problem.

detailed information being collected later in the interview only on the number of incidents then mentioned. This technique—first used in the 1966 NORC survey (Ennis 1967), and continued in the NCS—imposes an almost impossible mnemonic burden on respondents who have been victims on more than one occasion; the result is almost certainly an undercount of the numbers of such persons in the population.[27]

Many other examples of inefficient questionnaire design can be found in the NCS and other victimization surveys done to date. For example, it has been known since (at least) the NORC survey that use of "proxy" respondents—i.e. one member of a household who reports on other members' experiences as well—leads to incomplete reporting of the others' victimization, since the proxy respondent may not remember (or even know of) his or her spouse's or child's experience. Yet the practice of using proxy respondents persists in the NCS, since (as noted earlier) only one member of each interviewed household is asked about "household" crimes such as burglary and motor vehicle theft. In a series of analyses of NCS responses carried out by Richard Dodge of the Census Bureau (Dodge 1975, 1976, 1977) it was found that substantial proportions of all such "household" incidents mentioned in the NCS were first mentioned in response to *individual* screen questions; had questions about burglary and motor vehicle theft been explicitly asked of all members of each interviewed household, the numbers of such incidents reported would no doubt have been even higher. Dodge also found that not inconsequential proportions of mentioned incidents were mentioned in response to general "catch-all" questions, which ask about "anything" being stolen, without reference to a particular context or type of property.

It is sometimes suggested (e.g. Levine 1976) that survey respondents may deliberately fabricate crime that never actually

[27] Compare, for example, the investigation of people's work histories. Nobody in his right mind would try to do this by asking "How many jobs have you had?" Instead, respondents are asked what work they are now doing, what they did before that, what they did before that, and so on. (Alternatively, they may be asked about their first job, then their next, and so on.) Even these techniques by no means guarantee success; but they are far more likely to produce accurate answers than a global "how many?" question.

occurred, so that surveys overstate the incidence of crime. I
know of nobody experienced in actually doing this kind of research who believes such fabrication to be a serious problem. It
may be, however, that some respondents—desirous of saying
what they think the interviewer wants to hear—will recount as
their incident something which in fact happened to their neigh-
bor, or to them at some earlier time; it is possible that this is
part of the explanation for the higher rates of victimization
yielded by interviews which are not "bounded" in the sense
explained in section III above.[28] A further problem, to which
insufficient attention has yet been paid by those doing victimization survey research, concerns the imputations of intention
which respondents must often make when defining a situation
as one which involved a crime. Suppose the respondent returns
home to find a window broken or a door damaged. Was the
damage accidental, or the result of an attempted burglary? In
principle, such imputations of intention can be evaluated, if
enough detailed information about incidents is obtained. No
attempt has been made to do this, however, in the NCS or in
any other survey done to date.[29]

Indeed, the whole problem of how respondents define
situations—both at the time they occur and when an interviewer asks about them at a later time—has been generally neglected. Suppose that A and B have an argument in a bar; A
strikes the first blow, but is later knocked out by B; the bar-
tender calls the police, who arrest A for assault; both A and B go
away believing they won the fight. Which (if either) of the two
is more likely to see this situation as involving an "assault" if

[28] A usual explanation for this difference is that some incidents are "telescoped" in
memory by respondents: see, for example, Sudman and Bradburn 1974. However, as I
have argued elsewhere (Sparks 1980c) this explanation—which rests on no psychological
evidence or theory whatsoever and flies in the face of a good deal of evidence on im-
precision of recounting—may be mistaken. The problem may instead be that present
NCS procedures do not make sufficiently clear to respondents the beginning of the
period about which they are asked.
[29] Incidents are classified as crimes of different kinds, according to definitions not
unlike those used in the UCR, by a computer algorithm which examines details of
mentioned incidents (e.g. use of a weapon, infliction of injury) and classifies the incidents into categories like "assault." Interviewers do record a verbatim account of
"what happened," at the end of the list of structured questions; but this account is not
used in classifying mentioned incidents. For a further discussion of classification (and
the problem of deciding whether a mentioned incident constituted a "crime" or not), see
Ennis 1967; Sparks, Genn, and Dodd 1977.

asked about it five months later? The relatively low proportions
of assaults mentioned in the Census Bureau's three pretests may
be due in part to the fact that the respondents came to regard
the violence used against them as within culturally permissible
limits and thus not as "criminal." Evidence from one of these
pretests (NILECJ 1972) suggests that this is especially likely to
happen when the assailant is known or related to the victim;
similar evidence emerged from the Canadian reverse record
checks (Catlin and Murray 1979). It is clearly a mistake to suppose that respondents' failure to mention incidents in which
they were victimized is due entirely to failures of memory. Not
only definitional factors but also affective ones (e.g. shame, embarrassment) may also lead respondents to fail to recount their
experiences.[30]

For a variety of reasons, then, the NCS and other victimization surveys done to date almost certainly understate, by an
unknown but possibly large amount, the victimization experienced by their respondents. The surveys thus underestimate
levels of victimization in the population, even of the types they
purport to measure. To the extent that measurement errors in
surveys like the NCS remain constant over time, the surveys
may still accurately reflect *trends* in victimization, of course,
even if they understate absolute levels. But it is far from clear,
in the case of the NCS, that measurement error has remained
constant since 1972; thus even data on trends in crime and victimization may be suspect.[31]

B. Response Biases

If measurement error—caused by poor memory, incompetent
questioning,   or   whatever—were   a   reasonably   random

---

[30] Fox and Tracy (1980; see also Tracy and Fox 1979) have suggested that "randomized response" interviewing procedures might be used to overcome respondents'
reluctance to mention certain types of incidents (e.g. rape). The efficacy of "randomized
response" methods is still a matter of much dispute, however; and it is also doubtful
that these methods could or should be used in surveys carried out by the Census
Bureau. Cf. Penick and Owens 1976, p. 74.

[31] As mentioned in n.12 above, it was the case until 1975 that the "household respondent" could be a person aged 14 to 17 who knew little about victimization against
others. The classification by interviewers of incidents as "series" also fluctuated somewhat in earlier years of the NCS; and the proportion of interviews done by telephone
has also increased substantially over time.

phenomenon, it might not matter too much. To the extent that it is not systematically associated with types of persons, incidents, or other objects of survey research (and provided that it is not too great), the undercounting of victimization incidents may pose no more of a problem than any other kind of measurement error to which social science research techniques are subject. Unfortunately, there is good reason to believe that is not so and that data from many victimization surveys, in particular the NCS, are severely biased in several respects. These biases make doubtful a number of inferences which might be made (and have been made) from survey data.

One of the most serious of these biases concerns the almost certain effect on survey responses of social-class-linked variables, in particular educational attainment. "Being a survey respondent" is, in many ways, a middle-class game; it requires a certain amount of verbal fluency and a capacity for abstract conceptualization, both of which are to some extent concomitants (if not consequences) of formal education. In a victimization survey, the tasks which a respondent must perform involve casting one's mind back over a particular period in one's past and fitting descriptions given by the interviewer's questions ("Did anyone break into your house?") to the events which may have occurred in that time. It would not be surprising to find that these classroom-like tasks would be better performed by those with more practice (in the classroom) at them; and there is increasing evidence that this is precisely what happens.

Some evidence of this kind of "education effect" was first noted by Biderman, in his survey for the 1967 President's Commission (Biderman et al. 1967) though since no validating data were available for this pilot study the evidence was suggestive at best. In the survey which my colleagues and I carried out in London, for which validating data from police records were available, there were also suggestions that reporting of incidents to interviewers was associated with level of educational attainment; those respondents who had finished their secondary education before or at the compulsory school-leaving age (i.e. in most cases 15 or 16) were twice as likely *not* to mention crimes which had in fact happened to them as persons who had continued in their secondary education; and those who had had no college or other further education were also more likely to be nonreporters of their victimization than those who had (Sparks, Genn, and Dodd 1977, pp. 58–59). Neither of these associations reached statistical significance; but they suggested, as had Biderman's findings, that the survey findings were to some extent biased by differences in question-answering ability, even though random memory failure appeared to be a more important problem.

Even stronger evidence of a bias associated with educational attainment can be found in published data from the more recent years of the NCS. Table 2, which is based on data contained in the 1977 NCS report, shows victimization rates (per 1,000 persons aged 25 and over), by number of years of school completed, for offenses of aggravated and simple assault. It will be seen from this table that for both black and white respondents

TABLE 2

Victimization Rates per 1,000 Persons Aged 25 and Over, by Race and Level of Educational Attainment

Years of School Completed	Aggravated Assault	Simple Assault
	Whites	
0–4	4.3	7.2
5–7	4.4	5.0
8	3.1	3.9
9–11	6.9	8.0
12	5.4	10.7
13–15	8.0	16.0
16+	6.3	13.6
	Blacks	
0–4	5.1*	2.3*
5–7	7.9	4.6*
8	9.6*	4.0*
9–11	9.0	7.2
12	13.4	9.2
13–15	16.4	10.2
16+	6.0*	25.6

Source: U.S. Department of Justice 1979, table 16.
*Estimate, based on ten or fewer sample cases, is statistically unreliable.

there is a general tendency for victimization rates to *increase* with years of education, so that, for white respondents, those with some college have a rate of aggravated assault over twice as high as those who have only completed eighth grade; similarly, among black respondents, those with some college had twice the rate of aggravated assault victimization as those with less than an eighth-grade education. The differentials for simple assault are if anything even greater: for whites, those with some college reported over four times as much simple assault as those who had gone no further than the eighth grade; black college graduates reported rates of simple assault that are about six times the rates for those whose education ended in elementary school.

Similar trends are evident in the data (in the 1975–77 NCS reports) for reported rates of both armed and unarmed robbery and for personal larceny with and without contact. While these trends may at first sight seem plausible (better educated people tend to be richer, hence have more to steal), there is no ground whatever, either in criminological theory or common sense, for supposing that college graduates are about twice as likely to suffer aggravated assault as those who never even got to high school. Between believing such a wild implausibility, and doubting the validity of the survey data, the choice should be clear: table 2 reflects clear evidence of response bias. This bias is all the more serious in view of the strong associations which exist in contemporary American society between educational attainment and other demographic and social variables which are important both for criminological theory and for public policy concerning crime: that is, variables such as age, sex, race, income, area, and region of residence.[32] A response effect due to educational attainment is thus likely to infect pretty well any inference about victimization which might be made from NCS data. Yet at no time has this ever been mentioned, in any official NCS publication; nor am I aware that any academic

[32] Thus, for example, blacks, older persons, females, lower-income persons, southerners, and rural residents are, on average, less educated than their counterparts; the interrelations between these things, and the effects of those interrelations on educational attainment, may be extremely complicated.

analysis of crime or victimization based on NCS data has yet attempted to control for educational attainment.[33]

I noted earlier that there is evidence that assaults in which the offender was known or related to the victim are less likely to be mentioned to survey interviewers than those in which the assailant was a stranger. To the extent that this is the case, the picture of crime which emerges from survey data will be not only incomplete but biased—in a way which, given public concern about "the problem of violence," may have serious practical consequences.[34] But the differential definition of situations involving interpersonal violence (which is what is at issue here) may be a function not only of particular types of incidents but of subcultural variations among different groups; to the extent that such variation influences survey responses, comparisons of those groups' experiences (as revealed by survey data) may be misleading. Table 2 illustrates this point. Overall rates of assault victimization (aggravated and simple combined) are about the same, according to the NCS, for whites and blacks; in fact, in 1977, the rate was 26.8 per 1,000 persons aged 12 and over for whites, and 27.9 per 1,000 for blacks (U.S. Department of Justice 1979, table 7). But it will be seen from table 2 that, in general, white respondents mention more *simple* assaults; for most educational levels, the ratio of simple to aggravated is about 2:1. Black respondents, by contrast, are more likely to mention *aggravated* assaults; for all groups except college graduates, the ratio of simple to aggravated is about 1:2, or just the reverse of that for whites. (It is of interest to note that the ratio for blacks shifts slightly as educational level increases, being about 1:1.5 for high school graduates and those with some college. The ratio of 1:4 for black college graduates in table 2 is probably due to the

---

[33] See, for example, Hindelang, Gottfredson, and Garofalo 1978, where the subject is not even mentioned. Admittedly it is not easy to introduce such controls, especially for relatively rare types of crime.

[34] Thus, for example, early NCS reports stated baldly that most violent crime was committed by strangers; this statement was repeated by President Ford in his message to Congress on crime, on 19 June 1975 (see the *LEAA Newsletter*, June–July 1975, pp. 1–2). Presidents' pronouncements, of course, can be no more sensible than the briefings they receive; would that they were never less so.

statistically unreliable aggravated assault rate of 6.0 per 1,000 for that group in 1977; comparable tables for earlier years show a ratio near to 1:1). These data may conceivably reflect a real difference in the experiences of blacks and whites; that is, it may be that blacks, *if* assaulted at all, are more likely to be assaulted with a weapon, or to receive serious injury, than whites. But it seems at least as likely that the data reflect a response effect, with blacks (especially the less educated ones) being much less likely to mention simple assaults to interviewers than are white respondents. (For evidence of a similar response effect linked to social class rather than race, see Sparks, Genn, and Dodd 1977, pp. 79–80.)

C. Time-in-Sample Bias

Two other important kinds of response biases are known to be present in the NCS and should be taken into account by anyone attempting to use the data from those surveys. The first is known as "time-in-sample" or "rotation group" bias. Respondents in the NCS are supposed to be interviewed a total of seven times, at six-monthly intervals. Analyses of NCS data by Woltman and Bushery (1975, 1977a, 1977b) have shown, however, that there is a monotonic decrease in victimization rates, as the number of interviews increases; that is, respondents are less likely to mention incidents at their second, third, . . . seventh interviews. I suppose this might conceivably be due to a kind of "insulating" effect of participation in the survey itself; respondents, more mindful of crime, might take more precautions against it and thus lower their later victimization rates. But "rotation group" bias has been found in a number of other panel surveys as well (see Bailar 1975); and a much more plausible explanation for its appearance in the NCS is that some of those who have mentioned incidents in earlier interviews, only to be asked a barrage of detailed and time-consuming questions about those incidents, are less willing to be cooperative in later interviews. (Again, it may be that this is especially true for the small but important group of "multiple victims.") Since the beginning of 1977, the NCS sample is supposed to contain about equal numbers of persons interviewed one, two, . . . seven times. In earlier years, however, this was not the case; and estimates of changes in victimization rates across those years may thus be affected to some extent by time-in-sample bias. Again, it is not known how this phenomenon may affect different subgroups of the sample, e.g. blacks or the elderly.

D. Method of Interview

The second source of almost-certain bias in the NCS is due to the fact that some respondents are interviewed in person, whereas others are interviewed by telephone. Recent research by the Census Bureau (Woltman and Bushery 1978; see also Turner 1977) showed that respondents interviewed in person reported higher rates of victimization, for almost every type of offense and category of respondent, than those interviewed by telephone. Other researchers have found that telephone interviewing did not reduce reported victimization rates (Catlin and Murray 1979; Tuchfarber and Klecka 1976); and there are special methods of telephone interviewing (e.g. using computer assistance: Rustmeyer and Levin 1977) that are undoubtedly more efficient than the present NCS practice, which merely involves reading out over the telephone a questionnaire designed for face-to-face interviewing. Nonetheless, the use of the telephone now appears to result in some undercounting in the NCS;[35] this affects the interpretation of existing data from the NCS, since the proportion of interviews conducted by telephone has risen steadily, from about 25 percent in 1974 to over 60 percent in 1980.[36]

E. Movers and Stayers

A further methodological problem is, for the moment, unique to the NCS, because only that series of victimization surveys has

[35] In addition, the use of the telephone for interviewing may introduce some *sample* bias into surveys, since the 5 percent of American households without a telephone are disproportionately nonwhite and low-income. See Groves 1977 for a discussion. "Random-digit dialing" methods (advocated by Tuchfarber and Klecka 1976, among others) would thus certainly bias NCS results in a quite serious way.

[36] Personal communication from Bruce Taylor of the Bureau of Justice Statistics.

been designed in such a way that the problem could arise; we might term the problem one of "failed ambition." I noted earlier that respondents in the NCS are in theory interviewed seven times, at six-monthly intervals, over a period of three years. In principle, then, it is possible to obtain from the NCS genuine over-time data on the same individuals, which would permit the study of the *effects* of victimization on individuals' later behavior, attitudes, or further experience as a victim of crime. Similarly, it would be possible to obtain over-time data from the NCS which would throw light on the *causes* of victimization. All the other victimization surveys done to date—including the Nordic ones (Aromaa 1974a, 1974b; Wolf and Hauge 1975) and the NCS "high impact" and five largest city-level ones (see Bibliographic Note), in which the same populations were surveyed at two points in time—have used cross-sectional designs in which information was obtained from respondents at one point in time only. It is of course possible to make some inferences about the causes or consequences of victimization from such cross-sectional data. But—especially where possible changes in attitudes or behavior are the object of study—it is far better to obtain data from repeated measurements on the same individuals, at two or more points in time. Persons interviewed today, who report having been robbed three months ago, may say that they now go out of the house much less frequently;[37] but is this really the case? The only sure-fire way of knowing is to observe their behavior, assess their attitudes, etc., at t_1, t_2, ... t_k, and compare measurements before and after their victimization. The great strength of the NCS panel design is that it permits this kind of repeated measurement.

Unfortunately, the potential of this design has not so far been realized in practice. To begin with, the design is affected by the geographical mobility of the American population. About one-seventh of all American households (including one-seventh of

---

[37] Cf. the not-very-adept question asked in the "attitude questionnaire" administered to half of the respondents in the NCS city-level surveys: "Do you go out [in the evening for entertainment] more or less now than you did a year or two ago?" There may be some point in asking questions of that form; but it would be rash in the extreme to take the answers at face value.

those in the NCS sample) change their residences each year (Murphy and Cowan 1976). This does not mean that particular rotation groups in the NCS sample have lost half of their original members by the end of seven six-monthly interviews; some addresses are occupied by "stayers" and some by "movers," and the latter account for about one-seventh of the sample dwelling units, which thus may over a three-year period contain a number of different households. Furthermore, even in dwelling units in which the household remains the same for seven interviews, about 5 percent of the individual members of those households change, e.g. as couples divorce or separate, children go away to work or to college, or grandparents die or go into nursing homes.

At the present time, "movers" in the NCS sample are not followed to their new residences. Where a whole household moves, its replacement household (if any) at the selected dwelling unit is interviewed in its place; and the members of households interviewed at any particular time will be interviewed if they are present, and not if not, regardless of whether they were there to be interviewed on any previous occasion. The result is that a substantial proportion of the NCS sample is not interviewed seven times, as the design intends; a fair number must be interviewed only once or twice. Yet there is good reason to believe that the more mobile households and persons have different amounts and kinds of experience of victimization than those who stay in one place (and thus in the sample) for as long as three years. (It may well be that some of the movers moved precisely *because of* victimization.) There is evidence (Murphy and Cowan 1976) that replacement households, and persons not previously interviewed, have higher rates of victimization than the rest of the NCS sample. This may be due in part to the fact that their interviews are not "bounded" in the sense explained above; it may also reflect, to some extent, the effects of time-in-sample bias. But it also seems clear that the higher victimization rates of "in-movers" are due in part to characteristics of the persons themselves, and are not merely artifactual. Households that were previously noninterview or not in the sample, while making up about 4 percent of all interviews, contribute about 6 percent of all victimizations. But replacement households—which represent primarily "movers"—account for about 10 percent of all interviews but for 18 percent of all victimizations in the NCS (Murphy and Cowan 1976, p. 11). Conceivably some of this last group may have had some things stolen during the move to their new addresses—a category of offenses now missed entirely in the NCS, or at least not explicitly asked about.

Sample mobility, and the failure to follow those respondents who move after being interviewed one or more times, also limit the efficacy of the bounding procedure which is a feature of the NCS design. The first interviews conducted at a selected dwelling unit are used for bounding only, and not for estimation purposes. But the second (and subsequent) interviews at that dwelling unit *are* used to estimate victimization rates in the population, even if those interviews are with members of replacement households (or members of existing households who were not previously interviewed); these interviews are "unbounded." It is known that unbounded interviews yield more mentions of victimization than bounded ones, and there is reason to think that this is because respondents in some unbounded interviews mention things that happened to them before the beginning of the six-month period on which they are supposed to report; the purpose of the bounding procedure is precisely to eliminate this kind of overreporting. I have argued elsewhere (Sparks 1980c) that the bounding procedure may be based on mistaken assumptions; it is in any case expensive, since it involves, in effect, throwing away about 15 percent of the data collected in the NCS.[38] However that may be, the procedure is now ineffective for about one-seventh of the NCS interviews.

Disregarding these complications, one might suppose that the NCS, because of its design, now produces genuine longitudinal data, e.g. on changes in victimization rates over time. In fact, however, this is not the case, at least for the data analyses conducted by the Census Bureau and published by the

[38] For a further discussion of this point, and some alternatives to the present "bounding" procedure, see Sparks 1980c.

Bureau of Justice Statistics. Those data analyses make no use whatever of the fact that most members of the NCS sample are interviewed between two and seven times. Several analyses of changes in victimization rates over time have been done in recent years (see e.g. U.S. Department of Justice 1980b); but these involve comparisons of population estimates of victimization for successive years and provide no information on individuals' experiences in two or more successive time periods. Thus, for example, none of the Census Bureau's analyses makes it possible to determine whether an individual was victimized in, say, 1977, given that he or she was also victimized in 1976; nor do they make it possible to determine whether being a victim in t_1 reduces the risk of victimization in t_2, t_3, etc. (perhaps because of increased precaution-taking or changes in lifestyle). In other words, as the Census Bureau now analyzes the NCS data, the elaborate panel design is used merely as a convenient way to obtain successive cross-sectional estimates of victimization in the population and to try to minimize the response effects discussed earlier; those things aside, the samples interviewed in successive six-month periods might as well be completely different individuals.

It is possible (though exceedingly difficult) to stitch together data from successive interviews (for those interviewed more than once), using data tapes obtainable from the Census Bureau so as to conduct genuine longitudinal analyses. One such longitudinal data set exists and is currently being analyzed by Professor Albert J. Reiss, Jr., at Yale University. At some time in the future, presumably, this data set will be archived and made available to other researchers. It appears, however, that there are no plans for the Census Bureau to carry out longitudinal analyses which would make use of the panel feature of the NCS design.

F. Missing Variables

A final limitation of the NCS, and of a good many other victimization surveys done to date, is that very little other information is obtained from respondents that might help us to understand why some people become victims whereas others do not. All surveys have obtained basic demographic data on respondents; most have also obtained data on some socioeconomic variables (e.g. current employment, family income, years of education, marital status, time at same address). But only a few (e.g. Biderman et al. 1967; Sparks, Genn, and Dodd 1977) have gone beyond this to ask about respondents' lifestyles, attitudes to the police, beliefs about the prevalence of crime in their neighborhoods, or other things which might be either causes or consequences of their victimization. The National Academy of Sciences panel, in its evaluation of the NCS, referred to a "need for independent variables" (Penick and Owens 1976, pp. 93–101); but this is a somewhat misleading account of the problem. The additional variables which need to be measured are not primarily variables that might be found to predict or explain victimization (in the way that, for example, seriousness of offense and prior record might be used to predict severity of sentences imposed on offenders). Instead, they are variables which are needed in order to make sense of victimization rates: to enable us to assert that, say, 27 assaults per 1,000 persons per year is a "high" rate of assault rather than a "low" one. They are thus variables which measure, in a fairly obvious common-sensical way, different groups' exposure to the risk of criminal victimization. How often do people go out in the evening for entertainment or recreation? Where do they tend to go, and how do they get there? How much property do they have—or how much *stealable* property? What measures do they take to protect their dwellings, motor vehicles, or other property? What kinds of jobs do they do—and with what kinds of people do they interact at those jobs? In what sorts of neighborhoods do they live—and in what sorts of neighborhoods do they *think* they live? It is only by relating peoples' experiences of victimization to data from questions like these—questions about their lifestyles (cf. Hindelang, Gottfredson, and Garofalo 1978)—that those experiences can be meaningfully assessed: as I have said too often, in too many other places, it is not illuminating to be told that a man who never goes out of his house will never be robbed in the street.[39]

I would emphasize again that it remains to be determined just how serious the problems discussed in this section will eventually turn out to be, where the interpretation of data already collected (in the NCS and other surveys) is concerned. It may be that, for example, there will turn out to be no very important differences in the patterns of responses obtained by telephone versus personal interviewing, for those incidents which are mentioned by respondents interviewed in each way; and it may be that even if (as some research suggests) telephone interviews are less "productive" of victimization incidents than personal ones, the losses are more or less random (cf. Catlin and Murray 1979). Again, it may be that most purely mnemonic losses are more or less random in surveyed populations; to the extent that this is so, those losses will introduce no serious biases into inferences made from survey data. (It needs to be reiterated, however, that by no means all—perhaps not even most—of the losses in question are purely mnemonic.) A substantial program of analytical research is needed, however, before it can be determined whether or not these things are indeed so. Some research of this kind is now being done by the Census Bureau.[40] But much more expensive and complicated computing needs to be done before the error structure of existing survey data can be understood; and much more developmental work is needed, before the application of retrospective social survey techniques to crime can be used with anything approximating to complete confidence.

In the meantime, data from *all* victimization surveys done to date—in particular the NCS—should be treated with the

[39] Of course, such "opportunity" variables *will* predict victimization; the trouble is that those variables are essentially uninteresting, not to say boring. The proper procedure is thus to control for them, so that the effects of more interesting and important variables can be clearly seen. For a further discussion see Sparks 1980d.

[40] An irregular series of papers reporting analyses carried out by Census Bureau researchers is published from time to time, in mimeographed form. Some of these papers are also presented at professional meetings; some are published in learned journals; some important ones, however, are not. Those wishing to obtain copies of these papers should write to Mr. Robert Tinari of the U.S. Census Bureau (Demographic Surveys Division).

greatest caution, and with considerable skepticism. Findings concerning levels of victimization, in particular populations at particular times, should be treated as order-of-magnitude estimates only and as almost certainly understating the amount of crime which takes place. Any findings which seem counter-intuitive or even a little surprising—like the NCS data on assault and education, in table 2—should be disregarded on the ground that they are probably artifactual. In my opinion, NCS data on assault and rape should be ignored altogether, for the time being. (In the case of rape, in addition to probable underreporting and response bias, the extreme rarity of the crime makes survey estimates very unreliable.) Between-group comparisons of victimization rates should, at the very minimum, control for level of educational attainment, mode of interview, and (where the NCS is concerned) time in sample; the same goes for analyses of time trends, given the dramatic increase in recent years in the use of telephone interviews in the NCS. Analyses of the details of victimization incidents—e.g. of the proportions in which the police were said to have been notified—should take into account the characteristics of in-cidents which respondents failed to mention, again controlling for educational level and adjusting the results if any differences related to education are found.[41] Again, any findings should be treated as order-of-magnitude estimates only; the statistical significance (or lack of significance) of such findings can safely be entirely ignored.[42]

[41] Another example of this kind of adjustment is as follows. NCS data show that offenders (as described by victims) are disproportionately black. It is almost certain that black respondents understate their true experience of victimization; and most blacks are victimized by blacks. Thus offenders are almost certainly even more disproportionately black than the NCS data suggest.

[42] Much too much fuss is made, in practically all official·NCS publications, about statistical significance (i.e. allowance for sampling variability). A variety of standard errors and confidence intervals for NCS data are now routinely quoted in those publi-cations. Yet it is clear that nonsampling error is of far greater magnitude in the NCS; adjustments (like the one suggested in the preceding footnote) may offset some of this nonsampling error, though only in a ballpark way, which makes questions of sampling variability virtually irrelevant. My own view (not shared by all) is that if after common-sensical adjustment a trend or pattern appears which makes some sense, then it ought not to be disregarded even if it does not attain some magical level of statistical significance.

VI. Cui bono? Or, the Future of Victimization Surveying

At this point the reader may well wonder why this essay is subtitled "an optimistic assessment." Has it really been worthwhile to do fifteen years of extremely expensive research, merely to show that, Yes, Virginia, there really *is* a "dark figure" of unrecorded crime? Is it worth continuing to spend money on a research technique with an error structure of unknown but possibly enormous proportions, which may be producing findings that are not only mistaken but downright misleading? (There are probably some people who have no difficulty in believing that the college educated are more at risk of aggravated assault than those with an eighth-grade education.) Is the victimization survey technique ever likely to provide information about crime that will be useful to researchers, policy-makers, or administrators of the criminal justice system, and that could not be obtained in other (and less expensive) ways?

I believe that the answer to all of these questions is yes. At this point, I suppose I must declare an interest: I have invested about a decade of my professional career in this kind of research, and an investment of that magnitude is not calculated to make one condemn the method as worthless. That apart, I believe that good reasons can be given for continuing to improve the survey method, and for continuing to carry out a variety of types of victimization surveys in the future.

Perhaps the most important function of the victimization surveys done to date has been a latent one: by emphasizing the vast amount of criminal behavior which never comes to the attention of the police (or, if reported, is not recorded by them), the surveys have begun to undermine the credibility of police statistics as a measure of the true volume of crime. So far, they have only made a beginning at this, of course. The impact of most of the surveys done by academic researchers in the early 1970s has by now worn off to some extent; and there have so far been rather lengthy delays in publishing annual data from the NCS, so that the effect of comparison between the NCS and UCR data has been somewhat muted. (Typically, NCS data have been published about two years after the period to which they refer; thus, for example, the report on *Criminal Victimization in the United States, 1977* is dated December 1979. In part this is because data on victimization in 1977 were collected [owing to the NCS sample design] through May 1978. In part, however, it seems to be because the Census Bureau's analysis and tabulation procedures are just slower than they might be.) However, if the NCS surveys continue and improve, and the dissemination of their results becomes more timely, they should gradually lead researchers and policy-makers to see police statistics of crime for what they are—namely, the outcome of a mostly organized set of processes of reaction to crime—and to disregard the evidence of "crime waves" which many police forces still use their statistics to produce. At the very least, data from the NCS provide, for the first time, an alternative picture of crime—which can be used by legislators, administrators, the media, and the general public to put police statistics in perspective.

A separate but also important point is that victimization surveys in general, and the NCS in particular, may in time lead to improvements in police statistics—not only in their honesty, which is now greater than it was, say, thirty years ago, but in their completeness. Many police forces now routinely collect data on crime incidents (including data on victims) which they do not collate and publish; it is not inconceivable that the existence of an alternative statistical series generated by surveys will lead at least some big-city or state police forces to produce better data than they now produce.

This latent function has had its cost. From their inception to the present day, victimization surveys have been thought of, by most of those involved in conducting them, as well as by consumers and onlookers, primarily as a way of *counting crimes*—as a way of doing what police statistics of crime have done, only doing it better. (How else are we to explain the publication, in NCS reports, of the estimated total *number of victimizations* in the United States in a year—as if that number by itself had any meaning at all as an indicator of domestic tranquility?) But the victimization survey method offers much more than that. For one thing, it is a way of *counting victims*, and of identifying those groups that are, or are not, subject to specially high risks of suffering from crime. Inevitably, there is competition for the limited resources available to criminal justice systems; and this competition features claims by politically powerful groups, such as the elderly, for special measures on their behalf (see U.S. House of Representatives 1977a, 1978). For all of their imperfections, existing NCS data provide a data base against which such claims can be evaluated and more rational decisions reached. In addition, victimization surveys provide an opportunity to study the causes of victimization, and to assess its impact on society—not only in crude monetary terms, but in terms of changed attitudes and behavior, and the consequent "opportunity cost" which those changes may entail.[43]

These last objectives have not yet been fully realized, especially in the NCS, in which so little information relevant to the risk of victimization is now collected. The risk of becoming a victim of crime is, like all risks, conditional; that is, it reflects the probability of being victimized in some time period, given not only demographic attributes such as age and sex but also a particular lifestyle, certain social relations, a certain stock of stealable wealth, particular protective and policing arrangements, and so on. Without data on such risk-determining variables, we cannot make sense of observed victimization rates; we cannot say even if they are in some sense "low" or "high." Nor can we interpret changes in observed victimization rates, unless we know how far other things have changed as well. (For example, the fact if it is a fact that rates of personal victimization in some central cities have declined, or at least not increased much, may well be explained by the fact that people desert those cities at night, thus reducing their exposure to risk.) It is thus important for future surveys not only to mea-

---

[43] Questions of this kind belong, I suppose, to "victimology," assuming (what I am personally not prepared to concede) that there really is such a science. It is in fact questionable how far "victimology"—and its political arm, the victim-compensation movement—have influenced victimization surveying. It is clear, however, that victimization surveys can provide much valuable information relevant to compensation and restitution schemes, service delivery to victims, and the like.

sure victimization more accurately but also to obtain the contextual information which makes it possible to understand victimization rates.

Inevitably, the future of victimization surveying in the United States, and possibly elsewhere, is bound up with the future of the NCS; and it remains to be seen what that program will look like when the current redesign efforts are completed. Given the many different objectives of a large-scale survey program like the NCS, and the many different potential consumer constituencies which such a program must serve, it may be that no single survey will suffice. It may be instead that a number of different kinds of survey designs should be implemented. One possibility would be to ask some questions about victimization in other general-population surveys conducted by the federal government. For example, at the time of this writing legislation is being considered which would require data on burglary and household theft to be collected by the Annual Housing Surveys conducted by the Department of Housing and Urban Development. In a similar fashion, data on personal victimization could be collected in surveys carried out by the U.S. National Center for Health Statistics.[44] Again, there are some crimes which are reasonably well reported to the police, and thus reasonably well measured by the *Uniform Crime Reports;* car theft and commercial robbery and burglary are examples. These crimes might perhaps be dropped entirely from a future NCS, to make room for questions about crimes which are not well covered by the UCR.[45]

[44] See, for instance, U.S. National Center for Health Statistics 1965a, 1965b. It is not entirely clear, however, that adequate measures of criminal victimization can in fact be obtained by sticking one or two questions into a questionnaire that is primarily aimed at measuring something quite different; for what are probably mnemonic reasons, this seems likely to yield much lower estimates of victimization than would be obtained by a lengthier set of questions about crime. In England, for example, the Government Social Survey included two questions on burglary and household theft in the questionnaires used in its General Household Survey in 1972 and 1973; the yield of incidents mentioned in response to these questions was implausibly low. See Sparks, Genn, and Dodd 1977, p. 233.

[45] For a discussion of the problems of measuring commercial victimization, see Reiss 1969; Cutler and Reiss 1967. Note that while the UCR probably measures thefts *of* cars fairly well, it probably does not measure thefts *from* cars as efficiently. (I owe notice of this last point to Albert Biderman.)

Another possibility which deserves serious consideration is the splitting of the NCS itself into two or more separate components.[46] I noted earlier that it is important, for several reasons, to obtain and analyze genuine longitudinal data, from a sample interviewed at several points in time, with those who moved being followed to their new addresses. Such a sample need not be representative of the entire United States population; instead, it could be specially chosen, to represent (or overrepresent) those persons—mainly central-city residents—with relatively high rates of victimization. Data from such a longitudinal survey could tell us an enormous amount about the causes and consequences of victimization, and people's adaptations to crime. To supplement this longitudinal effort, one or more cross-section surveys could be carried out, using samples representative either of the population of the whole of the United States, or of smaller areas such as states. These surveys, which need not be conducted or published on an annual basis, would be less expensive than the present NCS; and they could be designed to include supplemental questionnaires which would obtain data on special topics of particular interest.[47]

It is to be hoped, however, that the future of victimization surveying will not lie entirely in large-scale efforts like the NCS, which in the nature of things can be afforded only by central governments. There is also room for local victimization surveys, and for smaller-scale studies by academic researchers and criminal justice agencies, for evaluation purposes and etiological studies. The survey of victimization is only one weapon in the researcher's arsenal, of course; no single research technique can do everything. But there is no doubt that it is a potentially powerful weapon—and one that can be used to great advantage against ignorance and misconception where many problems about crime are concerned.

[46] I am indebted to an unpublished paper by Dr. Robert Lehnen for this general strategy. He is not responsible for the use or misuse which I make of it here.

[47] One such supplement has already been used; this is a questionnaire devised by Dr. Marvin Wolfgang and his colleagues, for the National Survey on Crime Severity. The results of this survey are not yet published.

BIBLIOGRAPHIC NOTE

As explained in the text of this essay, the National Crime Surveys originally had four components, of which only one—the national household survey—is still in existence. The purpose of this note on publications on the National Crime Survey is to describe briefly the other three now-defunct components, and to summarize ways in which data from all four components are disseminated and may be obtained.

The City-Level Household Surveys

These surveys were based on samples of about 10,000 households (including about 22,000 persons aged 12 and over) in each of the surveyed cities. Interviewing was begun in July 1972 in the eight cities (Atlanta, Baltimore, Cleveland, Dallas, Denver, Newark, Portland Oregon, and St. Louis) included in the LEAA-funded "high impact" crime reduction program; beginning in January 1973, surveys were also carried out in the nation's five largest cities (New York, Chicago, Los Angeles, Detroit, and Philadelphia). A second round of surveys was conducted in all thirteen of these cities, in about March 1975. In addition, thirteen more city-level surveys were carried out in the first quarter of 1974, in Boston, Buffalo, Houston, Miami, Milwaukee, Minneapolis, Cincinnati, New Orleans, Oakland, Pittsburgh, San Diego, San Francisco, and Washington, D.C.; these cities were not resurveyed. At one time it was planned to carry out surveys in eleven more cities or groups of cities (see Penick and Owens 1976, p. 55, 183–84); but these plans were abandoned, and it is unlikely that any more surveys of this kind will be conducted under the NCS program.

The questionnaires used in these thirty-nine city-level household surveys were similar to those used in the NCS national household survey, except that respondents were asked about things that might have happened to them within the twelve months (rather than six months) preceding the interviews. (It should be noted that these interviews were not "bounded" in the sense explained in section III above; even in the thirteen cities in which two surveys were done, the samples were not based on the same set of addresses.) In addition, respondents in one-half of the interviewed households were asked a series of "attitude" questions, which in reality were not about attitudes but about shopping habits, beliefs about crime in the neighborhood, feelings of personal safety, and the like (for a description of some findings from this part of the questionnaire, see Garofalo 1977).

The National and City-Level Commercial Surveys

Surveys of commercial victimization took place in the same cities as the household surveys just discussed; samples varied in size from about 1,000 to 5,000 business establishments. In addition, a national survey of commercial victimization was carried out from mid-1972 to the end of 1977; this was based on a two-stage probability sample of businesses, containing in all about 39,000 establishments. The questionnaire used in both sets of commercial surveys asked only about incidents classifiable as burglary or robbery; no attempt was made to measure theft by employees, or victimization of customers or employees. It is unlikely that these surveys will be resumed in future, at least under NCS auspices.

Dissemination of Data

Data from the NCS are disseminated in three main ways. First, a series of detailed tabulations is routinely prepared by a special unit in the Census Bureau to specifications now provided by the Bureau of Justice Statistics (BJS). These tabulations are not routinely published in full, though BJS makes them available to police departments, planning agencies, and others upon request. (State-level data are available only for the ten largest states, for reasons of statistical reliability.) Second, BJS has arranged for the production of magnetic computer tapes, called "public use tapes," containing data from all of the various NCS surveys—national and city-level, household and commercial— done to date. These tapes contain "micro-data" (that is, data from each person's or organization's questionnaire responses), coded in such a way to preserve individuals' anonymity. (Census Bureau rules, however, prohibit the distribution of such tapes relating to any area with a population of less than 250,000; the purpose of this rule, which in the opinion of many is unnecessarily restrictive, is to minimize the possibility of identifying individuals—e.g. victims of rape or other rare offenses.)

These data tapes make it possible for individual researchers to carry out their own analyses of NCS data, using a computer. The tapes themselves, and their documentation, are relatively inexpensive to purchase. But owing to the size of the NCS data sets (in particular, those from the national household survey), and to the complicated way in which the data are arranged on the tapes, they pose considerable computing problems, and even the simplest of secondary analyses can be a very difficult and expensive task. The tapes and their documentation can be obtained through the Criminal Justice Archive and Information Network (CJAIN), which is located within the Inter-University Consortium for Political and Social Research, P.O. Box 1248, Ann Arbor, Michigan 48106; CJAIN may also provide special NCS data sets and data analyses, and their staff should in any case be consulted by anyone intending to use the NCS micro-data.

Finally, a number of fairly brief reports based on NCS data have been published by LEAA, since 1973. Single copies of these reports can be obtained at no charge from the National Criminal Justice Reference Service, P.O. Box 6000, Rockville, Maryland 20850; multiple copies are for sale by the Superintendent of Documents, U.S. Government Printing Office, Washington, D.C. 20402. Most of the earlier reports in this series had *report* numbers, e.g. SD-NCS-N-9; since 1978, however, all of these reports have been given *document* numbers prefixed with the letters NCJ. (Thus, for example, survey report SD-NCS-N-9, titled *Criminal Victimization in the United States, 1976*, is now also designated document NCJ-49593; document numbers were given retrospectively to earlier reports, though on some publications appearing since 1978 only document numbers appear).

The following lists give the titles of some of the various reports now available, followed by the year of publication in parentheses (since that typically does not correspond to the year for which survey results are reported), and the NCJ-prefixed document number of each report. A few earlier reports (usually interim or advance reports of relatively little importance) are now out of print and are not shown below; reports of pilot studies and of technical papers relating to the NCS are included in the list of references under the name of the author. Those NCS reports cited in the text are shown in the list of references under "U.S. Department of Justice." In all cases, the reports are published for the U.S. Department of Justice, Law Enforcement Assistance Administration, National Criminal Justice Information and Statistics Service (now called the Bureau of Justice Statistics), by the U.S. Government Printing Office, Washington, D.C.

1. The City-Level Surveys

Criminal Victimization Surveys in the Nation's Five Largest Cities: National Crime Panel Surveys in Chicago, Detroit, Los Angeles, New York and Philadelphia, 1972 (1976), NCJ-16909.

Criminal Victimization Surveys in Chicago, Detroit, Los Angeles, New York and Philadelphia: A Comparison of 1972 and 1974 Findings (1977), NCJ-36360.

Criminal Victimization Surveys in Eight American Cities [Atlanta, Baltimore, Cleveland, Dallas, Denver, Newark, Portland, and St. Louis]. *A Comparison of 1971/72 and 1974/75 Findings* (1977), NCJ-36361.

Criminal Victimization Surveys in Thirteen American Cities [Boston, Buffalo, Cincinnati, Houston, Miami, Milwaukee, Minneapolis, New

Orleans, Oakland, Pittsburgh, San Diego, San Francisco, Washington, D.C.] (1977), NCJ-18471. Separate volumes containing more detailed data for these cities are also available; titled *Criminal Victimization Surveys in* ———, these are documents NCJ-34818 through NCJ-34830. In addition, data from the "attitude supplement" to these city-level surveys are published in thirteen separate reports titled *Public Attitudes about Crime* plus the city name (1977–79; NCJ-46235 through NCJ-46247).

Crimes and Victims: A Report on the San Jose-Dayton Pilot Survey of Victimization (1976), NCJ-013314.

2. The National Surveys

Annual reports on the national household survey (including, until 1977, some data on commercial victimization) are published in reports bearing the general title *Criminal Victimization in the United States*, plus the calendar year (from 1973 onward) to which the data refer. All of these reports are in a similar format, though the more recent ones are more detailed; most have appeared about three years after the year to which they refer. Reference years and document numbers of reports so far published are: 1973, NCJ-34732; 1974, NCJ-39467; 1975, NCJ-44593; 1976, NCJ-49543; 1977, NCJ-58725; 1978, NCJ-62993.

In addition, a number of reports have presented year-by-year comparisons of victimization rates as estimated by the survey: these include 1973 and 1974, NCJ-34391; 1974 and 1975, NCJ-39548; 1975 and 1976, NCJ-44132; and 1976 and 1977, NCJ-52983. See also *Criminal Victimization in the United States: Summary Findings of 1977–78. Changes in Crime and of Trends since 1973* (1979), NCJ-61368.

Finally, a number of reports on selected topics, based on NCS data from one or more years since 1973, have been published. Recent examples include *The Cost of Negligence: Losses from Preventable Household Burglaries* (1979), NCJ-53527; *Intimate Victims: A Study of Violence among Friends and Relatives* (1980), NCJ-62319; and *Crime and Seasonality* (1980), NCJ-64818.

Data from the NCS have also been published in a variety of reports prepared under the Utilization of Criminal Justice Statistics project, funded by LEAA and directed by Professor Michael Hindelang of the School of Criminal Justice, State University of New York at Albany. Some of these reports (most of which have been published by LEAA) are cited in the references under the name of the author.

REFERENCES

Anttila, Inkere. 1964. "The Criminological Significance of Unregistered Criminality," *Excerpta Criminologica* 4:411.

Aromaa, Kauko. 1971. *Arkipaivan Vakivaltaa Suomessa* [Everyday Violence in Finland]. Helsinki: Kriminologinen Tutkimoslaitos. Series M:11.

———. 1973. "The Making of a Survey on Hidden Criminality in the Field of Labor Protection Laws in Finland, 1972," *International Journal of Criminology and Penology* 1(4):335–39.

———. 1974a. "Victimization to Violence: A Gallup Survey," *International Journal of Criminology and Penology* 2:333.

———. 1974b. *The Replication of a Survey on Victimization to Violence.* Helsinki: Institute of Criminology. Series M:36.

Aromaa, Kauko, and Seppo Leppa. 1973. *Omaisuusrikosten Yksilouhrien Tarkastelua* [A Survey on Individual Victims of Property Crimes]. Helsinki: Kriminologinen Tutkimoslaitos. Series M:26.

Bailar, Barbara. 1975. "The Effects of Rotation Group Bias on Estimates from Panel Surveys," *Journal of the American Statistical Association* 70:23–30.

Biderman, Albert D., Louise Johnson, Jennie McIntyre, and Adrianne Weir. 1967. *Report on a Pilot Study in the District of Columbia on Victimization and Attitudes to Law Enforcement.* U.S. President's Commission on Law Enforcement and Administration of Justice, Field Surveys I. Washington, D.C.: U.S. Government Printing Office.

Biderman, Albert D., Susan S. Oldham, Sally K. Ward and Maureen A. Eby. 1973. *An Inventory of Surveys of the Public on Crime, Justice and Related Topics.* Washington, D.C.: U.S. Government Printing Office.

Catlin, Gary, and Susan Murray. 1979. *Report on Canadian Victimization Survey Methodological Pretests.* Toronto: Statistics Canada.

Clarren, Sumner N., and Alfred I. Schwartz. 1976. "Measuring a Program's Impact: A Cautionary Note." In *Sample Surveys of the Victims of Crime,* ed. Wesley G. Skogan. Cambridge, Mass.: Ballinger.

Clinard, Marshall B. 1977. "Comparative Crime Victimization Surveys: Some Problems and Results," *International Journal of Criminology and Penology* 6:221–31.

———. 1978. *Cities with Little Crime.* Cambridge: Cambridge University Press.

Congalton, A. A., and J. M. Najman. 1974. *Unreported Crime.* Statistical Report No. 12, Department of the Attorney General. Sydney: New South Wales Bureau of Crime Statistics and Research.

Cutler, Stephen J., and Albert J. Reiss, Jr. 1967. *Crimes against Public and Quasi-Public Organizations.* A report submitted to the U.S. President's Commission on Law Enforcement and Administration of Justice. Mimeographed. Ann Arbor: Department of Sociology, University of Michigan.

Dodge, Richard W. 1975. "Analysis of Screen Questions on National Crime Survey." Unpublished memorandum dated 1 December 1975, U.S. Bureau of the Census, Washington, D.C. Mimeographed.

————. 1976. "National Crime Survey: Comparison of Victimizations as Reported on the Screen Questions with Their Final Classification, 1975." Unpublished memorandum dated 27 December 1976, U.S. Bureau of the Census, Washington, D.C.

————. 1977. "Analysis of Screen Questions on National Crime Survey." Unpublished memorandum dated 22 December 1977, U.S. Bureau of the Census, Washington, D.C.

Ennis, Philip H. 1967. *Criminal Victimization in the United States: A Report of a National Survey.* President's Commission on Law Enforcement and Administration of Justice, Field Surveys II. Washington, D.C.: U.S. Government Printing Office.

Fienberg, Stephen E. 1977. *Victimization and the National Crime Survey: Problems of Design and Analysis.* Technical report 291. Minneapolis: University of Minnesota, Department of Applied Statistics. Mimeographed. Also published, with additional testimony, in U.S. House of Representatives 1977b.

Fiselier, J. P. S. 1974. Personal communication on survey findings, reported in Sparks, Genn, and Dodd 1977, pp. 72–73.

Fox, James A., and Paul E. Tracy. 1980. "The Randomized Response Approach and Its Applicability to Criminal Justice Research and Evaluation," *Evaluation Quarterly.* In press.

Garofalo, James. 1977. *The Police and Public Opinion: An Analysis of Victimization and Attitude Data from Thirteen Cities.* U.S. Department of Justice, National Criminal Justice Information and Statistics Service, report NCJ-42018. Washington, D.C.: U.S. Government Printing Office.

Garofalo, James, and Michael J. Hindelang. 1977. *An Introduction to the National Crime Survey.* U.S. Department of Justice, National Criminal Justice Information and Statistics Service, report NCJ-43732. Washington, D.C.: U.S. Government Printing Office.

Gibbs, John J. 1977. *A Comparative Analysis of Personal Victimization*

Rates in Urban, Suburban, and Rural Areas. U.S. Department of Justice, National Criminal Justice Information and Statistics Service, report NCJ-53551. Washington, D.C.: U.S. Government Printing Office.

Groves, Robert M. 1977. "An Experimental Comparison of National Telephone and Personal Interview Surveys." Ann Arbor: University of Michigan, Survey Research Center. Mimeographed.

Harland, Alan. 1977. *Restitution to Victims of Crime*. Albany, N.Y.: Criminal Justice Research Center. Mimeographed.

Hawkins, Richard O. 1973. "Who Called the Cops? Decisions to Report Criminal Victimization," *Law and Society Review* 7(3):427–44.

Hindelang, Michael J. 1976. *Criminal Victimization in Eight American Cities: A Descriptive Analysis of Common Theft and Assault*. Cambridge, Mass.: Ballinger.

Hindelang, Michael, and James Garofalo. 1977. *An Introduction to the National Crime Survey*. U.S. Department of Justice, National Criminal Justice Information and Statistics Service, report NCJ-43732. Washington, D.C.: U.S. Government Printing Office.

Hindelang, Michael J., Michael R. Gottfredson, and James Garofalo. 1978. *Victims of Personal Crimes: An Empirical Foundation for a Theory of Personal Victimization*. Cambridge, Mass.: Ballinger.

Institute for Local Self-Government. 1969. *Criminal Victimization in Maricopa County*. Berkeley, Calif.

Kelling, George L., T. Pate, D. Dieckman, and C. E. Brown. 1974. *The Kansas City Preventive Patrol Experiment: A Technical Report*. Washington, D.C.: Police Foundation.

Kitsuse, John, and Aaron Cicourel. 1963. "A Note on the Uses of Official Statistics," *Social Problems* 11:131–39.

Levine, James P. 1976. "The Potential for Overreporting in Victimization Surveys," *Criminology* 14:307–27.

McClintock, F. H. 1971. "The Dark Figure." In *Collected Studies in Criminological Research*. Vol. 5. Strasbourg: Council of Europe.

McIntyre, Jennie. 1967. "Surveys of Public Attitudes to Crime," *Annals of the American Academy of Political and Social Science* 374:34–46.

Murphy, Linda, and Charles D. Cowan. 1976. "Effects of Bounding on Telescoping in the National Crime Survey." Paper prepared for presentation at the American Statistical Association meetings, Boston, 23–26 August 1976. Washington, D.C.: U.S. Bureau of the Census. Mimeographed.

National Institute of Law Enforcement and Criminal Justice. 1972. *San Jose Methods Test of Known Crime Victims*. Statistics Technical Report no. 1. Washington, D.C.: U.S. Government Printing Office.

Nelson, James. 1980. "Multiple Victimization in American Cities: A Statistical Analysis of Rare Events," *American Journal of Sociology* 85(4):870–91.

Neter, John and Joseph Waksberg. 1965. *Response Errors in Collection of Expenditures Data by Household Interviews: An Experimental Study.* U.S. Department of Commerce, Bureau of the Census, Technical Paper no. 11. Washington, D.C.: U.S. Government Printing Office.

Organization for Economic Cooperation and Development (OECD). 1976. *Data Sources for Social Indicators of Victimization Suffered by Individuals.* OECD Social Indicator Development Program, Special Studies, no. 3. Paris: OECD.

Penick, Bettye K. E., and Maurice E. B. Owens III, eds. 1976. *Surveying Crime.* Final Report of the Panel for the Evaluation of Crime Surveys, Committee on National Statistics, National Research Council. Washington, D.C.: National Academy of Sciences.

Reiss, Albert J. Jr. 1967. *Studies in Crime and Law Enforcement in Major Metropolitan Areas.* President's Commission on Law Enforcement and Administration of Justice, Field Surveys III, vol. 1. Washington, D.C.: U.S. Government Printing Office.

———. 1969. Appendix A to *Crime against Small Business*, a report of the Small Business Administration. U.S. Senate Document no. 91–14, 91st Congress, 1st session. Washington, D.C.: U.S. Government Printing Office.

Reynolds, Paul D., et al. 1973. *Victimization in a Metropolitan Region: Comparison of a Central City Area and a Suburban Region.* Minneapolis: Minnesota Center for Sociological Research. Mimeographed.

Rustmeyer, Anitra, and Arnold Levin. 1977. "Report on a Telephone Survey Using Computer Assistance." Unpublished paper, U.S. Bureau of the Census, Washington, D.C. Mimeographed.

Schneider, Anne L. 1976. "Victimization Surveys and Criminal Justice System Evaluation." In *Sample Surveys of the Victims of Crime*, ed. Wesley G. Skogan. Cambridge, Mass.: Ballinger.

———. 1978. *Portland Forward Records Check of Crime Victims.* U.S. Department of Justice, National Institute of Law Enforcement and Criminal Justice. Washington, D.C.: U.S. Government Printing Office.

Schwind, Hans Dieter. 1975. *Dunkelfeldforschung in Göttingen, 1973–74.* Wiesbaden: Bundesdruckerei.

Sellin, Thorsten. 1938. *Culture Conflict and Crime.* New York: Social Science Research Council.

———. 1951. "The Significance of Records of Crime," *Law Quarterly Review* 67:489–504.

Skogan, Wesley G. 1976. "Citizen Reporting of Crime: Some National Panel Data," *Criminology* 13:535–49.

———. 1977. "Public Policy and the Fear of Crime in Large American Cities." Paper presented to the Annual Meeting of the American Political Science Association, Chicago, May 1976.

Sparks, Richard F. 1980a. *Studying the Victims of Crime: Problems and Perspectives.* Crime and Delinquency Issues Monograph. National Institute of Mental Health. Washington, D.C.: U.S. Government Printing Office.

———. 1980b. "Multiple Victims: Evidence, Theory, and Future Research." Paper prepared for a Conference on Victimology, sponsored by the Mitre Corporation, MacLean, Virginia, March 1980.

———. 1980c. *Methodological Problems of Retrospective Social Surveys: With Special Reference to Surveys of Criminal Victimization.* U.S. Department of Justice, National Institute of Justice. Washington, D.C.: U.S. Government Printing Office.

———. 1980d. "Criminal Opportunities and Crime Rates." In *Social Indicators of Crime and Criminal Justice: Quantitative Studies,* ed. S. E. Fienberg and A. J. Reiss, Jr. Washington, D.C.: Social Science Research Council.

Sparks, Richard F., Hazel G. Genn, and David J. Dodd. 1977. *Surveying Victims: A Study of the Measurement of Criminal Victimization, Perceptions of Crime, and Attitudes to Criminal Justice.* London: John Wiley.

Stephan, Egon. 1974. *Dunkelfeld und Kriminalstatistik.* Freiburg: Max-Planck Institute.

Sudman, Seymour, and Norman M. Bradburn. 1974. *Response Effects in Surveys: A Review and Synthesis.* National Opinion Research Center Monographs in Social Research, no. 16. Chicago: Aldine.

———. 1977. *Improving the Quality of Surveys.* National Opinion Research Center Monographs in Social Research. Chicago: Aldine.

Tracy, Paul E., and James A. Fox. 1979. "A Field Validation of the Quantitative Randomized Response Approach." Paper prepared for presentation at the 1979 meetings of the American Society of Criminology.

Tuchfarber, Alfred J., and William R. Klecka. 1976. *RDD: Lowering the Cost of Victimization Surveys.* Cincinnati: Police Foundation.

Turner, Anthony G. 1975. "The Development of the National Crime Survey, 1970–74." Unpublished paper, U.S. Bureau of the Census, Washington, D.C. Mimeographed.

———. 1977. "An Experiment to Compare Three Interview Procedures in the National Crime Survey." Unpublished report dated December 1977, U.S. Bureau of the Census, Washington, D.C.

U. S. Bureau of the Census. 1970. "Victim Recall Pretest (Washing-

ton, D.C.).” Unpublished report dated 10 June 1970. Mimeographed.

U.S. Department of Justice. 1979. *Criminal Victimization in the United States, 1977*. National Crime Survey report NCJ-58725. Washington, D.C.: U.S. Government Printing Office.

———. 1980a. *Crime against Persons in Urban, Suburban, and Rural Areas: A Comparative Analysis of Victimization Rates*. National Crime Survey report NCJ-53551. Washington, D.C.: U.S. Government Printing Office.

———. 1980b. *Criminal Victimization in the United States: Summary Findings of 1978–79 Changes in Crime and Trends Since 1973*. NCS Report no. SD-NCS-N-18, NCJ-62993. Washington, D.C.: U.S. Government Printing Office.

U.S. House of Representatives. 1977a. *In Search of Security: A National Perspective on Elderly Criminal Victimization*. Report by the Subcommittee on Housing and Consumer Interests of the Select Committee on Aging, 95th Congress, 1st session, April 1977. Washington, D.C.: U.S. Government Printing Office.

———. 1977b. *Suspension of the National Crime Survey*. Hearings before the Subcommittee on Crime of the Committee on the Judiciary, 95th Congress, 1st session, 13 October 1977. Washington, D.C.: U.S. Government Printing Office.

———. 1978. *Research into Crimes against the Elderly*. Joint Hearings before the Select Committee on Aging and the Subcommittee on Domestic and International Scientific Planning of the Committee on Science and Technology, 95th Congress, 2d session. Washington, D.C.: U.S. Government Printing Office.

U.S. National Center of Education. 1978. *Violent Schools—Safe Schools*. Washington, D.C.: U.S. Government Printing Office.

U.S. National Center for Health Statistics. 1965a. *Reporting of Hospitalization in the Health Interview Survey*. Vital and Health Statistics. PHS Publication no. 1000, series 2-6. Washington, D.C.: U.S. Government Printing Office.

———. 1965b. *Comparison of Hospitalization Reporting in Three Survey Procedures*. Vital and Health Statistics. PHS Publication no. 1000, series 2-8. Washington, D.C.: U.S. Government Printing Office.

U.S. President’s Commission on Law Enforcement and Administration of Justice. 1967a. *The Challenge of Crime in a Free Society*. Washington, D.C.: U.S. Government Printing Office.

———. 1967b. *Task Force Report on the Assessment of Crime*. Washington, D.C.: U.S. Government Printing Office.

Waller, Irwin, and Norm Okihiro. 1978. *Burglary and the Public*. Toronto: University of Toronto Press.

Wheeler, Stanton. 1967. “Criminal Statistics: A Reformulation of the

Problem," *Journal of Criminal Law, Criminology and Police Science* 58:317–24.

Wilks, Judith. 1967. "Ecological Correlates of Crime and Delinquency." In U.S. President's Commission 1967b.

Wolf, Preben, and Ragnar Hauge. 1975. "Criminal Violence in Three Scandinavian Countries." In *Scandinavian Studies in Criminology*, vol. 5. London: Tavistock.

Woltman, Henry, and John Bushery. 1975. "A Panel Bias Study in the National Crime Survey." Paper prepared for presentation at the annual meetings of the American Statistical Association, Atlanta, 25–28 August 1975. Washington, D.C.: U.S. Bureau of the Census. Mimeographed.

————. 1977a. "Update of the NCS Panel Bias Study." Unpublished memorandum dated 11 July 1977. U.S. Bureau of the Census, Washington, D.C. Mimeographed.

————. 1977b. "Optimum Number of Times to Retain a Panel in Sample in the NCS." Unpublished memorandum dated 11 July 1977, U.S. Bureau of the Census, Washington, D.C. Mimeographed.

————. 1978. "Results of the NCS Maximum Personal Visit-Maximum Telephone Interview Experiment." Unpublished report dated 9 December 1977. U.S. Bureau of the Census, Washington, D.C. Mimeographed.

Yost, Linda R., and Richard W. Dodge. 1970. "Household Surveys of the Victims of Crime, Second Pretest (Baltimore, Maryland)." Unpublished report, U.S. Bureau of the Census, Washington, D.C. Mimeographed.

Martin T. Orne

The Use and Misuse of Hypnosis in Court

ABSTRACT

Hypnosis may be helpful in the context of criminal investigation and under circumstances involving functional memory loss. Hypnosis is not useful in assuring truthfulness since, particularly in a forensic context, subjects may simulate hypnosis and are able to lie wilfully even in deep hypnosis; most troublesome, actual memories cannot be distinguished from confabulations—pseudo-memories where plausible fantasy has replaced gaps in recall—either by the subject or by the hypnotist without full and independent corroboration. While potentially useful to refresh witnesses' and victims' memories to facilitate eyewitness identification, the procedure is relatively safe and appropriate only when neither the subject nor the authorities nor the hypnotist has any preconceptions about the events under investigation. If such preconceptions do exist, hypnosis may readily cause the subject to confabulate the person who is suspected into his "hypnotically enhanced memories." These pseudo memories, originally developed in hypnosis, may come to be accepted by the subject as his actual recall of the original events; they are then remembered with great subjective certainty and re-

Martin T. Orne is director of the Unit for Experimental Psychiatry at The Institute of Pennsylvania Hospital and professor of psychiatry at the University of Pennsylvania.

An earlier version of this essay appeared in the Monograph Issue of the *International Journal of Clinical and Experimental Hypnosis* on the forensic uses of hypnosis, 27 (4) (1979): 311–41. The substantive work carried out in our laboratory relevant to this paper and its preparation was supported in part by grant MH 19156 from the National Institute of Mental Health and by a grant from the Institute for Experimental Psychiatry. For their help in clarifying the issues involved, I wish to thank especially my colleagues at the Unit for Experimental Psychiatry: Emily Carota Orne, David F. Dinges, William M. Waid, William H. Putnam. Special appreciation is due to John F. Kihlstrom and Robert A. Karlin for their substantive suggestions. I am particularly grateful to Nancy K. Bauer, Lani Pyles MacAniff, Joanne Rosellini, and Mae C. Weglarski for their assistance in the editing, formatting, and referencing during the preparation of this manuscript.

62   Martin T. Orne

ported with conviction. Such circumstances can *create* convincing, apparently objective "eyewitnesses" rather than facilitating actual recall. Minimal safeguards are proposed to reduce the likelihood of such an eventuality and other serious potential abuses of hypnosis.

Over the years, much of the forensic interest in hypnosis has dealt with the question of whether an individual can be compelled to carry out antisocial behavior[1] and the implications that such a possibility would have for the concept of legal responsibility. More recently, however, there has been a sudden upsurge of legal cases throughout the country which have involved the use of hypnosis in an entirely different context. These cases employ hypnosis (*a*) to enhance defendants' memories in order to bring out new information which might clear them of accusations against them, or (*b*) to increase the recall of witnesses or victims who have observed a crime, either to facilitate the pretrial investigation or to enhance memory sufficiently so that following hypnosis the individuals can serve as eyewitnesses in court. Finally, hypnosis has been used to help in the psychological and psychiatric evaluation of defendants, especially to determine their state of mind (Kline 1979). Although this application will not be discussed substantively in this essay, all the limitations of hypnosis for the proof of fact generally apply even more strongly to its use to document the fact of a state of mind.

Because of our laboratory's work on the nature of hypnosis, I have become involved in a number of cases where our work was directly relevant to the proposed forensic use of hypnosis. Of particular relevance were our empirical studies dealing with the nature of hypnotic age regression (O'Connell, Shor, and Orne 1970; Orne 1951), the potential use of hypnosis in interrogation (Orne 1961), the question of whether antisocial behavior can be elicited by the use of hypnosis (Orne 1962, 1972a; Orne and

[1] For a detailed discussion of these issues, see Barber (1961), Orne (1960, 1962), Orne and Evans (1965), and the *International Journal of Clinical and Experimental Hypnosis* 20 (2) (1972), a special issue of the journal which includes relevant papers by Coe, Kobayashi, and Howard (1972), Conn (1972), Kline (1972), Orne (1972a), and Watkins (1972).

Evans 1965), the nature of posthypnotic behavior (Orne 1969; Orne, Sheehan, and Evans 1968; Sheehan and Orne 1968), the simulation of hypnosis (Orne 1971, 1972b, 1977), and posthypnotically disrupted recall (Evans and Kihlstrom 1973; Kihlstrom and Evans 1976, 1977; Nace, Orne, and Hammer 1974; Orne 1966).

This essay reviews the major issues concerning some of the forensic uses of hypnosis, illustrates the difficulties which may be encountered by examining the relevant scientific evidence as well as some of the relevant legal cases, and finally proposes some general guidelines for the use of hypnosis that should minimize the likelihood of serious miscarriages of justice.

I. The Use of Hypnosis to Legitimize New Information and Increase Credibility

In the past few years there has been a sharp increase in the use of hypnosis—by prosecutors and defendants, plaintiffs and respondents alike—to enhance memory for events associated with a crime or civil suit. In most cases, the courts ultimately refused to admit hypnotically elicited material as evidence. An examination of some of these cases illustrates many problems that can occur in the forensic use of hypnosis if appropriate safeguards are not employed.

A. To Exonerate a Defendant

At one time, both hypnosis and "truth serum" (sodium amytal and pentothal administered intravenously) were thought of as techniques which could elicit truthful information. Since it is widely believed by laymen that there is a virtual certainty of obtaining truthful information when a subject's critical judgment is diminished by either hypnosis or a drug, it is hardly surprising that efforts have been made to introduce hypnotic testimony in court as a way for the defendant to demonstrate his innocence to a jury. The courts, however, have recognized that hypnotic testimony is not reliable as a means of ascertaining truth and appropriately have rejected both these techniques as means of determining factual information.

Although these early decisions were usually accompanied by gratuitous deprecatory remarks about hypnosis, the wisdom of the decisions themselves is supported by scientific data. Thus, experience with a research design where deeply hypnotized subjects and unhypnotizable subjects instructed to feign hypnosis are seen by hypnotists who are unaware of the subjects' actual status (Orne 1959, 1971, 1972b) has shown that it is possible to deceive even highly experienced hypnotists (Hilgard 1977; Orne 1977; Sheehan 1972). Not only can individuals fake hypnosis, but even subjects who are genuinely in deep hypnosis are nonetheless able wilfully to lie (Orne 1961).

While the courts have usually rejected the use of hypnosis as a truth-telling device, recognition of hypnosis as a valid therapeutic method by the American Medical Association and the American Psychological Association has contributed to a new trend in the use of hypnosis in legal cases. Hypnosis has been widely used in a therapeutic context to help individuals remember material they had forgotten. Many defendants claim to be unable to remember the events for which they are being tried, and so it seemed reasonable to consider that hypnosis might help refresh their memories so that they might better assist in their own defense. In other cases it has been proposed that hypnosis could be useful in ascertaining the defendant's state of mind at the time of the crime. By this back door then, the role of hypnosis in facilitating the recall of otherwise "forgotten" facts or memories of the state of mind was reintroduced into the courtroom, and efforts were made to introduce hypnotically elicited testimony to juries.

An excellent example of this strategy occurred during the retrial of a convicted murderer in Ohio (State v. Papp, No. 78-02-00229, Com. Pleas Ct., Summit Co., Ohio, 3/23/78). The defendant claimed to be unable to remember some of the events at the time of the crime, and the court ordered that he be hypnotized to assist in his defense. Using the procedure of hypnotic age regression, the defendant apparently relived the period of the crime and exonerated himself, leading the press throughout the state to proclaim his innocence. After viewing the videotape record of the hypnotic session, which, according to the prosecution experts, revealed some anomalies in Papp's response to hypnosis, the hypnotist hired by the defense was persuaded to administer specific tests to assess possible simulation. The defendant behaved in a manner typical of those who are pretending to be hypnotized, and the result recorded on videotape was sufficiently clear that it was not effectively disputed by the defense. Consequently, no attempt was made to introduce the videotape recording purportedly demonstrating the defendant's innocence in court.

Criminal defendants have a clear self-interest in the outcome of hypnosis; accordingly great care must be taken in the interpretation of hypnotic material. It must also be kept in mind that the hypnotic session, which may involve displays of considerable feeling, is extremely arousing and compelling to the untrained observer. For example, in the case of People v. Ritchie, No. C-36932, Super. Ct., Orange Co., Calif., 4/7/77, the defendant was accused of killing a 2½-year-old child. When confronted with an overwhelming amount of circumstantial evidence, the defendant requested that he be hypnotized to enable him to remember details which he could not recall. Under hypnosis he relived the experience in an exceedingly dramatic fashion, remembering material indicating that his wife committed the murder and clearing himself. Through an analysis of the videotape recording of the hypnosis session, it was possible to document how the defendant had inadvertently been led by the hypnotist and also to demonstrate a number of intrinsic inconsistencies which clearly indicated that the version the defendant relived under hypnosis was either confabulated or a conscious lie designed to serve the needs of his case. After extensive testimony, the court excluded the hypnotic evidence because of its unreliability.

B. To Cause a Defendant to Confess

Confessions are regularly obtained by interrogators without the use of force, the threat of force, or even any obvious form of mental coercion, and even individuals who know that they would be better off not confessing often do so. There is general consensus that hypnotized individuals will not carry out activities which are morally unacceptable or inherently self-destructive. One would expect, therefore, that hypnosis should not cause a guilty individual to confess to a crime, since it is rarely if ever advantageous for a defendant to confess. The situation here is considerably more complex, however, since good interrogators frequently obtain confessions from defendants who know that they jeopardize their position by confessing. Somehow it is possible for the interrogator to make the relationship in the here and now seem more important than the eventual, detrimental consequences of having confessed. It seems clear that there are psychological needs which will be served by confessing, and that even in the usual waking state the relationship with a skilled interrogator may tap that psychological balance. It would hardly be surprising, therefore, that in some instances confessions have been obtained in a context of hypnosis. In the New York case of the People v. Leyra, 302 N.Y. 353, 98 N.E. 2d 553 (1951) the defendant was accused of the hammer murder of his mother and father. A psychiatrist retained by the district attorney's office saw him in jail and elicited a full confession. A tape recording of the session was available which showed that the psychiatrist identified himself as a physician there to help the defendant, massaged his forehead and temple repeatedly, demanded the defendant look into his eyes, told him that he was not morally responsible for what he had done, suggested that he had picked up the hammer and struck his parents, and even threatened to give him an injection if he failed to cooperate. The confession was introduced at the trial and the defendant convicted. On appeal, the judgment was reversed on the grounds that the confession was involuntary and coerced. The defendant was retried and again convicted. On appeal to the U.S. Supreme Court, the defendant prevailed (Leyra v. Denno, 347 U.S. 556 [1954]). While hypnosis is not explicitly mentioned, Justice Black's opinion in writing for the majority points out that "suspect's ability to resist interrogation was broken to almost *trance-like submission* by the use of the arts of a highly skilled psychiatrist. Then the confession petitioner began making to the psychiatrist was filled in and perfected by additional statements given in rapid succession to a police officer, a trusted friend, and two state prosecutors" (emphasis added; *id.* at 561).

It is worth noting that false confessions may also be elicited under hypnosis for the same kind of complex reasons that cause innocent individuals to assert their guilt whenever there is a well-publicized crime. It is important to recognize that merely because certain individuals, originally seen as witnesses, begin to relive the events of a crime during hypnosis and clearly implicate themselves one should not accept their actions as necessarily indicating guilt. An example of this kind involved a distinguished physician, an authority on the use of hypnosis, who at the request of the police department sought to facilitate the recall of a purported murder witness. Surprisingly, under hypnosis incriminating statements were made which would have implicated the witness as the perpetrator of the crime. The witness then became a suspect. Fortunately, subsequent investigation did not corroborate any of the statements made under hypnosis, including the location of the possible murder weapon, and the case turned out to be an inadvertent false confession obtained under hypnosis (see Kroger 1977).

In every instance where the courts have become aware that hypnosis has been used in an effort to obtain confessions, such confessions have been excluded. Consequently, everyone agrees that hypnosis should not be used in such a manner. While the likelihood of obtaining false confessions is not widely understood, it is a moot issue because care is taken to avoid the use of hypnosis with any possible suspect. Indeed, most prosecutors recognize that if they hypnotize a witness who later turns out to be implicated as a defendant, they will significantly complicate his or her ultimate prosecution.

C. To Recall Relevant Details in Civil Suits

Hypnosis has been used to help plaintiffs in accident cases remember details of the incidents. For example, in a Canadian case (Crockett et al. v. Haithwaite et al., No. 297/73, Sup. Ct., British Columbia, 2/10/78), a woman and a male passenger were found in a car which had run off the road and hit a tree. The passenger was dead and the driver seriously injured. British Columbia law is such that if the driver had been careless or distracted, her insurance would be liable to the estate of her dead passenger and she herself would have no substantial claim; however, if another car caused her to run off the road, her insurance company would not be liable and she herself would be able to recover very substantial damages from a special fund set up to compensate those injured by unidentified drivers. At the time of the accident, however, the woman reported no recollection of such a car. Some time later her attorney referred her to a psychiatrist for help with emotional difficulties stemming from the accident, and also requested that he might seek to facilitate her memory of the accident. There is little doubt that the driver and her lawyer were clearly aware of the substantial difference it would make whether or not another vehicle had been involved in the accident; thus it is hardly surprising that under hypnosis she remembered a van coming toward her and forcing her off the road. If the driver had simply stated that one day she suddenly remembered that a van had forced her off the road, a jury would be likely to reject such "spontaneous" memories as self-serving and not trustworthy. Memories which are recalled via the use of hypnosis, however, are more apt to be taken at face value. This case was ultimately settled on the courthouse steps. Even so, it represents a use of hypnosis closely analogous to hypnotizing a defendant and open to all the caveats involved in such a use.

II. The Nature of Hypnotic Recall

When hypnosis is used with a defendant or plaintiff who has much to gain by recalling one set of memories rather than another, motivational factors are superimposed upon the basic mechanisms involved in hypnotically aided recall. While these motivational factors complicate the picture, the basic facts about the phenomenon of hypnosis and its effects on recall apply to all circumstances where hypnosis is employed. The unreliability of hypnotic recall is due both to factors inherent in the nature of hypnosis and properties of the human memory system. This section reviews relevant research findings concerning the nature of hypnotic age regression, the effect of direct suggestions to remember material that was apparently forgotten, some aspects of memory as they are relevant to hypnotically aided recall, and the mental mechanisms which may account for the apparent increase in recall, including the tendency to confabulate, that is, to make up plausible pseudo memories for those portions of an event that the person is unable to recall. Finally, some aspects of the hypnotist's behavior characteristic of the hypnotic context which tend to alter the quality of recall are discussed.

A. Age Regression

While direct suggestion is sometimes used to facilitate recall in hypnosis, the procedures most widely employed involve some form of hypnotic age regression. This dramatic phenomenon appears to enable individuals to relive an event which might have occurred many years past. It is also a method that can be equally effective in helping an individual relive recent events, particularly if they involve some trauma leading to motivated forgetting manifested by the inability to recall significant events. Not only are extensive clinical observations available concerning hypnotic age regression, but it has also been studied systematically in the laboratory, providing data which shed much light on the nature of the process, and on the critical issue of the historical accuracy of hypnotically elicited recall.

When a hypnotized individual is told that he is 6 years old and at his birthday party, for example, he will begin to act, talk, and to some degree think like a child. He may play as a child would; address the friends who apparently were at his birthday party; and describe in detail the room where the party is occurring, the people who are in attendance, and the presents he is receiving. The naturalness with which these descriptions are given and the conviction that is communicated by the individual are compelling even to trained observers. The feelings which are expressed appear appropriate to a child more than to an adult, and the entire phenomenon is such that it is generally described as beyond the skills of even a professional actor. In a therapeutic setting, the material that is recovered during hypnotic age regression is often of great importance to a patient's treatment. As Breuer and Freud (1895) discovered at the end of the nineteenth century, the reliving of traumatic events may result in the cure of troublesome pathological symptoms, lending credence to the historical accuracy of these events. For these reasons, there is a widely held belief among both laymen and practicing clinicians that the events relived during hypnotic age regression are historically accurate.

Typically, age regressed individuals will spontaneously elaborate a myriad of details which apparently could be produced only by someone actually observing the events as they occurred. It is these details which sophisticated clinicians find most compelling and occasionally cause them to testify that they know with certainty that the individual was truly regressed. It is rare indeed, however, for the clinician to have the time, energy, or need to be certain that would cause him to attempt to verify the accuracy of an individual's description of events that actually happened many years ago in childhood. Unfortunately, without objective detailed verification, the clinician's belief in the historical accuracy of the memories elicited under hypnosis is likely to be erroneous. Freud's early "infantile seduction" theory of hysteria gives dramatic evidence of this.

Freud originally believed that seduction in childhood by an adult, usually the father, was the etiological factor in hysteria (see Ellenberger 1970) because in hypnosis his patients dramatically relived such an event and typically showed considerable subsequent improvement. It was some years later that Freud realized the seduction scene that the patients relived in treatment accurately reflected the fantasies of the patient but did not accurately portray historical events. Often the relived episodes combined several actual events and many fantasies. This in no way detracted from the usefulness of reliving these events in treatment where the purpose is to help the patient gain relief from his symptoms. Consider, however, the catastrophe which would have resulted if Freud had acted upon his patients' recollections and had urged the authorities to imprison the fathers for incest!

Experimental work with hypnotic age regression is possible because hypnosis is a phenomenon that can readily be induced in normal individuals. It is sometimes possible to obtain materials that an individual has not seen since the age of 6, then to age regress him back to that time, and while the subject is talking, acting, and writing like a child, to elicit these same materials—for example, childhood drawings. Characteristically, the productions superficially resemble those of a child. One tends to accept them as "typical" of what a 6-year-old would have done, *unless* they are compared to what the individual had actually drawn as a child. In an early study (Orne 1951), however, an expert in children's drawings examining a series of age regressed productions indicated that these were not done by children but showed "sophisticated oversimplification."

Since that time, other experimental studies have sought to document the historical accuracy of material produced during hypnotic age regression. The best known is an interesting monograph by Reiff and Scheerer (1959) who compared five highly responsive subjects age regressed to ages 10, 7, and 4 with three groups of role-playing subjects instructed to act as if they were 10, 7, and 4 respectively. The results seemed to document cognitive processes characteristic of children of the appropriate age in the age regressed subjects, but not in the controls. In our laboratory, this study was extended and replicated (O'Connell, Shor, and Orne 1970). With larger samples and controlling for subtle experimenter bias, it became clear that both modest increase in recall as well as increased confabulation occurred within the same subject in the same age regression session. There were many times that subjects provided us with what appeared to be factual material relating to events that occurred many years ago such as their school's name, their teachers' names, and the names of schoolmates who sat next to them in the fifth and second grades. The subjects would describe their classmates so vividly and with such conviction that we were surprised indeed to find, when we went to the trouble of checking the actual school records, that some of these individuals had not been members of the subject's class; nor was the factual recall better than that of the unhypnotized controls.

The hypnotic suggestion to relive a past event, particularly when accompanied by questions about specific details, puts pressure on the subject to provide information for which few, if any, actual memories are available. This situation may jog the subject's memory and produce some increased recall, but it will also cause the subject to fill in details that are plausible but consist of memories or fantasies from other times. It is extremely difficult to know which aspects of hypnotically aided recall are historically accurate and which aspects have been confabulated. The details of material that is confabulated depend upon the subject's total past experience and all available cues relevant to the hypnotic task. Subjects will use prior information and cues in an inconsistent and unpredictable fashion; in some instances such information is incorporated in what is confabulated, while in others the hypnotic recall may be virtually unaffected.

As a consequence of these limitations, hypnosis may be useful in some instances to help bring back forgotten memories following an accident or a crime while in others a witness might, with the same conviction, produce information that is totally inaccurate. This means that material produced during hypnosis or immediately after hypnosis, inspired by hypnotic revivification, may or may not be historically accurate. As long as this material is subject to independent verification, its utility is considerable and the risk attached to the procedure minimal. There is no way, however, by which anyone—even a psychologist or psychiatrist with extensive training in the field of hypnosis— can for any particular piece of information determine whether it is an actual memory or a confabulation *unless* there is independent verification. Thus, there are instances when sub-sequently verified accurate license plate numbers were recalled in hypnosis by individuals who previously could not remember them. In the Chowchilla kidnapping case (Kroger and Doucé 1979), the license plate number was helpful in the initial in-vestigation of the case (although ultimately not required in the courtroom because of the abundance of other evidence avail-able). On the other hand, a good many license plate numbers that have been recalled under hypnosis by witnesses in other cases in fact belonged to cars and drivers none of which, as it turned out after investigation, could have been involved.

B. Hypermnesia by Direct Suggestion

Another approach which has been used to increase memory is to give direct suggestions to the hypnotized individual that he will be able to remember crucial events which occurred some time ago. While generally used to enhance recall for recent events, it can also be employed to induce hypermnesia for the distant past.

Stalnaker and Riddle (1932) used direct suggestion to facili-tate recall of long forgotten memories, shedding light on the mechanism of hypermnesia. It was suggested to deeply hyp-notized subjects that they would recall prose and verse that they had committed to memory in grade school. In hypnosis, these subjects appeared to remember the material far more eas-ily, with far better recall, than they otherwise could. Careful analysis, however, showed that, while some additional material was recalled in hypnosis, the amount was far less than it first seemed; in fact, subjects showed a pronounced tendency to confabulate so that many of the new phrases "recalled" had simply been improvised in a style that superficially resembled the author's. Often these confabulations were sufficiently good so as not to be easily recognized as such on casual examination. This study clearly established two tendencies in hypnotic hy-permnesia: (a) a modest increase in the amount of material available to memory, and (b) a tendency to confabulate—to fill in those aspects which the subject cannot remember, in an effort to comply with the suggestions of the hypnotist. More recent studies, such as those of White, Fox, and Harris (1940), Sears (1954), and Dhanens and Lundy (1975), appear to show increased recall of meaningful, though nontraumatic, material in hypnosis. (No such effect has been demonstrated with nonsense syllables.) However, when the effects of hypnosis on increased memory are compared with those of increased motivation (Cooper and London 1973), and procedures analogous to hypnosis with unhypnotizable subjects (Dhanens and Lundy 1975), there is no significantly greater increase in recall with hypnosis. Thus, the widely held belief that hypnotic suggestion can not only increase the amount but also the reliability of the material recalled ignores motivational factors on the one hand, and the concurrent dramatic increase in the "recall" of inaccurate information on the other. This is illustrated in the Stalnaker and Riddle study (1932). Depending upon how they scored their material, these investigators could observe a 65 percent increase in memory for material learned many years earlier when recalled during hypnosis. Such a figure is obtained if one simply looks at the number of more accurate memories that are produced. At the same time, however, subjects in the hypnotic condition vastly increased the amount of inaccurate details that were "remembered."

The apparently increased recall in hypnosis can in large part be understood if one takes into account the deeply hypnotized individual's tendency to manifest a decrease in critical judgment. The same process that increases suggestibility by permitting subjects to accept counterfactual suggestions as real also makes it possible for subjects to accept approximations of memory as accurate. When not hypnotized they are unwilling to consider approximate or fragmentary memories as acceptable recall; in hypnosis, however, they alter their criterion of what is acceptable and express accurately recalled fragments mixed with confabulated material. When hypnosis is used in the context of gathering investigative leads, such a change in criterion is desirable since it will cause witnesses to produce bits of information which they would not otherwise have felt confident enough to report—*provided*, of course, one recognizes that these fragments are made available at the cost of adding other details which are likely to be inaccurate. Further, neither the subject nor the expert observer can distinguish between confabulation and accurate recall in any particular instance. This can be done only by corroboration extrinsic to the hypnotic situation.

C. Confusion of Memories during Hypnosis with Waking Recall

When subjects are hypnotized and told to remember the events of a particular day (and awakened without amnesia suggestions), they may be able subsequently, and not under hypnosis, to describe their recollections in hypnosis and clearly differentiate them from their earlier recollections before being hypnotized. It is another matter, however, if subjects are convinced before being hypnotized that they will have the "true facts" that they are now unable to remember, or if prior to awakening, they are given the suggestion that they will wake up and remember everything, including the details of what actually occurred on a particular day, and that they will be able to recall all details as vividly and clearly as in hypnosis. Under these circumstances, they will typically awaken and confound the hypnotic memories with their waking memories. Such suggestions, which are now widely used for forensic purposes, result in individuals' tending to accept the events relived in hypnosis as if they were what actually happened. The previous gaps or uncertainties in memory are now filled in, and the events as they were relived in hypnosis become recollections of what actually occurred on the day in question.

Witnesses who testify following such a procedure may even fail to be able to distinguish which memories occurred in hypnosis and which came about as part of the normal waking recollection. Instead of differentiating between earlier fragmentary recall and the gaps later filled in—perhaps by pseudo memories created during hypnosis—they experience the totality as their recollection of what had originally occurred. It is this new recollection that is convincingly reported when the individual is asked what happened. Even though prior to hypnosis they had been very uncertain about their memory, had changed their stories many times, and had not reported many of the details that emerged only during hypnosis, they will now report their "memories" consistently and with conviction. As a consequence, memories which occurred only during hypnosis may be incorrectly presented in court as though they represented recollections based on original memory traces of the events that actually occurred on the day in question, and of course they will be presented with the credibility attributed to sincere beliefs.

D. Hypnotic Recall as Part of Basic Memory Processes

The idea that one can in hypnosis somehow reactivate original memory traces stems from a popular view (shared among lay hypnotists) that memory involves a process analogous to a multi-channel videotape recorder inside the head which records all sensory impressions and stores them in their pristine form. Further, there is a belief that while this material cannot ordinarily be brought to consciousness, access to it can be obtained through hypnosis; this mechanism is presumed to make possible the phenomenon of age regression or revivification. Suffice it to say that such a view is counter to any currently accepted theory of memory and is not supported by scientific data (Hilgard and Loftus 1979; Jenkins 1974; Putnam 1979; Roediger 1979). As Bartlett (1932) pointed out many years ago, memory is continuously changing and is *reconstructive* as well as reproductive. It is possible that highly traumatic, emotional material that is repressed could be less subject to the kind of continuing changes seen with relatively neutral material, but even this is doubtful since, as has been pointed out earlier, many of the memories recovered in psychotherapy include material which is not historically accurate.

Particularly relevant to our consideration here, however, are the observations discussed by Hilgard and Loftus (1979) indicating that free narrative recall will produce the highest percentage of accurate information but also the lowest amount of detail. Conversely, the more an eyewitness is questioned about details, the more details will be obtained—but with a marked decrease in accuracy. This observation, based on research with unhypnotized individuals, is virtually certain to apply to hypnotized subjects as well.

E. From Hypnotic Enhancement of Recall to the Creation of Memory

While the laws that govern memory inevitably apply to hypnotic recall, it is difficult to disentangle which aspects of hypnotically enhanced memories represent accurate recall and which represent fantasies that are confabulated to approximate what might have occurred. The extent to which the process of confabulation may be stimulated by hypnosis becomes obvious when, instead of being asked to relive a prior event, the subject is given suggestions to experience a future event—about which no memories could possibly exist. For instance, in age progression (Kline and Guze 1951), a subject is given the suggestion that it is the year 2000 and asked to describe the world around him. Such a suggestion, given to the deeply hypnotized individual, will lead to a vivid and compelling description of all kinds of new, as yet unseen, scientific marvels. Obviously, the plausibility and the precise nature of a subject's description will depend upon the scientific knowledge, the reading, and the intelligence of that subject.

The same process that allows hypnotized individuals to hallucinate the environment of the year 2000 can also be involved when they are urged to recall what happened six months ago, especially if they lack clear, waking memories to permit them to recall details accurately. Unfortunately, such pseudo memories can and often do become incorporated into individuals' memories store as though they had actually happened. It is worth noting that this can occur even with bizarre memories such as when people "recall" their past lives and become convinced that these events really took place or, in other instances, when individuals under hypnosis remember encounters with flying saucers and become convinced they have actually communicated with beings from another galaxy. In such instances, the sophisticated listener smiles about the subject's assertions since it is obvious that they represent pseudo memories. Unfortunately, if such pseudo memories relate to events which occurred six months ago and are plausible, there is no way for either the hypnotist or the subject or a jury to distinguish between them and actual recall of what occurred.

The content of pseudo memories when they are wittingly or unwittingly induced during hypnosis is, of course, not random. If the subject has just seen a science fiction film, one can usually recognize elements of that film in the subject's description of what is going on about him or her in the year 2000; similarly, if a witness is hypnotized and has factual information casually gleaned from newspapers or inadvertent comments made during prior interrogation or in discussion with others who might have knowledge about the facts, many of these bits of knowledge will become incorporated and form the basis of any pseudo memories that develop. Furthermore, if the hypnotist has beliefs about what actually occurred, it is exceedingly difficult to keep from inadvertently guiding the subject's recall so that the subject will eventually "remember" what the hypnotist believes actually happened.

A simple experimental demonstration which I have often carried out is directly relevant to the circumstances of attempts hypnotically to enhance recall. First, I carefully establish and verify that a particular subject had in fact gone to bed at midnight on, say 17 February, and had arisen at 8 a.m. the following morning. After inducing deep hypnosis, it is suggested that the subject relive the night of 17 February—getting ready for bed, turning out the light, and going to sleep at midnight. As the subject relives being asleep, he is told that it is now 4 a.m. and then is asked whether he has heard the two loud noises. Following this question (which is in fact a suggestion), a good subject typically responds that the noises had awakened him. Now instructed to look around and check the time, he may say it is exactly 4:05 a.m. If then asked what he is doing, he may describe some activity such as going to the window to see what happened or wondering about the noises, forgetting about them, and going back to sleep.

Still hypnotized, he may relive waking up at 8 a.m. and describe his subsequent day. If, prior to being awakened, he is told he will be able to remember the events of 17 February as well as all the other things that happened to him in hypnosis, he readily confounds his hypnotic experience with his actual memory on awakening. If asked about the night of 17 February, he will describe going to sleep and then being awakened by two loud noises. If one inquires at what time these occurred, he will say, "Oh, yes, I looked at my watch beside my bed. It has a radium dial. It was exactly 4:05 a.m." The subject will be convinced that his description about 17 February is accurately reflecting his original memories.

The subject's altered memory concerning the night of 17 February will tend to persist (unless suggestions are given to the contrary), particularly because the subject was asleep at the time and there are no competing memories. The more frequently the subject reports the event, the more firmly established the pseudo memory will tend to become. In the experimental demonstration, we are dealing with an essentially trivial memory about which the subject has no strong inherent motivations. Nonetheless, the memory is created by a leading question, which, however, on casual observation seems innocuous.

In a life situation where hypnosis is used to enhance recall, the same mechanisms which we have purposively employed in the laboratory to create plausible pseudo memories which subjects accept as their own may easily occur inadvertently. It must be emphasized that one is not usually dealing with a conscious effort on the part of the hypnotist to distort witnesses' memories; on the contrary, the process by which hypnotized subjects are affected typically occurs outside of the hypnotist's awareness. Thus, if the hypnotist knows that two shots have been fired at approximately 4 a.m. on the night of 17 February, what seems more natural than to inquire of a witness whether he or she had heard any loud noises? Further, since usually the witness also knows something about the case and the kinds of memories which would be relevant and important, it may be sufficient simply to inquire at critical times, "Did you hear anything?" in order to lead the responsive hypnotized subject to create the desired "memories."

F. Lifting of Amnesia versus "Refreshing Memory"

Traditionally, hypnosis has been a widely used procedure to treat spontaneous amnesia. Similarly, when hypnosis has been used to treat traumatic neuroses, previously amnesic material would suddenly become accessible to consciousness, usually accompanied by profound affect as the patient relives the experience. As these internal emotions are relived, the patient's sudden awareness of a myriad of details becomes clear from the manner in which the events are reexperienced. The therapist, seeking to help the patient become aware of feelings, encourages the process of reexperiencing and allows the expression of affect to run its course. The therapist is careful to avoid interrupting the largely spontaneous experience of the patient; although he or she may well want to know more about some important details, questions are postponed in order not to interfere with the process.

It is characteristic of repressed memories that they suddenly come to consciousness as an entire experience rather than emerging detail by detail. In short, the procedure leads to a narrative exposition as the patient relives the experience. While there is no certainty about the historical accuracy of these memories, when they emerge largely spontaneously and without undue pressure, they are more likely to have been kept out of consciousness because of emotional reasons. To the extent that one is not dealing with the usual processes of forgetting but with material that is being kept out of awareness without having been forgotten, the likelihood of obtaining some accurate and important information seems greater. When the emotional blocks to recall are circumvented, one is more likely to obtain the important, and possibly accurate, information which had been remembered but kept out of consciousness than would be the case with neutral or irrelevant material that is forgotten over time.

Since these instances involved pathological conditions, the approach—even when legal issues were at stake—was essentially therapeutic, and hypnosis was carried out by psychologists or psychiatrists in the context of a traditional doctor-patient relationship. In contrast, hypnosis has more recently been used in circumstances where there is no evidence of pathological memory loss. Here, on the assumption that every memory is somehow recorded, hypnosis is purported to be simply a means of "refreshing memory." As such, it is claimed that there is no issue of therapy involved.

As a consequence, hypnotic technique is typically altered to prevent subjects from expressing intense feelings that would raise therapeutic issues and would tend to be frightening to lay observers. Thus, it is suggested to the subjects that they can visualize the events that they seek to recall on a special television screen; this screen can, as in televised sports events, move forward or backward through time, allowing events to be seen in instant replay, slow motion, or frame by frame. Further, it is explained to subjects that they need not experience any discomfort, that they are merely to observe the screen and see the events unfold—as if they were spectators rather than participants (e.g. Reiser 1974). Suggestions are given, such as "It is just like watching a television show except that you not only can see it but you can control and even stop the motion; you can be there, but you need not experience pain or fear." Since hypnotic subjects who have been emotionally affected are wont to take the opportunity to relive the experience, there is often some struggle between the hypnotist attempting to keep the affect bottled up and the subject seeking to express it.

This type of "objective" reliving, rather than the "subjective" reliving generally encouraged by trained therapists, seems to bring forth fragmentary recall based not so much on the subject's reliving the experience as upon the hypnotist's detailed questions about what is occurring. Typically, the subject is repeatedly asked to "stop the film and look at the face carefully," and is then asked further questions about the details of the face. The same is generally done in relation to all potentially important details. Since this type of procedure involves a great many questions about details, it will, of course, elicit many more details than a narrative. By the same token, as the work summarized by Hilgard and Loftus (1979) has indicated, it will result in vastly lowered accuracy of the material obtained. Further, such a procedure maximizes the potential input of the hypnotist about what is wanted, making it even more likely that the subject's memories will more closely resemble the hypnotist's prior conceptions than would ordinarily be the case.

It is, of course, quite useful at times to use metaphors such as "stopping a videotape" and "instant replay" when working with hypnosis. However, no competent hypnotherapist would, in using such a metaphor, confuse it with the manner in which memory is organized. The therapist would also recognize that great pressure is thus being put on the subject to produce something, and the greater the pressure, the more likely the development of guided confabulations.

Unfortunately, no meaningful research is available to document the relative merit of facilitating the reliving of a traumatic event versus attempting to prevent the affect from being relived by using specific suggestions and questions to increase the amount of memory-like material being brought forth. Considerable experience in the clinical and forensic use of age regression and related techniques suggests that patients have a higher likelihood of producing uncontaminated memories if allowed initially to relive the events without much questioning by the hypnotist. Further details can then be elicited by questioning the second or third time the material is brought forth. It is interesting that the interrogation technique advocated by Loftus (1979), based on an entirely different body of data with waking eyewitnesses, is remarkably similar to that which evolved with hypnotic subjects.

G. *The Effect of the Hypnotic Context on Refreshing of Memory*

While the effect of hypnosis is most clear-cut in the realm of memory when one is dealing with circumscribed areas of pathological amnesia, a dramatic lifting of amnesia (with which most laymen are familiar from its portrayal in films, novels, and the media) is the exception rather than the rule. With the increasing use of hypnosis, particularly with individuals *without* any obvious memory disturbance and *without* the ability to enter profound hypnosis, the clear demarcation between effects specific to hypnosis and what may occur in everyday interrogation with unhypnotized individuals becomes blurred. While there is no doubt that the kind of processes involved in hypnosis can also be shown to occur under many other circumstances and that the basic laws governing human memory are not negated because the individual is hypnotized, it would be quite wrong to assume that the hypnotic *procedure* brings about no important changes.

Some advocates of the wide use of "forensic hypnosis" have argued that we need not be concerned about the kinds of issues that have been described earlier, because these problems occur even in the waking state and are certainly negligible if the subject is only relaxed and not deeply hypnotized. It is ironic that this kind of disclaimer is made by the very persons who tout the unique effectiveness of hypnosis as an aid to criminal investigation. They cannot have it both ways! The reason hypnosis is used as a forensic tool is that it is effective in eliciting more details. This is so even with persons who are not particularly hypnotizable but who cooperate in the hypnotic situation. It is being in the hypnotic situation itself that may profoundly alter some aspects of the subjects' behavior and experience (London and Fuhrer 1961). Thus, there is a strong expectancy that hypnosis will facilitate recall. Subjects in the hypnotic situation feel relaxed and less responsible for what they say since they believe that the hypnotist is both an expert and somehow in control. The hypnotist in turn makes certain that subjects cannot "fail." Hypnotic technique involves the extensive use of reinforcers through frequent verbalizations, such as, "Good," "Fine," "You are doing well," and so on, which are novel, satisfying, and reassuring, particularly in a police interrogation situation. Not surprisingly, subjects want to maintain the level of approbation; consequently, when the hypnotist stops the expressions of approval (simply by not saying "Good"), he or she clearly communicates that something else or something more is wanted. It requires only a modest decrease in the level of support to alter subjects' behavior, after which there is a return to the previous frequent level of reassurance. Similarly, in the relaxed and apparently benign context of hypnosis, subjects may be generally less anxious and less critical—allowing themselves to produce bits of information about which they are uncertain but which may in fact be accurate and important—information that would not be forthcoming in contexts where the subjects are made to feel responsible for their memories and challenged about their consistency. Thus, one might say that the hypnotic situation itself serves to change the subject's "guessing strategy."

To date, little systematic research has sought to distinguish between different kinds of effects that the hypnotic situation may exert on recall. Some mechanisms may require a profound level of hypnosis and relate primarily to the recall of material which is actively kept out of awareness; other mechanisms may be involved in the recall of meaningful details in emotionally neutral contexts.

Finally, there are aspects of the hypnotic situation that are not related to hypnotic depth, but nonetheless facilitate the increased reporting and acceptance of detailed information. For example, once a series of details is reported and accepted as valid by the hypnotist, that very fact serves to help convince the subject about the accuracy of these memories—memories that might previously have been extremely tentative and about which the subject had little or no subjective conviction. While there has not been much systematic exploration of the means by which the hypnotic context itself may alter the experience of persons who are only lightly hypnotized, from a pragmatic point of view it is necessary to recognize that these effects exist and may be profound. While careful research will be needed to clarify precisely which kinds of subjects—under what circumstances, relating to what kinds of memories, and in response to which specific techniques—will be more or less likely to yield reliable information, in the absence of such data it seems best to illustrate these issues in a life context by a selective review of relevant legal cases.

H. The Use of Hypnosis with Witnesses or Victims to Enhance Memory

Given the limitations of the hypnotic technique to facilitate recall, it becomes crucial to distinguish between apparently similar applications which in fact are very different and which consequently range from entirely appropriate to completely misleading. The key issue is not only the possible benefits that material obtained under hypnosis might accrue but also the need to assess the potential harm that would be caused by erroneous information. The use of hypnosis in an investigative context, with the sole purpose being to obtain leads, is clearly the area where hypnotic techniques are most appropriately employed. We will contrast the investigative use of hypnosis with other uses where the purpose is oriented not to the task of providing leads subject to verification but more to providing witnesses who can testify in court. We will show that as emphasis shifts away from the search for clues that will lead to reliable independent evidence and focuses more on helping to prepare witnesses to give eyewitness testimony, the difficulties that hypnosis creates for the administration of justice become increasingly greater. Thus, we will distinguish between (1) the situation where hypnosis is used exclusively to provide leads in a context where facts are not known, (2) a superficially similar situation insofar as the witness was originally hypnotized ostensibly for investigative purposes but where, in fact, he or she became an eyewitness and the only real evidence against the defendant, (3) the circumstances where there is no concern with the uncovering of details unknown to the investigating officer but only to help the witness remember what happened so that he or she is able to give eyewitness testimony, and (4) yet a different situation where a witness may have given a number of conflicting statements where hypnosis is utilized to "help the witness remember what really happened," but the search is not for the facts nor is the emphasis on independent verification. Rather there is an effort to use the hypnotic session itself as a means of verifying a witness's statement. The overall effect is to help the witness become reliable in his statements while reassuring both the authorities and the witness himself about the validity of these statements.

I. When Facts Are Not Known or Presumed

There are many cases involving victims or witnesses to crimes who cannot recall potentially important details and where the enforcement authorities are equally in the dark. In cases of assault, for example, hypnosis has made it possible for the victim to recall the assailant's appearance, enabling police artists to draw a reasonable likeness. To the extent that the victim or witness, police, artist, and hypnotist alike share no preconceived bias about what might have occurred, the situation approaches the ideal case for hypnosis to be most appropriately employed: to develop investigative leads.

Hypnotic suggestions may directly or indirectly enhance memory by providing contextual cues, and the relaxed environment of a sensitively conducted session may help diminish the anxiety which otherwise interferes with attempts to recall. Several cases of this type are described by Kroger and Doucé (1979). Many of the limitations of the technique—even in such circumstances—have been emphasized earlier, and other pitfalls are described by Kroger and Doucé. Given appropriate care, however, hypnosis has provided important new information to the authorities in many instances. If the sole purpose of the hypnotic session is to provide clues which ultimately lead to incriminating evidence, the fact that hypnosis was originally employed becomes irrelevant. However, if there is even the vaguest possibility that hypnotically enhanced recall is to be used in court, it is essential that the entire contact of the hypnotist with the subject be recorded on videotape to allow an independent assessment of the events preceding, during, and following the hypnotic session to determine whether the memories might have inadvertently been guided by cues in the situation.

J. When Witness Hypnotized to Obtain Facts Becomes Eyewitness

The investigative use of hypnosis involves helping a witness or victim remember additional details in an investigation, perhaps even to make eyewitness identifications. Sometimes additional information produced during hypnosis does not result in verifiable leads, though it may result in an eyewitness identification. In these circumstances, the temptation to utilize the witness as the basis for an indictment and prosecution often proves irresistible. The problems here transcend even the very difficult issues involved with all eyewitness testimony since the hypnotic procedure makes the hypnotized individual unduly responsive to suggestions, a process which can result in the creation of memories. A recent case in Illinois (People v. Kempinsky, No. W80CF352, Cir. Ct., 12th Jud. Cir., Will Co., Ill. 12/21/80) illustrates this problem nicely. A young man was stabbed to death by two assailants in a residential suburb. By systematic canvassing, the police were able to determine that a young man had been sitting in a pickup truck facing in the right direction when the murder occurred at approximately 9:30 in the evening. When questioned, the young man indicated that he saw a man running toward him from a distance to a point which was approximately 250 feet away. He was being pursued by two others. The witness heard the sounds of a struggle when the three men were not in sight and then saw two figures running away. He was, however, unable to identify them because of the distance and the poor light. When hypnotized, he was told that he would be able to remember accurately everything that his visual system had seen, that he would be able to see things occurring on a screen which was like the videotape of a sporting event. It would allow him to speed up, slow down, or bring to a total stop what had happened. He could reverse and zoom in on all events. The subject described the scene and was asked to stop the motion while one of the presumed assailants was turned toward him. While he said he could not identify him initially, he then zoomed in on the assailant and brought him right up to where he was sitting; at that point he indicated that he could identify him. In fact, he first described him as ugly, then as short, later as normal, and then as tall, and eventually said he had known the individual in high school, that the assailant was a senior when he was a sophomore. He also indicated approximately where he lived. He then picked the presumed individual out of some mug books. Although there was no other apparent independent evidence to indicate that the suspect had been at the scene of the crime or was the actual murderer, he was nonetheless indicted and brought to trial.

This case is unusual because it was possible to demonstrate with the aid of a research ophthalmologist, appropriate weather charts, and studies of the available light at that time of the evening that the only kind of vision possible would be the relatively inefficient achromatic rod vision. The ability of the eye to resolve an image is sufficiently limited that it would be virtually impossible to identify a face beyond 30 feet, whereas the assailants had never been closer than well over 200 feet!

Thus, while in all instances hypnotically aided recall is an amalgam of actual recollection and confabulation, the extent to which one or the other factor predominates is all but impossible to determine outside of a laboratory experiment. In this situation, however, since true visual perception could not have taken place, the identification must have been based on confabulation, a point that was acknowledged by both the prosecution and defense experts. It was also possible for me to point to other clear inconsistencies of the apparent recall. The defendant had dropped out of high school in his sophomore year and could not have been the individual whom the witness remembered as having been a senior when he was a sophomore. His home also was in a very different area from where the witness had said he lived.

This case is particularly striking because of the fortuitous circumstances which made it obvious that the witness could not be testifying from his memory of the original event. It is worth noting, however, that he claimed to be testifying from his waking recall of the original events, obviously demonstrating the fallacy of accepting a witness's assurances in this regard after a hypnotic session. Further, the defendant was brought to trial solely on the unverified eyewitness identification which had occurred only during hypnosis. While in this instance it was possible to prove that the hypnotically created pseudo memory could not possibly be true recall, if by chance the assailant had run past the pickup truck where the witness was sitting, precisely the same psychological processes could have taken place but it would have been considerably more difficult to show the inherent problems created by the hypnotic session. In fact, no unverified hypnotic testimony should ever be permitted in court, and assertions by the waking individual that he actually had remembered the events prior to hypnosis are worthless because the witness is not in a position to determine whether that is or is not the case.

K. When Significant Facts are Known or Presumed

An increasing number of instances are finding their way into law courts where hypnosis is used to help "refresh" the memory of a witness or victim about aspects of a crime which are known to the authorities, the media, or the hypnotist and may involve presumed facts that in one way or another have been made available to the subject. Of course, witnesses or victims cannot testify on such matters unless they are able to remember them personally. Particularly when the interrogation focuses on some relevant detail and involves leading questions is there the greatest likelihood of mischief. A "memory" can be created in hypnosis where none existed before. While cases of this type were once rare, there has been a dramatic increase in recent years. Although the sources of the factual information may vary widely, all these cases have the quality that information is somehow introduced into subjects' memories which causes them to testify to the facts as if they were based on prior memories.

A Pennsylvania case, United States v. Andrews, Gen. Ct. Martial No. 75-14, N.E. Jud. Cir., Navy/Marine Corps Judiciary, Phila., Pa., 10/6/75, illustrates the kind of problem that may occur. Two seamen recuperating from illness were working in an office when a sailor appeared in the doorway, aimed a pistol at one of the sailors, shot at his head, and fled the scene. Fortunately, the intended victim moved quickly and suffered only a grazing wound to the ear. When the seamen were shown pictures of persons who might fit the description and could have been in the area, the victim was unable to identify anyone. The witness, however, identified one of the pictures as that of the assailant. Subsequently, at a preliminary hearing, the victim was present when the witness identified the defendant as the assailant. The victim, however, indicated that the accused looked like but was not the assailant. The victim was then hypnotized on two occasions by an experienced navy psychiatrist to facilitate his recall. During the first session, he was still unable to make an identification; however, during the second session he claimed to recognize the defendant who had previously been identified by the witness as the assailant.

At the general court-martial, the issue of the role of hypnosis was raised by the defense and I was asked to testify as an expert. My testimony pointed out that the victim's reaction to hypnosis would probably have been the same whether or not he could actually remember the assailant. Thus, if he continued to be unable to remember him—which was highly likely considering the difficulties encountered in eliciting the recollection—he would have been prone to confabulate an individual who appeared to be the most likely candidate. He had seen the defendant accused during the preliminary hearing, was aware that the witness had identified him with certainty, and knew also that it was the general belief of the prosecution that the defendant was guilty. The hypnotic session altered the victim's memory and, while he would now testify to what he erroneously believed his original memory to have been, he was in fact testifying on the basis of what he had been led to recall during hypnosis, which was quite different from his actual earlier memories.

In this instance, the military judge ruled as a matter of law that the victim could testify to those things that he had previously testified to but that since his memory was altered by hypnosis he was not permitted to identify the defendant. In the weeks following this event, two persons who had left for overseas the evening of the incident returned from Germany and independently corroborated the defendant's alibi, making it extremely unlikely that he was the actual assailant. In this case, it is interesting that the effect of hypnosis on the victim's memory persisted, and well over a year after the event he still asserted his conviction that the defendant had in fact fired the shot which nearly killed him.

Another example is a recent capital case in Milwaukee, Wisconsin, State v. White. No. J-3665, Cir. Ct., Branch 10, Milwaukee Co., Wis., 3/27/79. A 20-year-old Indian girl nicknamed "Sweetie Pie" had been found strangled several years before. The case had not been solved but had raised considerable attention and concern and had not been closed. Sometime later, another girl reported to the police that her boyfriend had beaten her several times and she wanted him to seek psychiatric help. When questioned, she admitted that on occasion he had choked her, presumably in an attempt to frighten her. The authorities became more interested at that point, particularly when it turned out that the boyfriend, also an Indian, had known "Sweetie Pie." At that point, the girlfriend became uncooperative because she had wanted only to induce the boyfriend to seek treatment and had no wish to have him become involved with the police. On further investigation, however, it was found that the boyfriend did not have an alibi for the time in question, and the authorities talked at length with his former wife, from whom he had been separated about a year, and her sister. Both women had lived with the defendant and had children by him.

The wife, who maintained some relationship with the defendant, was not particularly helpful to the authorities, but the sister, who was felt to be more willing to discuss matters, was interviewed on several occasions by police officers. She was asked whether she had been beaten up and indicated that there were times when this had occurred but claimed that she could not remember much else. When it was suggested that she and the former wife participate in a hypnotic session, they agreed to do so. The hypnotic session was carried out by a well-trained psychologist. Prior to hypnosis, he showed a gruesome picture of the dead body to the sister, who had also been a close friend of the murdered girl. He then induced hypnosis, and shortly thereafter said,

> For the moment I want you to think about just you and me and Sweetie Pie, who got strangled, thrown out on the road, taken to the morgue, put in a box, and buried in the ground. Now somebody did that. I don't know who, but you know that Joe White is a suspect in this case, don't you? Do you think that there is any reason why Joe White should or should not be a suspect in this case?

At the end of the session, which included an age regression-like procedure that did not work very well despite the subject's otherwise good response to hypnosis, there was a posthypnotic suggestion given that she would be thinking about telling the truth, how good it would feel to tell the truth, and that she was going to tell the truth. Within a week after the session, the sister called the police and told them how the defendant had often choked her, that he seemed to enjoy it, and that one time shortly after the murder he was choking her and said something to the effect, "If you don't behave, the same thing can happen to you that happened to Sweetie Pie." When she asked whether he had killed "Sweetie Pie," he allegedly broke down crying and said that he had not intended to but admitted that he had.

The case against the defendant was primarily based upon the sister's hearsay testimony which became available shortly after the hypnotic session. After a lengthy hearing, the court ruled that as a matter of law she could not testify before a jury because, thanks to the hypnotic session, the presumed memory was likely to have been created rather than remembered. It is unlikely that anyone will ever know for certain whether the defendant was or was not responsible for the murder. There was no doubt in the sister's mind, however, as to the kind of memory which was wanted, and the sister was amply motivated to testify against the defendant. She had continued to live with the defendant, supposedly knowing that he was a murderer, for many months until he rejected her. Consequently, her testimony would have been totally discounted if it had not come after the hypnotic session. The court recognized the danger of permitting hypnosis to be used in a context where it is more likely to create a memory than to refresh it.

Whereas in the first case the identity of the defendant became known to the victim during a pretrial hearing, and in the second case the nature of the memory was shaped by conversations with the police officers, with the sister, and particularly by the way the hypnotic session was conducted, it is equally possible for the suggestion about what to recall to come from entirely different sources unrelated to and long before hypnosis. For example, in the Minnesota case of State v. Mack, Dist. Ct., 4th Jud. Dist., Hennepin Co., Minn. (1979), a physician insisting that a laceration must have been made by a knife led to a total reorganization of an apparent victim's memory about how she had acquired an internal wound. In other cases, the media have provided the critical information, while in still others, the manner in which a lineup was conducted facilitated the creation of "memories" at hypnotic sessions conducted at a later date (e.g. State v. Peterson, No. CCR 79-003, Cir. Ct., Hamilton Co., Ind., 7/12/79).

In addition to criminal cases, it is not uncommon to find something of this kind in civil cases where persons are helped by hypnosis to remember details of accidents they had been unable to recall previously. By the time hypnosis is carried out, it is generally clear to subjects which of possible events that might have occurred would be most helpful to their particular cases. Although accurate information may be recovered, the important effects that motivation can exert on memory—hypnotically enhanced or otherwise—must be taken into account in assessing the "memories" obtained.

L. When Reliability of Witness's Statement Is to Be Affirmed

Many witnesses are unreliable in the sense that they tell somewhat different stories each time they are asked to tell what occurred. These differences may relate to important details of the crime. The adversary system upon which Anglo-Saxon jus-

tice is based relies upon cross-examination as the means of un-
masking the unreliability of witnesses before the finder of fact.

The effect of hypnotizing witnesses of this kind, presumably
to help refresh their memories, is generally dramatic. Even if
the subject is not particularly responsive to hypnosis, reviewing
the events in the hypnotic context and having the memories
legitimized by the hypnotist generally fixes one particular version of the testimony in the witness's mind which is then
faithfully and reliably reproduced every time. In these cases,
hypnosis does not serve to produce any new information, but
the procedure can bolster a witness whose credibility would
easily have been destroyed by cross-examination but who now
becomes quite impervious to such efforts, repeating one particular version of the story with great conviction.

To appreciate the effect of hypnosis in these kinds of cases, it
is important to view the use of the technique in its broader
perspectives. Often it will involve a witness about whom the
prosecution has considerable doubts. In one California case (*In
re Milligan*, No. J-17617, Super. Ct., Monterey, Calif., 6/29/78),
for example, the prosecution's star witness was a 14-year-old
girl who had told many different stories to the police at different times and readily changed her story during early de-
positions. Indeed, she repeatedly stated that it was impossible
for her to say whether her recollections were a dream or represented actual events. The case involved the murder of the witness's aunt, sister, grandmother, and cousin, and there was
some serious question as to the degree of possible criminal involvement of the witness herself.

The witness was hypnotized and again told her story to the
district attorney and the police. However, now it was during
hypnosis, which everyone agreed would reliably help her recall
and she would know whether her memories related to real
events or to her dreams. Simply carrying out the hypnotic session committed the prosecution to the view that the witness was
not criminally involved since it would not be permissible for the
state to hypnotize a defendant—especially a minor. Somehow
the witness became reassured that she would be safe and her

story became remarkably stable, virtually unshakable on cross-examination.

In a real sense, the hypnotic procedure also helped change the prosecution's attitude toward the witness. She was accepted as having no part in the crime, and instead of being considered an unreliable juvenile, became an exceedingly effective witness whose testimony led to the conviction of the other individuals involved. This was so despite the fact that the story she produced under hypnosis and on subsequent occasions contained a number of incorrect statements recognized as such by the hypnotist but ignored. Hypnosis had not resulted in accurate memories, but rather had served to produce consistent memories. Further, the technique served to reassure the law enforcement officials that the witness was in fact telling the truth, an aspect which was perhaps as important as the effect the hypnotic session had in stabilizing the witness's recollections.

The confounding effects of hypnosis in altering the views of the law enforcement agencies as well as the perceived credibility of the witness testifying before the finder of fact makes it essential that the use of hypnosis be disclosed to the other side whenever a witness has been hypnotized. Below I will spell out some relatively simple safeguards that must be adhered to in order to be able to assess the effect of hypnosis in a given case. Thus, unless proper videotape recordings are available of the hypnotic session as well as the interviews preceding and immediately following it, no witness who has been hypnotized should be allowed to testify.

M. The Consequences That Follow from the Inappropriate Use of Hypnosis

The attitude of law enforcement agencies toward the use of hypnosis is an important factor in the problems that may arise. In the case of *State v. White* (1979), referred to earlier, a senior law enforcement official was asked under oath about his views of hypnotically aided testimony and he succinctly expressed widely held beliefs when he testified that hypnosis lends "credibility and strength to your investigation." Perhaps the most interesting, as well as the most frightening, consequence of this belief is illustrated by a New Jersey case (State v. Douglas 1978). A woman was stopped at a light and two black men entered the car and forced her at gunpoint to drive to a deserted place on the outskirts of town. When they arrived there, the man in the front seat attempted to rape the woman. When she protested that she was pregnant, the man on the back seat with the gun told the attacker to stop. They took the woman's purse, made her leave the car, and threatened her that if she contacted the police, terrible things would happen to her family. On getting back to her home, the woman immediately reported the attempted rape, as well as the theft of her car and valuables. At the police station, she was shown mug shots and she identified one man and picked out another as a look-alike. Subsequently, she received several threatening notes which were turned over to the police. She continued to be unable to identify the second man involved in the crime, and finally the police persuaded her to undergo hypnosis. Although the police had videotape as well as audiotape recording equipment available, it was claimed that the equipment would not work, and hypnosis was carried out without any objective record of what occurred. During the hypnotic session, however, the victim identified the look-alike as the man who was involved in the crime.

It turned out that the district attorney had been quite skeptical about the case but was finally convinced to prosecute by the hypnotic session. It was only after the hypnotic session that indictments were brought against the two suspects. However, it was impossible for the defense to find out the details of what had occurred during the hypnotic session. As one might anticipate, the descriptions by the investigating officer and the district attorney of the events were quite different, and there was simply no way of ascertaining what had actually occurred. Nonetheless, when the district attorney learned that the use of hypnosis would be vigorously challenged and that the public defender's office was prepared to use this case as a vehicle to prevent the use of hypnosis by the police, she decided to have another look at the facts of the case. She was struck by the peculiarity of the handwriting in the threatening notes, and for the first time submitted these to a handwriting expert who identified the writing as that of the woman who had filed the charges. When the alleged victim was confronted with this fact, she confessed that there had never been an attempted assault, that she had never met the two men whom she had accused, and that she had generated the complaint and the threatening notes in an effort to reawaken the interest of her husband, who was in the process of filing divorce proceedings against her.

The appalling aspect of this case is that it was the hypnotic sessions that initially prompted the district attorney to cast doubt aside and proceed with the prosecution. The hypnotically enhanced memories would have been the basis for the victim's testimony and might well have led to the conviction of two innocent individuals who happened to have been in the collection of photographs available to the police and did not have excellent alibis. It was only when the district attorney became aware that the defense would have appropriate expert help to challenge the totally inappropriate way in which hypnosis was employed in this case that a more careful review of the evidence uncovered the true state of affairs. Far from being helpful to the prosecution, the manner in which hypnosis was employed actually served to confuse the authorities.

III. The Role of the Expert in Forensic Hypnosis

It is not possible in a single essay to more than touch upon the complex issues involved in the forensic use of hypnosis. However, it behooves those of us experienced in the clinical use of hypnosis to exercise extreme care when we use our skills in a forensic context. We should keep in mind that psychologists and psychiatrists are not particularly adept at recognizing deception. We generally arrange the social context of treatment so that it is not in the patient's interest to lie to us, and we appropriately do not concern ourselves with this issue since in most therapeutic contexts it is helpful for the therapist to see the world through the patient's eyes in order ultimately to help him view it more realistically. (See Lindner 1955 for a superb description of the kind of countertransference which leads to the uncritical acceptance of the patient's views that, on the one hand, makes treatment possible but, on the other, can be a source of serious difficulties.)

As a rule, the average hotel credit manager is considerably more adept at recognizing deception than we are. Not only does his livelihood depend upon limiting errors of judgment, but he is in a position to obtain feedback concerning those errors of judgment, whereas in most treatment contexts the therapist is neither affected by being deceived nor even likely later to learn that he or she has been deceived. While military psychiatrists and other health professionals who are required to make dispositional judgments on a daily basis do become adept at recognizing manipulation and deception, only a few health professionals who are experienced in the use of hypnosis have had this type of background. Consequently, they have little experience or concern about being deceived or used. On the other hand, a defendant in a murder trial or, for that matter, a witness or a victim in a crime of violence may well have an axe to grind, and it is essential for us to recognize that in a forensic context the unwary expert witness may become a pawn either for the prosecution or for the defense. With the increasing popularity of hypnosis in the courts, it is essential that those of use who have an interest in these matters develop the necessary sophistication and judgment in the forensic context, much as we have had to acquire it in the therapeutic context. It would be foolhardy indeed to assume that familiarity with one context is sufficient to allow us to function effectively in the other. On the contrary, the ground rules governing the two situations are vastly different, and we must guard against being co-opted— wittingly or unwittingly—by prosecution or defense.

The use of hypnosis and related techniques to facilitate memory raises profound, complex questions, and it is likely that the individual will be protected only if these issues are dealt with at the highest level of our court system. There are instances when hypnosis can be used appropriately provided that the nature of the phenomenon is understood by all parties concerned. It must be recognized, however, that the use of hypnosis by either the prosecution or the defense can profoundly affect the individual's subsequent testimony. Since these changes are not reversible, if individuals are to be allowed to testify after having undergone hypnosis to aid their memory, a minimum number of safeguards are absolutely essential. Based upon extensive review of the field and my own experiences in a considerable number of circumstances, I have proposed the following minimal safeguards in an affidavit (Orne 1978) in the case of *Quaglino v. California* which was filed with the Supreme Court of the United States (*cert. den.*, 99 S. Ct. 212 [1978]).

1. Hypnosis should be carried out by a psychiatrist or psychologist with special training in its use. He should not be informed about the facts of the case verbally; rather, he should receive a written memorandum outlining whatever facts he is to know, carefully avoiding any other communication which might affect his opinion. Thus, his beliefs and possible bias can be evaluated. It is extremely undesirable for the individual conducting the hypnotic sessions to have any involvement in the investigation of the case. Further, he should be an independent professional and not responsible to the prosecution or the investigators.

2. All contact of the psychiatrist or psychologist with the individual to be hypnotized should be videotaped from the moment they meet until the entire interaction is completed. The casual comments which are passed before or after hypnosis are every bit as important to get on tape as the hypnotic session itself. (It is possible to give suggestions prior to the induction of hypnosis which will act as posthypnotic suggestions.)

Prior to the induction of hypnosis, a brief evaluation of the patient should be carried out and the psychiatrist or psychologist should then elicit a detailed description of the facts as the witness or victim remembers them. This is important because individuals often are able to recall a good deal more while talking to a psychiatrist or psychologist than when they are with an investigator, and it is important to have a record of what the witness's beliefs are before hypnosis. Only after this has been completed should the hypnotic session be initiated. The psychiatrist or psychologist should strive to avoid adding any new elements to the witness's description of his experience, including those which he had discussed in his wake state, lest he inadvertently alter the nature of the witness's memories—or constrain them by reminding him of his waking memories.

3. No one other than the psychiatrist or psychologist and the individual to be hypnotized should be present in the room before and during the hypnotic session. This is important because it is all too easy for observers to inadvertently communicate to the subject what they expect, what they are startled by, or what they are disappointed by. If either the prosecution or the defense wish to observe the hypnotic session, they may do so without jeopardizing the integrity of the session through a one-way screen or on a television monitor.

4. Because the interactions which have preceded the hypnotic session may well have a profound effect on the sessions themselves, tape recordings of prior interrogations are important to document that a witness had not been implicitly or explicitly cued pertaining to certain information which might then be reported for apparently the first time by the witness during hypnosis. (Orne 1978, pp. 853–55)

Guidelines based upon these safeguards have been adopted by the courts in the *State v. White* (cited earlier), and in the State of New Jersey v. Hurd, 173 N.J. Super. 353, 362–63 (1980), and judicial notice has been taken of these guidelines by the Supreme Court of Minnesota in *State v. Mack* (cited earlier), and by the Supreme Court of Massachusetts (Commonwealth v. A Juvenile, S.2160, Supreme Judicial Court [1980]).

IV. Summary and Conclusions

An effort has been made to outline some of the major issues that must be considered for the forensic use of hypnosis, and particularly if hypnotically enhanced recall is to be used in court. It is possible to document, as has been done here, some of the circumstances where hypnosis has worked against the judicial process. Much of what has been said about memory and hypnosis in this essay has already been documented empirically; however, further rigorous research is needed. Future work will need to direct itself to the task of spelling out the circumstances under which the likelihood of confabulation is maximized, the specific effects which result from the hypnotist's preconceptions, the consequences of allowing the re-experiencing of relevant affect as opposed to suppressing it during the process of recall, the different effects which hypnosis may have on the recall of different kinds of material on the one hand and on the other to assess whether hypnosis has different effects in facilitating recall of material that was purposively learned as opposed to that incidentally noted. At the present state of knowledge, it is relatively easy to point to some clear-cut abuses and try to identify some relatively safe and appropriate applications of hypnosis. As serious research addresses the question of the effect of hypnosis and the hypnotic context on memory, it will become possible to be increasingly specific about other circumstances where hypnosis may play a legitimate role as opposed to those where its use will serve only to further confuse an already blind justice.

REFERENCES

Barber, Theodore X. 1961. "Antisocial and Criminal Acts Induced by 'Hypnosis': A Review of Experimental and Clinical Findings," *Archives of General Psychiatry* 5:301–12.
Bartlett, Frederick C. 1932. *Remembering.* Cambridge: Cambridge University Press.
Breuer, J., and S. Freud. [1895] 1955. *Studies on Hysteria.* Vol. 2. *The Standard Edition of the Complete Psychological Works of Sigmund Freud,* ed. and trans. J. Strachey. London: Hogarth Press.
Coe, William C., K. Kobayashi, and M. L. Howard. 1972. "An Approach toward Isolating Factors that Influence Antisocial Conduct

in Hypnosis," *International Journal of Clinical and Experimental Hypnosis* 20:118–31.

Conn, Jacob H. 1972. "Is Hypnosis Really Dangerous?" *International Journal of Clinical and Experimental Hypnosis* 20:61–79.

Cooper, Leslie M., and P. London. 1973. "Reactivation of Memory by Hypnosis and Suggestion," *International Journal of Clinical and Experimental Hypnosis* 21:312–23.

Dhanens, Thomas P., and R. M. Lundy. 1975. "Hypnotic and Waking Suggestions and Recall," *International Journal of Clinical and Experimental Hypnosis* 23:68–79.

Ellenberger, Henri F. 1970. *The Discovery of the Unconscious.* New York: Basic Books.

Evans, Frederick, and J. F. Kihlstrom. 1973. "Posthypnotic Amnesia as Disrupted Retrieval," *Journal of Abnormal Psychology* 82:317–23.

Hilgard, Ernest R. 1977. *Divided Consciousness: Multiple Controls in Human Thought and Action.* New York: Wiley.

Hilgard, Ernest R., and E. F. Loftus. 1979. "Effective Interrogation of the Eyewitness," *International Journal of Clinical and Experimental Hypnosis* 27:342–57.

Jenkins, James J. 1974. "Remember that Old Theory of Memory? Well, Forget It!" *American Psychologist* 29:785–95.

Kihlstrom, John F., and F. J. Evans. 1976. "Recovery of Memory After Posthypnotic Amnesia," *Journal of Abnormal Psychology* 85:564–69.

———. 1977. "Residual Effects of Suggestion for Posthypnotic Amnesia: A Reexamination," *Journal of Abnormal Psychology* 86:327–33.

Kline, Milton V. 1972. "The Production of Antisocial Behavior Through Hypnosis: New Clinical Data," *International Journal of Clinical and Experimental Hypnosis* 20:80–94.

———. 1979. "Defending the Mentally Ill: The Insanity Defense and the Role of Forensic Hypnosis," *International Journal of Clinical and Experimental Hypnosis* 27:375–401.

Kline, Milton V., and H. Guze. 1951. "The Use of a Drawing Technique in the Investigation of Hypnotic Age Regression and Progression," *British Journal of Medical Hypnotism* Winter:1–12.

Kroger, William S. 1977. *Clincial and Experimental Hypnosis.* 2d ed. Philadelphia: Lippincott.

Kroger, W. S., and R. G. Doucé. 1979. "Hypnosis in Criminal Investigation," *International Journal of Clinical and Experimental Hypnosis* 27:358–74.

Lindner, Robert. 1955. *The Fifty-Minute Hour.* New York: Holt, Rinehart and Farrar.

Loftus, Elizabeth F. 1979. *Eyewitness Testimony.* Cambridge, Mass.: Harvard University Press.

London, Perry, and M. Fuhrer. 1961. "Hypnosis, Motivation and Performance," *Journal of Personality* 29:321–33.

Nace, E. P., M. T. Orne, and A. G. Hammer. 1974. "Posthypnotic Amnesia as an Active Psychic Process," *Archives of General Psychiatry* 31:357–60.

O'Connell, Donald N., R. E. Shore, and M. T. Orne. 1970. "Hypnotic Age Regression: An Empirical and Methodological Analysis," *Journal of Abnormal Psychology* 76:1–32 (Monograph Supplement no. 3, pt. 2).

Orne, Martin T. 1951. "The Mechanisms of Hypnotic Age Regression: An Experimental Study," *Journal of Abnormal Psychology* 46:213–25.

———. 1959. "The Nature of Hypnosis: Artifact and Essence," *Journal of Abnormal and Social Psychology* 58:277–99.

———. 1962. "Antisocial Behavior and Hypnosis: Problems of Control and Validation in Empirical Studies." Paper presented at Colgate University Hypnosis Symposium, Hamilton, N.Y., April 1960.

———. 1961. "The Potential Uses of Hypnosis in Interrogation." In *The Manipulation of Human Behavior*, ed. Albert D. Biderman and H. Zimmer, pp. 169–215. New York: Wiley.

———. 1962. "Antisocial Behavior and Hypnosis: Problems of control and Validation in Empirical Studies." In *Hypnosis: Current Problems*, ed. George H. Estabrooks, pp. 137–92. New York: Harper and Row.

———. 1966. "On the Mechanisms of Posthypnotic Amnesia," *International Journal of Clinical and Experimental Hypnosis* 14:121–34.

———. 1969. "On the Nature of the Posthypnotic Suggestion." In *Psychophysiological Mechanisms of Hypnosis*, ed. Leon Chertok, pp. 173–92. Berlin: Springer-Verlag.

———. 1971. "The Disappearing Hypnotist: The Use of Simulating Subjects," *International Journal of Clinical and Experimental Hypnosis* 19:277–96.

———. 1972a. "Can a Hypnotized Subject Be Compelled to Carry Out Otherwise Unacceptable Behavior? A Discussion," *International Journal of Clinical and Experimental Hypnosis* 20:101–17.

———. 1972b. "On the Simulating Subject as a Quasi-Control Group in Hypnosis Research: What, Why and How." In *Hypnosis: Research Developments and Perspectives*, ed. Erica Fromm and R. E. Shore, pp. 399–443. Chicago: Aldine-Atherton.

———. 1977. "The Construct of Hypnosis: Implications of the Definition for Research and Practice," *Annals of the New York Academy of Science* 296:14–33.

———. 1978. Affidavit of Amicus Curiae, *Quaglino v. California*, U.S.

Sup. Ct. No. 77-1288, *cert. den.* 11/27/78. In *16th Annual Defending Criminal Cases: The Rapidly Changing Practice of Criminal Law*, chm. E. Margolin, 2:831–57. New York: Practising Law Institute.

Orne, Martin T., and F. J. Evans. 1965. "Social Control in the Psychological Experiment: Antisocial Behavior and Hypnosis," *Journal of Personality and Social Psychology* 1:189–200.

Orne, Martin T., P. W. Sheehan, and F. J. Evans. 1968. "Occurrence of Posthypnotic Behavior Outside the Experimental Setting," *Journal of Personality and Social Psychology* 9:189–96.

Putnam, W. H. 1979. "Hypnosis and Distortions in Eyewitness Memory," *International Journal of Clinical and Experimental Hypnosis* 27:437–48.

Reiff, Robert and M. Scheerer. 1959. *Memory and Hypnotic Age Regression: Developmental Aspects of Cognitive Function Explored Through Hypnosis*. New York: International Universities Press.

Reiser, Martin. 1974. "Hypnosis as an Aid in a Homicide Investigation," *American Journal of Clinical Hypnosis* 17:84–87.

Roediger, H. L. 1979. "Implicit and Explicit Memory Models," *Bulletin of the Psychonomic Society* 13:339–42.

Sears, Alden B. 1954. "A Comparison of Hypnotic and Waking Recall," *International Journal of Clinical and Experimental Hypnosis* 2:296–304.

Sheehan, Peter W. 1972. *The Function and Nature of Imagery*. New York: Academic Press.

Sheehan, Peter W., and M. T. Orne. 1968. "Some Comments on the Nature of Posthypnotic Behavior," *Journal of Nervous and Mental Disease* 146:209–20.

Stalnaker, John M. and E. E. Riddle. 1932. "The Effect of Hypnosis on Long-Delayed Recall," *Journal of General Psychology* 6:429–40.

Watkins, John G. 1972. "Antisocial Behavior Under Hypnosis: Possible or Impossible?" *International Journal of Clinical and Experimental Hypnosis* 20:95–100.

White, Robert W., G. F. Fox, and W. W. Harris. 1940. "Hypnotic Hypermnesia for Recently Learned Material," *Journal of Abnormal and Social Psychology* 35:88–103.

Elizabeth F. Loftus

Eyewitness Testimony: Psychological Research and Legal Thought

ABSTRACT

Most psychological studies of eyewitness testimony conducted during this century are aimed at discovering factors influencing the accuracy and completeness of an eyewitness account, with emphasis on those factors affecting the acquisition, retention, and retrieval of complex information. Recent studies have focused on some new issues, particularly the impact of eyewitness testimony in a legal proceeding. Research suggests that jurors place too much reliance on such testimony. Legal commentators have begun to realize the enormous impact of eyewitness testimony, and various safeguards have been devised to protect individuals from its damaging consequences. One solution, the use of expert psychological testimony on the reliability of eyewitness accounts, has been highly controversial and yet has spurred a new research effort designed to discover impact. Preliminary findings indicate that such testimony leads jurors to be cautious about the eyewitness testimony and not to accept it without scrutiny.

In the late nineteenth century, Harvard University, seeking a scholar to develop the new science of experimental psychology, was successful in capturing, with considerable effort, Hugo Munsterberg of Freiburg, Germany. When Munsterberg arrived early in the 1890s, he was received in a grand manner. After all, he was, and may still be, the most prolific writer in the history of American psychology (Hale 1980).

Elizabeth F. Loftus is professor of psychology, University of Washington, Seattle. The preparation of this manuscript was facilitated by grants from the National Science Foundation and from the National Bureau of Standards.

Some of Munsterberg's interests lay in the application of psychology to the law, an interest that was fueled by his involvement in two celebrated murder cases in the early 1900s.[1] Resulting publicity led Munsterberg to write a series of essays on the potential contributions of psychology to various legal problems, which were published in his classic book, *On the Witness Stand* (1908). Here Munsterberg demonstrated what psychology could contribute toward the correction of police procedures and courtroom behavior. Beginning with a discussion of eyewitness testimony in which he made the point that even the most honest and best-intentioned witnesses are fallible, and using data collected largely from his own laboratory and classroom, Munsterberg showed what enormous error can occur when people perceive and attempt to recall simulated "crimes." For example, in one demonstration a clown in a highly colored costume rushed into a room, followed by a black man with a revolver in his hand. A shooting ensued and finally both men left the room. The witnesses' accounts were highly variable. Only four people noted correctly that the black man had nothing on his head; others gave him a derby, a high hat, or some other head-covering. Although he wore white pants, a black jacket, and a large red tie, some "remembered" that he wore a red suit, others said it was brown, and still others recalled stripes. Modern demonstrations of this sort support the wide variation in eyewitness accounts and the widespread prevalence of error.

Munsterberg's book also covers such topics as false confessions, psychological detection of lying, and the prevention of crime. Because of its popular and occasionally sensational style, Munsterberg's book quickly became a best-seller (Moskowitz 1977), and his writings on the whole were more popular than

---

[1] The first case involved a self-confessed murderer of eighteen people, Harry Orchard, who accused others of having directed the murders. Munsterberg studied the behavior of Orchard in the courtroom and in private sessions, performed word-association and other tests on him, and decided that Orchard was not lying. His conclusions reached the popular press, which proclaimed that Munsterberg had invented a way to detect lies. Thus, the idea of the lie detector was launched. The second case involved a Chicago man who confessed to a brutal murder; the man was subsequently hanged. Munsterberg later reviewed the evidence in the case and concluded: "I have to say again that he was hanged for a crime of which he was no more guilty than you or I" (1908, p. 140). His opinion reached the popular press and he received a great deal of angry publicity.

scientific. They included very few original laboratory studies, in part because very few had been done. His work angered the legal profession (Wigmore 1909) but at the same time created a climate which gradually induced changes in traditional court-room procedures. These changes included the appearance of psychiatrists and psychologists as "expert witnesses" in trials, the use of the polygraph and psychological assessment as techniques in investigation, and the introduction of psychological training as a popular elective in law schools and prelaw studies.

Now, more than half a century later, it can no longer be said that original laboratory studies of eyewitness reliability are few. Three books on the psychological aspects of eyewitness testimony have recently been published (Clifford and Bull 1978; Loftus 1979; Yarmey 1979), all of which document the massive amount of psychological research that has been conducted in this area. A major purpose of this essay is to describe the psychological research on the eyewitness with special emphasis on research conducted since the publication of the three books mentioned. The identification by Penrod and Loftus (in press) of over sixty research articles and papers published in the years 1979 and 1980 alone attests to the rapidly growing interest in this field.

Relevant research can be organized into three distinct categories. First is the research on human perception, memory, and suggestibility as they relate to eyewitness ability. Results of these studies generally show that a person's perceptual and memorial systems do not passively record and store information from the environment. Rather, perceiving and remembering are constructive processes (Lindsay and Norman 1977). People are selective about what they pay attention to in the first place and selective about what they store in memory, and they differ in the extent to which they are susceptible to suggestion. Numerous other factors influence the accuracy of information that is stored and retained in the mind, and much of the psychological research on the eyewitness is aimed at discovering and illuminating those factors.

A second line of research concerns the impact of eyewitness testimony in a legal proceeding. These studies tend to suggest that jurors too easily believe eyewitness testimony. Jurors respond more to the confidence of the eyewitness than to the witnessing conditions themselves, even though confidence and accuracy are not necessarily related.

Taken together, these two areas of research suggest that, whether we are concerned with the identification of a person or the accurate recounting of the details of an event, there can be problems posed by evidence consisting of eyewitness testimony, either in a criminal case or a civil one. The problem can be stated rather simply: eyewitness testimony is not always reliable. It can be flawed simply because of normal and natural memory processes that occur whenever human beings acquire, retain, and attempt to retrieve information. Yet this testimony is very believable, can wield considerable influence over the decisions reached by a jury, and is sometimes the only evidence available.

What should be done? Several solutions have been proposed which have led to a third area of research designed to test their effectiveness. In 1967 the U.S. Supreme Court acknowledged the problem of identification of people and instituted some safeguards to limit the introduction of potentially unreliable evidence at trial (United States v. Wade, 388 U.S. 218 [1967]). These safeguards concerned the right of an accused to have an attorney present at any pretrial confrontation conducted for purposes of identification. Later decisions, however, chipped away at these safeguards. Another solution centered on the use by trial judges of cautionary instructions designed to focus the jury's attention on some of the problems with eyewitness testimony (United States v. Telfaire, 469 F. 2d 552 [1972]). However, these instructions have not gained widespread use. A third solution, involving the use of expert testimony on eyewitness reliability, has been controversial in the courts but has begun to excite new research on the impact of the expert testimony.

This chapter is organized in three major sections. The first, "The Psychology of Eyewitness Testimony," discusses the psychological research that bears on how witnesses *acquire* information into memory, *retain* that information in memory, and *retrieve* the information at some subsequent time. This section treats the many factors that influence the quality of a final eyewitness account. Facial recognition is considered separately, in part because there are some special phenomena (such as cross-racial identification) that pertain only to the recognition of human faces and not to memory for other sorts of details. The second major section, "Impact of Courtroom Eyewitness Testimony," considers the effect that eyewitnesses have in a courtroom and concludes that jurors give more weight to eyewitness testimony than perhaps they should. The third section, "The Eyewitness in the Legal System," discusses various methods for reducing the damage that faulty testimony can do in the courtroom. One practical solution has been the use of expert testimony on the reliability of an eyewitness account; such testimony causes jurors to scrutinize more carefully the eyewitness account.

The essay ends with a section, "Methodological Issues," that concerns researchers who study the eyewitness. As we shall see, a major concern has been with the external validity of the research. To what extent does laboratory research about eyewitness testimony tell us anything about real-world eyewitnesses or real-world reactions to eyewitness accounts?

I. The Psychology of Eyewitness Testimony

For most of this century basic research in experimental and social psychology was not conducted with the intention of applying results to the eyewitness situation. Yet it has now been found useful in understanding the eyewitness. Instead of reviewing the theoretical studies, however helpful they might be, this essay focuses on studies using fairly realistic materials.[2] This means studies in which subjects have been exposed to live incidents (e.g. Laughery, Alexander, and Lane 1971), movies or

[2] Basic research in human memory has similarly been concerned with how information is stored in memory and how it is later retrieved. In many experiments the materials to be remembered include lists of nonsense syllables, individual words, arrays of letters, or random dot patterns. There is some question as to how much of this work can be applied to a more naturalistic eyewitness situation. The more realistic the study, the greater the confidence one can have that the results can be applied to a natural eyewitnessing situation. Many reviews of the theoretical literature are available (e.g. Crowder 1976; Klatzky 1980; Loftus and Loftus 1976; Loftus 1980a).

film clips (e.g. Buckhout 1975), or individual photographs (e.g. Shepherd, Deregowski, and Ellis 1974). The review is not comprehensive because many other reviews exist. (In addition to the three recent books, see Bull and Clifford 1979, Goldstein 1977, and other articles cited throughout this essay.) This review is designed only to give the flavor of the research conducted in this area. A summary paragraph at the end of each subsection indicates what is and is not settled among researchers.

When we experience an important event, a complex process occurs. Nearly all the theoretical analyses of the process divide it into three stages (e.g. Crowder 1976; Loftus 1979). First, there is the *acquisition* stage—the perception of the original event—in which information enters a person's memory system. Second, there is the *retention* stage, the period between the event and the eventual recollection of a particular piece of information. Third, there is the *retrieval* stage, during which a person recalls stored information. Numerous factors in each of these stages can affect the accuracy and completeness of an eyewitness account. Examples are given in table 1.

Wells (1978) has cataloged the research in this area into two types. The first, system-variable research, investigates variables

TABLE 1

Factors Affecting Eyewitness Performance

Acquisition	
Event Factors	*Witness Factors*
Duration of event	Stress/Fear
Frequency of viewing	Age
Event complexity	Sex
Violence	Prior training
Seriousness	Expectation/Attitudes
	Personality characteristics
Retention	
Length of retention interval	
Change in appearance	
Intervening photographs	
Post-event suggestions	
Retrieval	
Method of questioning	
Identification procedures	
Status of questioner	
Nonverbal communication	

that are manipulable in actual legal proceedings (e.g. type of questions asked of a witness). The second, estimator-variable research, investigates variables that cannot be controlled in actual cases (e.g. how frightened the witness was at the time of the initial perception) but may be useful for evaluating the quality of an eyewitness account. Many of the factors that affect accuracy at the acquisition stage, such as the violence of the event, are estimator variables, whereas many of the factors occurring at the retrieval stage, such as question wording, are system variables. It is important to realize that both types of research can be valuable in different ways. For example, one cannot change the fact that the witness to an event is a child rather than an adult (age being an estimator variable). Knowing that young children are less accurate than adults can lead one to rely more heavily on an adult's eyewitness account if it is in conflict with that of a young child. Knowing that leading questions can bias an eyewitness account—a system variable—can suggest to investigators that they eliminate the use of these questions in their interrogations of witnesses.

A. Acquisition

At the acquisition stage, information about an event is perceived by the witness. The event may last a few seconds or, in some cases several hours. Factors such as exposure time (e.g. Laughery et al. 1971), violence of the event (e.g. Clifford and Scott 1978; Sanders and Warnick 1979), stress of the witness (e.g. Baddeley 1972), and expectations of the witness (e.g. Peterson 1976) are but a few of the factors that affect the quality of information stored in memory.[3] An examination in detail of one recent study will illustrate a typical methodology. Hollin

[3] Analytically the distinctions among acquisition, retention, and recall are clear, but behaviorally and experimentally they are not easily separated. To isolate the events responsible for memory failure or even to localize a source of failure in one of the stages often requires considerable ingenuity. Often it is impossible to conclude that a failure to recall is due to events occurring during at only one stage of the memory process. For example, numerous experiments report that the age of a witness affects the ability to perceive and remember an event. At present, it is impossible to determine unequivocally the locus of this effect. Are young children poorer at storing the event in the first place or in retrieving it at some later time? The important point here is that there will be disagreement as to whether the effects of some variables should be assigned to one memory stage or another.

and Clifford (1980) showed their subjects a black-and-white videotape of an event that was staged by members of a dramatic society. The tape showed a female walking, alone, toward the camera. In one version (the violent version) a male grabs her arm, forces her back against a wall, and then tears her bag from her grasp. He then runs away, leaving the female alone and sobbing. In the nonviolent version, the male approaches the female and asks for directions. After viewing the tape, the subjects were asked to recall the incident and to identify the male from a set of photographs. The results showed that accuracy of testimony was consistently poorer in the violent condition, replicating the earlier research.

The violence of an event is a factor that is inherent in the event itself. A second group, associated with the witness, includes such factors as age, sex, prior training, and intelligence.

Consider prior training. One question often asked is whether police officers are any better eyewitnesses than are lay people. As we shall see, training can help people notice certain kinds of details, but it is less able to help a person remember something that was not specially noted. Evidently the police are trained to look for both physical and behavioral clues that might escape the notice of someone without that training (Silberman 1978). For example, a jacket worn on a warm day might suggest a concealed weapon; a late-model car that has been repainted or a license plate that is too clean or shiny may suggest a stolen car. These are some of the subtle and not-so-subtle signals for which the police are alert and of which they may not even be conscious. Yet are police officers better at, say, recognizing the faces of strangers? A partial answer to this question has been provided by Woodhead, Baddeley, and Simmonds (1979), who evaluated an ongoing training course designed to improve the ability to recognize people. The training program, which had been operating for months prior to the study, involved three days of intensive training in which the trainees heard lectures, saw slides and film demonstrations, participated in discussions, handled case history materials, and performed exercises. Although the teaching was imaginative and enthusiastic, no examinations were given to find out if the training actually led to improvement. The three investigators found no evidence for any effect of the training course on the ability to remember photographed faces. It still remains to be discovered whether another type of training method could lead to enhanced acquisition and recall of human faces or whether training can enhance other kinds of memory, for example, accuracy concerning sizes, colors, and so on.

One question increasingly studied is the extent to which the witness's age affects eyewitness ability. Psychological research seems to indicate that young children make less good eyewitnesses than young adults do, whereas elderly individuals may or may not be less able than young adults.

Numerous studies have examined the eyewitness ability of children, an issue of practical importance since children are often called upon to give evidence in court. In some of this research, children of one age, say 6, have been studied with an eye toward discovering whether they are affected by particular independent variables such as questioning techniques (Dale, Loftus, and Rathbun 1978; Dent 1977, 1978). In other cases the ability of children of various ages has been examined. In much of the research reviewed in the three recent books, adults and older children outperform younger children. In fact, Clifford and Bull (1978) state that "children are inferior to adults in both the range and accuracy of their testimony, i.e., they give fewer items and what they do give is more likely to be inaccurate" (p. 156).

In light of this widespread belief, the results of a recent study showing minimal differences between children and adults were somewhat surprising (Marin et al. 1979). The study compared four groups of subjects: kindergarten and first grade, third and fourth grade, seventh and eighth grade, and college students. Each subject viewed a staged scenario in which a male entered the experimental room and, looking very upset, made some remarks to the experimenter. The entire interaction lasted about 15 seconds and, after a short delay, the subject was tested on his or her memory for the details of the event and ability to identify the intruder. Two weeks later, subjects returned for a second memory test designed to assess the extent to which subjects picked up misleading information during the initial interview and incorporated it into memory. The results showed that recall of both correct and incorrect items increased linearly with age and that there was a small but nonsignificant effect of age on ability to answer specific questions accurately and make accurate photo identifications, and on susceptibility to leading questions. These minimal effects (and those found by Cane, Finkelstein, and Goetze 1979) stand in sharp contrast to the generally accepted belief that young children are highly inaccurate and highly suggestive. This research together with the bulk of previous research that has shown much stronger effects suggests that an important task for future research is to discover the conditions under which children can be good eyewitnesses.

At the upper end of the age continuum, the situation is equally complex. The conventional wisdom is that old people have poor memories. Yet much of the evidence cited to support a decline in memory with advancing age comes from experiments with highly unrealistic materials (e.g. nonsense syllables) and thus may not generalize to natural memory situations (see Craik 1977 for a review). Studies using more realistic materials are scarce, but a few do exist. In one study (Farrimond 1968) subjects between the ages of 23 and 79 were shown some scenes recorded on silent film. For example, one scene showed a 4-second short of a young boy inflating a bicycle tire. Later all subjects were tested and an age decrement was observed, with recall being poorer for the older subjects than for the younger ones. One possible explanation for the decline with advancing age is that there is a narrowing of the field of attention, resulting in poorer memory, although this is by no means the only explanation.

More recently, other investigators have examined eyewitness ability in the elderly. For example, Brigham and Williamson (1979) showed photographs of faces of black and white individuals to subjects of both races who averaged 72 years in age. Later they were asked to identify the original photographs in a yes/no recognition test. The overall level of recognition accuracy for these elderly people was considerably lower than for college-age subjects who viewed the same slides in an earlier study (Brigham and Barkowitz 1978).

One must be cautious in comparing groups of subjects who were tested at different times and under somewhat different conditions. Yet the same decline in performance has been observed in eyewitness studies in which the elderly and young adults have been tested within the same experiment. This was the case in a recent study by Byrd and Thomson (1979). College students and elderly (over 65) subjects viewed a 7-minute videotape of eight people, some of whom were eventually involved in a purse-snatching incident. After an interval of time, subjects were tested for their ability to remember the details of the event and to identify the "thief." The overall pattern of results confirmed the finding of an age-related decrement in memory. This result occurs even though the studies have controlled for eyesight.

Although the cross-sectional studies comparing young and elderly adults might typically show age-related decrements, it is a mistake to assume that the elderly will invariably make poorer eyewitnesses. Many of the leading experts in the field of cognitive gerontology stress that while performance on some tasks, for example, memory for details, may weaken a bit with age, other cognitive skills are maintained with advancing age. Furthermore, there are great individual differences among people (Baltes and Schaie 1976).

In summary, there are numerous factors that influence the acquisition of information and its storage in the memory, and support for this influence can be found in the three major reviews of the eyewitness literature (Clifford and Bull 1978; Loftus 1979; Yarmey 1979). Witnesses are more accurate under the following circumstances:

1. Exposure time is longer rather than shorter.
2. Events are less rather than more violent.
3. Witnesses are not undergoing extreme stress or fright.
4. Witnesses are generally free from biased expectations.

5. Witnesses are young adults rather than children.

6. Witnesses are asked to report on salient aspects of an event rather than peripheral aspects.

There still exists some controversy over the following questions:

1. Are elderly witnesses invariably less accurate than young adults?

2. Which personality characteristics are associated with good witnesses?

3. How does the complexity of an event relate to its subsequent recall or recognition?

Some variables influence eyewitness performance in complicated ways. For example, the sex of a witness has a complex effect: women tend to be more accurate on items that they are interested in, and the same is true of men. Thus, women may more accurately store information about clothing while men are more accurate on the make and model of automobiles. Prior training can teach a witness to notice certain kinds of details, but it does not seem to enable them to remember more easily either the faces of strangers seen briefly or information that was not specially noted.

B. Retention

At the retention stage, new factors come into play. One of these is the length of the period between the event and the person's recollection of it. Occasional studies report little loss of memory over the course of a day or even a week (e.g. Saslove and Yarmey 1980; Laughery et al. 1974), but the more typical result is a decline in accuracy as the retention interval is lengthened. Thus, Shepherd and Ellis (1973) showed subjects photographs of faces and tested them either immediately, after six days, or after thirty-five days. Memory got progressively worse as time passed. Lipton (1977) showed subjects a film of an armed robbery and shooting and found that subjects tested one week after the event were substantially less accurate than were those tested immediately. Ellis, Shepherd, and Davies (1980) showed that verbal descriptions of human faces were adversely affected by long intervals of time. After a week's delay, descriptions of faces were briefer and less likely to lead to accurate identification than those made immediately or soon afterward. Furthermore, memory for the various features appeared to fade at much the same rate. This research generally supports Ebbinghaus's (1885) original research in showing that the longer the interval the more poorly people perform.[4]

What is important about the retention interval is not the mere passage of time but what goes on during that interval. After an event has happened, people talk about it, they overhear conversations, they may be asked leading questions by an investigator or may be asked to identify photographs. All these activities can cause new information to become available to the witness, and evidence is mounting to prove that information learned by eyewitnesses subsequent to observing an event can alter the witness's memory of that event. Loftus (1979) reports the results of numerous studies in which college students are presented with a film of a complex event (e.g. an accident) and immediately afterward are asked a series of questions. Typically, some of the questions are designed to present misleading information—that is, to suggest the existence of an object that did not in fact exist. Thus, in one study, subjects who had just watched a film of an automobile accident were asked, "How fast was the white sports car going when it passed the barn while traveling along the country road?" whereas no barn existed. Those subjects were substantially more likely to later "recall" having seen the nonexistent barn than were subjects who had not been asked the misleading question. These experiments, and others that used variations of this procedure, show that people will pick up information, whether it is true or false, and

---

[4] A central mystery of memory is how, physiologically, we manage to record and retain information. The answer lies somewhere in the billions of interconnected neuorons that make up the human brain. Many neurophysiologists believe that the storage of information somehow involves a temporary circulation of electrical impulses around complex loops of interconnected neurons. This is followed by a structural or chemical change during which long-term memory traces are created. Although some evidence exists for this view, the specific neurological changes that occur with learning and memory stubbornly elude researchers. (See Thompson 1975 for a complete discussion of the physiology of memory.)

integrate it into their memory, thereby supplementing or even altering their recollection (e.g. Brown et al. 1977; Dritsas and Hamilton 1977; Lesgold and Petrush 1977; Mand and Shaughnessy 1980). Lawyers routinely try to control testimony on deposition and in court by means of questioning techniques. It is important to realize that these questions may not only serve to elicit information from a witness, but they may be simultaneously delivering information and consequently altering memory at the same time.

Are people able to resist these suggestive influences? A study by Dodd and Bradshaw (1980) is especially important in showing the ability of people to resist misleading suggestions. Their subjects viewed an accident depicted in a series of slides. Misleading information that ostensibly came from a neutral source (e.g. a bystander) was incorporated into memory, but that same information, when attributed to a biased source (the driver who caused the accident), was not. Thus, happily, subjects are able to resist misleading post-event suggestions when they make the effort to do so.

Between an event and one's recollection, other activities occasionally intervene that can influence the quality of the final recollection. With a criminal incident, one such activity is the viewing of mugshots. In one study subjects viewed a videotape of three men whom they were later going to try to identify (Davies, Shepherd, and Ellis 1979). Those who searched through a sequence of one hundred mugshots to identify the targets were less accurate on a subsequent test than control subjects who had not searched through mugshots. There is some controversy on whether the intervening activity influenced the witness's internal criterion or whether it directly interfered with memory, but in either event the result has important practical implications.

Once an event is over, it is not uncommon for witnesses to either talk about it or to overhear the conversations of other witnesses. This can have both a positive and a negative effect. Post-event conversations that contain false information can have a deleterious effect on the first witness's memory. Yet occasionally the post-event conversations contain correct information, and the influence on any single witness's memory can be positive. This was shown in a study in which subjects first witnessed a brief videotaped crime incident and were subsequently tested on their memory for the incident (Warnick and Sanders, in press). Some subjects discussed the videotape with others before being tested. In general, those who discussed the incident responded more accurately than those who did not; specifically, those who discussed the incident made fewer errors of omission and were more accurate in their estimation of the duration of the incident. Those who discussed the incident also made slightly, although nonsignificantly, fewer errors of commission, that is, producing details that didn't actually occur (but, see Alper et al. 1974 for a study in which discussions produced more errors of commission). Presumably, then, when subjects discuss an incident with other subjects, they can correct some of their own errors and in this way benefit from the discussion. The danger of group discussion arises when pieces of erroneous information enter the conversation, for in this case the erroneous information can influence memory in a negative way (see Loftus and Greene, in press, for a related study).

In summary, many factors influence the retention of information in memory. There is general agreement on the following points:

1. Witnesses are better able to remember information that occurred a short rather than a long time before.

2. Between an event and one's recollection, new information can enter memory that can cause an alteration in that memory.

There is still considerable controversy over the issue of the permanence of memory. When forgetting occurs, does it consist of an actual loss of stored information, or does it result from a loss of access to information, which once stored, remains forever (Loftus and Loftus 1980)?

C. Retrieval

Witnesses to complex events retrieve information from memory in numerous ways. Sometimes they are asked open questions to which they report any details they wish. Sometimes they are asked very specific questions requiring short answers. Sometimes they are presented with objects, like people, for the purposes of identification. There is substantial agreement that eyewitness reports can be biased or distorted at the retrieval stage. How information is elicited from a witness is critical.

Both lawyers and social scientists are aware that the answer one receives depends on the question one asks, but very few people are fully aware of how subtle the influence of questions can be. A very early study on the influence of questions is one reported by Muscio (1916). Muscio presented motion pictures to subjects, each picture running for about half a minute. Pre-arranged questions were then asked about each of the films reflecting the objects or events shown. Muscio found that the most reliable type of question was one that explicitly mentioned the actual seeing of an event ("Did you see a gun?" rather than "Was there a gun?"), and which did not use either the definite article ("Did you see the gun?" versus "Did you see a gun?") or a negative ("Did you see a gun?" versus "Didn't you see a gun?"). Hunter (1964) found that "implicative" questions in which the questioner implies the presence of something that may have been absent (e.g. "What type of gun was it?") were highly suggestive. Modern researchers have confirmed these early studies in showing that small changes in question-wording can result in dramatically different answers. In recent investigations (reviewed in Loftus 1979) subjects were shown films of complex events which they later had to remember and report. In one study subjects who were asked questions using the definite article (e.g. "Did you see the broken headlight?") were more likely than subjects queried with the indefinite article ("Did you see a broken headlight?") to report having seen something that had not really appeared in the film. In another study, subjects who saw films of traffic accidents and were then asked, "How fast were the cars going when they smashed into each other?" reported a higher estimate of speed than other subjects who were asked, "How fast were the cars going when they hit each other?" Taken together, these experiments show that in a variety of situations the wording of a question about an event can influence the answer given. The legal system's partial recognition of this has resulted in the legal concept of a leading question and in legal rules indicating when leading questions are allowed (*Federal Rules of Evidence*, 1975). A leading question is simply one that, either by its form or content, suggests to the witness what answer is desired or leads him to the desired answer. However, while the rules of evidence and other safeguards provide protection in the courtroom, they are absent in the backroom of the precinct station. The protection offered in the courtroom is surely vitiated if it is applied only after information has been obtained earlier by the use of improper interrogation techniques.

One source of influence at retrieval is who is asking the questions. Some research indicates that high status interviewers (e.g. a police chief) obtain more information from witnesses than do low status interviewers (Marshall 1966). The suggestive influences of interviewers known to be biased can often be resisted by witnesses (Dodd and Bradshaw 1980).

As Dent (1978) has noted, the task of eliciting information from a witness can be thought of as one of helping the witness to create an accurate reconstruction of past events. In order to do this effectively, the interviewer must be aware of the ways in which a witness's recollection is likely to be affected by the different methods of elicitation. A large body of past research has shown that when witnesses are allowed to report freely rather than answer specific questions, they produce the most accurate but least complete initial recall (e.g. Lipton 1977). This has led researchers to suggest that optimal results will be achieved by an interviewing strategy which first allows the witness to report freely, and then requires the witness to answer specific questions to fill in gaps in the recollection. (See Loftus 1979 or Yarmey 1979 for a review of this literature.) Following up on this line of research, Dent and Stephenson (1979) explored whether initial use of the free report technique might not have a detrimental effect upon later, more structured recall. While no evidence for such a detrimental effect was found, these investigators did find that a delay before the first recall session had an adverse effect upon the completeness of recall. The moral is one that investigators have known since the days of Ebbinghaus—it is best to get to the witness as early as possible. Ask the witness to report freely and follow this with specific questions to fill in the gaps in the free report.

Some rather promising new work on methods of enhancing witness recollection can be found in Dent (1978). She compared the interviewing strategies of experienced and inexperienced interviewers. Each interviewer was asked to gather information from a child who had been exposed to a simulated crime. After the interview, each interviewer wrote a report of what he or she thought happened in the crime. Analyses revealed that the experienced interviewers elicited both more correct and more incorrect information. But more interesting, the experienced interviewers were more skilled at recognizing incorrect information—it tended to drop out when the final report was made. Whether this skill is exercised during individual interviews (say by discovering inconsistencies in a single subject's account) or whether it is based upon inconsistencies between the accounts of different subjects is not yet known. This is clearly an important question for further research.

One source of error in recollection comes from the fact that the context of the recollection is typically very different from the context in which the witness viewed the initial event. Basic research on context effects has shown that a person's ability to remember information is heavily influenced by the relation between the storage of that information and the retrieval context (e.g. Smith, Glenberg, and Bjork 1978). Two studies have attempted to reinstate event context at the time of retrieval, and in both cases superior memory performance resulted (Malpass and Devine 1980; Shaul 1978). In the Malpass and Devine study, for example, subjects viewed a staged vandalism and were interviewed five months later. Some of the subject-witnesses were reminded of the events of the evening of the vandalism in a detailed guided memory interview in which their feelings, their memory for details of the room, and their immediate reactions were explored. Following the interview the subjects tried to identify the vandal. Compared to control subjects, those whose memory had been guided were more accurate.

When it comes to recognizing people, studies have shown powerful effects of disguises and changes in expression (Patterson and Baddeley 1977; Covey and Scott 1980) and of instructions given at a lineup-type identification (Ellis, Davies, and Shepherd 1977; Egan and Smith 1979). Recognition is better when the individual looks similar at both the acquisition and retrieval stages, and is better when subjects are given strict instructions ("Be careful") versus lax instructions ("Don't worry about mistakes").

One of the most surprising results from eyewitness literature concerns the relationship between the confidence of an eyewitness account and the accuracy of that account. There is little doubt that the American judicial system relies heavily on eyewitness confidence as a predictor of eyewitness accuracy (e.g. Gardner 1933). Yet this strong faith in the adequacy of certainty as a predictor of accuracy is not at all supported by a recent review of forty-three separate assessments of the accuracy/confidence relation (Deffenbacher 1980). This critical review and analysis revealed that under low optimal viewing conditions, those mitigating against the likelihood of highly reliable testimony, there is no relationship between confidence and accuracy. These observations led the psychologist conducting the analysis to recommend that the judiciary cease its heavy reliance on witness confidence as an index of witness accuracy.

In summary, many factors influence the retrieval of information from memory. There is general agreement on the following points:

1. Witnesses produce the most accurate and complete accounts when they are first asked to recall in their own words, and then to answer specific questions about an event.

2. Biasing words in a question (e.g. "Did the cars smash into each other?" versus "Did the cars hit each other?") can contaminate a witness's recollection.

3. Instructions given to witnesses when they attempt to recollect a prior experience can influence the quality of the recollection. Lax instructions (e.g. "Don't worry about mistakes") result in more errors than do strict instructions (e.g. "Be careful of mistakes").

4. Returning a witness to a state that is similar to the one in which the witness had the original experience enhances the recollection. Witnesses who return to the original location or return to the same emotional state often recall more accurately than those who do not.

Vigorous research activity is still being undertaken on the important topic of developing ways to enhance witness recollection. The 1980s will enjoy substantial strides in this area.

D. Facial Recognition

Many reviews of the eyewitness literature split apart the studies of facial recognition, in part because there are some special phenomena that pertain only to the recognition of human faces and not to memory for particular sorts of details. Also, this literature is relatively vast, since there are large numbers of cognitive psychologists who have simply found it handy to use faces as their stimuli when conducting memory research. It is not difficult to become frustrated with the present state of research into facial memory. The faces chosen as targets and distractors in these studies are generally selected at random, giving rise to wide variations in hit and false-alarm rates between different experiments (Goldstein 1977).[5] Despite this problem, a few fairly reliable research findings have emerged from the literature on facial recognition that are particularly applicable to the study of eyewitness testimony.

1. Cross-racial identification. It is well established that there is generally a comparative difficulty in recognizing individual

---

[5] When a witness is tested, one of four different outcomes can occur. The face being viewed can either be one that was seen before (an old face) or one that was not (a new face). For both of these cases, a witness may respond "old" or "new." Two responses are correct (responding "old" to an old face, which is called a "hit," and responding "new" to a new face, which is called a "correct rejection"). The other two responses are incorrect and include responding "old" to a new face, which is called a "false alarm" and responding "new" to an old face, which is called a "miss."

members of a race different from one's own. The most widely cited study is that of Malpass and Kravitz (1969). These investigators used subjects from the University of Illinois, a predominantly white university, and Howard University, predominantly black. The experimental materials consisted of photographs of forty black and forty white males of college age, with each subject viewing ten black and ten white faces. After the faces had been presented, the subjects were shown the entire set of eighty faces, randomly ordered, and were asked to indicate which they had seen before. Overall, subjects recognized faces of their own race better than faces of the other race. For example, the white subjects from Howard University made an average of 2.14 false identifications when attempting to identify white faces, but they made an average of 5.86 false identifications when attempting to identify black faces.

Since this classic study many others have been conducted with slightly different results from one study to another but with a generally consistent pattern (e.g. Brigham and Barkowitz 1978; Luce 1974). Most of these studies have used photographs of faces. For example, Shepherd, Deregowski, and Ellis (1974) showed a set of white and black faces to white and black subjects from Scotland and Rhodesia. All subjects were later required to identify the original faces when they were mixed in with other faces. Not surprisingly, European subjects were superior at recognizing white rather than black faces, while for black African subjects the reverse was true: they were significantly better at recognizing black faces.

Many possible explanations of the cross-racial effects have been offered, for example that the effects are due to differential experience with members of a different race, to prejudicial attitudes about members of different races, or to different modes of processing faces of another race. Unfortunately the research relating to these various hypotheses has been inconsistent and inconclusive. (See Clifford and Bull 1978 for a comprehensive review.)

One group of researchers has recently asked whether the cross-racial effects, since they are largely obtained in studies using photographs, would apply in real-life situations. To explore this question, Brigham et al. (in press) used as subjects clerks working in small convenience stores in the Tallahassee area. Two experimental confederates posing as customers visited each store; one was black and one white. They each interacted with the cashier for a reasonably long period of time so that it would be possible for the cashier to make a subsequent identification, but not in such a bizarre way that all realism was lost. So, for example, one customer entered the store, purchased some cigarettes, and then apologetically paid for them with nothing but pennies. Then the customer asked for directions to a local shopping mall, hospital, or airport.

Originally, the researchers had planned to return twenty-four hours later to carry out the identification phase of the study; however, pilot research indicated that the identification rate was extremely poor. Thus, the retention interval was shortened to two hours. At this time two "law interns" returned and showed each clerk two sets of six photographs, one of whites and one of blacks. Even with this relatively short period of time, the general level of accuracy was not very high (approximately 34 percent correct identifications). More surprisingly, there was very little evidence of a cross-racial identification problem. There were too few black clerks to perform a decent analysis; however, the sixty-four white clerks made an incorrect identification 45 percent of the time for the white customer and 50 percent for the black customer. This is a rather small difference, when compared to the large differences obtained in studies on cross-racial identification using photographs, but it is still in the expected direction.

2. *Miscellaneous facts about faces.* Much has been discovered about ability to remember faces. The following list of findings will give the flavor of the types of issues that have been explored in the face-recognition area, and what is known about this complex ability.

1. Some faces are never falsely recognized whereas some faces are frequently falsely recognized (e.g. Goldstein, Stephenson, and Chance 1977). One reason why this may occur is that

some faces are more unusual than others. In fact, faces rated by people as being unusual are more easily recognized than are faces rated as being ordinary (e.g. Light, Kayra-Stuart, and Hollander 1979).

2. Upper face features attract more attention than do lower face features (Ellis, Shepherd, and Davies 1980).

3. Failure to recognize a face can sometimes be even more informative than positive recognition of a face (e.g. Wells and Lindsay 1980). When a witness says, "That's not the man!" this can be more reliable than the statement, "That is the man!"

4. Faces that are processed deeply (thought about carefully) are recognized better than faces that receive shallow processing (e.g. Mueller, Bailis, and Goldstein 1979).

5. The age of the witness affects face recognition. Ability to recognize faces is better for older children and adults than for younger children (e.g. Carey and Diamond 1977), and young adults appear to be better at recognizing faces than are the elderly (e.g. Smith and Winograd 1978).

6. The relationship between IQ and facial recognition ability appears to be negligible (e.g. Feinman and Entwisle 1976).

7. A number of personality characteristics such as field dependence are related to memory for faces (e.g. Hoffman and Kagan 1977). Field independence reflects the ability to focus attention on the important parts of a scene and to avoid the confusing influence of background factors. Field dependence is the converse of this.

8. Many individuals are unable to convey facial details clearly or fully, but they still may be able to recognize a previously seen face (Clifford and Bull 1978).

Psychological research has demonstrated that each stage of information processing is susceptible to the influence of different factors. Some of these factors influence the initial perception of an event, others influence the information as it is retained in memory, and still others can affect the accuracy of event retrieval. The retrieval stage is the point where maximal opportunity exists to use the results of psychological research in recommending changes in procedure that will enhance the accuracy of recollection. Little can be done at the acquisition stage, except perhaps an overall program of education designed to train people to be better observers. Yet all this research helps us to evaluate better the quality of eyewitness testimony; testimony with few problematic factors would, if the research is to be believed, be considered more trustworthy than testimony with many problematic factors.

II. Impact of Courtroom Eyewitness Testimony

Honest but mistaken identification by prosecution witnesses was the prime cause of two recent miscarriages of justice in England. Luke Dougherty had served nearly nine months imprisonment of a fifteen-month sentence for theft when a higher court overturned his conviction. Laszlo Virag had served nearly five years of a ten-year sentence for a number of offenses, including wounding a police officer, when he was granted a pardon by the queen. Both men were awarded payment for any suffering they might have undergone. In view of the serious questions raised by these two cases, a committee was appointed to look into the law and procedures relating to identification. The committee, chaired by Lord Devlin, held its first meeting in May 1974, and in April 1976 it reported with a number of recommendations (Devlin 1976).

The Devlin committee examined all lineups that were held in England and Wales during the year 1973. Of interest to the present discussion are the 347 people who were prosecuted even though the only evidence against them was the identification of one or more eyewitnesses. Of those 347 cases, 74 percent resulted in conviction. This figure of 74 percent indicates that when no other evidence is available, the testimony of one or more eyewitnesses is sufficient to convince a jury of a defendant's guilt. Unfortunately, the Devlin report did not indicate the extent to which the number of witnesses or the relationship between the witness and the defendant in a criminal case influenced the jury. It may seem that multiple witnesses would be more influential than a single witness. But it may also be the case that in many single-witness cases the relationship between the witness and the defendant is strong (e.g. a relative or friend versus a stranger).

Several psychological studies have addressed the question of the impact of eyewitness testimony, and all agree in showing that eyewitnesses are a potent influence on jury members. A partial answer was provided by Loftus (1974). In this study, subjects received a description of an armed robbery that resulted in two deaths. When subjects heard a version of the case with only circumstantial evidence, only 18 percent of them convicted. When other subjects heard the same weak evidence plus an eyewitness identification, the conviction rate rose to 72 percent.

Using different procedures, Wells, Lindsay, and Ferguson (1979) have shown the powerful impact of eyewitness testimony. Their study was conducted in two phases, the crime phase and the trial phase. During the crime phase, subjects (three in each session) sat for a few minutes, whereupon a "thief" entered, posing as a co-participant. She soon "discovered" a calculator that had apparently been left by a previous subject, and she left with it. Later the experimenter returned and asked the subject-witnesses to try to identify the thief. In the second phase of the study, the trial phase, a new group of subjects was asked to play the role of jurors and watch the cross-examination of one of the witnesses who had made an identification of the thief. Some of the jurors watched the testimony of a correct eyewitness while others watched the testimony of an incorrect eyewitness. Finally the jurors were asked for their reactions. The results were striking. Overall, the jurors tended to believe the eyewitness testimony about eighty percent of the time. However, the jurors were just as likely to believe a witness who had made an incorrect identification as one who had made a correct identification. Witness confidence, not accuracy, determined the jurors' decision to believe the eyewitness testimony, and yet confidence and accuracy were unrelated to one another. These results were replicated by the subsequent research of Lindsay, Wells, and Rumpel (1981). Although jurors showed some sensitivity to the viewing conditions, in general they overestimated the accuracy of eyewitness testimony.

In yet another study, Hastie (1980) used actual jurors on jury duty at the time, showing them a filmed reenactment of an armed robbery trial. At the end of the trial, each jury deliberated to reach a verdict, spending anywhere from one-half hour to over two hours. Of interest to the present discussion is the analysis of comments regarding the eyewitness. These comments revealed several weaknesses in the content of jury discussion of eyewitness testimony. For example, when assessing the accuracy of identifications, jurors relied too much on witnesses' statements showing their confidence in their identifications.

There is no doubt, then, that eyewitnesses are a potent source of influence on jurors, and legal commentators have recognized this (Kaplan 1979). In criminal cases, most of the eyewitness testimony is presented by the prosecution (Kalven and Zeisel 1966), after which the defense has the opportunity to challenge the testimony. Can such testimony, once offered, be discredited by an opposing attorney? A partial answer to this question was provided by Loftus (1974). Recall that subject-jurors who heard about an armed robbery/murder with only weak circumstantial evidence convicted the defendant 18 percent of the time, versus seventy-two percent when an eyewitness account was also offered. Most surprising were the results from a third group of subjects who heard the circumstantial evidence and the eyewitness identification, but this time heard the eyewitness discredited by the defense attorney, who showed that the witness had very poor vision. The eyewitness still insisted he was right, and the conviction rate dropped only slightly to sixty-eight percent.

The possibility that, once eyewitness testimony is heard, discrediting that testimony may be very difficult, raises some serious concerns. Many judges believe that the weaknesses in an eyewitness account can be revealed to a jury during cross-examination. The implication is that such weaknesses, if valid, will cause the jury to reduce the weight it gives to the eyewitness account or disregard the identification altogether. For example, one court recently said that witness credibility is properly tested "by examination and cross-examination in the forum of the trial court" (State of Washington v. Johnson, 12 Wash. App. 40 [1974]), and another agreed, adding, "Closing argument affords counsel the appropriate means to point out any weaknesses in eyewitness identifications" (State of Washington v. Jordan, 17 Wash. App. 542 [1977]).

Thus it is fortunate that researchers have begun to study the impact of eyewitness testimony, particularly the effects of discrediting that testimony. As Hatvany and Strack (1980) have pointed out, there are three possible effects that the discredited testimony might have: the jury might ignore the initial testimony after it has been discredited; the jury's judgment might "boomerang," so that the jury returns a verdict opposite to that indicated by the initial testimony of the eyewitnesses; or, alternatively, the jury might remain swayed by the initial testimony of the eyewitness. A plausible psychological rationale can be developed for each of the three possible effects of discrediting.

An examination of the literature here reveals that no single result has consistently been found. Cavoukian (1980) asked subjects to read a case summary containing either (1) no eyewitness testimony, (2) eyewitness testimony, (3) eyewitness testimony which was later discredited, or (4) forewarning of the subsequent discrediting. Discrediting the eyewitness testimony had no significant influence; that is, the eyewitness had the same effect regardless of whether the testimony had been discredited, replicating the results of Loftus (1974). However, forewarning subjects was effective and significantly decreased the weighting of the eyewitness account.

On the other hand, two studies, one by Weinberg and Baron (1980) and one by Hatvany and Strack (1981), failed to replicate the unsuccessful discrediting of the eyewitness. Why should discrediting work in some instances and not in others? The answer seems to lie in the nature of the discrediting. In the Hat-

vany and Strack research, subjects were exposed to two simulated courtroom trials. One dealt with a "dogbite suit" in
which it was alleged that the defendant's dog had bitten a pas-
serby, and the other dealt with a two-car accident. In both
these cases, after the eyewitness testimony was given, the opposing attorney proved to the jury that the original testimony
could not possibly have been right, and the eyewitness recanted
the testimony and then apologized for even having taken the
stand. Subject-jurors dealt with the discredited testimony logi-
cally, ignoring it. On the other hand, in the Loftus (1974)
study, the attorney showed that the eyewitness's vision was
quite poor, but the eyewitness—acknowledging his poor vision—
still insisted he had seen the defendant. Subject-jurors could still
believe the testimony if they chose to do so.

In short, the research in this area has consistently shown that
eyewitness testimony can powerfully influence the outcome of a
trial. Discrediting eyewitness testimony is likely to be difficult
at best, but probably not impossible. In the extreme case in
which an eyewitness retracts an earlier position, the influence
on jurors will be reduced.

III. The Eyewitness in the Legal System

The potential for faulty eyewitness testimony has not escaped
the attention of the Supreme Court and various appellate
courts. Three safeguards designed to reduce the likelihood of
faulty testimony influencing the jury have been considered.
They include: (1) right to assistance of counsel during
identification procedures, (2) use of cautionary jury instructions, and (3) use of expert testimony on the reliability of
an eyewitness account.

A. Right to Counsel

In 1967 the U.S. Supreme Court decided the landmark tril-
ogy of cases, United States v. Wade, 388 U.S. 218 (1967), Gilbert v. State of California, 388 U.S. 263 (1967), and Stovall v.
Denno, 338 U.S. 293 (1967) and thereby addressed the
problems of inaccurate eyewitness testimony. The Court noted

that a confrontation between an accused and the victim or witnesses to a crime to elicit identification evidence is "particularly riddled with innumerable dangers and variable factors which might seriously, even crucially, derogate from a fair trial." The Court held that holding a lineup in the absence of the accused's counsel violated his or her Sixth Amendment right to counsel.

In 1972, five years later, the Court heard Kirby v. Illinois, 406 U.S. 682 (1972). In *Kirby*, the Court held that the right to counsel was applicable only after adversary judicial criminal proceedings had begun, that is, after the suspect had been officially charged with the crime. The result has been that police now often delay formal charges until after the identification has been made, and thus *Kirby* has been viewed as the beginning of a gradual dismantling of the constitutional safeguards provided by the 1967 decision.

No psychological research has been done to investigate the particular problems of accuracy of lineup identifications with or without counsel. It seems likely, however, that the presence of counsel would have a beneficial effect. Many variables influence the fairness of a lineup, such as the similarity of the nonsuspects to the suspect (Doob and Kirshenbaum 1973; Wells, Leippe, and Ostrom 1979), and these are variables over which counsel could have some control.

B. Cautionary Jury Instructions

Another proposed safeguard is to have the judge give a special cautionary instruction to the jury in cases in which eyewitness testimony is introduced. The issue of cautionary instructions was an important one in United States v. Telfaire, 469 F. 2d 552 (1972). In that case, defendant Telfaire was convicted of robbery and he appealed. The case had turned on the testimony of a single witness. The court of appeals held that failure of the trial court, in the absence of request, to give special instructions on identification was not prejudicial. However, the court adopted model special instructions on identification to be used in future cases. These instructions were designed to focus the jury's attention on the identification issue by stressing several factors affecting witness perception and memory that the jury should consider when evaluating the eyewitness account.

Cautionary instructions provide some protection against faulty eyewitness testimony but probably not enough. Judges' instructions tend to be long and tedious, and much of the research on them indicates that they are rather poorly comprehended by jurors (Charrow and Charrow 1979; Sales, Elwork, and Alfini 1978). An instruction on eyewitness identification would usually be embedded in a long, difficult list of instructions and thus very likely not receive the careful attention that it deserved.

A further problem with the *Telfaire* instruction is that it is highly controversial. At least one appellate court has explicitly said that this instruction "is impermissibly slanted and should not be given in this state" (State of Washington v. Jordan, 17 Wash. App. 542 [1977], p. 543).

C. Expert Psychological Testimony

A final proposed safeguard to the problem of jurors' overreliance on eyewitness testimony is to allow judge and jury to hear an expert witness present psychological testimony about factors affecting the reliability of eyewitness accounts. The psychologist typically describes research studies illustrating people's ability to perceive and recall complex events. Factors that may have affected the accuracy of the particular identification in the case at bar are explained to the jury. The goal is to provide jurors with sufficient information with which to evaluate the identification evidence fully and properly. Such expert testimony, although already allowed in numerous states around the country, is highly controversial. Some lawyers and judges worry that it invades the province of the jury, that it will have undue influence on the jury, that it is well within the common knowledge of the jury, or that it will lead to a battle of experts that will detract from the real issues in the case.

The leading appellate decision on the subject is United States v. Amaral, 488 F. 2d 1148 (9th Cir. 1973). Defendant Amaral was charged with the robbery of two national banks. Later that year, at Amaral's trial, defense counsel moved to introduce the testimony about the unreliability of eyewitness identification, particularly in a stressful situation. The trial court refused to admit the testimony on the grounds that "it would not be appropriate to take from the jury their own determination as to what weight or effect to give to the evidence of the eyewitness . . . and to have that determination put before them on the basis of the expert witness testimony as proffered" (488 F.2d 1148, 1153). Amaral appealed on the ground that the trial court had erred in refusing to admit the expert testimony. The Ninth Circuit Court of Appeals affirmed the conviction and noted that the defense had uncovered no uncertainty as to the identity of the robber in any of several witnesses. Moreover, the court suggested that defense counsel could question the witnesses at cross-examination to ascertain their capacity and opportunity for observation.

Despite the affirmation of Amaral's conviction, the Amaral decision is significant in part because it reiterated the general principles regarding expert testimony so that they might be applied to this new type of expert: the witness must be a qualified expert, the testimony must concern a proper subject matter, the testimony must be in accord with a generally accepted explanatory theory, and the probative value of the testimony must outweigh its prejudicial effect. In addition, the court noted that the trial judge has broad discretion in whether to admit the testimony or not.

In a thoughtful analysis of *Amaral*, Woocher (1977) remarked that the appellate decision failed in one important way: it did nothing to establish any guidelines to aid the trial judge in exercising his or her discretion. How is the trial judge to decide whether the expert witness is truly qualified or whether the testimony concerns a proper subject matter or whether it conforms to a generally accepted explanatory theory? What standards should the judge use to weight its probative value against its potentially prejudicial effects?

Numerous psychologists and legal commentators have considered these four criteria and have concluded that expert testimony by research psychologists on the issue of the credibility of an eyewitness is proper (Addison 1978; Katz and Reid 1977; Sobel 1972; Loftus and Monahan 1980; Woocher 1977). Some have worried that the data upon which such testimony rests may be overly conflicting and inappropriate (e.g. Clifford 1979). A growing number of appellate decisions have discussed this issue, and most have either agreed with the *Amaral* decision regarding the broad discretion of the trial judge or have taken a generally negative posture toward the testimony. Several courts, for example, have concluded that the expert testimony on this subject is not beyond the knowledge and experience of a juror and thus is not a proper subject of expert testimony (Dyas v. United States, 376 A.2d 827 [1977]; State of Iowa v. James Thomas Galloway, 275 N.W.2d 736 [1979]; Nelson v. State of Florida, 362 So.2d 1017 [1978]). In *Dyas*, the court wrote, "We are persuaded that the subject matter of the proffered testimony is not beyond the ken of the average layman nor would such testimony aid the trier in a search for the truth" (p. 832). Citing from the Florida case, "We believe it is within the common knowledge of the jury that a person being attacked and beaten undergoes stress that might cloud a subsequent identification of the assailant by the victim. As such, the subject matter was not properly within the realm of expert testimony" (p. 1021). This remark is particularly interesting when considered in light of Hastie's (1980) study of the deliberations of actual jurors. He found that over 90 percent of the juries made at least one remark implying that perception is impaired when one is under stress; however, an equal number made at least one remark implying the opposite, that events perceived under stress result in especially vivid and enduring memories.

When evaluating the negative comments about expert psychological testimony, one must recognize that the decision to admit or exclude the testimony is discretionary, and that appellate courts seldom overrule a trial court's exercise of discretion. Moreover, for constitutional double jeopardy reasons, the state seldom can appeal a ruling to admit expert testimony in cases in which the defendant was acquitted. And, of course, the state does not appeal convictions. Thus, there will be few instances in which an appellate court has approved the admission of such testimony. Finally, since transcripts of trial court proceedings generally go unpublished, few records exist of cases in which the expert's testimony has been admitted. This fact occasionally escapes realization, as is indicated by a comment of one recent court that found no error in the trial court's refusal to admit the testimony: "Defendant has been unable to cite a published opinion which endorses the use of expert identification opinion evidence in a case such as this" (State of Kansas v. Reed, 226 Kans. 519, 522, [1979]).

D. Impact of Expert Testimony

Three studies on the impact of expert psychological testimony on eyewitness reliability have recently been conducted (Loftus 1980b; Wells, Lindsay, and Tousignant 1980; Hosch, Beck, and McIntyre 1980). These generally show that exposure to an expert reduces the impact of eyewitness testimony, perhaps by causing jurors to scrutinize that testimony more carefully. Loftus (1980b) presented written summaries of an assault case to subject-jurors, who were then asked to reach a verdict. Those whose summary contained expert psychological testimony were less likely to convict than those whose summary did not. In a follow-up study, six-person juries read the same case summaries and deliberated to reach a verdict. The juries whose summaries included expert testimony again convicted less often but also spent more time discussing the eyewitness testimony. Wells, Lindsay, and Tousignant (1980) had subjects view a videotaped cross-examination of an eyewitness and then reach a verdict. Prior to this, half the subjects viewed videotaped expert testimony. Again, those who viewed the expert testimony were less likely to believe the eyewitness. And finally, Hosch, Beck, and McIntyre (1980) asked community residents to serve as jurors in a videotaped burglary trial. As it happened, all juries acquitted the defendant; however, those who heard the expert testimony significantly lowered their judgments of the accuracy and reliability of eyewitness identification as well as its overall importance to the trial.

Further, those juries that heard the expert testimony spent a significantly longer time discussing eyewitness identification.

In sum, despite the controversial nature of the expert psychological testimony, it does have some benefit. When one considers the impact of eyewitness testimony on juror judgments, the inability of jurors to discriminate between accurate and inaccurate eyewitnesses, and the minimal ability of jurors to calibrate for the extent to which poor observing conditions may have undermined eyewitness accuracy, more research on the potential of expert testimony to alleviate some of these problems is clearly merited.

IV. Methodological Issues

Many psychologists believe that by studying behavior under conditions in which variables can be tightly controlled, one discovers principles which are then useful in interpreting human behavior in the world at large and in making wide-scale applications. In some areas of psychology, for example, the study of physiological or visual processes, psychologists almost never worry whether the specific behaviors that are studied in the laboratory have anything to do with behavior outside the laboratory. Not so when it comes to the study of less automatic processes. Here the external validity of laboratory findings, particularly those that use students as subjects, has been a matter of professional, as well as legal, contention for some time. A number of thoughtful articles have appeared on this subject in the past five years, nearly all of which focus on studies of jury behavior. This topic is directly relevant to the studies cited on the impact of eyewitness or expert witness testimony on jury decisions. Much less attention has been devoted to the generalizability of the research on factors affecting eyewitness reliability, but the results of at least one study are encouraging.

A. Studying Jury Decisions

The simulation method has the enormous advantage that the deliberations of a simulated or mock jury, unlike those of a real jury, can be recorded, dissected, and analyzed. Furthermore, the details in each mock trial can be controlled, and the experiments can then be replicated before large numbers of different panels. Hundreds of experiments have been conducted along these lines since the early years of this century, and a fraction of these have been concerned specifically with the reactions of jurors to eyewitness testimony.

In a simulated jury study, subjects are typically presented with a reconstruction of a real trial. Their reactions to the evidence and the means by which they reach a verdict are then observed. There are numerous variations of detail in the way this research is conducted. Despite the popularity of this research vehicle, mock-trial simulations have become the object of an increasing array of criticisms (Bray and Kerr 1979; Konecni and Ebbesen 1979 and in press; Vidmar 1979; Weiten and Diamond 1979).

Although the mock trial attempts to simulate events of the courtroom, these simulations are marked by procedural variations on a number of dimensions, for example, (1) population from which the subjects were drawn (e.g. students, actual jurors); (2) setting or location where the research transpired (e.g. classroom, courtroom); (3) stimulus mode of presenting the simulation (e.g. brief written summary, videotaped trial); (4) trial elements included in the simulation (e.g. voir dire, opening statements); (5) dependent variables used (e.g. guilt, believability of witnesses); (6) unit of analysis (individual jurors or juries) (Bray and Kerr 1979). When a simulation study differs from the "real thing" on any of these dimensions, its results are always open to uncertainty about whether they would change if observations were made in a more realistic environment. For the most part, however, it is safe to take the results of simulation studies as clues to what is likely to be influential in a real courtroom setting.

B. Studying Factors That Affect Eyewitness Reliability

Mock eyewitness simulations differ in numerous ways. Some use highly realistic simulations (e.g. Lindsay, Wells, and Rumpel 1981); others do not (e.g. Egan, Pittner, and Goldstein 1977; Brown et al. 1977). Viewing times differ widely, from less than 25 seconds (Brown et al. 1977; Lindsay, Wells, and Rumpel 1981) to more than a minute or two (Wells, Lindsay, and Ferguson 1979; Malpass and Devine 1980). The simulations vary in terms of how serious they are and how much arousal they can be expected to engender in witnesses. There are vast differences in terms of the retention interval, ranging from immediate to less than one hour (e.g. Leippe, Wells, and Ostrom 1978) to months (e.g. Malpass and Devine 1980). They vary in terms of the method of eliciting information from witnesses.

Despite these differences, mock eyewitness simulations have not tended to be subject to the same criticisms that have plagued the jury-simulation research. A few researchers have worried about the extent to which the simulations mirror real life and have attempted to use procedures that are as realistic as possible. One heroic attempt is that of Malpass, Devine, and Bergen (1980). Unaware that they were participating in an experiment, undergraduate students attended a voluntary lecture on biofeedback. During the demonstration-lecture, a man began tampering with the equipment and a violent argument between the intruder and the lecturer ensued. The equipment was thrown to the floor. Later, these students attended a lineup and attempted to identify the vandal. Some students were led to believe that, if identified, the culprit would suffer severe consequences; others were led to believe that the consequences would be trivial. Somewhat surprisingly, the percentage of witnesses making an identification in the "severe" case was substantially greater than the percentage in the "trivial" case. The error rates were quite high in both cases, roughly 50 percent.

Many researchers have taken the large error rates in experimental studies to imply that real eyewitnesses will be similarly unreliable. Yet, Sanders and Warnick (1980) have recently suggested that it is premature to suggest that real eyewitness testimony is inadequate since nearly all the experimental demonstrations of eyewitness fallibility (with the exception of the Malpass, Devine, and Bergen study, which was done at approximately the same time) have shared one crucial feature: witnesses were aware that their testimony would not actually be used. That is, in all of the research, subjects knew they were in an experiment and not in a real criminal investigation. Sanders and Warnick (1980), thus, explored the consequences of this important procedural feature. They compared eyewitness behavior in an explicitly experimental setting with behavior in a setting the subjects perceived to be real and in which loss of time, potential embarrassment and discomfort, a student's reputation, and the validity of a scholarship competition were at stake. Surprisingly, in two studies conducted, subjects were just as willing to offer information, just as willing to make a positive identification, and just as accurate in the real as in the experimental setting. These results offer encouragement to Ellis (1980) and others who have expressed concern about using mock eyewitnesses in studying eyewitness behavior. There have been few attempts to assess the generalizability of laboratory research to messy, real-life problems involving testimony, and more are obviously needed. One obvious difference that remains to be studied between real and hypothetical eyewitnesses is the likely effects on memory of a witness's extreme excitement or fear when viewing criminal acts. As Ellis (1980) notes, it is virtually impossible to simulate such crimes in the laboratory without crossing ethical boundaries, and so the relationship between the state of arousal experienced by a witness and his or her subsequent memory can be assessed only from actual case studies.

The ethical issue is an important one when it comes to research on eyewitness testimony. The Malpass, Devine, and Bergen (1980) study involving violent vandalism shocked and outraged the college community when it was discovered to be a psychological experiment. In a letter to the local newspaper, one student wrote, "I sincerely grieved for the faculty during the 'act.' I was genuinely hurt to think that someone would disrupt their presentation and destroy their guest's equipment. These emotional reactions clearly carried over into several aspects of my daily functioning a few days following. I feel hurt, betrayed,

angry, humiliated, and fraught with cynicism as a result of the
entire incident. Do you think the same degree of trust I once
had can be regained?" (*Rutland Herald*, Letters to the Editor, 25
February 1980). The researchers justified their experiment on
the grounds that its potential benefits outweighed the negative
aspects. They felt they could not conduct a meaningful experiment without deception. Some questions still remain as to why
the subjects in this experiment reacted so strongly when the
accounts of other researchers do not contain reactions that are
even remotely similar. Perhaps it was because the Malpass
group succeeded in achieving the high level of realism they had
hoped for, whereas other researchers have not. As Clifford and
Bull (1978, p. 50) have said, "laboratories are not emotionally
charged, but crime episodes are, and the eyewitness is left with
an aftermath of outrage, confusion, fear and shock." The Malpass group appears to have achieved a level of outrage, confusion, fear and shock that usually distinguishes the laboratory
simulations from natural events. But not without cost. In any
event, future researchers will be forced to balance scientific
usefulness and ethical boundaries in their pursuit of knowledge
in this field.

V. Conclusions

This review has provided a catalog of psychological research
relevant to the evaluation of the reliability of eyewitness testimony. When witnesses attempt to give truthful testimony
about directly experienced natural events, there are a vast
number of threats to the accuracy and completeness of their accounts. Of course, this is not a novel conclusion. Munsterberg
(1908) made the same point at the turn of the century, and even
then he was echoing European social scientists.

But we have come some way since Munsterberg in demonstrating that existing psychological research can explain, in a
systematic way, the bases of eyewitness unreliability. This
knowledge can now be used to reduce the unreliability in eyewitness reports and improve the quality of judgments that must
inevitably be based upon them. The task for the future will be
to continue to accumulate and apply this knowledge.

Some knowledge about eyewitness performance can usefully be conveyed to jurors who must weigh eyewitness evidence. One method for conveying this knowledge is through the appearance of research psychologists as expert witnesses in trials. The psychological expert could summarize the relevant scientific facts. A judge or jury would then decide the extent to which these facts apply to the particular facts in dispute.

One fruitful area for future research is the relationship between the apparent psychological premises of the law of evidence and the data of modern experimental psychology. In some cases there appears to be a contradiction. For example, one of the major exceptions to the hearsay rule that operates even though the declarant is available as a witness is the "excited utterance." According to the *Federal Rules of Evidence* (1975) an excited utterance is "a statement relating to a startling event or condition made while the declarant was under the stress of excitement caused by the event or condition" (Rule 802, p. 102). This rule presupposes that statements of people under stress are more reliable and accurate than statements not made under stress, which is precisely counter to a good many of the findings in experimental psychology. How many other psychological premises of the law are either contradicted or at least unsupported by psychological research? Consider the rule, "Present Recollection Revived," which is a trial tactic in which counsel shows a witness on the stand some item, be it a physical object, a previous statement, or a newspaper article, and asks whether the object refreshed the witness's recollection. If the witness claims that he or she can testify from a true recollection, the testimony will be permitted. This rule rests on the psychological assumption that accurate impressions of events reside somewhere inside a witness's memory and that the object merely elicits that memory without giving rise either to suggestion or to confabulation. Whether the object leads to the recovery of a real memory or causes a supplementation or change in memory is an issue that is far from settled. Similarly, the dying declaration exception to the hearsay rule, which permits a statement made by a person "while believing that his death was imminent, concerning the cause or circumstances of what he believed to be his impending death" (Rule 804) may rest on faulty psychological assumptions. Who is to say that the declarations of a dying person are any more accurate or truthful than those of one who is not dying? Discovering methods for testing the validity of this psychological assumption would, of course, require a high degree of ingenuity. Nonetheless, these examples indicate that an important direction for the future is the exploration of the validity of the psychological premises of various rules of evidence.

Another topic ripe for study is the judge and jury who are obviously witnesses to any trial. We know little about their ability to record, store, and retrieve information accurately. Much of what is known about the memory of eyewitnesses may apply to this novel situation, but some of it may not.

REFERENCES

Addison, B. M. 1978. "Expert Testimony on Eyewitness Perception," *Dickinson Law Review* 82:465–85.
Alper, A., R. Buckhout, S. Chern, R. Harwood, and M. Slomovitz. 1974. "Eyewitness Identification: Accuracy of Individual vs. Composite Recollections of a Crime." Report CR-10. Center for Responsive Psychology, Brooklyn College, C.U.N.Y.
Baddeley, A. D. 1972. "Selective Attention and Performance in Dangerous Environments," *British Journal of Psychology* 63:537–46.
Baltes, P. B., and K. W. Schaie. 1976. "On the Plasticity of Intelligence in Adulthood and Old Age," *American Psychologist* 31:720–25.
Bray, R. M., and N. L. Kerr. 1979. "Use of the Simulation Method in the Study of Jury Behavior: Some Methodological Considerations," *Law and Human Behavior* 3:107–19.
Brigham, J. C., and P. Barkowitz. 1978. "Do 'They All Look Alike'? The Effect of Race, Sex, Experience, and Attitudes on the Ability to Recognize Faces," *Journal of Applied Social Psychology* 8:306–18.
Brigham, J. C., L. D. Snyder, K. Spaulding, and A. Maass. 1980. "The Accuracy of Eyewitness Identifications in a Field Setting." Unpublished manuscript, Department of Psychology, Florida State University.

Brigham, J. C., and N. L. Williamson. 1979. "Cross-Racial Recognition and Age: When You're over 60, Do They Still 'All Look Alike'?" *Personality and Social Psychology Bulletin* 5:218–22.

Brown, L., S. Heymann, B. Preskill, D. Rubin, and T. Wuletich. 1977. "Leading Questions and the Eyewitness Report of a Live and a Described Incident," *Psychological Reports* 40:1041–42.

Buckhout, R. 1975. "Nearly 2000 Witnesses Can Be Wrong," *Social Action and the Law* 2:7.

Bull, R., and B. Clifford. 1979. "Eyewitness Memory." In *Applied Problems in Memory*, ed. M. M. Gruneberg and P. E. Morris. London: Academic Press.

Byrd, M., and D. M. Thomson. 1979. "Age Differences in Eyewitness Testimony." Unpublished manuscript. University of Toronto.

Cane, L. R., R. K. Finkelstein, and H. J. Goetze. 1979. "The Effect of Age on the Accuracy of Eyewitness Accounts." Unpublished manuscript. Hofstra University, Hempstead, N.Y.

Carey, S., and R. Diamond. 1977. "From Piecemeal to Configurational Representation of Faces," *Science* 195:312–14.

Cavoukian, A. 1980. "Eyewitness Testimony: The Ineffectiveness of Discrediting Information." Paper read at 1980 meeting of the American Psychological Association, Montreal. (Abstracted 1980. *Personality and Social Psychology Bulletin* 6:174.)

Charrow, R. P., and V. R. Charrow. 1979. "Making Legal Language Understandable: A Psycholinguistic Study of Jury Instructions," *Columbia Law Review* 79:1306–74.

Clifford, B. R. 1979. "The Relevance of Psychological Investigation to Legal Issues in Testimony and Identification," *Criminal Law Review* 1979:153–63.

Clifford, B. R., and R. Bull. 1978. *The Psychology of Person Identification*. London: Routledge and Kegan Paul.

Clifford, B. R., and J. Scott. 1978. "Individual and Situational Factors in Eyewitness Testimony," *Journal of Applied Psychology* 63:352–59.

Covey, K., and B. Scott. 1980. "Variations in a Mugshot Display: An 'Unobtrusive Creation' of an Eyewitness' Memory for a Criminal Defendant." Unpublished manuscript. Oklahoma State University, Stillwater.

Craik, F. I. M. 1977. "Age Differences in Human Memory." In *Handbook of the Psychology of Aging*, ed. J. E. Birren and K. W. Schaie. New York: Van Nostrand.

Crowder, R. G. 1976. *Principles of Learning and Memory*. Hillsdale, N.J.: Erlbaum Press.

Dale, P. S., E. F. Loftus, and L. Rathbun. 1978. "The Influence of the Form of the Question on the Eyewitness Testimony of Pre-school Children," *Journal of Psycholinguistic Research* 7:269–77.

Davies, G., J. Shepherd, and H. Ellis. 1979. "Effects of Interpolated Mugshot Exposure on Accuracy of Eyewitness Identification," *Journal of Applied Psychology* 64:232–37.

Deffenbacher, K. 1980. "Eyewitness Accuracy and Confidence: Can We Infer Anything about Their Relationship?" *Law and Human Behavior* in press.

Dent, H. R. 1977. "Stress as a Factor Influencing Person Recognition in Identification Parades," *Bulletin of the British Psychological Society* 30:339–40.

———. 1978. "Interviewing Child Witnesses." In *Practical Aspects of Memory*, ed. M. M. Gruenberg, P. E. Morris, and R. N. Sykes. London: Academic Press.

Dent, H. R., and G. M. Stephenson. 1979. "An Experimental Study of the Effectiveness of Different Techniques of Questioning Child Witnesses," *British Journal of Social and Clinical Psychology* 18:41–51.

Devlin, Hon. Lord Patrick. 1976. *Report to the Secretary of State for the Home Department of the Departmental Committee on Evidence of Identification in Criminal Cases*. London: H.M. Stationery Office.

Dodd, D. H., and J. M. Bradshaw. 1980. "Leading Questions and Memory: Pragmatic Constraints," *Journal of Verbal Learning and Verbal Behavior* in press.

Doob, A. N., and H. M. Kirshenbaum. 1973. "Bias in Police Lineups—Partial Remembering," *Journal of Police Science and Administration* 1:287–93.

Dritsas, W. J., and V. L. Hamilton. 1977. "Evidence about Evidence: Effects of Presuppositions, Item Salience, Stress, and Perceiver Set on Accident Recall." Unpublished manuscript. University of Michigan, Ann Arbor.

Ebbinghaus, H. E. [1885] 1964. *Memory: A Contribution to Experimental Psychology*. New York: Dover Publications.

Egan, D. M., M. Pittner, and A. G. Goldstein. 1977. "Eyewitness Identification—Photographs vs. Live Models," *Law and Human Behavior* 1:199–206.

Egan, D. M., and K. H. Smith. 1979. "Improving Eyewitness Identification: An Experimental Analysis." Paper read at October 1979 meeting of the American Psychology–Law Society Convention, Baltimore.

Ellis, H. D. 1980. "Psychology and the Law," *Science* 208:712–13.

Ellis, H. D., G. M. Davies, and J. W. Shepherd. 1977. "Experimental Studies of Face Identification," *Journal of Criminal Defense* 3:219–34.

Ellis, H. D., J. W. Shepherd, and G. M. Davies. 1980. "The Deterioration of Verbal Descriptions of Faces over Different Delay Intervals," *Journal of Police Science and Administration* 8:101–6.

Farrimond, T. 1968. "Retention and Recall: Incidental Learning of Visual and Auditory Material," *Journal of Genetic Psychology* 113:155–65.

Federal Rules of Evidence for United States Courts and Magistrates. 1975. St. Paul, Minn.: West Publishing Co.

Feinman, S., and D. R. Entwisle. 1976. "Children's Ability to Recognize Other Children's Faces," *Child Development* 47:506–10.

Gardner, D. S. 1933. "The Perception and Memory of Witnesses," *Cornell Law Quarterly* 18:391–409.

Goldstein, A. G. 1977. "The Fallibility of the Eyewitness: Psychological Evidence." In *Psychology in the Legal Process*, ed. B. D. Sales. New York: Spectrum.

Goldstein, A. G., B. Stephenson, and J. Chance. 1977. "Face Recognition Memory: Distribution of False Alarms," *Bulletin of the Psychonomic Society* 9:416–18.

Hale, M. 1980. *Human Science and Social Order: Hugo Munsterberg and the Origins of Applied Psychology.* Philadelphia: Temple University Press.

Hastie, R. 1980. "From Eyewitness Testimony to Beyond Reasonable Doubt." Paper read at 1980 meeting of the Law and Society Association, Minneapolis.

Hatvany, N., and F. Strack. 1981. "The Impact of a Discredited Key Witness," *Journal of Applied Social Psychology.* In press.

Hoffman, C., and S. Kagan. 1977. "Field Dependence and Facial Recognition," *Perceptual and Motor Skills* 44:119–24.

Hollin, C. R., and B. R. Clifford. 1980. "The Effect on Eyewitness Memory of the Nature of the Witnessed Incident." Unpublished manuscript. North East London Polytechnic, London.

Hosch, H. M., E. L. Beck, and P. McIntyre. 1980. "Influence of Expert Testimony Regarding Eyewitness Accuracy on Jury Decisions," *Law and Human Behavior.* In press.

Hunter, I. 1964. *Memory.* Harmondsworth: Penguin Books.

Kalven, Harry and H. Zeisel. 1966. *The American Jury.* Boston: Little, Brown.

Kaplan, J. 1979. Foreword to E. Loftus *Eyewitness Testimony.* Cambridge, Mass.: Harvard University Press.

Katz, L. S., and J. F. Reid. 1977. "Expert Testimony on the Fallibility of Eyewitness Identification," *Criminal Justice Journal* 1:177–206.

Klatzky, R. L. 1980. *Human Memory: Structures and Processes.* 2d ed. San Francisco: Freeman.

Konecni, V. J., and E. B. Ebbesen. 1979. "External Validity of Research in Legal Psychology," *Law and Human Behavior* 3:39–70.

————. In press. "A Critique of Theory and Method in Social-Psychological Approaches to Legal Issues." In *Perspectives in Law and Psychology. Volume 2: The Jury, Judicial and Trial Process*, ed. B. D. Sales. New York: Plenum Press.

Laughery, K. R., J. E. Alexander, and A. B. Lane. 1971. "Recognition of Human Faces: Effects of Target Exposure Time, Target Position, Pose Position, and Type of Photograph," *Journal of Applied Psychology* 55:477–83.

Laughery, K. R., P. K. Fessler, D. R. Lenorovitz, and D. A. Yoblick. 1974. "Time Delay and Similarity Effects in Face Recognition," *Journal of Applied Psychology* 59:490–96.

Leippe, M. R., G. L. Wells, and T. M. Ostrom. 1978. "Crime Seriousness as a Determinant of Accuracy in Eyewitness Identification," *Journal of Applied Psychology* 63:345–51.

Lesgold, A. M., and A. R. Petrush. 1977. "Do Leading Questions Alter Memories?" Unpublished manuscript. University of Pittsburgh, Pittsburgh.

Light, L. L., F. Kayna-Stuart, and S. Hollander. 1979. "Recognition Memory for Typical and Unusual Faces," *Journal of Experimental Psychology: Human Learning and Memory* 5:212–28.

Lindsay, P. H. and D. A. Norman. 1977. *Human Information Processing: An Introduction to Psychology*. New York: Academic Press.

Lindsay, R. C. L., G. L. Wells, and C. Rumpel. 1981. "Can People Detect Eyewitness-Identification Accuracy within and across Situations?" *Journal of Applied Psychology* 66:79–89.

Lipton, J. P. 1977. "On the Psychology of Eyewitness Testimony," *Journal of Applied Psychology* 62:90–95.

Loftus, E. F. 1974. "Reconstructing Memory: The Incredible Eyewitness," *Psychology Today* 8:116–19.

————. 1979. *Eyewitness Testimony*. Cambridge, Mass.: Harvard University Press.

————. 1980a. *Memory*. Reading, Mass.: Addison-Wesley.

————. 1980b. "Impact of Expert Psychological Testimony on the Unreliability of Eyewitness Identification," *Journal of Applied Psychology* 65:9–15.

Loftus, E. F., and E. Greene. In press. "Warning: Even Memory for Faces May Be Contagious," *Law and Human Behavior*.

Loftus, E. F., and G. R. Loftus. 1980. "On the Permanence of Stored Information in the Human Brain," *American Psychologist* 5:409–20.

Loftus, E. F., and J. Monahan. 1980. "Trial by Data: Psychological Research as Legal Evidence," *American Psychologist* 35:270–83.

Loftus, G. R., and E. F. Loftus. 1976. *Human Memory*. Hillsdale, N.J.: Erlbaum.

Luce, T. S. 1974. "Blacks, Whites, and Yellows: They All Look Alike to Me," *Psychology Today* (November) 106–08.

Malpass, R. S., and P. G. Devine. 1980. "Guided Memory in Eyewitness Identification." Unpublished manuscript. State University of New York, Plattsburgh.

Malpass, R. S., P. G. Devine, and G. T. Bergen. 1980. "Realism vs. the Laboratory." Unpublished manuscript. State University of New York, Plattsburgh.

Malpass, R. S. and J. Kravitz. 1969. "Recognition for Faces of Own and Other Race," *Journal of Personality and Social Psychology* 13:330–34.

Mand, J. L., and J. J. Shaughnessy. 1980. "How Permanent Are Memories for Real Life Events?" Unpublished manuscript. Hope College, Holland, Mich.

Marin, B. V., D. L. Holmes, M. Guth, and P. Kovac. 1979. "The Potential of Children as Eyewitnesses: A Comparison of Children and Adults on Eyewitness Tasks," *Law and Human Behavior* 3:295–306.

Marshall, J. 1966. *Law and Psychology in Conflict*. New York: Bobbs-Merrill. (Reprinted 1969. New York: Anchor Books, Doubleday.)

Moskowitz, M. J. 1977. "Hugo Munsterberg: A Study in the History of Applied Psychology," *American Psychologist* 32:824–42.

Mueller, J. H., K. L. Bailis, and A. G. Goldstein. 1979. "Depth of Processing and Anxiety in Facial Recognition," *British Journal of Psychology* 70:511–15.

Munsterberg, H. 1908. *On the Witness Stand*. New York: Doubleday.

Muscio, B. 1916. "The Influence of the Form of a Question," *British Journal of Psychology* 8:351–89.

Patterson, K. E., and A. D. Baddeley. 1977. "When Face Recognition Fails," *Journal of Experimental Psychology: Human Learning and Memory* 3:406–17.

Penrod, Steven and E. Loftus. 1980. "The Reliability of Eyewitness Testimony: A Psychological Perspective." In *The Psychology of the Courtroom*, ed. R. Bray and N. Kerr. New York: Academic Press.

Peterson, M. A. 1976. "Witnesses: Memory of Social Events." Ph.D. dissertation, U.C.L.A.

Sales, B. D., A. Elwork, and J. J. Alfini. 1978. "Improving Comprehension for Jury Instructions." In *Perspectives in Law and Psychology*. Volume I: *The Criminal Justice System*, ed. B. D. Sales. New York: Plenum Press.

Sanders, G. S., and D. H. Warnick. 1979. "Some Conditions

Maximizing Eyewitness Accuracy: A Learning/Memory Model."
Unpublished manuscript. State University of New York, Albany.
(Presented in part at the 1979 American Psychology–Law Society
Convention, Baltimore.)

———. 1980. "Truth and Consequences: The Effect of Responsibility
on Eyewitness Behavior." Unpublished manuscript. State University of New York, Albany.

Saslove, H., and A. D. Yarmey. 1980. "Long-Term Auditory Memory: Speaker Identification," *Journal of Applied Psychology* 65:111–16.

Shaul, R. D. 1978. "Hypnotic Hyperamnesia, Cognitive Strategy,
and Eyewitness Testimony." Ph.D. dissertation, Brigham Young
University.

Shepherd, J.W., J. B. Deregowski, and H. D. Ellis. 1974. "A
Cross-Cultural Study of Recognition Memory for Faces," *International Journal of Psychology* 9:205–11.

Shepherd, J. W., and H. D. Ellis. 1973. "The Effect of Attractiveness
on Recognition Memory for Faces," *American Journal of Psychology*
86:627–33.

Silberman, C. E. 1978. *Criminal Violence, Criminal Justice*. New York:
Random House.

Smith, A. D., and E. Winograd. 1978. "Adult Age Differences in
Remembering Faces," *Developmental Psychology* 14:443–44.

Smith, S. M., A. Glenberg, and R. A. Bjork. 1978. "Environmental
Context and Human Memory," *Memory and Cognition* 6:342–53.

Sobel, N. R. 1972 (1979 Supplement). *Eye-Witness Identification: Legal
and Practical Problems*. New York: Clark Boardman.

Thompson, F. R. 1975. *Introduction to Physiological Psychology*. New
York: Harper & Row.

Vidmar, N. 1979. "The Other Issues in Jury Simulation Research: A
Commentary with Particular Reference to Defendant Character
Studies," *Law and Human Behavior* 3:95–106.

Warnick, D. H., and G. S. Sanders. In press. "The Effects of Group
Discussion on Eyewitness Accuracy," *Journal of Applied Social Psychology*.

Weinberg, H. I., and R. S. Baron. 1980. "The Discredible Eyewitness." Paper read at the 1980 meeting of the Midwestern Psychological Association, St. Louis.

Weiten, W., and S. S. Diamond. 1979. "A Critical Review of the
Jury Simulation Paradigm: The Case of Defendant Characteristics,"
Law and Human Behavior 3:71–94.

Wells, G. L. 1978. "Applied Eyewitness-Testimony Research: System Variables and Estimator Variables," *Journal of Personality and
Social Psychology* 36:1546–57.

Wells, G. L., M. R. Leippe, and T. M. Ostrom. 1979. "Guidelines for Empirically Assessing the Fairness of a Lineup," *Law and Human Behavior* 3:285–94.

Wells, G. L., and R. C. L. Lindsay. 1980. "On Estimating the Diagnosticity of Eyewitness Nonidentification," *Psychological Bulletin* 88:776–84.

Wells, G. L., R. C. L. Lindsay, and T. J. Ferguson. 1979. "Accuracy, Confidence, and Juror Perceptions in Eyewitness Identification," *Journal of Applied Psychology* 64:440–48.

Wells, G. L., R. C. L. Lindsay, and J. P. Tousignant. 1980. "Effects of Expert Psychological Advice on Human Performance in Judging the Validity of Eyewitness Testimony," *Law and Human Behavior.* In press.

Wigmore, J. H. 1909. "Professor Munsterberg and the Psychology of Evidence," *Illinois Law Review* 3:399–445.

Woocher, F. D. 1977. "Did Your Eyes Deceive You? Expert Psychological Testimony on the Unreliability of Eyewitness Identification," *Stanford Law Review* 29:969–1030.

Woodhead, M. M., A. D. Baddeley, and D. C. V. Simmonds. 1979. "On Training People to Recognize Faces," *Ergonomics* 22:333–43.

Yarmey, A. D. 1979. *The Psychology of Eyewitness Testimony.* New York: Free Press.

Michael Ignatieff

State, Civil Society, and Total Institutions: A Critique of Recent Social Histories of Punishment

A B S T R A C T

Three books published during the seventies, by Michel Foucault, Michael Ignatieff, and David Rothman, greatly revised the history of the penitentiary. Contrary to the received wisdom which located the penitentiary's origin in the altruism of Quakers and other humanitarian reformers, and portrayed it as a humane advance from the squalid jails and workhouses, corporal and capital punishment, and transportation that preceded it, the revisionist accounts characterized the penitentiary, and other nineteenth-century "asylums" as weapons of class conflict or instruments of "social control." Social theories on a grand scale, such as Marxism or structural-functionalism, however, claim too much. The revisionist historiography of the prison followed these theories into three major misconceptions: that the state controls a monopoly over punitive regulation of behavior, that the state's moral authority and practical power are the major sources of social order, and that all social relations can be described in terms of power and subordination. The next generation of historical writing on crime and punishment must subject these distorting misconceptions to empirical examination.

Until recently, the history of prisons in most countries was written as a narrative of reform. According to this story, a band of philanthropic reformers in the second half of the eighteenth century, secular Enlightenment theorists like Beccaria and Bentham and religious men and women of conscience like the Evangelicals and the Quakers, set out to convince the political

Michael Ignatieff is a Fellow of King's College, Cambridge.

153

leadership of their societies that public punishments of the body like hanging, branding, whipping, and even, in some European countries, torture were arbitrary, cruel, and illegitimate and that a new range of penalties, chiefly imprisonment at hard labor, could be at once humane, reformative, and punitive. This campaign in Europe and America was powered by revulsion at physical cruelty, by a new conception of social obligation to the confined, and by impatience with the administrative inefficiency manifested in the squalid neglect of prisoners. The Enlightenment critique of legal arbitrariness and the vernacular of religious humanitarianism gradually created a moral consensus for reform which, after many delays and reversals, culminated by 1850 in the curtailment of hanging, the abolition of branding and the stocks, and the widespread adoption of the penitentiary as the punishment of first resort for major crime (Whiting 1975; Cooper 1976; Condon 1962; Stockdale 1977; O. Lewis 1967; Teeters 1935; D. Lewis 1965).

All of these accounts emphasized conscience as the motor of institutional change and assumed that the reformative practice of punishment proposed by the reformers was both in intention and in result more humane than the retributive practices of the eighteenth century. A third common feature of these accounts was their administrative and institutional focus on change within the walls and within the political system which ratified or resisted these changes. With the exception of Rusche and Kirchheimer's work (1939) on the relation between prison routines and emerging patterns of labor market discipline after 1550, few studies of imprisonment ventured beyond the walls of the prison itself.

The history of prisons therefore was written as a sub-branch of the institutional history of the modern welfare state. As such it has had an implicitly teleological bias, treating the history as a progress from cruelty to enlightenment. In the early sixties, historians in a number of fields, not just in the history of prisons but also in the history of mental health, public welfare, juvenile care, hospitals, and medicine, began to point up the political implications of this history of reform. To interpret contemporary institutions as the culmination of a story of progress was to justify them at least in relation to the past and to suggest that they could be improved by the same incremental process of philanthropic activism in the future. A reformist historiography thus served a liberalism of good intentions, which in turn seemed to legitimize dubious new initiatives—psychosurgery, chemotherapy, and behavior modification—as legitimate descendants of the reforming tradition. It was in part to question the legitimacy of these "reforms" in the present that a new group of revisionist historians set out to study the reforms of the past. Another broader motive was perhaps at work too—the libertarian, populist politics of the 1960s revised historians' attitudes toward the size and intrusiveness of the modern state; the history of the prison, the school, the hospital, the asylum seemed more easily understood as a history of Leviathan than as a history of reform.

Some, if not all, of the new historiography was avowedly political. Moreover, it saw itself offering intellectual support for the welfare rights, mental patients' rights, and prisoners' rights campaigns of the time. These motives inspired an outpouring of new revisionist history on the modern urban school (Katz 1968; Lazerson 1971), the welfare system (Piven and Cloward 1971), the asylum (Scull 1979), the juvenile court (Platt 1969), and the prison. Three works best embody the revisionist current as far as prisons were concerned. The first was David Rothman's *The Discovery of the Asylum* (1971), an ambitious and justly well-received attempt to relate the emergence of the penitentiary, the mental institution, juvenile reformatory, and the urban school to the transformation of American society from the late colonial to the Jacksonian period. The second major work, dealing with France, was Michel Foucault's *Discipline and Punish* (1978), which followed his studies of the origins of the mental institution (*Madness and Civilization* 1967) and the origins of the hospital (*Birth of the Clinic* 1973) and his work on the evolution of the social and natural sciences in the eighteenth and nineteenth centuries (*The Order of Things* 1970). *Discipline and Punish* was not only about imprisonment but about the disciplinary ideology at work in education and in the army, and in the new psychology and criminology which claimed to offer a scientific analysis of criminal behavior and intention. The third major work of the revisionist current was my own *A Just Measure of Pain: The Penitentiary in the Industrial Revolution* (1978). Narrower in scope than the others, it concentrates only on the penitentiary's emergence in England in the period from 1770 to 1840.

Despite these differences of scope and intention, all three agreed that the motives and program of reform were more complicated than a simple revulsion at cruelty or impatience with administrative incompetence—the reformer's critique of eighteenth-century punishment flowed from a more not less ambitious conception of power, aiming for the first time at altering the criminal personality. This strategy of power could not be understood unless the history of the prison was incorporated into a history of the philosophy of authority and the exercise of class power in general. The prison was thus studied not for itself but for what its rituals of humiliation could reveal about a society's ruling conceptions of power, social obligation, and human malleability.

Within the last two or three years, however, as the wider political climate has changed, these revisionist accounts have come under increasing attack for overschematizing a complex story, and for reducing the intentions behind the new institution to conspiratorial class strategies of divide and rule. The critique has put into question the viability of both Marxist and structural-functionalist social theory and historical explanation, not only in the area of prisons, but by extension in other areas of historical research. These larger implications make the revisionist anti-revisionist debate of interest to readers beyond the historians' parish.

What this review of the debate hopes to show is that revisionist arguments, my own included, contained three basic misconceptions: that the state enjoys a monopoly over punitive regulation of behavior in society, that its moral authority and practical power are the binding sources of social order, and that all social relations can be described in the language of subordination. This does not, by implication, make the counter-revisionist position correct. Insofar as it is a position at all, it merely maintains that historical reality is more complex than the revisionists assumed, that reformers were more humanitarian than revisionsits have made them out to be, and that there are no such things as classes. This position abdicates from the task of historical explanation altogether. The real challenge is to find a model of historical explanation which accounts for institutional change without imputing conspiratorial rationality to a ruling class, without reducing institutional development to a formless ad hoc adjustment to contingent crisis, and without assuming a hyper-idealist, all triumphant humanitarian crusade. These are the pitfalls; the problem is to develop a model that avoids these while actually providing explanation. This paper is a step toward such a model, but only a step. Since I am a former, though unrepentant, member of the revisionist school, this exercise is necessarily an exercise in self-criticism.

The focus on three books, and on a narrow if crucial period, is necessary because this is where debate has been most pointed and most useful. With the exception of David Rothman's *Conscience and Convenience* (1980a), Steven Schlossman's *Love and the American Delinquent* (1977), James Jacobs's *Stateville* (1977), and Anthony Platt's *The Child Savers* (1969), the revisionist and counter-revisionist debate has not extended itself into the terrain of the twentieth century. We are still awaiting a new historiography on the disintegration of the nineteenth-century penitentiary routines of lockstep and silence; the rise of probation, parole, and juvenile court; the ascendancy of the psychiatrist, social worker, doctor, and the decline of the chaplain within the penal system; the history of drug use as therapeutic and control devices; the impact of electric and TV surveillance systems on the nineteenth-century institutional inheritance; the unionization of custodial personnel; the impact of rising standards of living upon levels of institutional amenity and inmate expectation; the long-term pattern of sentencing and the changing styles of judicial and administrative discretion; the history of ethnic and race relations within the walls; the social and institutional origins of the waves of prison rioting in the 1950s and late 1960s. This is the work that needs to be done if historians are to explain the contemporary crisis in prison order epitomized at Attica and more recently at Santa Fe (Wicker 1975; Silberman 1978; for England, see Fitzgerald 1977). The classics of prison sociology in the forties and fifties described prisons as communities, guaranteeing a measure of order and security through a division of power between captors and captives (Sykes 1958; Clemmer 1940). Why has this division of power broken down so often in the sixties and seventies? Thus far, only Jacobs's exemplary study of Stateville penitentiary in Illinois has offered a truly historical answer integrating changes in institutional governance, inmate composition and expectation, and the racial politics of the outside world into a working explanation. His conclusions, that prisoners were often surer of their physical safety under the tighter and more self-confident authoritarian regimes of the forties than they were under the well-meaning but confused reformist regimes of the sixties, might appear to suggest that a return to authoritarianism is the best way to guarantee prisoners' and guards' physical security, if nothing else. Unionized guards and the militant prisoners of today will not permit a return to the prisons of the forties. But if we cannot and ought not repeat history, we can at least learn from history where we went wrong. In the market place of good ideas—decarceration, inmate self-management, due process grievance procedures, institutional redesign, token economies, behavior modification—history offers a reliable guide to consumer choice and its invariable lesson in *caveat emptor*. Criminal justice activists may be disappointed by the literature I will review here because no answers are offered to the question, What is to be done? I do hope there is use, however, in learning some of the subtler errors which good intentions can entrain.

I. What Happened: the Revisionist Account

Let me begin by describing the revolution in punishment between 1780 and 1850. Rothman, Foucault, and my own work may differ about explanation but we do agree about what happened. In each society the key developments seem to have been:

The decline of punishments involving the public infliction of physical pain to the body. Beccaria's campaign against the death penalty in the 1760s, the Pennsylvania statute of 1786, the reformed codes of the "enlightened despots," the French revolutionary decrees against the capital penalty, and Romilly and MacIntosh's capital statutes campaign in England culminated by the 1850s in the restriction of the death penalty to first degree murder and treason. The form of execution was also changed—in France the guillotine was adopted in 1792 as a scientific instrument of death sparing the victim the possible incompetence of the hangman; the traditional Tyburn processional of the condemned through the streets of London was abolished in 1783 in order to curtail the public symbolism of the death spectacle (Foucault 1978; Linebaugh 1975, pp. 65–119; Linebaugh 1977, pp. 246–70); public executions in England ended in the 1860s, and hanging henceforth took place behind prison walls (D. Cooper 1974). The lesser physical penalties were also curtailed or abolished (abolition of branding in England, 1779; pillory, 1837; whipping of women, 1819; see also Perrot 1980, pp. 59–60, for France). By 1860 the public ritual of physical punishment had been successfully redefined as a cruel and politically illegitimate means of inflicting pain.

The emergence of imprisonment as the preeminent penalty for most serious offenses. Imprisonment had been used as punishment on a selective but insubstantial scale prior to 1770. Places of confinement were generally used as waystations for persons awaiting trial, for convicted felons awaiting execution or transportation, and crucially for debtors. Nearly 60 percent of the institutional population in Howard's census of 1777 were debtors (Ignatieff 1978, p. 28; Pugh 1968; Sheehan 1977). Vagrants and disobedient servants convicted for a range of minor, work-related property offenses punishable at summary jurisdiction were confined at hard labor in houses of correction (Innes 1980b; DeLacy 1980, chap. 1; Beattie 1974, 1977). This use of imprisonment increased in the eighteenth century, for reasons we do not yet understand. In England it was not until the suspension of transportation in 1776 that English JP's and assize judges began to substitute sentences of imprisonment for sentences of transportation (Webb and Webb 1963; Ignatieff 1978, chap. 4). At first criminal law reformers like Beccaria showed no particular enthusiasm for imprisonment itself, preferring to replace hanging with penalities ranging from hard labor in public to fines. It was only after 1776 in America and after 1789 in France that imprisonment began to replace hanging as *the* penalty appropriate to modern, enlightened republics (Foucault 1978, p. 115; Rothman 1971, p. 59).

The penitentiary came to be the bearer of reformers' hopes for a punishment capable of reconciling deterrence and reform, terror and humanity. In England between 1780 and 1812, half a dozen counties built small penitentiaries mostly for the control of minor delinquency. The first national penitentiary, Millbank, was opened in 1816. An enormous warren of passages and cells built in the style of a turreted medieval fortress near the Houses of Parliament, it soon was condemned as a costly failure—the prisoners were in revolt against the discipline more or less continuously in the 1820s; a violent outbreak of scurvy closed the prison for a year in 1824; but the lessons of failure were learned at Pentonville, opened in 1842. Its penitential regime of solitude, hard labor, and religious indoctrination became the model for all national penal servitude prisons and most county prisons besides. In America the key developments of the penitentiary regime occurred between 1820 and 1830—Auburn, 1819–23; Ossining, 1825; Pittsburgh, 1826; Philadelphia, 1829 (Rothman 1971, pp. 80–81), and in France, La Petite Rocquette, 1836, and the juvenile reformatory at Mettray, 1844 (Perrot 1980, pp. 60–1).

As systems of authority, the new prisons substituted the pains of intention for the pains of neglect (Ignatieff 1978, p. 113). Reformers like Howard were appalled that the squalor in neglected institutions was justified for its deterrent value. Accordingly, regular diets replaced the fitful provision of food in eighteenth-century institutions; uniforms replaced rags and personal clothing; prisoners received regular medical attention, and new hygienic rituals (head shaving, entrance examination, and bath) did away with the typhus epidemics which were an intermittent feature of eighteenth-century European prison life.

These hygienic rituals in turn became a means of stripping inmates of their personal identity. This indicates the ambivalence of "humanitarian" reform: the same measures that protected prisoners' health were explicitly justified as a salutary mortification of the spirit (Ignatieff 1978, p. 100).

The new prisons substituted the rule of rules for the rule of custom and put an end to the old division of power between the inmate community and the keepers. All accounts of eighteenth-century prisons stress the autonomy and self-government of prisoner communities. Since common law forbade the imposition of coercive routines on prisoners awaiting trial and debtors, they were able to take over the internal government of their wards, allocating cells, establishing their own rules, grievance procedures, and punishments (Innes 1980a, 1980b; Sheehan 1977, p. 233; De-Lacy 1980, chap. 2). The implied authority model of the colonial American and British prison was the household. The keeper and his family often resided in the institution and the prisoners were called "a family." They did not wear uniforms, they were not kept to routines, and they defended an oral and common law tradition of rights, privileges, and immunities (Rothman 1971, p. 55). By the 1840s in all three societies, a silent routine had been imposed to stamp out the association of the confined and to wipe out a subculture which was held to corrupt the novice and foster criminal behavior. Under the silent associated system of discipline, prisoners were allowed to congregate in workshops but were strictly forbidden to communicate. In the separate system at Pentonville and Philadelphia, prisoners were kept in complete cellular isolation and were forbidden any form of communication or association (Rothman 1971, p. 81; Ignatieff 1978, chap. 1; Henriques 1972). While advocates of both systems argued fiercely over their respective merits, they both agreed in principle on the necessity of suppressing the prison subculture and ending the tacit division of authority between captors and captives which had prevailed in the *ancien régime*. From a positive point of view, solitude exposed the individual prisoner to the obedience training of routine and the religious exhortation of the chaplain.

The chaplain, not the doctor or the governor, became the chief ideologist of the penitentiary, justifying its deprivations in the language of belief.

The new institutions enforced a markedly greater social distance between the confined and the outside world. High walls, sharply restricted visiting privileges, constant searches and patrols ended the mingling of outside and inside in the unreformed prison. Before reform, visitors enjoyed the run of the yards, women commonly brought their husbands meals, and debtors and outsiders drank together in the prison taproom. The aim of reform was to withdraw the prisoner from the corrupting influence of his former milieu and, at the same time, to inflict the pains of emotional and sexual isolation. Once again the mixture of humane and coercive motivations becomes apparent. As an unintended consequence, however, the check to the power of institutional personnel offered by constant visitors was reduced. The new institutions, therefore, did not resolve the old question, Who guards the guards? Instead they posed the question in a new and thus far more intractable way (Ignatieff 1978, conclusion; DeLacy 1980, conclusion).

All three versions agree that the emergence of the modern prison cannot be understood apart from the parallel history of the other total institutions created in this period—the lunatic asylum, the union workhouse, the juvenile reformatory and industrial school, and the monitorial school. Besides being the work of the same constituency of philanthropic and administrative reformers, these institutions enforced a similar economy of time and the same order of surveillance and control. They also expressed a common belief in the reformative powers of enforced asceticism, hard labor, religious instruction and routine.

The preceding paragraphs provide a schematic summary of the revolution in discipline as the revisionist account would have it. Before considering the explanations offered for this revolution, we ought to pause to consider the objections that have been raised to the revisionist account as valid description. A number of theses and monographs completed within the last couple of years have insisted that the descriptive picture is more complex, contradictory, and inchoate than Foucault, Rothman, or I have suggested.

Margaret DeLacy's excellent Princeton dissertation on county prison administration in Lancashire, 1690–1850, argues that even a relatively dynamic county administration like Lancashire lacked the resources to impose the highly rationalized Pentonville model on all the county institutions (1980). Many of these remained much the same as they had been in the eighteenth century. Eighteenth-century historians, particularly Joanna Innes, have argued that the prereform prison was neither as squalid nor as incompetently administered as the reformers made it out to be (Innes 1980b). By implication, therefore, the revisionist account may have been taken in by the reformers' sources. It is less clear, therefore, that the history of the institution between 1780 and 1840 can be described as a passage from squalid neglect to hygienic order.

Michelle Perrot and Jacques Leonard have made the same case for France, arguing that the highly rationalized institutions like La Rocquette and La Mettray cannot be taken as typical of the mass of local lockups, jails and hulks in mid-nineteenth-century France. In these institutions, the persistence of disease and the continued use of whipping and chains would appear to suggest a melancholy continuity with the worst features of the *ancien régime* (Perrot 1980).

It appears then that the revolution in punishment was not the generalized triumph of Weberian rationalization which the revisionist account suggested. Foucault's work (and my own as well) remained captive of that Weberian equation of the *ancien régime* with the customary, the traditional, and the particularistic, and of the modern with the rational, the disciplined, the impersonal, and the bureaucratic. The gulf between the reformers' rationalizing intentions and the institutionalized results of their work ought to make us rethink this equation of modernity and rationalization, or at least to give greater room for the idea that modernity is the site of a recurring battle between rationalizing intention and institutions, interests and communities which resist, often with persistent success.

Yet even if we admit that Pentonville and the Panopticon (Bentham 1791), Auburn and La Rocquette were "ideal types" rather than exemplary realities of their time, we still have to explain why it became possible between 1780 and 1840 and not before to conceive and construct them. However much else remained unchanged in the passage from the *ancien régime* to the industrial world of the nineteenth century, the penitentiary was something new and unprecedented and was understood as such by the great observers of the age, Alexis de Tocqueville, Charles Dickens, and Thomas Carlyle. A counter-revisionist account that considers only the local institutions, which went on much the same as before, will miss what contemporaries knew had to be explained about their own age.

II. Jacksonian America: The Emergence of the Asylum

Let us turn to this business of explanation and let us begin with the American case, with the work of David Rothman. In Rothman's account, the new total institutions of the Jacksonian period emerged in an overwhelmingly rural and agricultural society, growing beyond the boundaries of the colonial past yet still a generation away from the factory system, industrialism, European immigration, and the big city. It is a fundamental mistake, he argues, to interpret the total institution as an "automatic and inevitable response of an industrial and urban society to crime and poverty" (Rothman 1971, p. xvi). Americans were anxious about the passage of colonial society and the emergence of a restless, socially mobile population moving beyond the controls of family, farm, and town meeting, but there was nothing in this process which itself required the emergence of the new asylums and prisons. The catalyst for institutionalized instruction was not social change itself but the way it was organized into an alarmist interpretation of disorder and dislocation by philanthropic reformers. Crime was read for the first time not as the wickedness of individuals but as an indictment of a disordered society. This explains the emergence of new institutions aiming at the reformation and discipline of the deviant, disorderly, and deranged.

For a society which interpreted crime as the sign of the passing of the colonial order, the penitentiary symbolized an attempt to re-create the godly superintendence and moral discipline of the past within a modern setting. Rothman demonstrates brilliantly that the language developed in a society to explain disorder and deviance also defines the solutions it develops for these problems. An environmentalist theory of crime and faith in the reformative effects of isolation from the environment were linked together in a system of ideas, each legitimizing the other.

Rothman is better at re-creating the reformers' systems of belief than in locating these beliefs in a believable social and economic context. We need to know something about actual trends in crime during 1780–1820 if we are to understand the changing fit between reform and rhetoric and their social context. In the absence of such data, crime becomes a static and empty category in Rothman's analysis, and the reformers' alarmist discourse drifts away from any point of reference.

Why, we need to know, were the Jacksonians so specially anxious about change and disorder, and why did they look back with such nostalgia to colonial society? Rothman simply accepts the Jacksonian reformers' picture of the stable pre-revolutionary society they were leaving behind, but surely this was a questionable historical fable. Many eighteenth-century Europeans regarded colonial America as a restless, rootless, dynamic, and explosive society. Tom Paine's Philadelphia was no deferential idyll (Foner 1976). Yet Rothman never questions the Jacksonian's rosy image of their own past, never asks how their account of it should have been so out of joint with what we know of colonial society.

One would also have liked Rothman to explore the relationship between the rise of the total institution and the theory and practice of Jacksonian democracy. This was after all the period of the extension of universal manhood suffrage in the United States. Tocqueville himself thought the relation was one of contradiction: "While society in the United States gives the example of the most extended liberty, the prisons of the same country offer the spectacle of the most complete despotism" (Beaumont and Tocqueville 1964, p. 79). As Tocqueville suggested in the "tyranny of the majority" sections of *Democracy in America*, democratic republics which represent law and order as the embodied will of all the people treat disobedient minorities more severely than monarchical societies which have no ideological commitment to the consensual attachment of their citizens. Rothman suggests but leaves unexplored the possibility of a connection between Jacksonian popular sovereignty, an environmentalist theory of crime as being the responsibility of society, and an interventionist social therapy taking the form of the "total institution."

III. Sovereignty and the Margin of Illegality

If we turn to Foucault, we find that the relation between forms of sovereignty outside the walls and carceral regimes inside constitutes the main axis of his interpretation. Public executions, which the reformers of the Enlightenment condemned as a carnal and irrational indulgence, can be read, Foucault argues, as symbolic displays of the highly personalized sovereignty of the king and of his alternatively vengeful, merciful relation toward his wicked subjects.

The execution suited a philosophy of order that ignored minor delinquency to concentrate instead on the ritualized dispatch of selected miscreants. This exercise of sovereignty in turn implied a loosely articulated political nation in which

> each of the different social strata had its margin of tolerated illegality; the non-application of the rule, the non-observance of the innumerable edicts or ordinances were a condition of the political and economic functioning of society. . . . the least favoured strata of the population did not have in principle any privileges, but they benefited within the margins of what

was imposed on them by law or custom, from a space of tolerance, gained by force or obstinacy. (Foucault 1978, pp. 84–5)

The illegalities of the poor, like the tax exemptions of the rich, were tolerated because of the persistent weakness of an underfinanced, chronically indebted state, the tenacious survival of regional and local immunities, and the persistent countervailing power of the *parlements* (see Montesquieu, *The Spirit of the Laws*, 1748), the judiciary, and the nobility. Above all, the margin of illegality enjoyed by the poor reflected a ruling conception of national power as the sovereign's will rather than the operation of a bureaucratic machine. The state, moreover, shared the punitive function with civil society, in the double sense that its public rituals (execution, pillory, whipping, and branding) required completion by the opprobrium of the crowd if they were to have full symbolic effect, and in the sense that household heads, masters, and employers punished directly without invoking the state's power.

Independently of Foucault, Edward Thompson and Douglas Hay seem to have reached a similar description of the exercise of sovereign power in eighteenth-century England. They put the same emphasis on the symbolic centrality of the public hanging in reproducing awe and deference before the sovereign's mighty but merciful power, and they describe a philosophy of order essentially similar in its permissive approach to the small fish.

Permissive, however, is too nostalgic or sentimental a word for a tactics of order uneasily poised between an obvious and sometimes brutal concern to defend property rights and an equal distaste, moral, libertarian and economic, for the apparatus of state police (Hay 1975, pp. 17–65; Thompson 1975, conclusion). The Revolution Settlement and the common law tradition imposed limits on the discretionary power of eighteenth-century magistrates, and the common people themselves were quite capable of forcibly reminding magistrates of "the rights of free born Englishmen" and of the protocol of customs guaranteeing free assembly (Thompson 1971). It is possible that there was no corresponding corpus of rights in common law available to the French poor, but is is hard to believe that they did not hold to some customary beliefs and traditions about the proper bounds of monarchical "police."

Hay's and Thompson's works show up Foucault's tacit assumption that the only limits on public order policy were the mental assumptions of the authorities themselves and the structural weaknesses of the state apparatus. What is missing in his work is the idea that public order strategies were defined within limits marked out not only by the holders of power but also by those they were trying, often vainly, to persuade, subdue, cajole, or repress. Foucault's account consistently portrays authority as having a clear field, able to carry out its strategies without let or hindrance from its own legal principles or from popular opposition. Power is always seen as a strategy, as an instrumentality, never as a social relation between contending social forces. We need to know much more about the social process by which the margin of illegality enjoyed by the poor in the *ancien régime* was established before we conclude with Foucault that it owed its existence to the toleration of the authorities.

IV. Class Conflict and the Prison

However we interpret the margin of popular illegality under the *ancien régime*, Foucault and I agree that the penitentiary formed part of a new strategy of power aiming at its circumscription between 1780 and 1850. This new strategy was the work of Burke's "sophisters, economists, and calculators"—the monarchical administrators like Turgot and Le Trosne, and gentry men of letters like Beccaria. In England, the new ideology found expression in Henry Fielding's proposals for reform of London police in the 1760s, in Howard's penitentiary scheme of the 1770s, and in the hospital and asylum reforms led by the provincial Nonconformist professional classes in the 1790s (Ignatieff 1978, chap. 3). In the

1780s, too, Bentham and Romilly began their campaigns for the codification of law and for the curtailment of public executions.

The ideal of reforming through punishment and of apportioning just measures of pain to crimes previously tolerated or ignored was compatible with the democratic ideals of the French Revolution—equal rights, equal citizenship, equal punishment—but it proved no less compatible with Napoleonic centralism and the Bourbon Restoration. Beneath the whole surface play of debate about political rights and regimes between the 1770s and 1840s, Foucault argues, a new "carceral archipelago" of asylums, prisons, workhouses, and reformatories slipped into place. The political divisions over regimes and rights hid a deeper, unstated consensus among the ruling orders on the exercise of power over the criminal, the insane, and the pauper. This ideology forged in the 1760s by the Enlightenment reformers and opponents of the *ancien régime* was transmitted and reproduced by social interests in the Restoration and the July Monarchy often deeply hostile to the rationalist or egalitarian spirit of the philosophers themselves.

In England, the first bearers of the new disciplinary ideology were the reforming county magistrates and the Dissenting professional classes of the provinces—reformist in politics, scientific in mental outlook, rational and improving in their management of labor, county finance, and personal estates. The new asylums, prisons, workhouses, and schools which they built appealed to their residual religious asceticism, to their scientific and rationalist outlook, and to their impatience with the administrative incompetence and political corruption of the *ancien régime*. In the crisis years of early industrialization after 1815, the disciplinary ideology was taken up by the evangelized professional, mercantile, and industrial classes seeking to cope with the dissolution of a society of ranks and orders and the emergence of a society of strangers. The philanthropic campaigns to reform old institutions and to build new asylums, workhouses, prisons, and hospitals gave expression to a new strategy of class relations. In return for the humanity of minimal institutional provision, the disobedient poor were drawn into a circle of asceticism, industriousness, and obedience. They would return to society convinced of the moral legitimacy of their rulers. The persistent ideal of prison reform was a kind of punishment at once so humane and so just that it would convince the offender of the moral legitimacy of the law and its custodians. The penitentiary was designed to embody this reconciliation of the imperatives of discipline with the imperatives of humanity.

My own account places more stress than Foucault's on the religious and philanthropic impulses behind institutional reform. His version of the disciplinary ideology retains the secular rationalist tone of its initial Enlightenment formulation, while mine stresses the fusion of the secular rationalism embodied in Benthamism with the Quaker and Evangelical language of conscience epitomized by Elizabeth Fry. The penitentiary in England had at its core the religious discourse of the chaplain, just as the new Evangelical language of class relations had at its core the idea of rich and poor bound together in the common experience of sin and the common salvation of faith and industry.

My own account also places more stress than Foucault's upon the reformers' concern to defend and explain institutional routines to the confined. As a consequence I have put more emphasis on the humanitarian intentions of the reformers. They were genuinely repelled by the chains, squalor, and neglect they discovered in existing institutions, especially because these compromised the moral legitimacy of the social system in the eyes of the confined. In their theory of the reform of character, the crucial task was to persuade the poor to accept the benevolent intention behind institutional deprivations. Once convinced of the benevolence of the system, reformers argued, prisoners would be unable to take refuge from their own guilt in attacking their confiners. Personal reformation thus meant succumbing to the benevolent logic of their captors. In Foucault's account on the other hand, reformers were not centrally concerned to legitimize new penal measures as humane.

Reformers in his account simply took the humanity of their measures for granted and looked to the discipline to routinize the habits of the poor. My model of the reform of character is one of symbolic persuasion; Foucault's is of disciplinary routinization.

We both agree, however, on the relation between this new strategy of power and the social crisis of the post-1815 period, exemplified in recurrent surges of distress-related crime, pauperism, and collective pauper unrest. Foucault is sketchy in the extreme about the causation of this social crisis, but it is clearly implied as the backdrop of the institutional revolution in France. My account likewise does not purport to be a social history of crime and pauperism in the 1815–48 period, but it does locate three major sites of crisis. The first was the breakdown of social relations in the agricultural counties of the southeast between 1815 and 1831 as a result of the casualization of the agricultural proletariat. Rising rates of vagrancy, pauperism, and petty crime through the 1820s and the explosion of the Swing Riots in 1831 are the symptoms of this crisis in rural social relations. The second site of crisis was in London, where the Anti–Corn Law Riots of 1815, the Spa Field disturbances of 1816, and the riots attendant upon Queen Caroline's trial proved that the existing parish constabulary was hopelessly outdated in coping with urban crowd control while the soldiery brought in upon these occasions was a clumsy, brutal, and therefore alienating instrument of order (Silver 1967). In addition there was growing anxiety among magistrates and philanthropists about the rising incidence of juvenile crime in the metropolis after 1815. Masterless apprentices, orphans, underemployed youths, child prostitutes, all seemed to symbolize a breakdown in the order of the family, the parish, and the workshop. The third site of crisis lay in the new northern industrial towns where regional labor markets tied to single industries like cotton proved extremely vulnerable to cycles of demand in the international economy. Mass unemployment in "bad years" like 1826 threw up the specter of recurrent breakdown in labor market disciplines (Ignatieff 1978, chap. 6).

There cannot be much doubt that the new strategy of mass imprisonment, the creation of the Metropolitan Police in 1829, and the diffusion of paid constabularies through the agricultural counties and the industrial towns in the 1830s, 40s, and 50s must be seen as a "response" to this crisis of public order (Storch 1975). The creation of permanent police courts, the expansion of the scope of the vagrancy and trespass statutes, and the formation of the union workhouse system in 1834 represented additional attempts to "grapple for control," to cope with a social order problem the size and magnitude of which clearly grew faster than any of the authorities anticipated (Silver 1967; Hart 1955, 1965; Radzinowicz 1968, vol. 5; DeLacy 1980; Philips 1977).

Yet there are dangers of social reductionism in this explanation. Institutional reformers did not justify their program as a response to the labor discipline needs of employers. Indeed the reform discourse antedates the labor discipline crisis. Howard's penitentiary schemes, the police theory of the late Enlightenment, the hospital and asylum campaigns of the 1790s, all anticipated the post-1815 crisis. Moreover, as Rothman pointed out in the American case, the fact of crisis itself would not explain why authorities chose the particular remedies they did, why they put such faith in institutional confinement when greater resort to hanging or to convict gang labor in public might have been equally eligible responses to the perceived breakdown of social controls.

A. Divide and Rule

Foucault's argument and mine nonetheless is that the massive investment in institutional solutions would have been inconceivable unless the authorities had believed that they were faced with the breakdown of a society of stable ranks and the emergence of a society of hostile classes. This diagnosis of the malaise of their times in turn suggested an institutional solution. Mass imprisonment offered a new strategic possibility—isolating a criminal class from the working class, incarcerating the one so that it would not corrupt the industriousness of the other. The workhouse likewise would quarantine pauperism from honest poverty (Foucault 1978, pp. 276–78). Beneath the surface debate over whether these institutions were capable of reforming or deterring their target populations, Foucault argues, lay a deeper consensus among the ruling orders about using institutionalization to manufacture and reproduce social divisions within the working classes between working and criminal, rough and respectable, poor and pauperized. Foucault claims that this strategy of division actually worked—that the institutional quarantine of the criminal did create a criminal class separate from the working-class community. In this lay the secret "success" of prison, beneath all its apparent failures as an institution of reform and deterrence.

The divide and rule argument works best in respect to the workhouse, where the creation of the Bastilles of 1834 (see Babington 1972) does appear to have succeeded in making pauperism disgraceful to the poor. Before the Bastilles, the poor conceived of relief as a right and did not look upon it as a disgrace; afterwards while many continued to insist on their rights, working-class respectability came to insist on avoiding the degradation of appealing for relief and ending one's days in the public ward. The Bastilles do seem to have dug the gulf deeper between pauperism and poverty within the value system and the social behavior of the poor themselves.

As regards imprisonment, however, the divide and rule argument seems to me now to have fallen prey unwittingly to the problem inherent in what criminologists call "labeling theory." The notorious difficulty with this approach is that it makes the state's sanctions the exclusive source of the boundary between the deviant and the respectable. This would seem to ignore the degree to which, in the nineteenth as in the twentieth century, the moral sanctions condemning murder, rape, and sexual and personal assault were prior to and independent of the punitive sanction, commanding assent across class lines. In punishing these offenses, the state simply ratified a line of demarcation already indigenous to the poor. Even in the case of petty property crime, it is not clear that the criminal sanction was labeling acts which the poor excused as an inevitable response to distress or which they justified in the vernacular of natural justice. The poor, no less than the rich, were victims of property crime, and any study of London police courts in the nineteenth century shows they were prepared to go to law to punish members of their own class (Davis 1980; Philips 1977). If a constant process of demarcation was underway between criminals and the working classes, it was a process in which the working classes themselves played a prominent part, both in their resort to law and in the informal sanctioning behavior which enforced their own codes of respectability. Doubtless there was sympathy for the first-time offenders and juveniles convicted for minor property offenses during hard times; doubtless there were offenders whom working people felt were unjustly convicted. Certainly repeated imprisonment did isolate the criminal from his own class. But it is a serious overestimation of the role of the state to assume that its sanctioning powers were the exclusive source of the social division between criminal and respectable. The strategy of mass imprisonment is better understood in class terms as an attempt by the authorities to lend symbolic reinforcement to values of personal honor which they themselves knew were indigenous to the poor.

The behavior of the politicized sections of the working classes leaves no doubt that they drew a very strict demarcation between themselves and the criminal. Michelle Perrot's study of French prisons in 1848 shows that the revolutionary crowds who stormed the prisons reserved liberation for prostitutes, political offenders, and conscripts, not for ordinary criminal offenders (Perrot 1980, p. 241). In England, while political radicals often cited the criminal statistics as proof of the grinding pressure of distress on the poor, they never questioned the ultimate legitimacy of their convictions (Ignatieff 1978, chap. 4; DeLacy 1980).

B. Class Fear

Thus if fears by the ruling orders of a potential union of interest and action between the criminal and working classes are

to be regarded as having had some influence in generating public support for mass imprisonment, it must be recognized that
these fears were without actual sociological foundation. We are
dealing with a form of social fantasy detached from observable
reality. Moreover, it is not clear how general these fantasies of
revolution were or even how influential they were in galvaniz-
ing public opinion in support of the total institution. The difficulty with arguments from class fear is that they are simply too
vague, too global, to account for the specific timing of institutional or legislative change. Class fear among educated
public opinion in the 1820s and 1830s may have contributed
something to the consensus that public order was too parlous
and insecure to go on with the haphazard punishment and
police strategies of the eighteenth century. But class fear cannot
account for the specific idiosyncrasies of the institutional solution—the faith in silence, solitude, religious indoctrination,
and hard labor.

If we return to what reformers said they were doing, it becomes clearer to me now than it was when I wrote *A Just Measure of Pain* that the adoption of the penitentiary in particular
and the institutional solution in general cannot be explained in
terms of their supposed utility in manufacturing social divisions
within the working class. This is because at bottom reformers
like most of their own class understood deviance in irreducibly
individual rather than collective terms, not ultimately as collective social disobedience, however much distress and collective
alienation influenced individuals, but as a highly personal de-
scent into sin and error. Given this individualist reading of deviance, the appeal of institutional solutions lay in the drama of
guilt which they forced each offender to play out—the drama of
suffering, repentance, reflection, and amendment, watched over
by the tutelary eye of the chaplain. Foucault's neglect of the
religious vernacular of reform argument obscures the deep hold
which this symbolic drama of guilt and repentance held for the
Victorian imagination. To be sure, this hypothetical drama
bore little if any relation to what actually happened in prisons,
asylums, and workhouses, and many Victorians, Charles Dick-

ens among them, knew this full well. But nevertheless, even
skeptics like Dickens and Mayhew were not immune to the appeal of a symbolic system of associations in which the reform of
the guilty criminal was held to reveal the triumph of good over
evil, conscience over desire, in all men and women. If there was
a social message in the ideal of reform through institutional discipline it was that the institutional salvation of the deviant acted
out the salvation of all men and women, rich and poor alike.

V. Who Directed the Carceral Archipelago?

Where does all this leave the problem of agency? Whose interests did the new institutions serve? In whose name were the
reformers speaking?

A. Foucault and the Disciplinary "Savoir"

On these questions of agency, Foucault's answers are notori-
ously cloudy. At some points, he refers to the "bourgeoisie"
though this is hardly an adequate categorization of the shifting
alignment of class fragments, aristocrats, financiers, professionals, industrialists, who competed for power in France
between 1815 and 1848. At other points, Foucault slips into a
use of the passive voice which makes it impossible to identify
who, if anyone, was the historical agent of the tactics and strategies he describes. Yet before we condemn them out of hand it
is worth noting that Foucault is trying to work free of what he
regards as the vulgar Marxist conception of agency according to
which the prison is a tool of a definable class with a clear-
sighted conception of its strategic requirements. He also rejects
the functionalist model according to which the prison is the
designated punitive instrument within a social division of labor.
In place of these accounts, he argues that punitive power is
dispersed throughout the social system: it is literally
everywhere, in the sense that the disciplinary ideology, the *savoir*
which directs and legitimizes power, permeates all social groups
(with the exception of the marginal and deviant), ordering the
self-repression of the repressors themselves. The prison is only
the most extreme site for an exercise of power which extends

along the whole continuum of social relations from the family, to the market, to the workplace, and to citizenship. If prisons and factories came to resemble each other in their rituals of time and discipline, therefore, it was not because the state acted in response to the labor discipline strategies initiated by employers but because both public order authorities and employers shared the same universe of assumptions about the regulation of the body and the ordering of institutional time.

Given that all social relations were inscribed within relations of domination and subordination, ordered, so he says, by a continuous disciplinary discourse, it is impossible to identify the privileged sites or actors that controlled all the others. The disciplinary ideology of modern society *can* be identified as the work of specific social actors but once such an ideology was institutionalized, once its rationality came to be taken for granted, a fully exterior challenge to its logic became impossible. The institutional system took on a life of its own. One cannot say, Foucault argues, that the political apparatus of modern states actually controls the prison system. There is a formal chain of delegation and responsibility from the legislature to the bureaucracy, from the bureaucracy to the warden, and from the warden to guards and prisoners, but this does not take into account the way institutional systems develop their own inertial logic which each "actor" feels powerless to change (even those at its very summit).

Since the appearance of *Discipline and Punish*, Foucault has reformulated this problem of agency as one of historical causation, putting a new stress on the way in which the new institutions emerged as the unintended consequence of levels of change, which in themselves were independent of each other— the new discourse on discipline in the Enlightenment, the search by the propertied for stricter legal and social protection, and the crisis in public order. The new discourse emerged prior to the social revolution of the nineteenth century and prior to the labor discipline needs of employers, but once in play ideologically, it provided the program around which constituencies assembled their response to social turbulence and

labor indiscipline. Once the disciplinary discourse's independence of its social grounding is granted, it becomes possible to work free of the various traps which the problem of
agency has caused for historians—the conspiratorial all-seeing
ruling classes of the Marxist account; the low rationality model
of ad hoc responses to social crisis, and the hyperidealist version
of reform as a humanitarian crusade (see Foucault's interview in
Perrot 1980).

B. The Middle Class as a Ruling Class

But where does this leave the concept of a ruling class as the
historical actor behind the making of the penitentiary? My own
work has been criticized for using middle class as a synonym
for ruling class in a period in which it would be more accurate
to speak of a bewilderingly complex competition for political
power and social influence by different class fractions, professionals, industrialists, and merchants, aristocratic magnates,
and small gentry farmers. While it is a convention of Marxist
argument that such division of interest and jockeying for power
were stilled whenever "the class as a whole" felt threatened
from below, my own work on the intense debates about social
order policy suggests that choral unanimity was rare even in
moments of universally recognized crisis. Unquestionably justices, members of Parliament, and philanthropists recognized
each other as the rich and regarded vagrants, pickpockets, and
the clamoring political mob as the lower orders, but their sense
of "we" versus "they" was not enough to make the ruling class
into a collective social actor. One can speak of a ruling class in
the sense that access to strategic levers of power was systematically restricted according to wealth and inheritance, but one
cannot speak of its acting or thinking as a collective historical
subject. One can only ascribe historical effectivity to identifiable social constituencies of individuals who managed to secure
political approval for penal change through a process of debate
and argument in the society's sites of power. It would be wrong
to think of these constituencies of institutional reformers as
acting for their class or expressing the logic of its strategic im-

peratives. This would make them into ventriloquists for a clairvoyant and unanimous social consensus. In fact they managed to secure only the most grudging and limited kind of approval for their program. The penitentiary continued to be criticized from multiple and contradictory points of view: it was inhumanly severe; it was too lenient; it was too expensive; it could not reconcile deterrence and reform; the reformation of criminals was a sentimental delusion; and so on.

In his most recent reflections, Foucault himself admits that the new carceral system was not the work of an overarching strategic consensus by a ruling class, but instead fell into place as a result of a conjuncture between transformations in the phenomena of social order, new policing needs by the propertied, and a new discourse on the exercise of power.

Yet for all his disclaimers, Foucault's conception of the disciplinary world view, the *savoir* as he calls it, effectively forecloses on the possibility that the *savoir* itself was a site of contradiction, argument, and conflict. In England at least, for example, a preexisting legal tradition of rights imposed specific limits to the elaboration of new powers of arrest, new summary jurisdiction procedures, just as habeas corpus limited carceral practice toward the unconvicted. At every point, new proposals for police, prisons, and new statutory powers raised the question of how to balance the changing conceptions of security against preexisting conceptions of the liberty of the subject. Foucault makes no mention of these legal limits.

There is more than a touch of Marxist reductionism in Foucault's treatment of law as a pliable instrument of the ruling class. Recent Marxist legal theory describes the autonomy of law as a historical sedimentation of the outcome of earlier struggles over the competing rights of subjects which as such imposes rules not only on subjects but on rulers themselves. The jury system, the legal criteria of evidence and proof, and the legal ideology of the "rights of free-born Englishmen" constituted a court of appeal in England against plans or projects for tightening the law's grip (Pashukanis 1978; Renner 1949; Fine et al. 1979, pp. 22–24; Thompson 1975, conclusion). Penal practice, far from representing the unfolding of an all-embracing disciplinary *savoir*, should be seen as embodying the compromise outcomes of often heated political and legal debates. Foucault seems to ignore the possibility of conflict between the claims of private wealth and the requirements of public order. Compromise was also required between the desire to punish minor delinquency more strictly and the desire to avoid criminalizing normally law-abiding members of the popular classes through mass imprisonment. The conflict between these two imperatives frequently pitted policemen against magistrates, and magistrates against employers (Ignatieff 1978, pp. 186–87). The erratic line of policy traced out by these conflicts could be said to have been functional to the reproduction of a ruling class only in the relatively trivial sense that the existing distribution of social relations was not overthrown by revolution; but once the elaboration of carceral policy is seen as the unplanned outcome of compromise and conflict, it seems rationalist and conspiratorial to call it an unfolding strategy of a carceral *savoir*.

VI. "Social Control" as Historical Explanation

These questions about the ruling class as a historical actor ought to be connected to earlier questions raised about the role of prisons in disciplining the working class. Given the frequency with which the popular classes themselves sought to invoke the penal sanction against members of their own social group, it would be difficult to maintain that they were simple objects of the punitive sanction. While the majority of punished offenders undoubtedly came from the popular classes, it would not follow from this that the function of imprisonment was to control those classes as such. Foucault's and my own work, I think, confused statements about the social fears motivating the construction of institutions with statements about their actual function.

The "social control" model of the prison's function which informed my own work assumed that capitalist society was systematically incapable of reproducing itself without the constant interposition of state agencies of control and repression. This model essentially appropriated the social control models of American Progressivist sociology according to which society was a functional equilibrium of institutional mechanisms in the family, the workplace, and marketplace working together to ensure the cooperation of individuals in the interests of social order (Stedman Jones 1977; Rothman 1980b; Muraskin 1976). As Stedman Jones has pointed out, the Marxist version of this idea, and the structuralist version of it reproduced in Foucault, carries on the assumption of society as a functionally efficient totality of institutions. When applied to prison history, this model implies that institutions "work," whereas the prison is perhaps *the* classic example of an institution which works badly and which nonetheless survives in the face of recurrent skepticism as to its deterrent or reformative capacity. Instead of looking for some hidden function which prisons actually succeed in discharging, we ought to work free of such functionalist assumptions altogether and begin to think of society in much more dynamic and historical terms, as being ordered by institutions like the prisons which fail their constituencies and which limp along because no alternative can be found or because conflict over alternatives is too great to be mediated into compromise.

The second assumption in Marxist social control theory is that the use of the state penal sanction is essential to the reproduction of the unequal and exploitative social relations of the capitalist system. Marx himself qualified the centrality of state coercion, arguing that while the hangman and the house of correction were central in the "primitive accumulation" process, that is, in the forcible establishment of wage relations, once such wage relations were in place, "the silent compulsions of economic relations" "set the seal on the domination of the capitalist over the worker." The extra-economic coercion of the state penal sanction was then invoked only in "exceptional" cases (Marx 1976, p. 899). My own work on the expansion of vagrancy, trespass, and petty larceny statutes in the 1820s and 1830s suggested that state penal sanctions were required by employers, especially in the agricultural counties, to prevent their chronically underemployed casual labor force from passing out of the wage system into theft and vagrancy (Ignatieff 1978, pp. 180–83; also Linebaugh, forthcoming).

Important as the penal sanction may have been in sustaining discipline in pauperized labor markets, or in constituting wage discipline itself in the face of worker resistance, we ought not to take these instances as typical of the role of state force once the wage bargain has been broadly accepted. We ought not to assume that exploitative social relations are impossible to reproduce without threat of force. Even in objectively exploitative, underpaid, and unhealthy conditions of labor, one can conceive of men and women voluntarily coming to work not in the sense that they are free to choose wage labor but in the specific sense that they derive intrinsic satisfaction from the sociability of labor, from the activity itself, from the skill they manage to acquire, and from the pride they take in their work. Marxist theories of labor discipline consistently ignore these aspects of submission to the wage bargain and consequently overstate the centrality of penal force in reproducing those relations. The fact that workers do submit to the wage bargain need not imply that they accept the terms of their subordination as legitimate; it is a cliché of labor history that those whose wage levels, skill, and pride in craftsmanship gave them the most reasons for satisfaction with industrial labor were often the most militant in their political and moral challenge to it as a system. The point is simply that the punitive sanction of the state need not be regarded as decisive in the reproduction of exploitative and unequal social relations.

Going still further, it could be asked whether force itself, apart from its specific embodiment in state apparatuses of coercion, is decisive to the maintenance of social order. The tacit social theory of Foucault's *Discipline and Punish* describes all social relations in the language of power, domination, and subordination. This would imply that individuals are naturally unsocial or asocial, requiring discipline and domination before they will submit to social rules. Not surprisingly, therefore,

Foucault sees the family as an authority system, linked to the carceral system of the state outside:

> We should show how intra-familial relations, essentially in the parent-children cell, have become "disciplined," absorbing since the classical age external schemata first educational and military, then medical, psychiatric, psychological, which have made the family the privileged locus of emergence for the disciplinary question of the normal and the abnormal. (Foucault 1978, p. 215)

Can fathers' or mothers' social relations toward their children really be defined only in terms of Foucault's disciplinary question? Foucault would seem to be taking to the limits of parody a fashionable current of thought, nourishing itself in the Freudian analysis of Oedipal conflict and in the feminist critique of patriarchal domination, which has, to my way of thinking, "over-politicized" family social relations, neglecting the collaborative and sacrificial elements of family attachment and over-emphasizing the power aspects of family interaction. This makes it easy to locate the family as an institution of domination on a continuum with the prison, enforcing the same over-arching disciplinary rationality, but it does so by ignoring obvious distinctions between the basis of our obligations as family members and our obligations as citizens to the law. It also neglects the extent to which loyalty to one's family or the desire to maintain one's authority as a family head can constitute the basis for rejection of state authority, for example, in resistance by families to the introduction of compulsory school attendance.

By describing all social relations as relations of domination, Foucault neglects the large aspects of human sociability, in the family and in civil society generally, which are conducted by the norms of cooperation, reciprocity, and the "gift relationship." He neglects that human capacity which Adam Smith called "sympathy," by which we voluntarily adjust our behavior to norms of propriety in order to stand well in the eyes of our fellows (Smith 1759). In Smith's social theory the order of civil society was reproduced, without state direction or class design, by an uncoordinated molecular process of individual self-regulation. Our obedience to legal norms could be understood both in terms of this largely subconscious order-seeking behavior and as an expression of conscious belief in the utility and the justice of such rules in themselves. In Smith's theory threat of penal sanction was not necessary to the reproduction of normal patterns of obedience. Punishment did not constitute the order of civil society; rather, it gave ritual and symbolic expression, in retributive form, to the moral value attached by individuals to rule-obedient behavior (Smith 1763).

Smith's theory of social order may underestimate human beings' mutual malignity, and it is justly criticized by Marxists for writing the facts of power, domination, and subordination out of its account of the social process. But precisely because it tried to think of social order in terms that go beyond the language of power, it offers a more persuasive account of those social activities which we do experience as uncoerced subjects than one which conceives of order as the grid imposed by a carceral archipelago.

My point here is not to argue the virtues of Smithian social theory as against Foucault's structural functionalism or Marxist social control, but rather to use Smith to point to hidden features of both: their state-centered conception of social order and their tendency to reduce all social relations to relations of domination.

How then are we to think through a theory of the reproduction of social life which would give relative weights to the compelled and the consensual, the bound and the free, the chosen and the determined dimensions of human action in given historical societies? Contemporary social theory is increasingly aware that it has been ill-served by the grand theoretical tradition in its approach to these questions—a Parsonian functionalism which restricts human action to the discharge of prescribed roles and the internalization of values; a Marxism which in its hostility to the idealist account of human subjectivity went a long way toward making the active human subject the determined object of ideological system and social formation; and a structuralism which likewise seems to make individual intellectual creativity and moral choice the determined result of cultural and discursive structure (Giddens 1976). Work-a-day historians and sociologists of criminal justice may well ask at this point what this high-flown theoretical debate has to do with them, or what they could possibly contribute to it. Its relevance is that any theory or history of punishment must make some ultimate judgment about what weight to attach to the state's penal sanction in the reproduction of obedient behavior. What weight you give depends ultimately on how much importance you attach to the consensual and voluntary aspects of human behavior. The social control theory of the 1920s, as Rothman points out in an excellent review of that literature, placed so much stress on the consensual that it neglected the coercive; the social control literature of the seventies exaggerated the coercive at the expense of the consensual (Rothman 1980b). The first step back to a balance between these perspectives will require us to ask how crucial the state has been historically in the reproduction of the order of civil society. My suspicion is that the new social history of law and punishment in the seventies exaggerated the centrality of the state, the police, the prison, the workhouse, and the asylum.

If we are going to get beyond our present almost exclusive focus on the state as the constitutive element of order, we will have to begin to reconstitute the whole complex of informal rituals and processes within civil society for the adjudication of grievances, the settling of disputes, and the compensation of injury. Historians have only just begun to study dispute and grievance procedures within civil society in the same way as these are studied in the anthropology of law (Diamond 1974; Roberts 1980). Among such studies are Edward Thompson's discussion of the "rough justice" rituals of sixteenth- and seventeenth-century English villages, by means of which wife-beaters, scolds, and couples who married out of their age cohort were subjected to public scorn and humiliation by their neighbors (see also Davis 1975; Thompson 1972; Thomas 1971). Because studies of such grievance procedures exist only for the early modern period, it would be easy to conclude that the state expropriated such functions in its courts and prisons in the course of consolidating its monopoly over the means of legitimate violence (Weber 1947, pp. 324–37).

But the idea that the state enjoys a monopoly over legitimate means of violence is long overdue for challenge. The crimes which it visits with punishment ought to be interpreted as the tip of an iceberg, as a small part of those disputes, conflicts, thefts, assaults too damaging, too threatening, too morally outrageous to be handled within the family, the work unit, the neighborhood, the street. It would be wrong, I think, to conclude that early modern English villages were the only communities capable of exercising these de facto judicial powers. Until recently, social histories of the working-class family and the working-class neighborhood were too confined within their subdisciplines to include discussion of the anthropology of dispute settlement and the social history of relations with the police, the courts, and the prisons. But what is now opening up as an area of study is the social process by which crime was identified within these units of civil society, and how decisions were taken to channel certain acts or disputes for adjudication or punishment by the state. The correlative process, from the state side, is how agents like the police worked out a tacit agreement with the local enforcers of norms, determining which offenses were theirs to control, and which were to be left to the family, the employer, or the neighborhood (Fine et al. 1979, pp. 118–37). Such research would indicate, I think, that powers of moral and punitive enforcement are distributed throughout civil society, and that the function of prison can only be understood once its position within a whole invisible framework of sanctioning and dispute regulation procedure in civil society has been determined. We have always known that prisons and the courts handled only a tiny fraction of delinquency known to the police. Now we must begin, if we can, to uncover the network which handled the "dark figure," which recovered stolen goods, visited retribution on known villains, demarcated the respectable, hid the innocent, and delivered up the guilty. This new area of research will not open up by itself. Empirical fields of this sort become visible only if theory guides historians to new questions. This essay amounts to a plea to historians, criminologists, and sociologists to involve themselves seriously with texts they have been apt to dismiss as abstract and ahistorical—the classical social theory tradition of Smith, Marx, Durkheim, and Weber. The involvement ought to take the form of self-criticism, for if I have argued correctly, these texts are the hidden source of some basic misconceptions—that the state enjoys a monopoly of the punitive sanction, that its moral authority and practical power are *the* binding sources of social order, and that all social relations can be described in the language of power and domination. If we could at least subject these ideas to practical empirical examination, a new social history of order, authority, law, and punishment would begin to emerge.

REFERENCES AND SELECTED BIBLIOGRAPHY

Babington, Anthony. 1971. *The English Bastille.* New York: St. Martin's Press.
Bailey, Victor. 1975. "The Dangerous Classes in Late Victorian England." Ph.D. dissertation, Warwick University.
Beattie, J. M. 1974. "The Pattern of Crime in England, 1660–1800," *Past and Present* 62:47–95.
———. 1977. "Crime and the Courts in Surrey, 1736–53." In *Crime in England, 1550–1800,* ed. J. S. Cockburn. London: Methuen.
Beaumont, Gustave de, and de Tocqueville, Alexis. 1964. *On the Penitentiary System of the United States.* Reprint. Carbondale: Southern Illinois University Press. Originally published 1835.
Bellamy, John. 1973. *Crime and Public Order in England in the Later Middle Ages.* London: Routledge and Kegan Paul.
Bentham, Jeremy. 1791. *Panopticon; or the Inspection House.* London: T. Payne.

Branch, Johnson W. 1970. *The English Prison Hulks*. Chichester: Phillimore.

Chill, Emmanuel. 1962. "Religion and Mendicity in Seventeenth Century France," *International Review of Social History* 7:400–25.

Clemmer, Donald. 1940. *The Prison Community*. New York: Holt, Rinehart and Winston.

Cockburn, J. S., ed. 1977. *Crime in England, 1550–1800*. London: Methuen.

Condon, R. 1962. "The Reform of English Prisons, 1773–1816." Ph.D. dissertation, Brown University.

Cooper, David D. 1976. *The Lesson of the Scaffold: The Public Execution Controversy in Victorian England*. London: Allen Lane.

Cooper, Robert Alan. 1976. "Ideas and Their Execution: English Prison Reform," *Eighteenth Century Studies* 10:73–93.

Davis, Jennifer. 1980. "The London Garroting Panic of 1862: A Moral Panic and the Creation of a Criminal Class in Mid-Victorian England." In *Crime and Law in Western Societies: Historical Essays*, ed. V. A. C. Gatrell, B. Lenman, G. Parker. London: Europa.

Davis, Natalie. 1975. "The Reasons of Misrule." In her *Society and Culture in Early Modern France*. Stanford, Calif.: Stanford University Press.

DeLacy, Margaret Eisenstein. 1980. "County Prison Administration in Lancashire, 1690–1850." Ph.D. dissertation, Princeton University.

Diamond, Stanley. 1974. "The Rule of Law versus the Order of Custom." In his *In Search of the Primitive: A Critique of Civilization*. New Brunswick, N.J.: Transaction Books.

Donajgrodzki, A. P., ed. 1977. *Social Control in Nineteenth Century Britain*. London: Croom Helm.

Evans, Robin. 1975. "A Rational Plan for Softening the Mind: Prison Design, 1750–1842." Ph.D. dissertation, University of Essex.

Fine, Bob, R. Lea J. Kinsey, S. Picciotto, and J. Young, eds. 1979. *Capitalism and the Rule of Law: From Deviancy Theory to Marxism*. Harmondsworth: Penguin.

Fitzgerald, Mike. 1977. *Prisoners in Revolt*. London: Penguin.

Fitzgerald, Mike, and Joe Sim. 1979. *British Prisons*. Oxford: Basil Blackwell.

Foner, Eric. 1976. *Tom Paine and Revolutionary America*. London: Oxford University Press.

Foucault, Michel. 1967. *Madness and Civilization*. Translated by Richard Howard. London: Tavistock.

———, ed. 1973. *Moi, Pierre Rivière . . . un cas de parricide au XIXe siècle*. Paris: Gallimard Julliard.

————. 1976. *La volonté de savoir: histoire de la sexualité*. Paris: Gallimard.

————. 1978. *Discipline and Punish*. Translated by Alan Sheridan. New York: Pantheon.

Giddens, Anthony. 1976. *New Rules of Sociological Method*. New York: Basic Books.

Goffman, Erving. 1961. *Asylums*. Garden City: Doubleday/Anchor.

Gramsci, Antonio. 1971. *Prison Notebooks*. London: Lawrence and Wishart.

Hart, Jennifer. 1955. "Reform of the Borough Police, 1835–1856," *English Historical Review* 70:411–27.

————. 1965. "Nineteenth Century Social Reform: A Tory Interpretation of History," *Past and Present* 31:39–61.

Hay, Douglas. 1975. "Property, Authority and Criminal Law." In *Albion's Fatal Tree*, ed. D. Hay, P. Linebaugh, J. Rule, E. P. Thompson, and C. Winslow. London: Allen Lane.

Henriques, Ursula. 1972. "The Rise and Decline of the Separate System of Prison Discipline," *Past and Present* 54:61–93.

Himmelfarb, Gertrude. 1968. *Victorian Minds*. New York: Harper.

Ignatieff, Michael. 1978. *A Just Measure of Pain: The Penitentiary in the Industrial Revolution, 1750–1850*. New York: Pantheon.

Innes, Joanna. 1980a. "The King's Bench Prison in the Later Eighteenth Century: Law, Authority and Order in a London Debtor's Prison." In *An Ungovernable People: Englishmen and the Law in the 17th and 18th Centuries*, John Brewer and John Styles. London: Hutchinson.

————. 1980b. "English Prisons in the Eighteenth Century." Ph.D. dissertation, Cambridge University.

Jacobs, James. 1977. *Stateville: The Penitentiary in Mass Society*. Chicago: University of Chicago Press.

Katz, Michael. 1968. *The Ironies of Early School Reform*. Cambridge, Mass.: Harvard University Press.

Labour History Society, Great Britain. 1972. *Bulletin: Crime and Industrial Society Conference Report*.

Lasch, Christopher. 1973. "The Discovery of the Asylum." In his *The World of Nations*. New York: Vintage.

Lazerson, Marvin. 1971. *The Origins of the Urban School*. Cambridge, Mass.: Harvard University Press.

Leroy, Ladurie E. 1973. "La décroissance de crime au XVIIIe siècle: bilan d'historiens," *Contrepoint* 9:227–33.

Lewis, W. David. 1965. *From Newgate to Dannemora: The Rise of the Penitentiary in New York, 1796–1848*. Ithaca, N.Y.: Cornell University Press.

Lewis, Orlando F. 1967. *The Development of American Prisons and Prison Customs, 1776–1845*. Reprint. Montclair, N.J.: Patterson Smith. Originally published 1922.

Linebaugh, Peter. 1975. "The Tyburn Riot against the Surgeons." In *Albion's Fatal Tree*, ed. D. Hay, P. Linebaugh, J. Rule, E. P. Thompson, and C. Winslow. London: Allen Lane.

———. 1976. "Karl Marx, the Theft of Wood and Working Class Composition: A Contribution to the Current Debate," *Crime and Social Justice* 6:5–16.

———. 1977. "The Ordinary of Newgate and His Account." In *Crime in England, 1550–1800*, ed. J. S. Cockburn. London: Methuen.

———. Forthcoming. *Crime and the Wage in the Eighteenth Century*.

McConville, Sean. 1977. "Penal Ideas and Prison Management in England, 1700–1850." Ph.D. dissertation, Cambridge University.

McKelvey, Blake. 1977. *American Prisons*. Montclair, N.J.: Patterson Smith.

Marx, K. 1976. *Capital*, I. Harmondsworth: Penguin.

Muraskin, W. A. 1976. "The Social Control Theory in American History: A Critique," *Journal of Social History* 11:559–68.

Pashukanis, B. 1978. *Law and Marxism: A General Theory*, 3d ed. London: Ink Links.

Perrot, Michelle. 1975. "Delinquance et systèmes penitentiaire en France au XIXe siècle," *Annales: économies, sociétés, civilizations* 30:67–91.

———, ed. 1980. *L'impossible prison: recherches sur le système penitentiaire au XIXe siècle*. Paris: Seuil.

Philips, David. 1977. *Crime and Authority in Victorian England: The Black Country, 1835–60*. London: Croom Helm.

Piven, Francis F., and Richard Cloward. 1971. *Regulating the Poor*. New York: Vintage.

Platt, Anthony M. 1969. *The Child Savers: The Invention of Delinquency*. Chicago: University of Chicago Press.

Playfair, Giles. 1971. *The Punitive Obsession*. London: Victor Gollancz.

Pugh, R. B. 1968. *Imprisonment in Medieval England*. Cambridge: Cambridge University Press.

Radzinowicz, Sir Leon. 1948–68. *A History of English Criminal Law*. Vols. 1–6. London: Stevens.

Renner, Karl. 1949. *The Institutions of Private Law and Their Social Functions*. London: Routledge and Kegan Paul.

Roberts, Simon. 1980. "Changing Modes of Dispute Settlement: An Anthropological Perspective." Paper presented at the Past and Present Society Conference on Law and Human Relations, London, 2 July 1980.

Rothman, David J. 1971. *The Discovery of the Asylum*. Boston: Little, Brown.

———. 1980a. *Conscience and Convenience: The Asylum and Its Alternatives in Progressive America*. Boston: Little, Brown.

———. 1980b. "Social Control: The Uses and Abuses of the Concept in the History of Incarceration." Department of History, Columbia University. Unpublished paper.

Rusche, George, and Otto Kirchheimer. 1939. *Punishment and Social Structure*. New York: Columbia University Press.

Schlossman, Steven L. 1977. *Love and the American Delinquent: The Theory and Practice of "Progressive" Juvenile Justice, 1825–1920*. Chicago: University of Chicago Press.

Scull, Andrew T. 1977. *Decarceration: Community Treatment and the Deviant—a Radical View*. Englewood Cliffs, N.J.: Prentice-Hall.

———. 1979. *Museums of Madness*. London: Allen Lane.

Shaw, A. G. L. 1971. *Convicts and the Colonies*. London: Faber.

Sheehan, W. J. 1977. "Finding Solace in 18th Century Newgate." In *Crime in England, 1550–1800*, ed. J. S. Cockburn. London: Methuen.

Silberman, Charles E. 1978. *Criminal Violence, Criminal Justice*. New York: Random House.

Silver, Alan. 1967. "The Demand for Order in Civil Society: A Review of Some Themes in the History of Urban Crime, Police and Riot." In *The Police: Six Sociological Essays*, ed. D. Bordua. New York: Wiley.

Smith, Adam. 1976. *The Theory of Moral Sentiments*. Edited by D. D. Raphael. Oxford: Clarendon Press. Originally published 1759.

———. 1978. *Lectures on Jurisprudence*. Edited by R. L. Meek, D. D. Raphael, and P. G. Stein. Oxford: Clarendon Press. Originally delivered 1763.

Stedman Jones, Gareth. 1971. *Outcast London*. London: Penguin.

———. 1977. "Class Expression versus Social Control?" *History Workshop Journal* 4:163–71.

Stockdale, Eric. 1977. *A Study of Bedford Prison, 1660–1877*. London: Phillimore.

Storch, Robert D. 1975. "The Plague of the Blue Locusts: Police Reform and Popular Resistance in Northern England, 1840–1857," *International Review of Social History* 20:61–90.

Stone, Lawrence. 1979. *Family, Sex and Marriage in England, 1500–1800*. Harmondsworth: Penguin.

Sykes, Gresham. 1958. *The Society of Captives*. Princeton: Princeton University Press.

Teeters, Negley D. 1935. *The Cradle of the Penitentiary: The Walnut Street Jail at Philadelphia, 1773–1835*. Philadelphia: Lippincott.

Thompson, E. P. 1963. *The Making of the English Working Class*. New York: Pantheon.

————. 1971. "The Moral Economy of the English Crowd," *Past and Present* 50:76–136.

————. 1972. "Rough Music! le charivari anglais," *Annales: économies, sociétés, civilisations* 27:285–312.

————. 1975. *Whigs and Hunters*. London: Allen Lane.

————. 1980. *Writing by Candlelight*. London: Merlin.

Tobias, J. J. 1972. *Crime and Industrial Society in the Nineteenth Century*. New York: Schocken.

Tocqueville, Alexis de. 1969. *Democracy in America*. Edited by J. P. Mayer. New York: Doubleday/Anchor.

Tomlinson, Margaret Heather. 1975. "Victorian Prisons: Administration and Architecture." Ph.D. dissertation, Bedford College, London University.

Trumbach, Randolph. 1978. *The Rise of the Egalitarian Family: Aristocratic Kinship and Domestic Relations in 18th Century England*. London: Academic Press.

Webb, Beatrice and Sidney. 1963. *English Prisons under Local Government*. London: Frank Cass. Originally published 1922.

Weber, Marx. 1947. *The Theory of Social and Economic Organization*. Edited by Talcott Parsons. Glencoe: Free Press.

Whiting, J. R. S. 1975. *Prison Reform in Gloucestershire, 1775–1820*. London: Phillimore.

Wicker, Tom. 1975. *A Time to Die*. New York: Quadrangle.

Clifford D. Shearing and Philip C. Stenning

Modern Private Security: Its Growth and Implications

A B S T R A C T

On the North American continent, in Europe and elsewhere, the dramatic growth in private security in the past several decades has reshaped the structure and function of modern policing. The development of private security has been facilitated by fundamental shifts in the nature of property relations. These changes have encouraged the development of a preventative mode of policing consistent with the principles and hopes of nineteenth-century police reformers, but they also suggest that we are moving in the direction of a new disciplinary society and raise fundamental questions with respect to sovereignty, justice, and individual liberty now almost entirely unrecognized. In particular, the legal institutions regarding private property operate to enhance the potential threat to individual liberty posed by the development of modern private security.

In the thirty-five years since the Second World War, we have witnessed what can fairly be described as a quiet revolution in the policing and social control systems of many countries of the world. To the general public, the major manifestation of this change has been the transformation of the public police through more sophisticated management techniques and the application

Clifford D. Shearing is Coordinator of Graduate Studies and Senior Research Associate in the Centre of Criminology, University of Toronto. Philip C. Stenning is Consultant and Special Lecturer, in the Centre of Criminology, University of Toronto.

In this review we have drawn considerably on our previous research and writings on the subject. In order to avoid repetitious self-citation we have not referenced much of this material. These sources include the following: Stenning 1975; Stenning and Cornish 1975; Farnell and Shearing 1977; Freedman and Stenning 1977; Shearing and Stenning 1977; Shearing, Farnell, and Stenning 1980; Stenning and Shearing 1980; Shearing and Stenning, forthcoming. We are grateful to our colleague John Ashley Friendly for his assistance in the preparation of this essay.

of elaborate technology. But at the forefront of the changes taking place in the arrangements for policing in many societies is a phenomenon whose growth has only occasionally attracted public attention and has only recently become the subject of serious study by criminologists and others traditionally concerned with developments in policing and social control. This is the phenomenon of private security.

In this essay we consider the development and significance of modern private security in various countries and its implications for the nature and scope of policing in those societies. We begin with a discussion of some of the problems of defining private security for the purposes of research and analysis and then go on to describe, to the extent that available statistics permit, the size and growth of private security in a number of different jurisdictions. An attempt is also made to contrast the growth of private security with the growth of public police forces in those same jurisdictions. A description of the role and functions of private security follows, as well as a discussion of the relationships which exist between private security and the public police. This descriptive material forms the basis for a discussion of some of the possible explanations advanced for the modern developments of private security. We endeavour to place these explanatory theories within the historical context of public and private initiatives in policing. The essay then turns to the nature and scope of legislative responses to the development of private security in various countries. Finally, we conclude with some thoughts on the more general implications of private security for the public police and criminal justice systems. In doing so we identify what we consider to be the critical issues to be addressed in responding to private security systems and the systems of justice within which they operate.

I. What Is "Private Security"?

While it is often referred to as "the private security industry," this label does not do justice to the phenomenon of private security, for two reasons. In the first place, while it is true that there is a thriving private security industry—comprised of all manner of businesses providing various security services to clients for hire—this contract security industry represents only one side of the many-sided phenomenon of private security. Equally important is the development of the so-called "in-house" side of private security, which has resulted in sometimes very substantial investments by large corporations and institutions in developing their own internal security systems.

The second reason why the term "private security industry" is not adequate to describe the phenomenon of private security involves an appreciation of the wider social and political ramifications of the phenomenon. For just as one would not dream of trying to describe the nature of public policing solely by reference to the institution of the public police, but rather by reference to the whole framework of public criminal justice of which the public police represent one critical part, so in understanding private security it is necessary to consider the wider context of private justice systems of which private security is merely the most visible and easily identifiable manifestation. We shall have more to say about these "private justice systems" below.

In defining what is usefully comprehended within the categories of "private security," we may start by considering the scope of "security." One way to go about defining security would be to list the variety of services associated with the term. Such a list would include guard, patrol and investigation services, alarms, safes, armoured transportation services, document shredders, identification systems, courier services, electronic surveillance equipment, guard dogs, sensor devices, etc. The ever-changing growth of new technologies, however, ensures that this approach toward defining security will never remain exhaustive for long. What is perhaps more useful is to identify the unifying theme which makes all of these services "security services." That theme, we believe, is protection against depredation, and in particular the protection of information, persons, and property.

Most descriptions of private security start with a general distinction between manned private security and the hardware sector. Manned private security includes the provision of personnel to perform security work of various kinds. Such personnel include guards, watchmen, patrol persons, floor detectives, investigators, escorts, couriers, alarm respondents, auditors, and security consultants. What distinguishes such persons as private security personnel is the fact that they are (*a*) privately employed and (*b*) employed in jobs whose principal component is some security function. These criteria allow private security personnel to be distinguished from public security personnel (e.g. government guards and investigators, and public police) and from other members of the public who may perform security functions as an incident to, rather than as a central component of, their regular occupation (e.g. receptionists and secretaries).

Even this definition of manned private security, however, presents some problems, largely because it is not always a simple matter to characterize a security person as unquestionably privately employed or publicly employed. Between the obviously public character of a municipal police officer and the equally obviously private character of a company guard lies a whole grey area populated by quasi-public institutions (e.g. some universities, transportation and utility companies, etc.) whose security personnel cannot so easily be fitted into discrete public/private categories. The practice, common in many jurisdictions, of "deputizing" security personnel (or granting them "special constable status") serves merely to blur still further the demarcation between private and public security personnel. The result seems to be something in the nature of a public/private security continuum, rather than two clear and distinct categories of "private security" and "public security." Where on this continuum any given security employee should be placed depends, we believe, not only on who his immediate employer is but also on what legal powers he possesses and to whom he is accountable for the exercise of those powers.

Such distinctions, of course, are of great importance in assessing comparative international statistics on the size and growth of private security in different jurisdictions. For it is not uncommon to find that the statistical data prepared in relation to one jurisdiction include within the category of "private security" classes of security personnel who, in the statistics prepared with respect to another jurisdiction, would not be so included.[1] It must be frankly admitted that these definitional problems have not yet been adequately resolved in the research literature, including our own. In these circumstances, a detailed accounting of what classes of personnel are included in a definition of "manned private security" is of great importance for valid comparative research.

A further important distinction within "manned private security" is the distinction between "contract" and "in-house" security. This distinction is of importance in many jurisdictions, not only from the point of view of its implications for the locus of legal liability for the actions of security personnel when performing their duties, but also because it is frequently the basis for determining the applicability of schemes of governmental licensing and regulation to security organizations. Such schemes are the subject of further discussion below.[2]

The hardware sector of private security is concerned almost exclusively with the manufacture, distribution, and servicing of a wide variety of security equipment, ranging from alarm systems to weapons, from electronic monitoring equipment to lie-detectors, and from armored vehicles to guard dogs. In many jurisdictions there is undoubtedly some overlap between the security hardware industry and the contract manned security industry, such as in the provision of security consultant services by security hardware firms or of alarm response services by alarm system manufacturers. The significance of the security hardware industry for a study of private security lies, of course, in the transformations being effected in security procedures as a result of technological developments in the production of such

---

[1] For example, figures for public security personnel in some jurisdictions include "government guards" and various specialized police forces, whereas in others they do not; in some jurisdictions, figures for "contract security" personnel include persons employed in the manufacturing sector of the security industry, while in others they do not. See, for example, the discussion of the United Kingdom statistics below.

[2] See the section "Responses to the Phenomenon of Private Security" below.

equipment. This industry, however, has so far been the subject of almost no systematic research, despite the fact that there is good reason to suspect that it is the most rapidly growing sector of private security.[3] Beyond acknowledging the undoubted importance of this sector of private security in understanding the total phenomenon of modern private security, we do not say very much about it here because not much is known about it. From a research point of view, this is clearly a gap which needs to be filled.

II. The Size and Growth of Modern Private Security

Although private security is commonly thought to be a largely American phenomenon, available data indicate that it is to be found in one form or another in almost every developed country of the Western world. Comparative data on the size and growth of private security internationally, however, are extremely uneven and often difficult to interpret with confidence.

In presenting the following brief survey of international data, we should caution the reader against drawing any but the most tentative conclusions comparatively. Despite serious efforts to improve matters in a number of jurisdictions (notably the United States) current statistical information on the size and growth of private security remains very crude. Estimates of expenditures on private security, for instance, vary wildly and standard categories for determining the number of persons involved have not been developed sufficiently to support comparative analysis across national borders.

This problem is compounded by the fact that in many jurisdictions there is a wide range of estimates to choose among. One's conclusions will depend on whether one examines government censuses, labor and business statistics, licensing records, or independent surveys, each mapping slightly different but overlapping populations and using different criteria. De-

---

[3] According to a 1974 Predicast Inc. market analysis the increase in security equipment sales will more than double the growth of (manned) protective services between 1971 and 1985.

termining which set of figures is the most accurate or useful therefore is a precarious endeavor. These difficulties are exacerbated in the case of studies undertaken by private consulting firms and industrial associations as they typically do not make their methodologies explicit.

A. Private Security Personnel

A massive program of research in the United States, sponsored by the Department of Justice's Law Enforcement Assistance Administration, has produced data on private security which are more comprehensive than that available for most other jurisdictions. In 1969 the first major study of private security in the United States was conducted by the Rand Corporation (Kakalik and Wildhorn 1971) but it was not until 1977 when the authors revised their findings in light of 1970 census data that a reasonably complete picture of size and growth trends for the decade 1960–70 became available.

TABLE 1

Private Security Personnel: United States, 1960, 1970

	(000s)		Change (percent)	
	1960	1970	1960–70	Yearly Average
Total security personnel	549	775	41	3.5
Total public security	327	494	51	4.2
Police strength	258	390	51	4.2
Government guards	69	104	51	4.2
Total private security	222	281	27	2.4
Guards	198	256	29	2.6
In-house	175	203	16	1.5
Contract	23	53	130	8.7
Investigators	24	25	4	0.4
In-house	17	17	...	...
Contract	7	8	14	1.3
Total in-house	192	220	15	1.4
Total contract	30	61	103	7.4
Ratio police/private security	6:5	7:5		
Ratio in-house/contract	6.4:1	3.6:1		

Source: Adapted from table 2.11, "Security Employment Trends by Type of Employer" (Kakalik and Wildhorn 1977, p. 43).
Note: Figures rounded.

As table 1 indicates, public security personnel outgrew their private sector counterparts by a factor of almost two to one with the ratio of public police to total private security rising from 6:5 to 7:5.[4] Within private security the contract sector grew at a rate almost seven times that of the in-house sector and more than twice that of the public police. This remarkable growth was accounted for almost exclusively by the 130 percent increase in contract guard strength. This is reflected in the fall of the in-house/contract ratio from just over 6:1 in 1960 to less than 4:1 in 1970.

Until the 1980 census figures are available or the next phase of research is complete,[5] predictions of growth in the United States for 1970–80 must of necessity be based on estimates which, if previous experience is a guide, cannot be relied upon. For example, the number of private security personnel in the United States has been estimated at 881,245 at a time (1975) when total police employment was 669,518. Since both these figures include part-time as well as support staff, they cannot be directly compared to the 1970 census figures. The former figure is a projection based on an American Society for Industrial Security survey responded to by one-third of its membership (U.S. Department of Justice 1976, pp. 414–15). According to these calculations, over 590,000 private security employees were working in the contract sector in 1975. This seems unrealistically high especially in the face of alternative estimates which place contract security strength at 175,000 (see table 2), 250,796,[6] and 278,165[7] in that year.[8]

---

[4] To those readers familiar with Kakalik and Wildhorn's earlier estimates of a 1969 police/private security ratio of 1:1 and 1:2, these figures will come as a surprise and serve to highlight the very serious problems involved in estimating private security growth rates and contrasting them with those of the public police.

[5] On 15 September 1980 the National Institute of Justice, U.S. Department of Justice, awarded Hallcrest Systems Inc. a $254,952 grant to conduct a study on "The Utilization of Private Security in the United States," which will, among other things, "profile the growth and changes in the private security industry in the last decade" (Security Management 1980, p. 43).

[6] Based on the U.S. Bureau of the Census County Business Patterns 1971 and 1973: see U.S. Department of Justice 1976, app. 9, table III, p. 404.

[7] See U.S. Department of Justice . . . 1976, app. 9, table IV, p. 405.

[8] A recent item in the *New York Times*, however, cites "trade executives" as suggesting that the security industry in the United States currently employs "nearly a million" persons: "Protection of Celebrities Remains a Small Part of Security Business," 21 December 1980.

The only available estimates for the United States for the
entire decade are those of Predicasts Inc. (1974) reproduced in
table 2. These are considerably lower than the survey figures
cited above, but they seem to duplicate the trends established in
the earlier census material, namely, contract growth greater
than the police rate, which is in turn greater than that of private
security taken as a whole. Furthermore, the in-house/contract
personnel ratio is estimated to have declined as it did between
1960 and 1970. Similarly, Predicasts Inc. estimates a continued
gradual increase in the public police/private security ratio (7.6:5
in 1975).

As depicted in table 3, research by Farnell and Shearing
(1977) and Friendly (1980) indicates that between 1971 and
1975 the total number of public and private security personnel
in Canada increased by just under 29 percent. While public
police and private security manpower each increased by about
30 percent during this period,[9] the contract sector of private
security showed a 65 percent growth compared with a 14 per-

TABLE 2

Private Security Personnel: United States,
1971, 1975, 1980

| | (000s) | | | Change (percent) | | | |
	1971	1975	1980	1971–75	Yearly Average	1971–80	Yearly Average
Police strength	575.5	669.5	NA	16	3.9	...	...
Private security	397	435	476	10	2.3	20	· 2.0
In-house	246	260	271	6	1.4	10	1.1
Contract	151	175	205	16	3.8	36	3.5
Ratio police/private security	7:5	7.6:5	...				
Ratio in-house/contract	8:5	3:2	4:3				

Source: Adapted from table V.2, "Protective Service Workers" (Predicasts Inc. 1974,
p. 26) and from table 3, U.S. Department of Justice, LEAA, and U.S. Bureau of the
Census, "Trends in Expenditure and Employment Data for the Criminal Justice System
1971–77" (Washington D.C.: U.S. Government Printing Office 1979). Note: These are
total employee figures and therefore cannot be compared with police strength figures
provided by the census in table 1.

[9] The figures are 7,895 in 1971; 13,381 in 1975; 17,285 in 1980. Source: Registration
Branch, Ontario Provincial Police.

cent growth rate in the in-house sector. By 1975, therefore, the ratio of public police to private security personnel in Canada had decreased from 1.09 to 1.07:1. This is in contrast to the increase in this ratio for the United States. However, the direction of the in-house/contract ratio is the same in both countries and by 1975 that ratio was identical (3:2).

Patterns of growth in contract security in Ontario—which Farnell and Shearing (1977) suggest can be used as a guide to Canadian trends—suggest that since 1975 we have witnessed a sharp decline. The growth rate appears to have dropped from 69 percent in the period 1971–75 to 29 percent in the period 1975–80.[10] These figures suggest a surge in the early seventies and more modest growth after 1975.

Recently, the British Home Office assembled census and police survey data on private security for 1971 (United Kingdom, Home Office 1979). These are shown in table 4. Other estimates available suggest that if one includes the manufacturing sector of the security industry, 40,000 people were em-

TABLE 3

Private Security Personnel: Canada, 1971–75

			Change (percent)	
	1971*	1975†	1971–75	Yearly Average
Total security personnel	89,734	115,443	28.7	6.5
Total public security	53,209	67,663	27.0	6.2
Police strength	39,724	51,243	30.0	6.6
Government guards	13,485	16,420	21.8	5.0
Total private security	36,525	47,780	30.8	6.9
Guards	33,430	46,060	37.8	8.3
Investigators	3,295	1,720	−91.7	−15.0
In-house	25,200	28,756	14.1	3.4
Contract	11,525	19,024	65.1	13.3
Ratio police/private security	1.09:1	1.07:1		
Ratio in-house/contract	2.2:1	3:2		

*1971 figures adapted from Farnell and Shearing (1977).
†1975 figures adapted from Friendly (1980).

[10] A slower rate of growth (21.8 percent) in government guard forces accounts for the lower overall figure of 29 percent.

ployed in 1970. Otherwise, the total is 25,000 (Randall and Hamilton 1972).

Using figures supplied by the British Security Industry Association (which claims to represent "about 90 percent by volume of the British security industry" (Wright 1978), the Home Office estimated that contract security manpower (excluding the manufacturing sector) had increased from 30,000 to 40,000 between 1971 and 1978. This is an increase of 33 percent whereas public police strength grew only 12 percent; this trend is similar to those we have described for Canada and the United States. It is also noteworthy that the Home Office estimates for 1978 suggest the same 3:2 in-house/contract security ratio in Britain as has been estimated in North America for 1975.

B. Private Security Market Statistics

A wide variety of financial and market estimates with respect to private security in the United States, Canada, and England are available. However, their reliability and accuracy are as doubtful as are the personnel statistics just described. In particular, the possibility of confusion between expenditure and sales figures presents problems. The extent to which many of the estimates of expenditures purport to include expenditures

TABLE 4

Private Security Personnel: United Kingdom, 1971–78

	(000s)		Change (percent)	
	1971	1978	1971–78	Yearly Average
Public police*	97.3	109	12	1.6
Private security†	80	100	25	3.2
In-house	50	60	20	2.6
Contract	30	40	33	4.2
Ratio police/private security	6:5	1.09:1		
Ratio in-house/contract	5:3	3:2		

*Source: Reports of Her Majesty's Chief Inspector of Constabulary for the years 1971 and 1978 (app. I, "Total Police Strength not including Civilians, Special Constables and Staff") (London: H. M. Stationery Office, 1972 and 1979).
†Source: United Kingdom, Home Office 1979, p. 3.

on in-house security (especially in-house personnel), rather than merely describing the contract security industry (as the sales figures do) is usually unspecified. Since, as we have seen, the in-house sector is estimated to account for two-thirds of all private security manpower in many jurisdictions, this is obviously a matter of considerable importance in accurately estimating the extent of private security investment.

In the United States there is evidence from a variety of sources that the rapid development of the contract security industry involved thousands of new companies entering the security services and products market. Kakalik and Wildhorn (1971, 2:34), for instance indicate that between 1958 and 1967 the number of establishments with payroll[11] rose from 1,525 to 2,547 (up 67 percent). They also indicate that, despite this market expansion, in 1967 "four firms . . . , with less than 6 percent of all establishments, accounted for half the revenues of this industry" (1971, 1:11–12).

Nossov (1975) shows that this growth continued into the early 1970s. He reports that between 1967 and 1973 the number of contract security establishments grew from 2,558 to 4,182 (up 63 percent).[12] From survey data which the Task Force obtained in St. Louis, they also noted the possibility that the hegemony of the large national corporations over the private security labor force in the United States, to which Kakalik and Wildhorn drew attention in the early 1970s, may have been somewhat eroded by the entry of smaller local security firms (U.S. Department of Justice 1976, pp. 34–40).

In summarizing their early findings, Kakalik and Wildhorn concluded that during the 1960s: "Whether viewed in terms of revenues or expenditures, growth in private contract protective

[11] If companies without payroll are included, the figures are 2,831 and 4,280, respectively.
[12] The U.S. Task Force (U.S. Department of Justice 1976, p. 405), using estimates derived from a survey of 31 states, indicates that in 1975 there were 7,421 applications for security business licenses processed in those states. It is not clear, furthermore, whether this figure includes businesses without payroll. Its comparability with figures cited from Nossov (1975) and Kakalik and Wildhorn (1971) above, therefore, is doubtful.

services (guards, investigators, armoured car, central station alarm) averaged 11 to 12 per cent per year" (1971, 1:13).

While market analysts traced similar annual security industry growth rates of from 10 to 12 percent during the early part of the 1970s (Little 1973; Frost and Sullivan 1975), more recent research on the size and growth of private security indicates that some important changes have occurred since the mid-seventies. For example, the federal Task Force on Private Security Standards and Goals predicted in 1976 that "with the 'encroachment by electronic technology,' growth rates for guard, armored car, and courier services will be modest compared to the 10 to 12 per cent annual growth of the past few years" (U.S. Department of Justice 1976, p. 34). This prediction has been supported by *Business Week* (13 November 1978, pp. 160–61) which stated that the annual growth rate of 17 percent between 1968 and 1974 has slowed to a 4.5 percent average since then. However, evidence on this question appears to be contradictory.[13]

While estimates of expenditures on private security services vary greatly in the literature, they all indicate a substantial increase during the 1970s. In this context, the Rand Corporation's estimate of $3.3 billion for 1969 (Kakalik and Wildhorn 1971, 1:12), which was comparable to figures produced by other analysts (see Little 1973; Frost and Sullivan 1975) may be compared with recent estimates of $11–$12 billion for 1979 (see Cory 1979; Bailey 1979).[14] In 1976, the U.S. Task Force on Private Security Standards and Goals (U.S. Department of Justice 1976, p. 37) estimated that 50 percent of the private security market serviced industrial and transportation clients, 30 percent serviced financial, commercial, and retail institutions, while the remaining 20 percent was accounted for by schools, hospitals, universities, and residential and other in-

[13] A recent item in the *New York Times* (see n.8) cites "trade executives" as indicating that the security business is continuing to increase by "about 12 per cent a year."

[14] Predicasts Inc. has predicted "increases in the security device and protective service business from $6 billion in 1978 to $21 billion by 1990" (see *New York Times* article cited in n.8).

stitutions. Since the basis for calculating the above estimates is seldom made explicit in the literature, they must be regarded as tentative.

Our own research into private security in Canada reveals striking similarities to the phenomenon in the United States. This may well be a consequence, at least in part, of the branch-plant character of Canadian private security. A study of the manned contract security industry in Ontario, for instance, has revealed that in 1976, 20 percent of the licensed agencies in the province were foreign-owned. Five agencies (approximately 10 percent of all agencies) accounted for almost 50 percent of all the employees in these industries, and three of these five companies were foreign-owned (Shearing, Farnell, and Stenning 1980). From these data it is apparent that a large proportion of the licensed contract security industry in the province is controlled by foreign-owned companies, most of which are based in the United States. Although comparable research has not been undertaken in other provinces, government reports in British Columbia and Quebec have alluded to similar levels of foreign control of the contract security industry in each of those provinces (Draper and Nicholls 1976; Quebec, Commission de Police 1976). Available information also suggests that the alarm and equipment sector of the security industry in Canada (which is not licensed) is similarly dominated by a small number of foreign-owned companies (mostly American and British) (Stenning 1975). Add to this that many of the large corporations which employ in-house security forces are also foreign-owned (e.g. oil companies, electronics and auto manufacturing companies, hotel chains), and it becomes clear that similarities between Canadian and American private security are to be expected.

Research on private security in Britain has been less systematic than comparable research in North America, with the result that accurate and reliable statistics on the size and growth of private security there are even harder to come by. The available information provides varying estimates but is virtually unanimous in suggesting that private security is somewhat less developed in Britain than in North America. Since the basis for most of the published figures is usually not revealed, however, it is difficult to say with confidence whether they provide a true picture of private security in Britain.

Randall and Hamilton (1972) found annual turnover (sales) had grown from £5 million to £55 million between 1950 and 1970. This has since increased to an estimated £135 million in 1976 (United Kingdom, Home Office 1979, chap. 1).

The Home Office also found that of the 741 private security organizations known to the police in 1971, some 80 percent of the firms operated in only one police force area, and only about a dozen operated nationally. On the basis of a more detailed analysis of a sub-sample of 529 security organizations, they report that 84 percent of the employees work for 2 percent of the security organizations (United Kingdom, Home Office 1979, p. 3).

Despite the obvious shortcomings of these statistics, they suggest a similar domination of the contract security market by a few large companies. Although no systematic research appears to have probed the question of foreign ownership of the private security industry in Britain, there are indications that some of these large firms are foreign-owned. Bunyan (1976), for instance, indicates that the second largest security company in Britain is Swedish-owned. He further notes that the largest company in the business, which is a British company, has 30 percent of its staff working outside the United Kingdom. This suggests that foreign ownership is probably a significant factor in the European private security industry as well as in the industry in Britain and Canada. Bunyan's claims in this regard seem to be corroborated by other commentators on the British security industry (see Draper 1978; Dun and Bradstreet 1979, p. 314).

Published information on private security in other countries of the world is extremely sparse. Such information as is to be found concentrates almost exclusively on the contract security industry and often echoes the themes of rapid growth and domination by a small number of large firms which have become so familiar to observers of private security in North America and Britain. Thus Magnusson asserts: "The industrial security service branch in Sweden is dominated by one company, Securitas Security Service, Ltd., which is part of the Securitas concern. In the concern, whose mother company is Securitas International, Ltd., one finds another six Swedish security services. Securitas covers about 60% of all security service in the country. The remaining activities are rather equally divided between three groups of companies. One group is made up of the other companies belonging to the Securitas concern, a second group consists of the state owned National Security Service, Ltd., with daughter companies and a third group consists of all other companies" (1979, p. 172).

A recent article in *Forbes* magazine (October, 1979) describes the rapid growth and market domination of Security Patrols, Ltd., in Japan. The article refers to the transformation of an "$11,000 investment into a company that will gross just short of $200 million this year," over a period of fourteen years (1965–79). The article claims that this company now controls 60 percent of the contract security market in Japan. Apparently emulating many of its British and North American counterparts, the company, faced by increasing costs in the labor-intensive guard market, responded by diversifying into the security hardware industry.

Similar references to rapid growth of private security in Australia (Grabosky 1977, p. 160), Israel (Hovav and Amir 1979, p. 14) and France, Belgium, the Netherlands, and West Germany (Heijboer 1979, pp. 8–9) are to be found in the literature, but we have not yet encountered substantial statistical material to support these assertions.

The two most significant trends revealed by these international comparisons are those of market concentration and foreign ownership within private security. The concentration of private security in the hands of vast conglomerates within a country raises questions as to the locus of sovereignty in that country, for sovereignty has traditionally been associated with control over the order maintenance process. These questions become even more intriguing when one considers the facts of concentration alongside those of foreign ownership. Do these trends suggest the beginnings of a shift in sovereignty from governments to multinational corporations who may control international security organizations of immense proportions? These are questions that deserve more thorough investigation than we have been able to give to them here, but they should be borne in mind in terms of their possible relevance to other important implications of private security discussed below.

III. The Role of Private Security

In considering the development of private security forces two related questions arise: What do they do? And how does what they do relate to what the public police do? It is to these questions that we now turn.

It will be evident from the foregoing discussion that private security is not a simple phenomenon. Rather, it is a phenomenon manifested in a variety of different forms. Included in our definition of private security are diverse organizations which exist for diverse purposes and which pursue diverse philosophies and policies. Furthermore, private security serves, or forms a part of, organizations and interest groups which exist for widely differing objectives, ranging from the profitable to the charitable and philanthropic. We have noted that one of the defining characteristics of private security is that private security organizations exist essentially to serve the interests of those who employ them, rather than some more or less clearly defined "public interest" which purportedly lies at the heart of the public police mandate. It is in this sense that they can be said to undertake private rather than public policing.

In these circumstances, it is difficult to describe the "role of private security" as such, without including endless qualifications which will take account of the great variety of objectives for which private security is employed. This is because the role of any particular private security organization is usually defined principally, and sometimes exclusively, by its "clients," i.e. those who employ it. In saying this, we intend to refer not only to "contract" security, but also to "in-house" security, since in both cases it is the employer who defines the role.

In the following discussion we argue that, in general terms, the role of private security may be characterized by its emphasis on a preventative approach to the protection of assets and the maximization of profits. We shall argue, further, that this emphasis serves to distinguish the role of private security from that of the typical public police organization. We should emphasize at the outset, however, that we recognize that not all private security organizations can be accommodated neatly within such an analysis. In some cases, private security organizations appear to be organized and to operate according to principles and role definitions which are barely distinguishable from those of the public police. Having said this, however, we should nevertheless caution against a too ready reliance on form as an indicator of role. Behind a private security organization's adoption of "police-like" methods and strategies (e.g. emphasis on investigation, apprehension, and prosecution) will often be fundamental philosophical differences of approach and orientation from those of the public police. Thus, for instance, even when a private security organization is committed to a mode of policing in which investigation, apprehension, and prosecution are dominant strategies, it will often be found that the bases for such an organization's exercise of discretion within this mode are markedly different from those of the public police. In particular, the exercise of discretion by such private security personnel will often be far more influenced by their perceptions of the interests of their immediate employer than by any generalized conception of the public interest. What principally distinguishes private security from the public police in this regard is that private security personnel are generally not under any legally defined public duty to perform their duties in the public interest, as public police personnel (by virtue of their oath of office) generally are. Even private security organizations which *appear* to be functioning similarly to the public police, therefore, are not necessarily always fulfilling a role which is identical or similar to that of the public police. With these caveats in mind, we can now turn to a discussion of what we conclude, on the basis of available research, is the dominant role of most private security organizations.

In examining what private security forces do it is instructive to consider what private security executives say their organizations do in their promotional material and trade journals. On analysis these materials reveal that private security executives are in almost unanimous agreement that private security is fundamentally a preventative force. While both public and private security forces engage in both prevention and apprehension they differ fundamentally, it is argued, in the emphasis they accord to each of these objectives. The public police are distinguished by their emphasis on apprehension, an emphasis which finds its expression in the attention paid to clearance rates, the status of the criminal investigation branch within police departments, the importance of "good pinches" for a police officer's career prospects, and so on. In contrast, private security is distinguished by its preventative emphasis, an emphasis which finds its expression in the relative lack of concern with clearance rates, the disparagement of the public police's investigative mentality, the importance of restitution, profit maximization, and so on.

Modern developments in the philosophy of the public police role can be seen to be moving in a direction which might seem to be eroding this distinction. The current public police emphasis on preventative roles, and on a return to more "traditional" functions (witness the current interest in reviving foot patrols), is of obvious importance in this regard. It remains true, however, that in general terms the organization and structure of modern public police forces have evolved much more slowly toward the preventative philosophy than have those of private security organizations, which have been able to develop without the constraints which a close association with the public criminal justice system have imposed upon the public police (Goldstein 1977, pp. 21–24). These constraints are reflected in another critical distinction which has emerged between private security and the public police, namely, their different characterizations of "prevention." While the preventative role of the public police is almost universally referred to in terms of "*crime* prevention," private security typically refer to their preventative role as one of "*loss* prevention" (see, for example, Curtis 1971), thereby acknowledging that their principal concern is the protection of their clients' assets (Shearing, Farnell, and Stenning 1980). In a study of contract security in Ontario, for instance, we found that while private security executives acknowledged that they engaged in crime prevention, they argued that this is but an aspect of a more general concern with loss prevention and profit maximization. In making this point, contract security agencies made clear to potential clients that if they were to employ them it would be their corporate concerns and needs as potential victims, rather than those of the state or "public interest," that would be given precedence. As one agency put it, private security offers a "calculated strategy" tailored to the needs and requirements of each client. Although it is seldom, if ever, explicitly stated, these promotional arguments clearly imply that clients would be better off dealing with a security force that gave priority to their interests rather than relying on the public police whose first commitment is to public order and the state. As this emphasis on "policing for profit" (Spitzer and Scull 1977b) suggests, private security's clientele, whether in-house or contract, is heavily dominated by large institutions who view security as a managerial cost-cutting function (Kakalik and Wildhorn 1971; Shearing, Stenning, and Farnell 1980).

While the point about the preventative emphasis of private security is made with monotonous regularity within the trade literature, it is much less informative with respect to just what loss prevention is. At most one will find the occasional reference to what is regarded as a particularly useful preventative strategy. Nonetheless it is possible from a review of these illustrations, and more particularly from a review of what little research has been done on the activities of private security persons, to identify what it is that private security does do. What this research (see especially Shearing, Farnell, and Stenning

1980) reveals is that the feature uniting the diverse activities undertaken by private security under the heading of prevention is surveillance. This theme is nicely illustrated by the slogan originally adopted by the Pinkerton Detective Agency, which described itself as "the eye that never sleeps" (Morn 1975).

Surveillance, despite the somewhat sinister connotations of the term and the vivid imagery of the Pinkerton slogan, is in practice a very mundane activity made up of a multitude of functions that when viewed in isolation seem too trivial to warrant the label "surveillance." Foot patrol for instance, which is the activity performed most often by contract security guards, basically involves nothing more than keeping an eye out for potential security problems and applying simple remedies to any that are discovered. In our study, for example, we found that security guards spent much of their time checking security barriers such as locks, doors, and fences, checking for fire hazards, closing windows, and attending to a host of similar mundane security details. In addition to this concern with security hazards, and corresponding safeguards, we found that security guards devoted much of their time to controlling access and egress to and from the areas for which they were responsible. For example, 68 percent of the security guards reported that they were involved on a daily basis with the screening or escorting of visitors or both. Similarly, searches of employees (34 percent) and of vehicles (16 percent) also proved to be important features of many of their jobs. However, each of these seemingly separate activities involves the security guard in surveillance in one form or another.

As this description of the nature of security work suggests, what the growth of private security has meant is that the *scope* of surveillance undertaken by security forces has increased enormously. What is not so evident is that the *nature* of surveillance has also been transformed in the process. Let us consider first the question of scope. Unless they receive specific legal authorization to do otherwise, the surveillance that the public police engage in is legally limited to public areas. In practice what this means is that the police generally restrict their routine surveil-

214 Clifford D. Shearing and Philip C. Stenning

lance to publicly owned areas, primarily public streets. Private security forces, on the other hand, operate primarily in areas of private property to which the public police do not have routine access. Because of this, their growth has meant that surveillance by security forces has been extended into private areas that were previously largely immune from such organized scrutiny. Furthermore, such private property has come increasingly to include areas which can only be regarded as public places, insofar as they are routinely frequented by the general public at the invitation of their private owners. Numerous examples of such places come readily to mind—shopping malls, recreational facilities, condominium and public housing developments, educational institutions.

The significance of this geographic extension of surveillance lies, in our view, in its implications with respect to the *objects* of such surveillance, that is, with respect to its nature. The public police, with their apprehension orientation, have tended to direct their surveillance toward potential troublemakers, that is, to what Spitzer (1975) has called "problem populations." While this is undoubtedly an activity that private security persons also engage in—for instance in the detection of shoplifting (Jeffries 1977)—this focus on breaches of the law is only one aspect, and probably the least important one, of private security surveillance. Private security's emphasis on prevention directs its surveillance not so much to breaches of the law (or of organizational rules) as to *opportunities* for such breaches. As a consequence, the objects of private security surveillance tend to be not just potential troublemakers but also those who are in a position to create such opportunities for breaches. Thus, the target population is greatly enlarged. For example, within a business setting the focus of surveillance is not simply potential rule-breaches but any person who might contribute to the creation of an opportunity for a breach of a rule. This feature of private surveillance is nicely illustrated by a surveillance strategy commonly used by private security and described in an article on corporate headquarters security by Jack Luzon, under the revealing heading "Further Loss Prevention Refinements":

In support of the project drive for theft reduction, Atlantic Richfield security instituted an evening patrol still in effect.

For each risk found, the patrolling officer fills out and leaves a courteous form, called a "snowflake," which gives the particular insecure condition found, such as personal valuable property left out, unlocked doors, and valuable portable calculators on desks. A duplicate of each snowflake is filed by floor and location, and habitual violators are interviewed. As a last resort, compliance is sought through the *violator's* department manager. (1978, p. 41; our emphasis)

As this example illustrates, when the surveillance spotlight is turned from those who commit breaches of rules to those who create opportunities for such breaches a new class of "delinquent" is created; the category "offender" is expanded to include those who violate security procedures as well as those who commit traditional criminal and other offenses. This characteristic of security work is very evident from our own research. For instance, the security problem that the security guards in our Canadian study reported encountering most often was the carelessness of others. This involved responding to straightforward but potentially very costly problems of precisely the kind mentioned by Luzon, such as confidential documents and other valuables left unprotected, doors and windows left open, electrical appliances left on, and cigarette butts left smoldering.

As the "snowflake" strategy implies, the loss preventative role of private security, in creating a new category of delinquents, also creates a new category of person requiring reformation. Loss prevention implies remedial activity directed at those persons who create opportunities for breaches. Our own research revealed that the reports written by security guards at the end of each shift documented "breaches of security" and were used both as a means of increasing the "security consciousness" of employees and as an impetus for improving existing security measures. This concern with identifying and eliminating loopholes in security procedures also proved to be a central feature of investigative work. Private investigators typically proved to be much more interested in preventing future losses than they were in establishing a case related to one or more employees.

Although the activities of private security we have been discussing may be contrasted with those of the public police, they, ironically, conform surprisingly well with the objectives of the "new police" as these were first conceived by Sir Robert Peel and his fellow police reformers. While this irony may be glimpsed in Peel's famous maxim that "the police are the public and the public are the police" (since private security persons, unlike the public police, are legally only private citizens), it runs far deeper than this. Sir Robert Peel, and the commissioners whom he appointed to head the Metropolitan Police Force in London, conceived of their new police as a preventative force whose success was to be judged by the "absence of crime" and not by "the detection and punishment of the offender after he has succeeded in committing the crime" ("General Instructions" of 1829 cited by Radzinowicz 1968, p. 163). "Foremost amongst the means by which it was hoped prevention might be achieved was an *unremitting watch* upon the whole area for which the Metropolitan Police became responsible" (Radzinowicz 1968, p. 164; our emphasis).

In planning a police force that was to achieve this preventative end, the nineteenth-century police reformers argued for a bureaucratically organized and salaried force to be deployed on foot on a grid system that would permit them to keep all parts of the city under surveillance "at every hour of the day and night" (Radzinowicz 1968, p. 164). While the first public police forces closely approximated this model, today the foot patrol officer has given way to a motorized patrol officer whose primary job involves reacting to citizen requests for service (Rubinstein 1973; Reiss 1971) and who works within an organization which measures effectiveness primarily in terms of detection and punishment (see, for example, Manning 1980, p. 226). This reactive mode has remained predominant despite recent initiatives to reintroduce the more "traditional" foot patrol function. In contrast, private security forces are not only committed to prevention but have selected foot patrol as their principal means of surveillance. What is more, private security forces, far from abandoning a preventative emphasis, have worked to refine and extend the strategies advocated by the early police reformers. The foot patrol officer has been supplemented by electronic equipment which serves to enhance the patrol officer's effectiveness. Further, as we have already noted, surveillance itself has been extended beyond traditional "problem populations" to include a more broadly defined class of persons considered as legitimate subjects of security interest.

This ability of private security both to fulfill and extend the preventative ideas of police reformers can be traced to the access to private areas which they enjoy. The notion of an "unremitting watch" of an entire geographic area has implicit in it the assumption that the watchers will have access to the entire area to be watched. Although this assumption proved valid for the essentially *private* Thames police where the police reformers' ideas were first put to the test (Radzinowicz 1968), this was not the case when this experiment was generalized to public policing. The difficulties the public police have confronted, since their inception, in securing access to private property lie at the heart of the problem they have faced in remaining true to a preventative philosophy (Elliott 1973). Of course, as the public police have ready access to public property, such as public streets, their difficulties in preventing criminal activities in these places have been less acute and are more easily remedied. However, as public places come increasingly under private control (see below) the ability of the public police to prevent wrongdoing even in these areas is being progressively undermined.

The picture that emerges from this discussion of the principles of police reform is that modern policing is gradually being restructured in such a way as to bring it more closely in line with Peel's dream of a truly preventative police force. But it is through private security rather than through the public police that this has been most substantially accomplished.

To seek an understanding of the nature of this accomplishment it is useful to note that one of the most striking features of private security is that so much of it, as the activities referred to above bear witness, seems to be so "mickey mouse." This categorization is interesting not only because it captures the common popular and public police conception of private security, but also because it serves to trivialize the most significant aspects of the phenomenon. Its "mickey mouse" nature means that private security work does not have the appearance of importance normally attached to apprehension-related activities (such as the making of arrests or laying of charges). This view of private security work, which incidentally makes it appear nonthreatening, arises from its most fundamental features. It tends to have a low visibility; it tends to be continuous rather than occasioned; it is a part of the institutional structures it operates to control, rather than outside them; it seems not to be backed by "authority"; persons who work in private security are frequently "unskilled"; it is "integrative" rather than "segregative" (Spitzer 1975, p. 648) in its response to offenders; and it seldom involves physical coercion.

All these features are significant because they characterize what Michel Foucault has called a "disciplinary society": a society that is based not on physical coercion but on a more subtle and pervasive form of coercion that draws its power from surveillance, that is, from the very same "unremitting watch" advocated by the nineteenth-century police reformers. In such a society "observation, surveillance, and inspection" become the principal modes of social control; here, "the gaze is not a passive entity but an active force engaged in its own strategy of domination" (Megill 1979, p. 492). The techniques generally employed to achieve a disciplinary society also appear at first sight to be "mickey mouse," as disciplinary social control does not find its expression in the spectacle of punishment or in "the brilliance of those who exercise it" (Foucault 1977, p. 220) but in strategies that are characterized by a minute concern for apparently insignificant detail (Foucault 1977, pp. 213–14). In a society in which the mechanisms of control are at once "immense and minute" the qualifications of the controllers dwindle in importance so that "it does not matter who exercises power. Any individual taken almost at random can operate the machine" (Foucault 1977, p. 202). In the disciplinary society it is "the small techniques of discipline," the "insignificant tricks," that count (Foucault 1977, p. 223).

That the appearances presented by private security can be very misleading is simply but effectively summed up by Pleece, a British police officer who after attending the "gate-keeping duties" session at the training center of Group 4 Total Security, one of the largest contract security companies operating in Britain, wrote: "I now know, as opposed to suspect, that there can be rather more to this function than preventing the gates from being stolen! So it appears with most guard and patrol services provided on a commercial basis. What is sold seems consistently to be more than meets the eye" (1972, pp. 42–43).

IV. Relationships between Private Security and the Public Police

The modern development of private security has, of course, raised both conceptual and practical questions about what the relationship between private security and the public police is and should be. In seeking to answer these questions, public police and private security officials have tended to rely on the prevention/apprehension distinction to define the nature of their relationship. The view most frequently cited in the trade literature, and the one that appears to receive the widest support from within the private security community, is that both private security and the public police are committed to similar general objectives and that private security makes its contribution to these objectives by complementing the public police. Given that a passive nonthreatening face is one which private security executives often assume to avoid provoking a negative response from the public police, it is not surprising that advocates of this view tend to minimize the extent to which the interests and activities of private security and the public police conflict. (See, for example, Kobetz and Cooper 1978).

Despite attempts by the police to reestablish their preventative role, police executives appear, by and large, as comments on private security in police journals testify, to be prepared to accept the claim that private security fulfills preventative functions that the public police remain ill-equipped to provide. Pleece, for instance, in advocating, and seeking to legitimate, this division of labor defines private security as an extension of the principle of self-help (see also Becker 1974) as follows:

Although the community has delegated much of its responsibility for the prevention and detection of crime and the protection of life and property to its police forces, fortunately this neither legally nor morally relieves property owners from taking security measures on their own initiative. This is the sphere in which the security industry deploys the majority of its uniformed security forces. . . . I see such services, therefore, as an extension of traditional responsibilities in a property-owning democracy and, as such, ideologically and professionally unobjectionable. (1972, p. 44)

Kakalik and Wildhorn, who pioneered research on private security in the United States, offer a similar definition when they argue that private security begins where the public police leave off and therefore does not encroach on the public police because it undertakes what "the public police either do not perform because of resource limitations or cannot perform because of legal constraints" (1971, 1:19). For Kakalik and Wildhorn (and in this they state a view commonly expressed by police officers writing on the subject) private security forces not only do but should function as junior partners in law enforcement, who fill gaps and take up the slack left by the public police.

In specifying where the function of the public police leaves off, some advocates of this "partners in order maintenance" view use the distinction between public and private property to distinguish between the proper spheres of each of the partners. Thus, for instance, Sir Roland Howe, formerly assistant commissioner of the London Metropolitan Police, and later chairman of the board of directors of Group 4 Total Security in

Britain, has argued that in "beginning where the policeman's guard and patrol function ends" private security starts "at the factory gates" (cited in Pleece 1972, p. 44). The public police, however, are far more leery of accepting this distinction as the basis for cutting up the security pie, as the public/private property distinction places all security tasks that relate to private property, including criminal investigation, in the hands of private security. While this, as we will argue below, reflects the de facto nature of private security work, it is not something that the police take kindly to; rather, they are more likely to regard private security involvement in criminal investigatory activity as a serious encroachment on what should be the exclusive jurisdiction of the public police. Recently, for example, a British detective inspector, in commenting on the involvement of private security forces in England in investigative work, argued that this was a practice "fraught with danger" and concluded that private security should be restricted to the defensive and passive stance which their preventative role implied (French 1979, p. 29). Similarly, in the United States, the Law Enforcement/Private Security Relationships Committee of the Law Enforcement Assistance Administration's Private Security Advisory Council has identified precisely this issue as a critical factor in conflict between the public police and private security (U.S. Private Security Advisory Council 1977, p. 9).

This conflict over private security's involvement in investigative work raises questions about the theory that the relationship between the public police and private security is complementary. Further, the fact that private security executives, notwithstanding that they are well aware of the involvement of private security in investigative functions, cling tenaciously to the complementarity view suggests to us that its utility arises from the political function it serves in avoiding police hostility and police resistance to the growth of private security and not from its theoretical value.

In seeking to accommodate the evidence that private security forces do engage in investigative functions, Kakalik and Wildhorn propose that where overlap exists between the public

police and private security, private security be viewed as supplementing the public police (1971, 1:18). This analysis
identifies private security forces as playing a subsidiary role and
is, like the associated notion of complementarity, politically
useful from the point of view of both these security forces.

As we have already implied in our discussion of private security and the preventative philosophy of policing advocated by
Sir Robert Peel, it is possible, on the basis of the existing evidence, to conceive of private security and the public police as
competing security forces. This position was put forward in a
relatively early analysis of modern private security by Scott and
McPherson, who argued that private security in the United
States has historically provided a wide range of policing activities and that today these forces "perform functions which
are virtually identical in many respects to those carried out by
the public police" (1971, pp. 273–74). What distinguishes private security and the public police, they reasoned, is not what
they do but the fact that they perform their activities "for other
private individuals" who pay them for their services (p. 274).

In disputing that private security and the public police can be
distinguished on the basis of either the nature of their activities
or on the public or private nature of the property where these
activities occur, this competitive view directs attention to the
context of control in which private and public security forces
operate. In arguing for this orientation, Flavel points out that it
has the advantage of moving the discussion from consensus assumptions which imply by inference that private security forces
"act in the best interests of society as a whole" (1973, p. 6) to a
position in which the issue of whose interests private security
serve becomes an empirical question. In Flavel's opinion such
an empirical examination leads to a rejection of the "social service view" of private security advanced by Kakalik and Wildhorn, in favor of what he terms an "interest group view" which
holds that private security "is more appropriately viewed as a
range of services designed to protect the immediate interests of
those groups in society who, in various situations, own or control valued property" (1973, p. 14). This view is consistent with

our findings which, as we have already mentioned, indicate that private security regards its first and most important obligation as being to its clients and that in exercising this responsibility its foremost concern is protecting client interests by minimizing losses. This overriding concern with loss frequently leads private security to avoid bringing problems it encounters to the attention of the police even when these problems would be regarded by the public police as criminal offenses. For instance, employee theft, whether of the blue collar or the white collar variety, is more often than not regarded as an in-house matter to be dealt with within the client organization, that is, within a private rather than a public system of "justice."

A number of other important considerations must be borne in mind if the relationships between private security and the public police are to be properly understood. In the first place, as research in the United States (Kakalik and Wildhorn 1971, 1:75–76) and Britain (Bunyan 1976, pp. 239–40), as well as our own research in Canada (Shearing and Stenning 1977, p. 49; Jeffries 1977, p. 38; Shearing, Farnell, and Stenning 1980), has made clear, there is a very significant interchange of personnel between private security and public police organizations. Not only do many potential recruits see private security as an effective stepping stone to a career in the public police, but it is also clear that private security represents an important source of "second career" opportunities for police personnel, who frequently have limited promotional opportunities and become eligible to retire on full pension many years before the end of a natural working life.

In addition, in many jurisdictions, public police personnel frequently perform private security work during their off-duty hours—a situation which has led to much criticism, including allegations by the contract security industry itself of unfair competition (Distelhorst 1977, p. 65). The opportunities which private security thus offers to public police personnel to supplement their police salaries, however, must be regarded as a further significant factor in the relationships of the two institutions.

The implications of this substantial interchange of personnel for relationships between private security and the public police are of great significance. Not only does it ensure that the personnel in both sectors (especially at the senior levels) are likely to share similar experiences, attitudes, and social backgrounds, but it also contributes significantly to the ease with which information may be shared between the private and public sectors of policing, and mutual cooperation and accommodations may be achieved. Clearly, with the burgeoning of private security and of information and retrieval technology, this last issue is one which will be of growing significance for relations between the public police and private security in the future.

Second, in many jurisdictions, as we shall note further below, there are very direct controlling relationships between the public police and the contract security industries. Not only are many of the statutes providing for licensing of contract security administered directly by the public police, but matters such as the granting of permission to carry firearms and deputization (or the granting of special constable status) also commonly lie within the jurisdiction of the public police.

A further significant aspect of the relationship between the police and private security is their mutual consumption of each other's services. As with most other aspects of the relationship, the exact nature and extent of this phenomenon is not yet clear. Nor are the factors which govern this particular aspect of the relationship. It is clear, however, that many private security forces (both in-house and contract) maintain policies under which security employees are required to call in the public police to take over a "case" as soon as any significant law enforcement powers are considered necessary, despite the fact that in most cases the security employees possess quite adequate legal powers themselves (Shearing, Farnell, and Stenning 1980). Furthermore, once an arrest for a criminal offense has been made, the law in many jurisdictions requires that the public police be brought in.

Reliance on public police support by the private security industry is not limited to situations involving criminal investigations. Indeed, one of the most problematic instances of such reliance in recent years has arisen out of the phenomenal growth of the alarm industry. The extent to which the development of this industry had made additional demands upon police manpower (primarily through the need to respond to an ever-increasing volume of alarm calls, many of which turn out to be "false" in the sense that they were not caused by human interruption) led one Canadian police department to impose a charge on businesses for responding to alarms which sounded "falsely" more than a certain number of times in one year (see Stenning 1975).

Public police, however, also rely to some extent on private security for some services and will sometimes seek the cooperation of private security personnel in complex or technically difficult investigations (e.g. commercial fraud cases or cases involving highly technical equipment such as computers, polygraphs, etc.) (Shearing, Farnell, and Stenning 1980).

Most important, however, it is our view that the relationships between private security and the public police can be properly assessed only when the context within which private security operates is fully understood. Just as the role of the public police can be properly understood only within the context of the public criminal justice systems which constrain and circumscribe so much of their activities, so private security must be viewed in the context of the private justice systems within which they primarily operate. By the term "private justice systems" we mean to include dispute resolution practices such as grievance procedures, commonly found in collective agreements, which may be used as alternatives to the public criminal justice system to resolve a variety of problems, including some that have traditionally been dealt with as crimes within that system.

As yet we have little knowledge about the structures and dynamics of such systems, the way they shape the activities of private security, and their impact on the relationships between private security and the public police and public criminal justice systems. Preliminary observations, however, indicate that such private justice systems do not conform to any uniform model but do share relatively informal negotiated procedures and outcomes in common. Individual "incidents" tend to be dealt with in terms of wider problems, with the overall success of the enterprise, rather than any fixed or predetermined concepts of "justice" in the individual case, seen as the major objective. Although many features of the public criminal justice system are to be found in private justice systems, such systems characteristically bring into play a radically different set of assumptions, objectives, processes, and outcomes (see Stenning and Shearing 1980, pp. 133–39, for a more elaborate discussion). Although we do not propose to discuss the evolution of such private justice systems in any further detail here, we do believe that this is an important subject for further research in the future.

V. Reasons for Growth

In considering the explanations that have been offered for the development of private security, it is useful to begin with the position implicit in the complementarity view discussed above, if only because this explanation is the most widely held and has an immediacy and simplicity which makes it attractive. The historical position advanced by those who hold to the complementarity view is that private security develops to fill the vacuum created by the absence of the public police and decreases in importance as the public police expand to cover the full range of security functions themselves (for a review of this position see Carson and Young 1976). The implication is that private security would not exist today if the growth of the public police had not been limited. The public police, if they had been permitted to develop fully, would have been able to meet the demands for order maintenance unaided. This argument typically identifies the "economic crisis of the state" as the principal, if not the only, reason for the reemergence of private security in the latter half of the twentieth century. Advocates of this position sometimes refer back to the fact that in the early nineteenth century the development of Peel's "new police" in England led to the demise of the large number of varied private arrangements which had developed to deal with the breakdown of traditional methods of crime control (see, for example, Kakalik and Wildhorn 1971).

The difficulty with this vacuum theory of the development of private security, as Carson and Young (1976) have pointed out, is not so much that it is wrong but that it is too narrow and limited. Certainly the fiscal restraints that have affected public police budgets are real enough and this most assuredly has had some influence on the growth of private security. However, a limited focus on this, and other "proximate causes" (Carson and Young 1976) of modern private security, in the absence of a historically grounded analysis of the structural changes at work, results in both an inadequate explanation of the development of private security and a distorted picture of the historical nature of the relationship between private and public security forces.

In seeking such a structural analysis it is useful to consider the arguments presented by Spitzer and Scull (1977a, 1977b). In their consideration of the history of public and private policing initiatives since the eighteenth century, these authors tend to rely too heavily on a fiscal crisis argument. Nonetheless, they contribute significantly to our understanding of the conditions necessary for the existence of private security by drawing attention to the geographic consequences of changes in economic structures.

In explaining the development of private security at the turn of the century in the United States, they note that this period of industrialization was associated with the emergence of industrial towns which developed around large-scale primary industry. These private towns proved to be functional "analogue[s] of the feudal manor" (1977b, p. 22) as they "brought together vast numbers of unskilled laborers within geographically circumscribed areas" (p. 21) who could be privately policed under a system of "paternalistic domination" (p. 22).

Spitzer and Scull develop this geographic argument further when they consider the subsequent development of capitalism. They argue that while the direct control over policing that the

industrial towns afforded "captains of industry" proved beneficial, the changing "structure of the capitalist economy and
changes in the organization of capitalist enterprise" (1977b, p.
22) undermined their ability to maintain this system of direct
control and this in turn permitted the development of the tendency toward monopoly over policing which the public police
enjoyed into the 1960s. In expanding upon this inverted vacuum theory, Spitzer and Scull argue that what eroded "the
basis for and feasibility of private control" (1977b, p. 23) of
policing was the fact that corporate activity became increasingly
"geographically dispersed and decentralized" (1977b, p. 23).
Consequently it was no longer possible, within the new economic environment, to establish viable private policing initiatives because "under conditions of high labor mobility, 'open
towns' and fluid markets the first businessman to underwrite
the costs of preserving order would be at a competitive dis-
advantage. He could be forced to face increased costs of production while other capitalists could benefit from domestic
tranquillity at no cost to themselves" (1977b, p. 23). In short,
outside the context of private towns, industrialists faced a
"free-rider problem" (Olson 1965; Buchanan 1968) which made
it impossible to continue to rely on private policing initiatives
and encouraged them to rely on the state as a mechanism that
would permit them to share in the cost of policing. Unfortunately, these authors fail to develop and extend this line of
reasoning when they consider the most recent growth of private
security. As a result they miss the opportunity of developing a
general explanation of the structural relationship between public and private security forces.

One of the most striking features associated with private security is the fact that it appears to be correlated with shifts in
property relationships. The most significant of these shifts,
from our point of view, are those toward and away from "mass
private property." By this term we mean control over large
tracts of property by corporate interests dominated by relatively small numbers of people. Whenever one finds a shift in
property relations toward such large geographically connected

holdings of mass private property one also finds a shift toward private policing initiatives. Similarly, shifts toward small individual landholdings appear to be associated with a shift toward public policing initiatives. In other words "private towns," be they the feudal manor, early nineteenth-century industrial towns, or the large industrial, commercial, and residential complexes with their miles of "private streets" that characterize our modern urban environments, tend to be privately policed while public areas tend to be policed by a public authority.

The reasons for this correlation between property relationships and modes of policing are not hard to find. One of the consequences of mass private property, as we have already implied, is the development of public places on private property. One consequence of this is that the private "persons" who control this property have an interest in policing these places. Furthermore, because this correlation of public place with private property is, in the case of mass private property, frequently associated with wealth and administrative resources, these private interests have the capacity to hire a security force. Not only is mass private property associated with the capacity and motivation to establish private security forces, but it facilitates their development because on mass private property the free-rider problem is eliminated.

Today, as this generalization suggests, it is the large corporations controlling extensive industrial and commercial facilities, as well as large residential complexes, who are the principle users of modern private security rather than local grocery stores and individual homeowners. This merely reflects a historical pattern in which organizations that have traditionally operated within a context of mass private property (e.g. certain religious establishments and universities) have persistently resorted to private security in one form or another.

VI. Responses to the Phenomenon of Private Security

The similarity of much private security work to police work has probably been the most significant factor to influence the legislative reaction in many jurisdictions toward regulation of private security. In some jurisdictions this trend toward formal regulation of private security began quite early; in Canada, for instance, Ontario's first Private Detective Act was enacted in 1909. Even early statutes such as this, however, displayed many of the features that have characterized such legislative regulatory schemes throughout most of their history. In the first place, until very recently, they have almost all been limited exclusively to the contract security industry, more particularly to the contract guard and investigation industries. Second, they all appear to have been concerned to control competition between the contract guard and investigation industries and the growing public police forces. This intention may be inferred not only from the frequency with which regulation of these industries has in practice been given to public police authorities themselves[15] but also from provisions in such legislation that are aimed specifically at regulating "moonlighting" in the private security field by public police personnel.

Third, until very recently legislative regulatory schemes regarding contract security have typically conferred on regulatory authorities extraordinarily broad and ill-defined discretion with respect to the issuance or denial of the requisite license or certification. Thus, in most jurisdictions the regulatory agency is free to deny such a license or certification on the grounds that the applicant's character or competency is in question; yet the criteria on which character and competency are to be judged are usually not spelled out in the legislation, but are left to the discretion of the regulatory agency. Again, until recently such decisions were not subject to any appeal in most jurisdictions.[16]

The early legislative schemes were primarily concerned with controlling private detectives and seem to have been intended to protect the budding detective function in public police departments. The infamous involvement of private security guard

[15] There are, of course, other reasons why responsibility for regulating private security is so often given to the public police. See the discussion below, and Stenning and Cornish 1975, pp. 58–68, in this regard.

[16] In this respect, of course, regulation of private security has merely reflected more general trends in administrative regulation (see, for example, Nonet 1969).

forces in situations of labor unrest in the early decades of this century in the United States (see Johnson 1976) and other jurisdictions (see Jamieson 1968), however, served to shift the emphasis of such legislation in the direction of curbing the contract guard business. The involvement of the Pinkerton's Agency in the Homestead riots in 1892 led to hearings by a subcommittee of the House Judiciary Committee and the passage by Congress of the so-called Pinkerton Law a year later. This law, which is still in effect, prohibited the employment of Pinkerton's, or any "similar agency," by the U.S. government.[17] Forty years later the involvement of contract security agencies in industrial espionage, union infiltration, and strikebreaking (Lipson 1975, chap. 3) led to another congressional inquiry under the chairmanship of Senator Robert LaFollette. This senate committee recommended legislative remedies which "should be designed to prohibit labor espionage and the rough shadowing, coercion and intimidation of workers in ordinary times, and to restrict company police to company property during times of strike." The committee concluded that "a statutory prohibition of these practices of private police systems, carefully defined, will also cover the similar practices of detectives and strikebreaking agencies" (U.S. Senate Committee on Education and Labor 1971, p. 218).

At the present time, legislative licensing or certification schemes exist in most of the states of the United States, in all but one of the provinces of Canada, in New Zealand, in many of the states of Australia, in Israel, and in some European countries (West Germany, Holland, Belgium, Sweden). In addition, model licensing statutes have been developed by the U.S. Justice Department's Private Security Advisory Council (see U.S. Private Security Advisory Council 1975 and 1976).

Typically, such regulatory statutes apply only to the contract guard and investigation businesses, although there is a trend

---

[17] 27 Stat. 591, 5 U.S. Code 53 (3 March 1893); revised as Pub. L. 89-554, sec. 3108, title 5 U.S.C.A. in a slightly altered form. But as Lipson points out "in practice this provision as interpreted by various Comptroller Generals has been no barrier to the use of private security firms, either directly or indirectly by the United States government" (1975, p. 163).

toward the inclusion of other contract security businesses (e.g. alarm installers, locksmiths, armored car companies, couriers, security consultants, guard dog suppliers) and some jurisdictions are moving toward the regulation of in-house security personnel (e.g. Ontario and Quebec in Canada). Generally, such statutes require employees as well as businesses to be registered, certified, or licensed. Criteria for license eligibility almost always include the absence of any (or specified) convictions for criminal offenses and of any substantial evidence indicating an applicant's bad moral character or "unfitness" to be licensed. Citizenship of, or residence in, the jurisdiction concerned is a common prerequisite for a business license. In addition, businesses are commonly required to be bonded or to hold liability insurance or both, and in many jurisdictions employees are also required to be bonded. Licensing authorities frequently have considerable powers of inspection of company books and other records, as well as powers to insist on minimum training standards, powers to approve company advertising materials, uniforms to be worn, and so forth, and to insist on the carrying and presentation of identification cards on demand by employees. Many can also determine whether employees will be permitted to carry firearms or other weapons, and under what circumstances.

Some, but by no means all, of the current statutes include explicit provisions for the receipt and disposition by the licensing authority of public complaints against licensees. Almost all licensing authorities have the power to suspend or revoke a license for cause, in some cases only after a hearing, and many of the statutes now contain provisions allowing appeals from decisions of the licensing authority (see e.g. Security Management 1980).

Authority to license private security personnel is frequently given to the public police, although in many jurisdictions it is given to a government department (e.g. an attorney-general's department) or to a specially created licensing commission. Whichever body has this ultimate authority, practical realities usually dictate that the necessary investigations of license appli-

cants are in fact undertaken by the public police. In the light of
the very considerable mutual dependence between the public
police and private security, discussed above, it may be argued
that such control over the licensing of private security personnel
has the potential for placing the public police in a position of
considerable conflict of interest.

In general, licensing statutes confer no additional powers on
private security personnel and indeed some of them contain
provisions specifically prohibiting licensees from being dep-
utized, holding special constable appointments, and so forth.
In most jurisdictions, however, licensees are free to accept such
appointments, and in some countries certain licensees routinely
hold police-like powers (see e.g. Magnusson 1979).

Despite the apparently expansive scope of these regulatory
schemes, research into the adequacy and effectiveness of such
schemes has not produced encouraging results. A survey of
regulatory agencies in the United States, conducted in 1971,
revealed that half of the responding agencies indicated that they
did not have sufficient personnel to perform assigned functions
adequately (Kakalik and Wildhorn 1971, 3:54). Our own research into the regulation of private security in Canada resulted
in similar conclusions (Stenning and Cornish 1975, chap. 6).
Regulatory agencies were typically understaffed and under-
budgeted, with the result that they could rarely perform more
than the most minimum of licensing functions. Administration
of such regulatory functions as inspections, competency tests,
the hearing and disposition of public complaints, and setting of
standards for advertising, uniforms, and equipment was typically minimal or nonexistent.[18] Since formal evaluation of such
agencies is virtually unheard of in most jurisdictions, this credi-

---

[18] Our own conclusions in this regard have recently been confirmed, for Ontario at
least, by the report of the Ontario Commission of Inquiry into the Confidentiality of
Health Information. Referring to the registration branch which has statutory authority
to license private security in the province, Mr. Justice Krever, the commissioner, concluded that "the Registration Branch seems to have viewed its function primarily as an
automatic licensing bureau. It did not, it appears, consider itself a regulatory agency
concerned with policing breaches, not only of the law relating to confidentiality, but of
all the laws affecting the entire range of an investigator's activities" (Ontario. Commission of Inquiry . . . 1980, 2:103).

bility gap goes largely unnoticed and rarely causes serious problems for the agencies themselves, which make suitable accommodations with the industries they are established to regulate.

Shortage of manpower and resources, however, is not the only reason why such regulatory agencies usually achieve unimpressive results. For in truth the real problems associated with private security can rarely be economically or effectively controlled through such schemes. One of the more important of these problems is the fact that much contract private security work is low status, largely unskilled, tedious, and unrewarding work which attracts a highly transient labor force. Attempts to impose sophisticated regulatory controls over industries with such a high turnover of personnel are almost inevitably doomed to failure.

In some jurisdictions, governments have specifically eschewed such formal regulatory schemes. Most notable among these is the United Kingdom (see U.K. Home Office 1979). In this jurisdiction the security industry has largely been left to regulate itself, the only regulatory legislation being the Guard Dogs Act of 1975, which prohibits the use of unaccompanied guard dogs for security purposes. Self-regulation of private security in Britain is accomplished largely through the influence of the British Security Industry Association and the National Supervisory Council for Intruder Alarms. Although agency membership of the B.S.I.A. is numerically small, it has been estimated that its members represent "at least 80 per cent of the total number employed by security firms outside of manufacturing and perhaps account for some 90 percent of the business (measured by turnover)" (U.K. Home Office 1979, p. 4). In addition, many in-house security personnel belong to the International Professional Security Association. Each of these organizations attempts to establish and maintain minimum standards for its members with respect both to recruitment, training, and employment of personnel and to the quality, advertising, and selling of security products and services. Membership in such organizations, however, is of course voluntary, and a large number of the smaller contract security businesses therefore fall outside the scope of this kind of industry self-regulation. A further important consideration is the fact that none of these organizations has an extensive enforcement capability equal to the standards it promotes. Because of these and other weaknesses in the comprehensiveness of self-regulation in the U.K., calls for the introduction of legislative regulation have persisted there (see, for example, Christie 1976, pp. 75–76; Wright 1978, pp. 6–8; Samuels 1978, p. 303).

Apart from regulatory statutes, a variety of other laws have direct relevance to private security. While general laws typically do not contain provisions enacted specifically with the needs and problems of private security in mind, there are some notable exceptions. Most prominent among these are statutes which give additional powers to private security personnel and those which restrict or prohibit specific activities which private security might otherwise engage in. In the former category are the so-called shoplifting detention statutes, now common in the United States (see Bassiouni 1977, chap. 9 and app. B), and statutes granting private security personnel special search powers to enforce airport security measures (e.g. the Federal Aeronautics Act in Canada, and the Protection of Aircraft Act in Britain). In the latter category are a variety of statutes dealing with such matters as the protection of privacy, access to criminal records information, and prohibitions on professional strikebreaking which are now being enacted in an increasing number of jurisdictions.

In treating private security personnel as if they are no different from ordinary citizens, the general law in all jurisdictions has failed to keep pace with the modern development of private security. Thus, a stranger to modern Western societies who merely read the law could scarcely guess that, in addition to publicly financed and controlled security forces (the public police), a massive private industry largely fulfilling similar functions also exists. We have argued, on a number of occasions (see, for example, Freedman and Stenning 1977, chap. 8) that this is a situation likely to lead to unfairness and injustice to the industry, to its employees, and to those members of the general public who come into daily contact with it. The law's blindness to the realities of modern private security in this regard is the subject of further discussion in the conclusions that follow.

VII. Conclusions

The issues discussed in this essay raise fundamental questions about the implications of modern private security for the nature of society. The striking similarity between the characteristics of Foucault's "disciplinary society" and the essential features of private security suggests that the reorganization of policing that private security is precipitating is part of a more general phenomenon in the transformation of social control. That is, it represents a move toward a society in which control takes the form of mere "snowflakes," rather than the more spectacular exploits of television "cops." Within this context, the philosophy enunciated by Sir Robert Peel is revealed as not just the basis for a new police force but the rationale for a mode of policing which can contribute toward the development of a disciplinary society. Further, within this context, the various stages in the historical development of policing may be viewed as mere way stations in the emergence of a society whose model Foucault argues can be found in Bentham's vision of the Panopticon. A fundamental prerequisite of such a society is the elimination of privacy through pervasive surveillance (Foucault 1977, p. 201). In profoundly undermining the institutions of privacy (Stinchcombe 1963) as a barrier to police surveillance, it is private security rather than the public police who seem to be leading the way to the new "disciplinary society."

To characterize private security policies and practices as essentially disciplinary in nature is likely to provoke some very negative reactions. But before jumping to conclusions about the possible undesirable consequences of moving away from a predominant reliance on traditional criminal justice processes toward modes of private justice (of which private security forms a part), it is as well to remember that private justice systems flourish to a considerable extent as a result of dissatisfactions with the public criminal justice system and a feeling that it fails to provide adequate solutions to the problems which we currently define as "crime." In this respect one may legitimately question whether the term "justice" as it is used in the context of public criminal justice may be as much a legitimizing euphemism as a descriptive term. Furthermore, if, as we have argued, private security and private justice systems flourish as a result of significant structural changes occurring in society, which seem unlikely to be reversed within the foreseeable future, then to propose a return to the "old" system as a solution to the potential dangers of a "disciplinary society" may be only tilting at windmills.

In our view, we are likely to be far more effective in responding to the possible threats to individual liberty that private justice poses if we face up to the new reality of policing and "justice" by seeking to isolate and respond to those features which appear to be the most potentially ominous. We believe that this suggests a major change of emphasis in the way society responds to private security, that attention should be focused less exclusively on forms of direct regulation (such as licensing) and that more effort should be made to reexamine, and perhaps redefine, some of the more fundamental legal institutions of relevance to the phenomenon. The starting point for such an approach is the situation of changing property relations which we have identified. The significance of this situation is that it has called into question the continued appropriateness of the traditional legal institutions of private property and privacy which have historically been so critical, not only as an essential basis for capitalist development, but also as a foundation for securing the liberty of individuals in the face of encroachments both by the state and by other private interests (Reich 1964).

These twin legal institutions of privacy and of private property lie at the heart of the way in which legal systems respond to private security. Both institutions, as we have pointed out, are critical in setting constraints on the role of the public police and thereby protecting the jurisdiction of private security. On the other hand, because private security personnel normally op-

erate as the agents of those who own or possess private property, they have access to most or all of the powers and authority
associated with the institution of private property and its protection. It is these powers (e.g. the right to control access to,
and use of, property and to impose conditions upon such access
and use) that form the basis for the most potentially disturbing
interferences with liberty and civil rights. Yet for the most part
such powers remain premised on assumptions about the nature
of property relations which no longer reflect modern realities
and which are being increasingly challenged by the development of what we have called mass private property. One of the
most important of these assumptions is the notion that places
which are privately owned and controlled are normally "private
places."

Historically, the notions of "private property" and "private
place" have never been recognized as entirely congruent by any
legal system. Yet most of the powers and authority of those
who own or possess private property have been premised on the
assumption that they usually are. The modern development of
mass private property, however, has resulted in more and more
areas of the urban environment which, although they are privately owned and controlled, are quite clearly not "private
places" in any meaningful sense. Yet those who own and control such places (including their private security agents) remain
free to exercise powers and authority originally conceived of in
terms of their appropriateness for the protection of private
rather than public places. And it is the exercise of these powers
(which are derived from the law of property and contract rather
than from criminal law and procedure) which pose the greatest
potential threats to individual liberty.

Most of the elaborate protections which have been
established to ensure the liberty of an individual when he is in a
publicly owned public place become subject to the property
rights of the owner and his agents as soon as that individual
steps into a privately owned public place. In the exercise of
such rights, the owner (or his private security agent) is free to
impose almost unlimited infringements on the liberty and pri-

vacy of the individual (e.g. a requirement to submit to search of his person or property, to be photographed, or temporarily to surrender his property) as conditions of access to or exit from the premises (see Stenning and Shearing 1980).

The need to reexamine these fundamental legal institutions on which the role, jurisdiction, and powers of private security are founded has, in our view, been obscured and neglected as a result of the concentration on licensing and other forms of direct regulation which has preoccupied public authorities in so many jurisdictions. For, as long as the fundamental institutions remain unexamined and unchanged, no amount of direct regulation of various parts of the contract security industry is likely adequately to resolve the dilemmas posed by the modern development of private security and private justice systems.

In considering threats to individual liberty in another context entirely, Reich (1964) some years ago came to the conclusion that changes in the nature of property required the development of a "new property" which would once again permit the legal definition of property to continue to fulfill its traditional role as a critical legal and social institution in the defense of individual liberty. In applying this thinking to the phenomenon of modern private security, it seems clear to us that the common legal analogy between individual property ownership and corporate property ownership must also be reexamined. As Flavel has pointed out:

> An important element in this approach is the realisation
> that there are significant differences between the ownership,
> control and security of personalised property, and of industrial and commercial property. The legal institution of property creates an impression of similarity but does not reflect the social and economic reality. The ownership and control of property in industry and commerce involves more than the right to control physical assets. It also extends to the control of people, as workers. Security in this situation is therefore particularly important. In immediate terms, security of personal property merely ensures continued enjoyment of prop-

erty objects. But in industry and commerce the function of
security in maintaining owner/management control of physical assets constitutes one element in the process through
which the power relationships between groups in the work
situation are preserved. (1973, p. 14)

The modern development of mass private property controlled
by vast corporate conglomerates, and so frequently consisting
of essentially "public places," is the critical change that has
paved the way for the modern growth and influence of private
security. And it is these developments that necessitate the kind
of fundamental reassessment which we are suggesting. The
courts, as well as legislators and law reformers, have only recently, and reluctantly, begun to perceive this need. In a recent
Canadian case, in which some of these fundamental issues were
pushed to the foreground, the Chief Justice of the Supreme
Court of Canada, in a dissenting opinion, captured the problem
succinctly when he observed: "It seems to me that the present
case involves a search for an appropriate legal framework for
new social facts which show up the inaptness of an old doctrine
developed upon a completely different social foundation" (Las-
kin, C.J.C., in Harrison v. Carswell, 25 C.C.C. (2d) 186 at 194
[1976]).

This is precisely the challenge which the modern development of private security and private justice poses; it requires a
response if we are to come to terms with private security, private justice, and more generally the disciplinary society of
which they are a part.

REFERENCES

Bailey, Maureen. 1979. "'It's a Jungle Out There'—So Companies
That Furnish Security Services Prosper Mightily," *Barron's*, 26
November.
Bassiouni, M. Cherif. 1977. *Citizen Arrest: The Law of Arrest, Search,*

and Seizure for Private Citizens and Private Police. Springfield, Ill.: Charles C. Thomas.

Becker, Theodore M. 1974. "The Place of Private Police in Society: An Area of Research for the Social Sciences," *Social Problems* 21:438–53.

Buchanan, J. M. 1968. *The Demand and Supply of Public Goods.* Chicago: Rand McNally.

Bunyan, T. 1976. *The History and Practice of the Political Police in Britain.* London: Julian Friedmann.

Carson, W. G., and P. Young. 1976. "Sociological Aspects of Major Property Crime." In *Major Property Crime in the United Kingdom: Some Aspects of Law Enforcement,* ed. P. Young. Papers presented at a conference held in September 1975. Edinburgh: School of Criminology and Forensic Studies, University of Edinburgh.

Christie, David P. 1976. "Legal Aspects of Enforcement and Control." In ibid.

Cory, Bruce. 1979. "Police for Hire—Fear Pays a Dividend to Those Who Guard," *Police Magazine,* September: 39–45.

Curtis, Bob. 1971. *Security Control: External Theft.* New York: Chain Store Age Books/Lebhar-Friedman.

Distelhorst, Garis F. 1977. "Remarks—Police/Private Security Interface." In *The Police Yearbook 1977.* Papers and proceedings of the Eighty-Third Annual Conference of the International Association of Chiefs of Police. Gaithersburg, Md.

Draper, Hilary. 1978. *Private Police.* Markham, Ont.: Penguin Books (Canada).

Draper, H. A., and A. A. Nicholls. 1976. *Task Force Report on Private Policing in British Columbia.* Vancouver: British Columbia Police Commission.

Dun and Bradstreet International. 1979. *Europe's 5000 Largest Companies 1979.* London and New York: Dun and Bradstreet International.

Elliott, J. F. 1973. *The "New " Police.* Springfield, Ill.: Charles C Thomas.

Farnell, M. B., and C. D. Shearing. 1977. *Private Security: An Examination of Canadian Statistics, 1961–1971.* Toronto: Centre of Criminology, University of Toronto.

Flavel, W. 1973. "Research into Private Security." Unpublished paper presented to the Second Bristol Seminar on the Sociology of the Police (April).

Forbes. 1979. "The Ga-a-do Man," *Forbes* 15 October:192.

Foucault, M. 1977. *Discipline and Punish: The Birth of the Prison.* New York: Pantheon.

Freedman, David J., and Philip C. Stenning. 1977. *Private Security, Police and the Law in Canada.* Toronto: Centre of Criminology, University of Toronto.

French, J. A. 1979. "Private Security Organisations—Threat or Benefit to Society?" *Police College Magazine* 15(2): 23–32.

Friendly, John Ashley. 1980. "Harbinger." Unpublished. Toronto: Osgoode Hall Law School.

Frost and Sullivan. 1975. *The Industrial and Commercial Security Market.* New York: Frost and Sullivan.

Goldstein, H. 1977. *Policing a Free Society.* Cambridge, Mass.: Ballinger.

Grabosky, Peter N. 1977. *Sydney in Ferment: Crime, Dissent, and Official Reaction 1788–1973.* Canberra: Australian National University Press.

Heijboer, H. J. 1979. "The (dangerous) Evolution of Private Police Forces," [De (gevaarlijke) ontwikkeling van een particulier politie wezen] *Delikt Delinkwent* 9(1):5–23.

Hovav, Meir, and Menachem Amir. 1979. "Israel Police: History and Analysis," *Police Studies* 2(2):5–31.

Jamieson, S. M. 1968. *Times of Trouble: Labour Unrest and Industrial Conflict in Canada 1900–1966.* Study no. 22. Ottawa: Task Force on Labour Relations.

Jeffries, Fern. 1977. *Private Policing: An Examination of In-House Security Operations.* Toronto: Centre of Criminology, University of Toronto.

Johnson, Bruce C. 1976. "Taking Care of Labor: The Police in American Politics," *Theory and Society* 3:89–117.

Kakalik, James S., and Sorrel Wildhorn. 1971. Vol. 1: *Private Policing in the United States: Findings and Recommendations* (R-869-DOJ); vol. 2: *The Private Police Industry: Its Nature and Extent* (R-870-DOJ); vol. 3: *Current Regulation of Private Police: Regulatory Agency Experience and Views* (R-871-DOJ); vol. 4: *The Law and Private Police* (R-872-DOJ); vol. 5: *Special Purpose Public Police* (R-873-DOJ). Santa Monica, Calif.: Rand Corp.

Kakalik, James S., and Sorrel Wildhorn. 1977. *The Private Police: Security and Danger.* New York: Crane Russak.

Kobetz, Richard W., and H. H. A. Cooper. 1978. "Two Armies: One Flag," *Police Chief* 45(6):31–33.

Lipson, M. 1975. *On Guard: The Business of Private Security.* New York: Quadrangle/New York Times Book Co.

Little, Arthur D. 1973. *Outlook for the U.S. Safety, Fire Protection and Security Business.* Cambridge, Mass.: Arthur D. Little.

Luzon, Jack. 1978. "Corporate Headquarters Private Security," *Police Chief* 45(6):39–42.

Magnusson, Dan. 1979. "The Private Police." In *Police and the Social Order*, Report no. 6, ed. J. Knutsson, E. Kuhlhorn, and Albert Reiss, Jr. Stockholm: National Swedish Council for Crime Prevention.

Manning, P. 1980. *The Narcs Game.* Cambridge, Mass.: M.I.T. Press.

Megill, Allan. 1979. "Foucault, Structuralism, and the Ends of History," *Journal of Modern History* 51(3):451–503.

Morn, F. T. 1975. "The Eye That Never Sleeps: A History of the Pinkerton National Detective Agency, 1850–1920." Ph.D. dissertation, University of Chicago.

Nonet, P. 1969. *Administrative Justice.* New York: Russell Sage Foundation.

Nossov, W. 1975. *The Security Enforcement Industry.* Merrick, N.Y.: Morton Research Corp.

O'Connor, J. 1973. *The Fiscal Crisis of the State.* New York: St. Martin's Press.

Olson, M. 1965. *The Logic of Collective Action: Public Goods and the Theory of Groups.* Cambridge, Mass.: Harvard University Press.

Ontario. Commission of Inquiry into the Confidentiality of Health Information. 1980. *Report.* 3 vols. Toronto: Queen's Printer.

Pleece, Sydney. 1972. "The Nature and Potential of the Security Industry," *Police Journal* 45 (Jan.–Mar.): 41–60.

Predicasts, Inc. 1974. *Private Security Systems.* Cleveland, Ohio: Predicasts, Inc.

Quebec. Commission de Police. 1976. *Etude en matière de sécurité privée.* Quebec City: Commission de Police de Quebec.

Radzinowicz, Sir Leon. 1968. *A History of English Criminal Law and Its Administration From 1750.* Vol. 4: *Grappling for Control.* London: Stevens and Sons.

Randall, W. E., and P. Hamilton. 1972. "The Security Industry in the United Kingdom: Its Growth, Role, Accountability and Future." In *The Security Industry in the United Kingdom: Papers Presented to the Cropwood Round Table Conference.* Cambridge: Institute of Criminology, University of Cambridge.

Reich, Charles A. 1964. "The New Property," *Yale Law Journal* 73:733–87.

Reiss, A. J. 1971. *The Police and the Public.* New Haven: Yale University Press.

Rubinstein, J. 1973. *City Police.* New York: Farrar, Straus, and Giroux.

Samuels, Alec. 1978. "Privacy and Business Espionage: II—A Legal View." In *Privacy*, ed. John B. Young. Toronto: John Wiley.

Scott, Thomas M., and Marlys McPherson. 1971. "The Development of the Private Sector of the Criminal Justice System," *Law and Society Review* 6(2):267–88.

Security Management. 1980. "Summary of State Legislation Affecting Private Security," *Security Management* 24(4):54–59.

Shearing, Clifford D., Margaret F. Farnell, and Philip C. Stenning. 1980. *Contract Security in Ontario.* Toronto: Centre of Criminology, University of Toronto.

Shearing, Clifford D., and Philip C. Stenning. 1977. "Private Security and Law Enforcement in Canada." Unpublished paper prepared for the Task Force on Law Enforcement, Ministry of the Solicitor General of Canada.

———. Forthcoming. "Snowflakes or Good Pinches? Private Security's Contribution to Modern Policing." Paper presented to a Symposium on Law Enforcement and Society, at the Canadian Police College, August 1980 (to be published in *Proceedings*).

Spitzer, Steven. 1975. "Towards a Marxian Theory of Deviance," *Social Problems* 22:638–71.

Spitzer, Steven, and Andrew T. Scull. 1977a. "Social Control in Historical Perspective: From Private to Public Responses to Crime." In *Corrections and Punishment: Structure, Function and Process*, ed. David F. Greenberg. Beverly Hills, Calif.: Sage Publications.

———. 1977b. "Privatization and Capitalist Development: The Case of the Private Police," *Social Problems* 25:18–29.

Stenning, Philip C. 1975. "Private Security in Canada," *Signal*, 1st quar.:10–14.

Stenning, Philip C., and Mary F. Cornish. 1975. *The Legal Regulation and Control of Private Policing in Canada.* Toronto: Centre of Criminology, University of Toronto.

Stenning, Philip C., and Clifford D. Shearing. 1980. *Search and Seizure: Powers of Private Security Personnel.* A study paper prepared for the Law Reform Commission of Canada. Ottawa: Ministry of Supply and Services.

Stinchcombe, Arthur L. 1963. "Institutions of Privacy in the Determination of Police Administrative Practice," *American Journal of Sociology* 69(2):150–60.

United Kingdom Home Office. 1979. *The Private Security Industry: A Discussion Paper.* London: H.M. Stationery Office.

U.S. Department of Justice. (LEAA, National Criminal Justice Information and Statistics Service.) 1979. *Sourcebook of Criminal Justice*

Statistics—1978. [Parisi, Gottfredson, Hindelang, Flanagan, eds.]. Albany, N.Y.: Criminal Justice Research Center.

————. (LEAA, National Advisory Committee on Criminal Justice Standards and Goals.) 1976. *Private Security: Report of the Task Force on Private Security.* Washington D.C.

U.S. Private Security Advisory Council. (Department of Justice, LEAA). 1975. *A Model Burglar and Hold-Up Alarm Business Licensing and Regulatory Statute.* Washington D.C. (April).

————. 1976. *A Report on the Regulation of Private Security Guard Services Including a Model Private Security Licensing and Regulatory Statute.* Washington D.C. (May).

————. 1977. *Law Enforcement and Private Security Sources and Areas of Conflict and Strategies for Conflict Resolution.* Washington D.C. (June).

U.S. Senate. Committee on Education and Labor. 1971. *Private Police Systems.* Senate Resolution 166, Subcommittee on Violations of Free Speech and Rights of Labor, R. M. LaFollette, Jr., Chairman, 1939. New York: Arno Press and New York Times.

Wright, K. G. 1978. "The British Security Industry," *Police Studies* 1(4):3–8.

David A. J. Richards

Rights, Utility, and Crime

ABSTRACT

John Rawls's *A Theory of Justice* (1971) launched important jurispru-
dential rethinking of criminal law doctrine, policy, and practice.
The opposing theories of Kant (natural rights) and Bentham
(utilitarianism) are brought into new perspective by the human
rights analysis flowing from Rawls's innovative theory. The traditional antagonism between the natural rights and utilitarian positions can no longer be sustained at least in its traditional form; the
human rights perspective becomes central in relation to decriminalization, mens rea, deterrence, prisons, capital punishment,
sentencing, probation, parole and other doctrines, and institutions
and principles of punishment under the criminal law.

We are in the midst of a major philosophical shift from the
positivist conception of the public official as a managerial tech-
nocrat ideally seeking the utilitarian goal of the greatest happiness of the greatest number to a natural law concern for rights.
This shift, dramatically apparent in the work of Ronald Dworkin (1978a) and others (Epstein 1973, 1974, 1975; Fletcher 1972,
1978; Michelman 1967, 1973), has not yet been fully and fairly
articulated. One cannot be certain of the final forms rights
theories will take or of the extent of their influence on thought
about law and how it is practiced. This shift was catalyzed by
the most serious and profound attack on utilitarianism since
Kant, namely, John Rawls's *A Theory of Justice* (1971; but see
Hart 1979) and the subsequent works of Robert Nozick (1974)

David A. J. Richards is Professor of Law at New York University Law School.

and Alan Gewirth (1978) which developed the neo-Kantian, deontological,[1] antiutilitarian thrust of Rawls's theory but in ways expressly critical of various aspects of Rawls's pathbreaking book. Legal theorists who are attempting to introduce these ideas into the analysis of legal doctrines and institutions correspondingly reflect these tensions among the theories of Rawls, Nozick, and Gewirth. Although the natural law conception of rights is of quite general significance for rethinking the normative foundations of legal doctrines and institutions, I will here address its specific relevance to rethinking criminal law and its institutions (see, in general, Fletcher 1978).

The tasks of a theory of criminal law, as is often the case in social theory, appear to be both explanatory and normative, concerned with both understanding and reform. With respect to understanding, an adequate normative theory of the substantive criminal law is needed to illuminate the rules of criminal liability—for example, the concurrence of *mens rea*[2] and *actus reus*,[3] the disfavor in the criminal law of strict liability, the place and forms of excuses (e.g. the insanity defense) and justifications (e.g. self-defense, necessity) in rebutting criminal liability, the form of mitigation doctrines such as provocation, the nature and proper scope of inchoate offenses like attempt and conspiracy, and the place of general requirements of legality and proportionality.

Many of these doctrines of criminal law are much disputed today. Accordingly, an adequate normative theory of the criminal law should clarify such controversies and indicate the reasonable direction of reform. To what extent, if at all, should traditional mens rea requirements or specific excuses (e.g. in-

---

[1] In an oversimplification: teleological theories are concerned with actions as means; deontological theories with actions as ends. Thus most utilitarians argue that the end of society is some form of the greatest aggregate social good; the morality of acts must be assessed in relation to attainment of that end. Most rights theories are deontological and assess the morality of acts without regard to their relation to achievement of any preconceived end.

[2] "A guilty mind": for all but strict liability offenses, the substantive criminal law specifies a mental state (purpose, knowledge, recklessness, or negligence) that must be proved before an individual may be convicted of an offense.

[3] The "actus reus" of an offense comprises the physical facts (acts, circumstances, results) that must be proved before an individual may be convicted of an offense. The intention to steal is a mental state (mens rea). The act of taking is the actus reus.

sanity) be eliminated to facilitate aims of therapeutic care and cure in place of retributive impulses (compare Wootton 1959, 1963, with Hart 1968, chaps. 2, 7, 8)? Should new excuses be recognized—for example, a defense of socioeconomic deprivation (see Bazelon 1976; Morse 1976)? Should proportionality requirements be more aggressively developed to invalidate various forms of criminal sanction? In what areas should the scope of the criminal sanction be contracted (e.g. consensual adult sexual relations, or use of certain drugs) or expanded (e.g. corporate wrongdoing)?

Similar controversies rage over various aspects of criminal law institutions. To what extent, if at all, should prisons be the main form of contemporary punishment? If prisons must be retained, should their design emphasize retributive or reform considerations? What kinds and degrees of punishment can be justified? To what extent should the scope of discretion in current sentencing, probation, and parole policies be delimited, and in what ways? An adequate normative theory of the criminal law should critically illuminate these controversies as well.

In this essay, I propose to show how the recent elaboration of rights theories transforms our perception of these questions, rendering sterile and anachronistic the familiar historical divisions between liberal humane reform (associated with utilitarianism) and conservative moralistic retributivism (associated with Kantianism). The essay begins, however, with a historical survey of the traditional antagonism between utilitarian and natural rights analyses of the criminal law and its persistence in recent thought and then returns to an exposition of the recent revival of neo-Kantian theory, largely prompted by Rawls's remarkable book. Later sections consider some of the implications of the reinvigorated rights perspective for the analysis and understanding of the criminal law and some of its institutions.

I. The Historical Antagonism between Utilitarianism and Natural Rights Theory

A reformist attitude to criminal justice arose during the Enlightenment, concerned to assess empirically, and with a mind to relieve unnecessary suffering, the sometimes brutal excesses of criminal justice systems in which all felonies (including sometimes minor larcenies) were capital crimes; where punishments often involved bodily disfigurements or public humiliations (see, in general, Rothman 1971) and capital crimes were the objects of death-dealing punishments of incredible barbarity (Foucault 1979); and where criminal sanctions could be imposed for entertaining the thought of your sovereign's demise, expressing the thought that Jesus of Nazareth might not be divine, or expressing the opinion that your current government was inefficient or corrupt. The Enlightenment attitude toward these practices received its most characteristic and brilliant expression in *On Crimes and Punishments*, a book by the liberal Italian Cesare Beccaria (1963) originally published in 1764.

Beccaria presents an argument which is an amalgam of all the tensions and strains within Enlightenment thought about criminal justice. He bases his argument, for example, both on ideas of contractarian natural rights and on utilitarian conceptions of maximizing the greatest happiness of the greatest number, two ideas which, later writers have argued, have very different implications. Beccaria's practical reforms sought to reduce the unwarranted degree to which existing criminal justice systems inflicted suffering without good deterrence evidence (pp. 42–52, 55–59) and the excessive invocation of the criminal sanction to enforce religious values (heresy, blasphemy, etc.) which he took to be inappropriate grounds for criminal sanctions in a liberal constitutional state based on tolerance among various religions and philosophies (pp. 86–89). His most striking attack is on the death penalty, which he argues can never be acceptable except in a very narrow range of cases (pp. 42–52).

Beccaria's argument is the foundation for all later assessments of criminal justice reform, depending on which prong of Beccaria's basic moral argument is selected for emphasis—his natural rights argument or his utilitarian concern with relieving suffering and increasing the maximum level of happiness. For present purposes, the views of two thinkers (Kant, for natural rights; Bentham, for utilitarianism) dramatically bring out tensions that Beccaria's argument concealed or left implicit.

Immanuel Kant took opposition to utilitarianism as a central tenet of his moral theory and outlook. In his most powerful statement of his general moral philosophy, Kant articulates a form of moral theory that we now conventionally refer to as deontological. Deontological moral theories, in contrast to teleological views, maintain that the concept of what is morally right *cannot* be defined in terms of whether something maximizes goodness in the world, whether goodness is understood in terms of pleasure, or satisfaction of desire, or display of talent, or whatever (see Rawls 1971, pp. 22–27). Kant, accordingly, repudiates utilitarianism because it is one form of teleological theory, namely, that form which defines the right in terms of maximizing the aggregate of pleasure over pain of all sentient creatures. For Kant, it is not pleasure or pain or anything of that kind which has controlling ethical significance but rather the capacity of each person to pursue higher-order interests in freedom and rationality whereby they critically reflect on, evaluate, revise, and take responsibility for their structure of ends as independent beings imposing structure on one's life in terms of arguments and evidence to which one freely and rationally assents. Kant calls this capacity autonomy (Kant 1959, pp. 5–64; cf. Rawls 1980, pp. 515–35). Moral right, for him, depends not on whether an action will have certain effects but on whether the principle which the action expresses has a certain form of justification, namely, whether the principle is one which persons, as free and rational creatures (i.e. autonomous), could offer and accept as principles of conduct in the context in question. This general form of analysis can be called the principle of autonomy (Kant 1959, pp. 49–64); for action on it insures that actions, to be deemed ethical, express respect, on fair terms to all, for a person's capacity for autonomy: for the capacity of each person to determine their own ends as free and rational creatures and to acknowledge the like capacity of other persons by acting on those standards of conduct (namely, ethics) which express this acknowledgment.

Human rights are forms of coercive claim justified by the principle of autonomy, which are, for Kant, specifically anti-utilitarian, assuring that no person is to be sacrificed for aggregate utility inconsistent with the principle of autonomy. These remarks about Kantian ethics are vague and sketchy, but they suggest, I hope, the kind of nobility and moving appeal that his abstract moral views have always had for serious students of ethics. In justice, however, we must note that these views are, in Kant, combined with other features which many find much less attractive. For example, Kant mixes together the ethical notion of autonomy, which underlies his moral analysis, with a notion of causal indeterminism or freedom of causal law (pp. 64–92), which the empiricist bent of the modern mind finds it difficult to accept. More important, Kant uses his moral philosophy to justify results which many humane people find horrifying. We may see one form of the complex reaction that Kant's views have elicited if we turn to his conception of criminal justice.

As one might have expected, Kant's theory of criminal justice rejects Beccaria's dependence on utilitarian arguments, and claims that he should have rested his reformist arguments solely on grounds of human rights, including concerns of free thought and expression, religious and philosophical tolerance, certainty and clarity in criminal laws, and proportionality in punishment; all of which Kant would defend as implicit in taking the dignity of man, and thus rights, seriously.[4] Kant departs from Beccaria in emphasizing that, whatever the unjust uses to which retributive arguments have been and can be put by tyrants and religious fanatics, they have, properly understood and interpreted, a humane and reasonable role to play in a just system of criminal law, namely, as a way of vindicating and expressing the ethical requirements imposed by the principle of autonomy. Kant interprets this role in terms of a substantive conception of moral wrongs which tracks the conventional moral values of his period (for example, Christian sexual morality) (Kant 1963, pp. 162–71) in a way which many find, however historically natural, singularly unimaginative and uncritical in a philosopher of Kant's stature (see Richards 1979a, pp. 1255–62). His views

---

[4] For Kant's general statement of his theory of punishment, see Kant 1965. For his general argument for liberal freedoms, see Kant 1964, 1965.

thus support the extension or retention of the criminal sanction in the area of "victimless" crimes which have been a traditional object of liberal criticism and reform. Within the substantive scope of the criminal law so defined, Kant's theory of punishment makes two distinct claims. First, Kant argues that ideas of human rights require that, notwithstanding utilitarian calculations of maximum social advantage, criminal sanctions only be applied to those who are personally morally guilty and that the levels of sanction correspond to the moral gravity of the underlying offense (Kant 1965, p. 100). But, second, Kant interprets the proportionality requirement of just punishment in a striking way: levels of criminal sanction are to be proportional to the moral gravity of the underlying offense in a manner of strict equivalence and with uncompromising moral necessity without concern for deterrent effects: the murderer *must* himself or herself be killed, the rapist castrated (pp. 100–107). Only in these ways, Kant argues, can we assure strict equality to all criminals, removing from the law unjust caprice which fails to treat persons equally (p. 101). Thus, while Kant agrees with many of Beccaria's recommendations, he does not follow, indeed severely criticizes, his most striking one: the attack on the death penalty. Kant criticizes Beccaria for his "sympathetic sentimentality and an affectation of humanitarianism" (pp. 104–5). In general, Kant's theory of just punishments in terms of in kind qualitative equivalences is one in spirit with the common forms of punishment in his period (before the dominance of prisons as a criminal sanction) although, of course, he was sharply critical of the barbarous punishments which exceeded these equivalences.

Another group of moral critics of the criminal law that derives from Beccaria are the classical utilitarians, notably the indefatigable Jeremy Bentham, who insisted on describing in excruciating and often unreadable detail *exactly* the reforms in criminal justice which were required by taking utilitarianism as the only ultimate moral value: creating the greatest net of pleasure over pain for all sentient creatures (see Halevy 1955). Bentham resolves the moral ambiguity in Beccaria's argument exactly conversely to Kant. Ideas of human rights, Bentham argues, are dangerous nonsense: they encourage the uneducated rabble to revolt;[5] and worse than nonsense, based as they are on vague and speculatively nonempirical self-evident truths unsupported by the kind of careful empirical studies that application of the utilitarian principle rationally requires. Accordingly, any form of argument for criminalizing certain conduct must, for Bentham, take the form of showing that the pain-producing effects of the conduct are best minimized by the effects of criminal sanctions in discouraging or reforming such conduct; and forms of criminal sanction, since they impose pains, must be shown to be so designed as best to maximize pleasure over pain overall in view of all the facts and circumstances (in terms of general deterrence effects on others, special deterrent effects on the criminal, protection of society from imminent recurring criminality, and reform of the criminal). For Bentham, as for utilitarians in general, there are no just concepts of morality or retributivism independent of maximizing the utilitarian aggregates. Implicitly, Bentham's view would urge the contraction of the scope of the criminal law to the extent a certain form of alleged wrongdoing did not cause pain or the use of criminal sanctions causes more pain than produces pleasure. For example, in a remarkable essay unpublished in his lifetime, Bentham argues on such grounds that consensual adult homosexuality should not be criminal (Bentham 1978).

Bentham's explicit use of such arguments focused on general deterrence and reform (see, generally, Bentham 1864, 1948). In contrast to Kant's disavowal of the relevance of any deterrence

[5] Bentham, like many Englishmen of his period, had in mind the excesses of the French Revolution. See "Anarchical Fallacies, Being an Examination of the Declaration of Rights, Issued During the French Revolution" (Bentham 1853, 2:488–526). Rather, Bentham urged the role of managerial technocratic experts: he courted, for example, the Russian tsars and thought he had discovered such a potential monarch in George Washington, whom he wrote regarding possible willingness to undertake utilitarian reforms from above. See, for example, J. Bentham, *Papers Relative to Codification and Public Instruction: Including Correspondence with the Russian Emperor, and Divers Constituted Authorities in the United States* (London, 1817). Eventually, he turned, in despair, to English parliamentary democracy: his "philosophical radicals" dominated parliamentary reforms in the nineteenth century in England both in extension of the franchise and reforms in the criminal justice system. See, in general, Halevy 1955.

evidence to consideration of just punishment, Bentham focused on deterrence evidence as *the* central question in determining just punishments; to the extent that any level of sanction was not required to secure deterrence, that punishment was, for Bentham, cruelly unjust. Bentham supposed such deterrence considerations to justify the place of requirements of personal culpability, legality, and proportionality in the criminal law; but, for him, unlike Kant, these concepts did not require any particular form or level of punishment independent of appropriate utilitarian calculations. The general thrust of Bentham's argument was to secure maximum deterrence at least cost, for example, by imposing less severe penalties more certainly. In particular, Bentham's focus on reform, as well as general deterrence at least cost, led to a pervading interest in prisons found neither in Beccaria or Kant, notably his famous "panopticon" (Bentham 1843, vol. 4).

Bentham's design was for a total institution which would secure maximum intrusive surveillance of each criminal, with no knowledge by the criminal of when he was being watched, or by whom. The almost naive manipulativeness and intrusiveness of Bentham's design has been described by Foucault (1977) as "panopticism," an approach to institutionalization for purposes of reform that could be and was generalized to other institutions (asylums, reformatories for juveniles, hospitals, and the like). For Bentham, this form of institution, whose history was importantly shaped by religious models of private remorse and reform (thus, the word "penitentiary"), could be given a purely secular justification in terms of the managerial utilitarian ethic of securing maximum deterrence and reform at least cost. In Bentham, there is no special emphasis on discretion as an instrument of reform, but of course, as Rothman's studies (1971, 1980) have made clear, discretion was a natural development from the objectives of reform that, at the expense of other purposes, increasingly dominated the institutions of panopticism.

The antagonism between natural rights and utilitarian theories in the context of criminal justice can be summarized in terms of four focal differences between Kant and Bentham.

First, in terms of the scope of the criminal law, Kant's theory appeared to justify much of the traditional concern of the criminal law in forms of "victimless" crime, whereas Bentham appears to have been critical of such concern. Second, both Kant and Bentham supported classic structural doctrines of the criminal law (personal culpability requirements, legality, proportionality), but Kant rested them on the principle of autonomy whereas Bentham regarded them as applications of general deterrence considerations. Third, Kant refused entirely to acknowledge the place of deterrence considerations in just punishment, emphasizing forms of in-kind equivalence that must mandatorily be imposed; Bentham emphasized general deterrence and reform, which gave a secular rationale to the emerging institutions of panopticism. Fourth, Kant acknowledged no room for discretion in punishment: his equivalences are intended to insure precisely equal treatment with no invidious caprice; Bentham's panopticism naturally lent itself to increasing emphasis on the exercise of discretion as a way of determining and expressing reform objectives.

Many of these differences were sharpened in the course of the nineteenth century when reformers and critics of criminal justice aligned themselves with natural rights or utilitarianism. Conservative defenders of existing institutions of criminal justice, whether in the form of philosophical (e.g. Bradley 1962, pp. 58–126, 160–206) or legal (Stephen 1967, 1885) argument, aligned themselves with Kantian deontology. Liberal reform, notably in John Stuart Mill's classic argument for decriminalization (1947), is phrased in utilitarian terms. In Mill, who combines doctrinal utilitarianism (1957) with remarkable sensitivity to Kantian values of autonomy (1947, chap. 3), we find bridge elements between the traditions, which we shall later emphasize.

II. Liberal Reform and H. L. A. Hart

H. L. A. Hart is a pivotal transitional figure, within the tradition of liberal reform, from the previously dominant utilitarian theories to the emerging theories of rights. Hart is the major contemporary exponent of legal positivism, the jurisprudence of utilitarian reform and reconstruction (Hart 1961b). His proposals for decriminalization, which have set the model for others, are characteristically utilitarian (1963). And, yet, at the same time, Hart's analyses of principles of just punishment (1968) made clear, prior to the recent reinvigoration of rights theories, that utilitarianism cannot explicate these principles.

A. Decriminalization and the Substantive Criminal Law

A remarkable fact, though one not usually perceived as such, is that the often eloquent literature calling for the decriminalization of "victimless crimes" (Kadish 1967; Packer 1968; Morris and Hawkins 1970) exclusively focuses on efficiency-based arguments of ending the pointless or positively counterproductive waste of valuable and scarce police resources expended in the enforcement of these laws. The pattern of argument and the litany of evils are familiar. The argument begins dismissively with H. L. A. Hart's tactical concession (1963, pp. 45, 52, 67–68), in his defense of the Wolfenden Report (Home Office 1957), that the acts in question (here, consensual adult homosexuality and prostitution) are immoral, and then discusses in detail the countervailing and excessive costs of law enforcement in this area. Commentators in the United States, following Hart's model, stress implicitly utilitarian pragmatist arguments, identifying tangible evils which intangible moralism appears quixotically and impractically to incur. The core problem is that these crimes are typically consensual and private. The absence of a complaining victim or a witness requires special enforcement efforts, including forms of police work (for example, entrapment) that are colorably unconstitutional, often clearly unethical, and eventually corruptive of police morals (see Skolnick 1966). Such high enforcement costs are then contrasted with the special difficulties in this area of securing sufficient evidence of conviction, of deterring the strong and ineradicable motives that often explain these acts, and of the opportunity costs thus foregone in terms of the more serious crimes on which police resources could have been expended. The utilitarian balance sheet, in conclusion, condemns the criminalization of such acts as simply too costly.

Such arguments proselytize the already converted and, remarkably, do not seriously engage the kind of justification to which proponents of "victimless crimes" traditionally appeal. Such proponents may reply that the consensual and private character of certain acts, and the consequent higher enforcement costs, should not suffice for decriminalization, for many such acts clearly are properly criminal (for example, dueling) and many other acts are also appropriately criminal though enforcement costs are comparable; many homicides, for example, are intrafamilial, thus involving high enforcement costs in intrusion into privacy and intimate relations (compare Junker 1972 and Kadish 1972). If there is good reason for criminalizing certain conduct, quite extraordinary enforcement costs will justly be borne. Accordingly, efficiency-based arguments for decriminalization, of the kind just described, appear to be deeply question-begging. They have weight only if the acts in question are not independently shown to be immoral or not seriously immoral, but the decriminalization literature dismissively concedes the immorality of such acts, and then elaborates efficiency costs that, apart from analysis of the morality of these acts, may properly be regarded as of little decisive weight.[6]

This remarkable absence of critical discussion of the focal issue that divides proponents and opponents of "victimless crimes" has made decriminalization arguments much less powerful than they can and should be. Indeed, utilitarian arguments may not have been decisive in the retreat of the scope of "victimless crimes," whether by legislative penal code revision or by judicial invocation of the constitutional right to privacy. In those areas where there has been wholesale or gradual decriminalization (for example, contraception, abortion, consensual noncommercial sexual relations between or among adults), the basis of change has crucially been one of moral judgments to the effect that these acts, traditionally believed to

[6] H. L. A. Hart, in this connection, draws a distinction between "conventional" and "critical" morality, but does not elaborate on the latter concept (1963, pp. 17–24).

be morally wrong per se, are not morally wrong (see Richards 1979a, 1979b). In order to complete and perfect decriminalization arguments so that they have the full force that they should have, one must supplement such arguments with moral analysis of a kind that they presuppose. The absence of such analysis has blinded us to the kinds of moral needs and interests that decriminalization serves. To this extent, legal theory has not responsibly brought to critical self-consciousness the nature of an important and humane legal development.[7]

This glaring gap derives from deeper philosophical pre-suppositions that the decriminalization literature appears often to assume—namely, the utilitarianism associated with Hart's legal positivism and, in the United States, the utilitarian prag-matism associated with legal realism (see Jacobsohn 1977; Twining 1973). From the publication of Holmes's *The Common Law* in 1881, American legal theory has followed the traditional legal positivist schizoid view about the proper analysis of moral values in the law. Traditional moral values underlying existing legal institutions are washed in cynical acid so that the legal institution may be analyzed without having to address any questions about its moral propriety (the separability of law and morals, which is the most characteristic mark of legal positivism as a philosophy of law; see Richards 1977a, pp. 11–22).[8] On the other hand, the enlightened moral criticism of legal institutions is conducted in terms of implicitly utilitarian calculations of maximizing the greatest happiness of the greatest number (Holmes 1881). There is not, because there cannot be, any seri-ous, nonutilitarian critical analysis of the moral values supposed to underlie "victimless crimes," because such values, being non-utilitarian, cannot be accommodated by the only enlightened critical morality that there is, namely utilitarianism.

[7] This is most evident in the area of commercial sex where the absence of critical moral thought about the putative immorality of prostitution has disabled reformers from identifying the best arguments in support of decriminalization in this area and has re-sulted in largely abortive attempts to achieve decriminalization. For an attempt to correct this defect, see Richards 1979a.
[8] The famous appeal to wash the law in cynical acid derives from Oliver Wendell Holmes's essay "The Path of the Law" (Holmes 1952, pp. 167–202).

B. The Principles of Just Punishment

The central feature of Hart's probing and incisive analyses of the moral foundations of the criminal law has been the incapacity of Benthamite utilitarianism to account for certain structural features of principles of just punishment in the way that Bentham supposed and a concomitant attack on the overemphasis on therapeutic reform which flowered in the work of critics and reformers who derive from Bentham. Both branches of Hart's analysis importantly anticipate the development of modern moral philosophies based on human rights.

Hart's attack on the utilitarian theory of just punishment focuses on Bentham's attempt to justify doctrines of personal culpability and fair warning, as preconditions of just punishment, on the basis of deterrence (Hart 1968, pp. 17–24). Bentham argues, for example, that Blackstone's insistence on personal culpability does not rest, as Blackstone supposed, on retributive ideas of an evil will but rather on the fact that only such requirements insure that the criminal law has some effect on conduct. Thus, an insane person who lacks capacity to conform conduct to law is exempt from criminal punishment not because he lacks personal culpability but because the criminal sanction can have no effect on such a person, and thus such pain would serve no purpose and be, on utilitarian grounds, immorally cruel. But, Bentham's argument, here and elsewhere, rests—so Hart points out—on "a spectacular non-sequitur" (p. 19); namely, it does not follow that, because the imposition of the criminal sanction would have no specific deterrent effect on a particular person, it would not have general deterrent effect on others. Indeed, it is not unlikely that, at least in some cases, emphasis on such general deterrent effects might make requirements of personal culpability and the like quite irrational, at least on utilitarian grounds. For example, the high costs of proving personal culpability and the risks of deception might make such requirements too costly; at least this might plausibly be true over some significant range of cases in which such costs might outweigh the insecurity people would feel at the absence of personal culpability requirements, for example, where general deterrence of very serious wrongs is demonstrably thus better secured and the insecurity is, in comparison, not significant. Nonetheless, Hart argues, we continue to regard the lack of personal culpability requirements in such cases as, *in principle*, unjust. In consequence, utilitarianism wholly fails to give proper expression to considered judgments of just punishment which even utilitarians claim to believe in.

Hart proposes that we reconceive the antagonism between natural rights and utilitarianism over the theory of punishment so that they address different normative issues. Natural rights theory argues that principles governing the *just distribution of criminal sanctions* (personal culpability requirements, fair warning, and the like) cannot be reduced to utilitarian aims and act as moral constraints on such aims. These principles, for Hart, are standards of fairness, which guarantee to persons the greatest liberty, compatible with an equal liberty for all, in planning, predicting, and controlling their lives so that they are subject to criminal sanctions only where they have fair capacity and opportunity to avoid such sanctions, and thus can fairly be regarded as personally responsible for the imposition of such sanctions on them (pp. 11–13, 40–50). While these ideas are not unlike Kantian concepts of moral autonomy, Hart, unlike Kant, does not argue that these ideas require any punishment in general or in particular. On this issue of the general *justifying aim for punishment*, Hart remains utilitarian (pp. 8–11, 71–89): within the constraints imposed by the principles of just punishment, the aim of punishment is broadly utilitarian, so that whether or how much to punish is determined by, inter alia, general deterrence evidence of how, at least cost, to secure conformity to desirable standards of conduct.

Hart's critical moral stance appears to be broadly one of moral pluralism; he attacks both utilitarianism and Kantian retributivism for making excessive claims, and tries to show, properly circumscribed, their respective roles in just punishment. His work in legal reform, like that of John Stuart Mill, evinces a deep attraction to Kantian ideas of personal autonomy, but, unlike Mill, also shows a clear sense of the limitations of utilitarianism as a comprehensive alternative moral theory.[9] Hart's work marks the transition to the theories of rights.

III. John Rawls and the Theory of Rights

John Rawls's *A Theory of Justice* (1971) attempts to state a defensible form of Kantian moral theory which preserves the attractions of Kant's general position without its nonempirical metaphysics or its sometimes unfortunate casuistry. For purposes of clarity of exposition, I first state the general matrix of values on which Kantian theory rests and its intuitive relation to ideas of human rights; then I turn to a summary of Rawls's construction and how it claims to explicate these values; finally, I sketch the views of later writers who derive from Rawls's pathbreaking book.

A. *Autonomy and Equality as the Values of Human Rights*

To think of persons as possessing human rights is to commit oneself to two crucial and interconnected normative assumptions: first, that persons have the capacity to be autonomous and, second, that persons are entitled, as persons, to equal concern and respect in exercising that capacity. When we accept these assumptions, we accept also the moral idea of rights (for expanded versions of the arguments in this section, see Richards 1977a).

Autonomy, in the sense fundamental to the theory of human rights, is an assumption about the capacities, developed or undeveloped, of persons. Persons have a range of capacities that enables them to develop, to want to act on, and to act on, higher-order plans of action that take as their object the individual's life and the way it is lived (see Richards 1971, pp. 65–68). For example, persons establish various kinds of priorities and schedules for the satisfaction of first-order, immediate desires. The satisfaction of certain wants, such as hunger, is regularized; the satisfaction of others is sometimes delayed. Indeed,

[9] For a striking attempt by Hart to construct a nonutilitarian theory of natural rights from Kantian premises, see Hart 1961a.

persons sometimes gradually eliminate certain self-criticized desires (smoking) or over time encourage the development of others (cultivating one's still undeveloped capacities for love and tender mutual response). Sometimes the exercise of such capacities of autonomy is rational or morally desirable; at other times it is irrational or morally wrong. Nevertheless, autonomy gives to persons the capacity to call their lives their own. The development of these capacities for separation and individuation is, from the earliest life of the infant, the central developmental task of becoming a person (see Mahler, Pine, and Bergman 1975; Kaplan 1978).

The concept of equality, treating persons as equals, is interpreted in terms of this capacity for autonomy. Because autonomy is so fundamental to the concept of what it is to be a person and because all are equal in their possession of it, all persons are entitled to equal concern and respect, as persons.

It is the autonomy-based interpretation of treating persons as equals, then, that underlies the notion of human rights. To attribute human rights to persons is to assess and criticize human institutions and relationships in terms of whether those institutions and relationships conform to principles of obligation and duty[10] that guarantee to each person equal concern and respect in exercising autonomy. The vision, ultimately, is one of persons, who, because of the effective exercise of their autonomy, are able to identify their lives as their own, having thus realized the inestimable moral and human good of having chosen one's life as a free and rational being.[11]

Accordingly, the revolution of human thought represented by the emergence and development of the idea of human rights derives from the fact that such rights recognize and foster equal concern and respect for the exercise of the autonomous capacities of persons. It is no accident that the progressive enlargement of the application of ideas of human rights, since Rousseau and Kant, has rested on the enlarged conception of

[10] For an account of principles of obligation and duty, see Richards 1971, pp. 92–106.

[11] A similar idea underlies John Stuart Mill's *On Liberty* (1947, especially chap. 3). For the idea of moral title to one's self, see Reiman 1976.

the class of humans believed to have autonomous capacities (e.g. racial and ethnic minorities and women) as well as the kinds of capacities that can be autonomously exercised (e.g. sexual autonomy).

Of course, people differ widely in their effective autonomy—the actual exercise of autonomous capacities. The idea of human rights, however, does not rest on actual autonomy, but only on the capacity for it. When John Stuart Mill eloquently argued against the subjection of women, he accepted for the purpose of argument that the women of his period were not actually autonomous (Mill 1970). His arguments for their rights rested not on their actual condition, which he conceded to be in large part slavish and emotionally dependent on men, but on their capacities for autonomy, however blunted and disfigured by traditional prejudices and conventions. Correspondingly, when people cogently vindicate the rights of putatively primitive people, their arguments do not rest on the idea that such people are effectively autonomous (although they may be), but on the assumption, at least, that these people have the capacity for autonomy.

Even in so-called developed countries, mature people differ widely in their effective autonomy. Human rights do not rest on effective autonomy, nor can they ensure its existence. Perhaps nothing can ensure effective autonomy. The process of achieving it is often risky and painful, and the process of maintaining it often incompletely secure. But the idea of human rights rests on the idea that seeing people in this way and regulating our conduct and institutions accordingly can facilitate the moving vision of persons as equals and independent, with servility and nonconsensual dependence reduced to a tolerable minimum.

The moral values of autonomy and equal concern and respect intuitively explain and justify features of the moral ideal of human rights: the character of rights as trumps over utilitarian considerations (Dworkin 1978a, pp. 90–94, 188–92), the weighing of rights only against other rights (pp. 184–205), and the special force of rights in justifying ultimate resistance (pp.

206–22). To see people as having the capacity for autonomy and entitled to equal concern and respect in the exercise of their personal independence is to deny the propriety of allowing utilitarian calculations of the greatest happiness of the greatest number to override the range of significant life choices facilitated by respect for rights and to require that considerations of rights be weighed only against considerations of rights of comparable weight. Utilitarianism, by definition, requires that the pattern of individual life choices be overridden if others are thus made better off in a way that maximizes utility over all. But this is precisely to assimilate human life choices into the judgments of one person, the sympathetic spectator whose pleasure is maximized if and only if the utilitarian principle is observed.[12] To treat persons in the manner required by utilitarianism is to focus obsessively on the aggregation of pleasure as the only ethically significant fact. Pleasure is treated as impersonal, and no weight is given to the separateness of individual interpretation of the creatures who experience it and, for whom, accordingly, it may have radically different weights and meanings. But, this treatment flatly ignores the ethically crucial facts that persons experience pleasure and that pleasure has moral significance only in the context of the life a person chooses to lead. In contrast, according rights rests on respect for autonomy—on the integrity of the person in leading his or her life (see Smart and Williams 1973, p. 77). Accordingly, the fundamental goal of morality must be, not the impersonal aggregation of pleasure, but the assurance that persons have been guaranteed conditions requisite for the developed capacity self-critically to choose how they will live their lives; ethical principles of obligation and duty rest upon and ensure that this is so, and correlatively define human rights.

B. Contractarian Theory and Human Rights

The task of interpreting human rights in terms of the focal values of autonomy and equal concern and respect has been

[12] For an account of the use of the device of a "sympathetic spectator" as a measure of social utility, see Richards 1971, pp. 86–91.

substantially furthered by the recent revival of contractarian theory in the work of John Rawls. His seminal writings explicate such rights and their institutionalization in American constitutional law in a way that the existing moral theories of constitutional thinkers—utilitarianism (see Thayer 1893; Bickel 1970, 1975) and value skepticism—cannot imitate.[13] The early great theorists of human rights—Locke, Rousseau, and Kant—whose ideas clearly influenced American constitutionalism, all invoked, explicitly or implicitly, contractarian metaphors in explaining the concrete implications of autonomy and equal concern and respect.[14] The basic moral vision of these theorists was that human institutions and relationships should be based on equal concern and respect for personal autonomy. The requirements of this moral point of view were expressed by the idea of a just society as one governed by an agreement or social contract arrived at by the consent of all persons, starting from a position of basic equality. Rawls's contractarian model has the great virtue of showing the continuing intellectual and moral vitality of this metaphor.

The basic analytic model is this: moral principles are those that perfectly rational persons, in a hypothetical "original position" of equal liberty, would agree to as the ultimate standards of conduct that are applicable to all (Rawls 1971, pp. 11–22). Persons in the original position are to be thought of as ignorant of any knowledge of their specific situations, values, or iden-

[13] See generally Judge Learned Hand's The Bill of Rights (1958). Also see Bickel 1970, in which a value skepticism similar to Hand's leads to a critique of moral reform through constitutional adjudication. Moral reflection and reform in the light of principles are to be replaced by unconscious moral historicism (pp. 174–75). These ideas represent a significant retreat from Bickel's earlier work (1962). Value skepticism and utilitarianism are often inextricably intertwined in the work of these theorists. The idea, invoked seminally by Holmes (1881), appears to be that one is skeptical of any nonutilitarian ideas but that utilitarian ideas are to be invoked in any proper policy analysis of the law. For a good statement of Holmes's value skepticism as a theory of the first amendment, see his dissent in Abrams v. United States, 250 U.S. 616 (1919). See also his famous dissenting observation: "The fourteenth Amendment does not enact Mr. Herbert Spencer's Social Statics," Lochner v. New York, 198 U.S. 45, 75 (1905).

[14] Kant did not expressly invoke a contractarian model in the way Locke and Rousseau did, but he clearly suggested it. See Kant, "Concerning the Common Saying: This May be True in Theory, But Does Not Apply in Practice" (1st ed. 1793), excerpted in Kant 1961. For Locke, see his Second Treatise, in Locke 1689. For Rousseau, see J. Rousseau, The Social Contract or Principles of Political Right (1st ed. Amsterdam 1762), reprinted in Rousseau 1950.

tities, but as possessing all knowledge of general empirical facts capable of interpersonal validation, and as holding all reasonable beliefs. They are not altruists but act from self-interest as representatives of themselves and their descendants. Since Rawls's concern is to apply this definition of moral principles to develop a theory of justice, he introduces into the original position the existence of conflicting claims to a limited supply of general goods and offers a specific set of principles to regulate these claims.[15]

The original position presents a problem of rational choice under uncertainty. Rational people in the original position have no way of predicting the probability that they will be rich or poor, black or white, of high or low social status, whether they will end up in any given situation of life. If a person agrees to principles of justice that permit deprivations of liberty and property rights and later discovers that he occupies a disadvantaged position, he will, by definition, have no just claim against deprivations that may render his life prospects meager and bitterly servile. To avoid such consequences, the rational strategy in choosing the basic principles of justice would be the conservative "maximin" strategy: one would seek to maximize the minimum condition, so that if one were born into the worst possible situation allowed by the adopted moral principles, he would still be better off than he would be in the worst situation allowed by other principles (Rawls 1971, pp. 150–61).

The choice of which fundamental principles of justice to adopt requires consideration of the weight assigned to general goods by those in the original position. "General goods"[16] are those things or conditions that all people desire as the generalized means to fulfillment of their individual life plans.[17] Lib-

[15] If there were goods in abundant superfluity or if people were more willing to sacrifice their interests for the good of others, the need for a moral system might be significantly different or even nonexistent. For David Hume's remarkable discussion of the conditions of moderate scarcity, see Hume, *A Treatise of Human Nature*, Bk. III, pt. II, sec. II (1st ed. 1739), reprinted in Hume 1961. See also Rawls 1971, p. 128.

[16] Rawls describes these general goods as "things which it is supposed a rational man wants whatever else he wants" (p. 92). The notion of rationality considered here is developed in Richards 1971, pp. 27–48, and in Rawls 1971, pp. 407–16.

[17] For the notion of a life plan, see Fried 1970, pp. 97–101, 155–82; Rawls 1971, pp. 407–16; Richards 1971, pp. 27–48, 63–74.

erty, understood as the absence of constraint, is usually considered to be one of these general goods. Similarly classifiable are powers, opportunities, and wealth (Rawls 1971, p. 92).

Among these general goods, self-respect or self-esteem, a concept intimately related to the idea of autonomy developed previously, occupies a place of special prominence (Rawls 1971, pp. 433, 440–46; Rawls 1980). Autonomy, seen now in the light of contractarian theory, is the capacity of persons to plan and shape their lives in accordance with changing desires and aspirations. As such, it involves such essentially human capacities as thought and deliberation, speech and craftsmanship. The competent exercise of such abilities in the pursuit of one's life plan forms the basis of self-respect—"the most important primary good" (Rawls 1971, p. 440)—without which one is liable to suffer from despair, apathy, and cynicism. Thus, persons in the original position, each concerned to create favorable conditions for the successful pursuit of their life plan, but ignorant of the particulars of their position in the resulting social order, would agree to regulate access to those general goods so as to maximize the possibility that every member of society will be able to achieve self-respect. Such considerations lead Rawls to interpret the general goods of liberty in terms of certain bundles of liberty which express respect for personal autonomy: liberties of thought and expression (freedom of speech, the press, religion, and association), civic rights (impartial administration of civil and criminal law in defense of property and person), political rights (the right to vote and participate in political constitutions), and freedom of physical, economic, and social movement.

Because such liberties are among the fundamental factors that shape a person's capacity to become a full rational being and to enjoy the life of such a being, the rational contractors of the model of political morality could not, consistent with the maximin strategy of rational choice, agree to any configuration of principles except the one providing equality in the distribution of these general goods. The maximin strategy calls for institutions that afford the most disadvantaged people a higher rational expectation of desire satisfaction than any alternative system would afford them. Use of the maximin strategy in choosing principles relating to liberty, then, tends to eliminate the disadvantaged class; the highest lowest condition is equality for all persons.

By contrast, once a certain minimum level of property and income is guaranteed, the rational interest in property and income is not as fundamental as that in liberty. Assuming the greatest amount of equal liberty and fair opportunity for all, inequalities in property and income above the minimum are tolerable if there are countervailing advantages. A relatively poor person, with full liberty and basic opportunity, may be better off in a system that allows inequalities in the distribution of wealth than in a system that requires equality: the consequences of inequality, for example, incentive effects on total production, may increase his absolute well-being although his relative share is less than it would be in a system with mandated equality of wealth.

For purposes of the theory of distributive justice which is his analytic concern, Rawls accordingly proposes (pp. 302–3) that the substantive principles of justice would include a principle of greatest equal liberty and opportunity consistent with a like liberty and opportunity for all; and, assuming that principle is fully satisfied, a principle permitting those differences in wealth which are necessary to make all classes better off than they would be under equality and make the worst off class as well off as possible (the difference principle).

Thus, Rawls's contractarian reconstruction provides an interpretation of the moral weight of autonomy (autonomy as a feature of the basic good of self-respect) and equality (the original position of equal liberty), and affords a decision-making procedure (the maximin strategy) which provides a determinate substantive account for the content of human rights as minimum conditions of human decency.

An important feature of the contractarian interpretation of autonomy is the assumption of ignorance of specific identity and the consequent requirement that a decision be reached on the basis of empirical facts capable of interpersonal validation. This assumption assures that the principles decided on in the original position will be neutral as between divergent visions of the good life, for the ignorance of specific identity deprives people of any basis for illegitimately distorting their decisions in favor of their own vision. Such neutrality, a fundamental feature of the idea of political right (see Dworkin 1978b; Richards 1980a) ensures to people the right to choose thei own lives autonomously.

C. Theorists of Rights in the Wake of Rawls

Rawls's book has given rise to an enormous and ever expanding literature of comment, criticism, and elaboration (see e.g. Daniels 1975; Wolff 1977; Barry 1973). The criticisms range from objections to the general model of morality (Barry 1973, pp. 10–33), to queries about the derivation of the substantive principles of justice Rawls offers from the model (Barry 1973, pp. 87–107), to various questions about the nature or interpretation of the substantive principles themselves (Daniels 1975, pp. 253–81).

We may broadly characterize that group of later commentators as theorists of rights who elaborate the paradigm that Rawls's work makes possible, in particular, continuing the antiutilitarian themes of Rawls's conception and the defensibility of some form of reconstruction of Kantian theory. These theorists of rights are, nonetheless, quite diverse. Some of them, like Robert Nozick (1974), focus on objections to certain specific aspects of Rawls's work, such as the egalitarian and redistributive implications of the difference principle and its underlying conception of human talents as subject to forms of regulation and incentive to advance the aims of the difference principle. Others, like Alan Gewirth (1978), present a striking alternative reconstruction of Kantian theory, which is broadly convergent with many of Rawls's substantive moral conclusons (see Richards 1979c, pp. 1409–14). Finally, legal philosophers have tried to show how the Rawls work clarifies general features of adjudication and the defensibility of some form of natu-

ral law theory (Dworkin 1978a) or specific controversies of adjudication or legislative reform (Richards 1973, 1974, 1977b,
1977c, 1979a, 1979b, 1979d). Others have developed general
conceptions of rights relevant to many areas of the law (Fried
1978) or specific neo-Kantian theories of specific substantive
bodies of law (e.g. Fletcher 1978; Epstein 1973, 1974).

These writers differ on many issues, but they appear to be at
one in their view of the implications of rights theories for an
alternative moral analysis of criminal law and institutions. Accordingly, I shall not here elaborate the nuances of difference
among them. Rather, for illustrative purposes and with no claim
to comprehensiveness, I shall use Rawls's general model to
examine the kind of analysis of the criminal law to which the
rights paradigm tends to lead. Rawls has not himself explicitly
focused his model on these questions (1971, pp. 575; cf. p. 241);
but two subsequent theorists who work within the rights perspective (Alan Gewirth and David Richards) have done so, and
I shall adapt contractarian theory to these questions in the spirit
of their work.

IV. The Moral Foundations of Criminal Law
and Institutions

It is commonly observed that the criminal law rests on the enforcement of public morality, that criminal penalties, inter alia,
identify and stigmatize certain moral wrongs which society at
large justifiably condemns as violations of the moral decency
whose observance defines the minimum boundary conditions of
civilized life (see e.g. Henry Hart 1958; Feinberg 1970). However, little critical attention has yet been given in Anglo-
American law to the proper elaboration of public morality in
light of considerations of the human rights to which constitutional democracy is in general committed. Rather, legal
theory and practice has tended to acquiesce in a quite questionable identification of the public morality with social convention.
We are now in a position to articulate an alternative account of
the moral foundations of the criminal law, which can illuminate

various criminal law doctrines, criminal justice institutions and practices, and the proper direction of criminal law reform.

The following discussion, adapting Rawls's maximining contractarian hypothesis to this issue, proposes certain basic principles that I believe would be agreed to as basic principles of critical morality which are to regulate conduct at large, because their observance would secure, at little cost to agents acting on them, forms of action or forebearance from action that rational persons would want guaranteed as minimal conditions of advancing the responsible pursuit of their ends, whatever they are.[18] Further, these principles will be so fundamental in securing the conditions of rational autonomy that, in general, coercion will be viewed as justified, as a last resort, in getting people to conform their conduct to these principles. Accordingly, these principles are commonly referred to as the ethical principles of obligation and duty, which define correlative rights.

One fundamental distinction between these principles of obligation and duty is that some apply in the state of nature, whether or not people are in institutional relation to one another, whereas others arise because of the special benefits that life in institutions and communities makes possible. I refer to the former as natural duties, the latter as institutional duties and obligations. With respect to natural duties, the principles include, at a minimum, a principle of nonmaleficence (not killing, not inflicting harm or gratuitous cruelty), mutual aid (securing a great good, like saving life, at little cost to the agent), consideration (not annoying or gratuitously violating the privacy of others), and paternalism (saving a person of impaired or undeveloped rationality from danger likely to cause death or severe and irreparable harm). With respect to institutional duties and obligations, the principles include basic principles of justice which regulate such institutions (legal and economic systems, conventions of promise-keeping and truth-telling, family and edu-

[18] For a detailed contractarian derivation of these principles, see Richards 1971, chaps. 7–10. The ideas developed in this and the following four paragraphs are developed at length in Richards 1971.

cational structure) and in appropriate circumstances require compliance with the requirements of such institutions (for example, paying taxes or respecting certain property rights). Now, all these principles of obligation and duty—natural and institutional—are formulated in quite complex terms; and priority relations are established among them to determine how, in general, conflicting obligations should be resolved and what the relative moral seriousness of offenses would be (the infliction of death, for example, is a graver violation of integrity than a minor battery). We do not have to pursue these complexities here. The general nature of such principles and their derivation from the moral imperative of treating persons as equals, however, seem clear: such principles secure to all persons on fair terms basic forms of action and forebearance from action which rational persons would want enforceably guaranteed as conditions and ingredients of living a life of self-critical integrity and self-respect. Correlatively, such principles define human or moral rights, whose weight as grounds for enforceable demands rests on the underlying moral principles of obligation and duty which justify such enforceable demands. Other moral principles are also agreed to or universalized, but they fall in an area, supererogation, which is not our present concern.

Because all the moral principles of obligation and duty are the proper objects of the use of force or coercion (an evil), ethical principles are agreed to or universalized that govern the distribution of this evil. Enforcement of such principles in the law takes place through the criminal law and the private remedies of the civil law (contracts, torts). While both the criminal and civil law rest on the moral foundations of the moral principles of obligation and duty, the grounds of enforcement differ in both cases: the criminal law rests on the punitive upholding of basic standards of moral decency, the civil law on moral principles of compensation. While some moral principles are enforced under both bodies of law (for example, the criminal and civil law of assault), others are enforced only under one body of law (for example, American law tends to prefer the civil law to remedy breaches of contract, where the promisee has the moral and legal right to extinguish or enforce the obligation).[19]

Our present concern is with ethical principles relevant to the just imposition of criminal sanctions, the principles of punishment. Generally, at least four relevant principles regulate the use of criminal sanctions to enforce moral obligations and duties.

First, the Kantian interpretation of treating persons as equals importantly puts special constraints on the imposition of criminal penalties for violations of moral duties and obligations, namely, that sanctions be applied only to persons who have broken a reasonably specific law, who had the full capacity and opportunity to obey the law, and who could reasonably have been expected to know that such a law existed. In this way, each person is guaranteed a greatest liberty, capacity, and opportunity of controlling and predicting the consequences of his or her actions compatible with a like liberty, capacity, and opportunity for all. Such a principle can be agreed to from the original position because it is a reasonable way to secure general respect for and compliance with moral principles at a tolerable cost. Because criminal sanctions are a form of humiliating stigma, persons in Rawls's original position would limit the application of such sanctions in order to secure their rational autonomy; for these conditions provide the fullest possible opportunity for people to avoid these sanctions if they so choose, or, at least, the fullest possible opportunity within the constraint that a system of coercive enforcement is justified to insure compliance with and respect for moral principles of obligation and duty. This principle forbids the application of criminal sanctions to an innocent person who has not broken the law or to persons lacking the liberty (the severely coerced),

[19] The moral analysis of why some of the principles of obligation and duty are enforced by the criminal law and others are not would require, I think, investigation of the costs of publicly enforceable sanctions versus the kind of gain to be obtained in greater regulation of conduct by the relevant principles. In general, public sanctions are expensive and draconian and would accordingly be reserved for the more serious moral offenses; others would be left to private law remedies and to informal forms of moral blame and criticism. For present purposes, it suffices that it is a necessary, though not sufficient, condition of criminal punishment that there be a violation of underlying moral principles of obligation and duty (see Richards 1971, chaps. 7–10).

the capacity (the insane, infants, involuntary acts) or full opportunity (those not reasonably apprised of the law) to regulate conduct by the relevant principles, even where the application of sanctions might have some deterrent effect in better enforcing moral principles. It also tends to render immune from criminal sanctions those unintentional actions that result from unforeseeable and unavoidable accidents, which there was no fair opportunity to avoid; or, at least, requires that liability only attach in such cases where the form of criminal sanction is not grave (e.g. where the penalty is a fine) or, perhaps, not an unfair risk of the conduct undertaken. In general, forms of mental state (intent, knowledge, and individualized standards of recklessness and negligence) are required as necessary moral conditions of just punishment because the presence of these mental states insures that the person may fairly be said to have had the capacity and opportunity to conform his conduct to the law. To the extent that intentional, as opposed to unintentionally negligent, actions involve easier or fuller opportunities to regulate conduct by principles, a higher gradation of sanction would, on this view, justly be applied to the former than the latter, other things being equal.

Second, given that the application of criminal sanctions is regulated by the principle of equal liberty, capacity, and opportunity, such sanctions must also observe two ethical principles of proportionality.

The first principle rests on the purpose of the criminal law to enforce and vindicate moral principles of obligation and duty: levels of sanctions must reflect the relative moral gravity of underlying moral wrongs. For example, since murder is morally graver than a minor battery, the level of sanction for murder must be greater than that for battery. This proportionality principle says nothing about the level at which sanctions should be set; it requires only that whatever sanctions may be justified on other grounds must reflect relative gravities of underlying moral wrongs.

The second moral principle of proportionality is more substantive. Since, from the ethical point of view of treating persons as equals, persons agree to or universalize principles of just punishment whether they are on the giving or receiving end, rational persons so situated are concerned to place substantive upper limits on the level of sanction that could be applied for moral wrongs in general or certain moral wrongs in particular. For example, certain forms of torture that are incompatible with respecting human dignity are ruled out, except in very extreme circumstances (see Shue 1978). In addition, rational contractors would place upper limits on sanctions for certain wrongs: death, for example, is never acceptable as an appropriate sanction for a minor battery or theft; such an extreme sanction cannot be rationally acceptable to persons who might be on the giving or receiving end, for the gains in moral conformity are incommensurate to the risks in punishment.

Third, within the contraints of all the above principles, criminal sanctions must satisfy the underlying purpose of affording an effective symbolic statement of minimal moral standards of decency. Effectiveness in this context should be measured by many factors—general deterrence, special deterrence, atonement, and moral reform. While theories of punishment commonly distinguish retributive and deterrent aims of criminal justice, I believe that, on analysis, these considerations are, within the contraints of the principles of equal liberty and proportionality, one: the justifying aim of criminal sanctions is to make a symbolic public statement about the importance of respecting certain basic human rights defined by moral principles of obligation and duty. There is, *pace* Kant (1965, pp. 99–108), no necessary connection between this aim and any particular form or level of criminal sanctions, including prisons.

There is no reason to accept intuitionistic notions of the intrinsic goodness of evil plus pain (Moore 1960, pp. 214–16; Ross 1930, pp. 57–58) or Kant's concept of the abstract obligation to punish evil in exactly the same kind. Rather, the central reasonable aim of criminal sanctions, from the point of view of treating persons as equals, is to make the required effective public statement justified by the special moral force of the underlying moral principles of obligation and duty and correlative moral rights. Which sanctions make this statement most effectively is a matter of humane empirical research among alternative forms of sanction to identify which ones best communicate respect for the underlying values of human dignity (Feinberg 1970, pp. 95–118), including, of course, forms of sanction that respect the moral personalities of offenders themselves. One corollary of this approach is that levels of sanctions must be rigorously scrutinized to ensure that the same level of effectiveness is not achievable with less severe sanctions, or less severe sanctions more certainly imposed. Any excess of sanctions above the level necessary for their effectiveness is morally gratuitous cruelty, because it is the infliction of pain not necessary to a purpose which rational persons would reciprocally agree to or universalize.

Fourth, on the assumption that a generally just legal system exists, rational persons would agree that the use of coercion in enforcing moral principles of obligation and duty, justified in an institutional state of nature, must be restricted to the legal system, except for certain special cases (for example, self-defense). The reason for this has been a prominent point made by the contractarian tradition, especially Locke (1689) and Kant:[20] when each person, in an institutional state of nature, himself acts as an enforcer of moral duties, he is judge, jury, and executioner in each case, including his own, and his judgment will often be distorted by personal interest and bias, selfish envy, and vindictiveness. The virtue of a just legal system, where the final appeal in the exercise of coercive power is to a group of impartial interpreters and executors of the law, is that distortions of judgments and execution are significantly reduced. This is simply to say that such legal institutions tend to be more just in their distribution of punishment: the persons who violate moral duties and obligations, which the law enforces, are more likely to be punished than in the state of nature, where distortions of judgments lead to applying coercion to the innocent, or applying coercion to the guilty to a degree

[20] On the grounds of the injustices endemic to the state of nature, Kant supposed there to be a moral obligation for persons to leave the state of nature and enter civil society. See Kant 1965, pp. 69–72.

that is out of all proportion to the requirements of effective deterrence. For this reason, when a just legal system exists, coercion is justified in enforcing moral duties and obligations, in general, only when these requirements can be effectively enforced by law;[21] those duties and obligations which cannot be effectively enforced by law must be, at best, left to informal forms of criticism and blame.

V. Concrete Implications for Criminal Law and Its Institutions

Theories should be judged by their explanatory power. As the preceding section suggests, the contractarian rights perspective importantly informs analysis of the scope of the criminal law, its provisions, and the sanctions which it occasions and legitimates.[22] Thus the criminal law's proviso that only voluntary acts be punished; the mens rea requirements that inflicted harms whether by commission or omission be made criminally culpable only when accompanied by a conscious purpose or knowledge or individualized standard of recklessness or negligence; and the existence of excusing defenses such as insanity and duress all derive from the notion that the criminal law is the way in which basic rights of moral decency, defined by ethical principles of obligation and duty, are enforced. Since the values underlying these rights are those of equal concern and respect for autonomy, people are only justly subject to such sanctions when each, compatible with like treatment for all, has been given a fair chance to avoid such sanctions. In short, per-

---

[21] For this purpose, I view both the criminal law and the remedies of the civil law as means of enforcement. Certain moral rights, relating, for example, to keeping informal promises and the like, may not be appropriately enforced either by the criminal or civil law, on the ground that they relate to forms of personal relationship that are more effectively regulated, given the interests involved, by forms of blame and criticism (see Henry Hart & Sacks 1958, pp. 477–78). Many times, the moral interests thus protected will be of acute human significance, for example, personal interests against the betrayals of friends or lovers. The underlying quality of informal and spontaneous attachment of such relationships, however, is not compatible with the forms of coercive enforcement by law.

[22] I have elsewhere attempted to elaborate the implications of rights theories on several such matters (Richards 1977a, 1979a, 1979c).

sons may justly be criminally sanctioned as an example to others only after a showing of the exercise or failure of exercise of capacities of choice and deliberation that could fairly have obviated the sanctions. Those basic criminal law requirements are a minimal aspect of this requirement, for, without it, people would be subject to criminal sanctions for conduct which bore no marks of personal responsibility (see Richards 1977a, pp. 199–202).

This final section outlines some of the implications of a rights perspective for thinking about two questions: decriminalization and the proper scope of the criminal law, and the proportional imposition of sanctions.

A. Decriminalization and the Scope of the Criminal Law

Students of the criminal law, like George Fletcher, who otherwise rightly urge the relevance of Kantian moral theory in understanding the substantive criminal law err in not applying moral theory to the question of the proper scope of the criminal law (see Fletcher 1978; Richards 1979c, pp. 1427–28). It is certainly true that not all unethical acts are criminal; even some acts violative of moral principles of obligation and duty are not criminalized. However, no act that is not, on examination, morally wrong is properly the subject of serious criminal penalties; to the extent the criminal law does criminalize such acts, it is justly the subject of moral criticism and constitutional attack. Theorists of the criminal law, who lavish much theoretical concern on understanding the moral foundations of mens rea or the excusing defenses and who justly criticize failures to conform to these foundations (e.g. Fletcher 1978; Hart 1968), should bring comparable energy to bear on the substantive scope of proper criminal liability. We do not, as judges or lawyers or persons, at any point abdicate our moral responsibility for applying to ethical questions the kinds of reasoning, treating persons as equals, that is alone properly ethical. (For recent philosophical attempts to explicate this idea, see Baier 1958; Donagan 1977; Fried 1978; Gauthier 1963; Gewirth 1978; Grice 1967; Hare 1963; Rawls 1971; Richards 1977a).

The rights perspective on the moral foundations of the criminal law enables us to reinterpret contemporary debates over decriminalization and the limits of the criminal sanction in a striking way that confirms the main conclusions of liberal reformers like John Stuart Mill but does so on the basis of a moral theory deriving from Kant. There is an important converging strain in the moral theories of Kant and Mill, namely, the central role in ethics of equal concern and respect for autonomy. Liberalism rests on a certain view of the *person*, namely, that persons, as such, have capacities I earlier described as the higher-order capacities self-critically to evaluate and order their first-order, immediate desires. Thus, Kant, who is the most profound philosophical theorist of liberalism, identifies personhood in the capacity of persons to be "sovereigns in the kingdom of ends," to be *ends in themselves* (Kant 1959, p. 53), to think self-critically about their ends and to take, as the central task of personhood, how to live their lives. When John Stuart Mill sought to elaborate similar values as at the core of liberal political theory, he wrote of the central importance of persons choosing plans of life for themselves, identifying persons' relations to their lives as the highest creative task of humans: "Among the works of man, which human life is rightly employed in perfecting and beautifying, the first in importance surely is man himself" (Mill 1947, p. 59). Mill's interpretation of autonomy supplements Kant's with a special concern for facilitating that independence from custom and convention by which a person is enabled, in Mill's memorable phrase, "to fit him with a life" (p. 68).

Kant and Mill unite in their focal emphasis on giving weight to respecting and fostering the natural capacity for independence of domination by others and for self-critical control over our lower-order desires. For Kant, ethics is the point of view which requires that we regulate our conduct by principles which respect the equal dignity of each person in exercising this capacity. Kant's theory of ethics is deeper than Mill's in explaining the ethical requirement of treating persons as equals in terms of this capacity; Mill ultimately interprets equality in terms of the capacity for pleasure or pain.[23]

The idea of human rights is a corollary of the Kantian interpretation of treating persons as equals by virtue of their autonomy. An important feature of this perspective, as Dworkin has noted (1978b), is a neutral theory of the good: the ethical principles which define rights assure to persons, on fair terms to all, their dignified independence in designing a life as free and rational creatures, and are accordingly broadly neutral on the question of what is good for any particular person. To say that these principles entertain a neutral theory of the good, however, is not to say that they do not take relevant consequences into account.[24] Clearly, the Kantian interpretation of treating persons as equals presupposes a certain view of human nature (for example, the natural capacity for autonomy); and, the content of needs rational persons tend to have (for example, not being killed or harmed; or, needs for food and shelter; or, the ingredients of the development of critical rationality). Such considerations, however, are compatible with many disparate visions of the good life. The idea of human rights, without answering the question of what is good for any particular person, secures the minimum conditions which enable free and rational persons to design their lives. Once rights are secured, persons are, to pursue Mill's aesthetic metaphor, to face the highest creative task of human life—to make a life. To this extent, rights embody a deontological concept: rights are defined independently of maximizing the good; they set the boundary conditions or constraints within which people on fair terms are free to define their own good.

This autonomy-based interpretation of treating persons as equals enables one to understand and defend, in terms of Kant-

[23] Mill appears to regard his analysis of autonomy as identifying an interest to which a person would rationally give a greater weight than other forms of desire satisfactions, and thus the greater weight of this form of desire satisfaction accounts for the normative weight which the utilitarian principle would give to the cultivation of this interest. For his distinction between higher and lower pleasures, see Mill 1947, chap. 2. For his statement about the rational attractions of autonomy, see Mill 1957, chap. 3.

[24] For examples of this mistake see Posner 1979 and Ackerman 1977.

ian ethics, Mill's general right "of framing the plan of our life to suit our own character . . . without impediment from our fellow creatures, so long as what we do does not harm them, even though they should think our conduct foolish, perverse, or wrong" (Mill 1947, p. 6). Mill's right of personal autonomy assumes as its background the moral principles of obligation and duty discussed earlier. Mill does not argue that the right of personal autonomy legitimates a general right of amoralism or immoralism, that is, not treating persons as equals. Indeed, the whole point of liberalism, correctly understood, is to make treating persons as equals the central tenet of political and constitutional morality. Mill's argument, rather, is that ethical principles, correctly understood, allow circumscription of personal autonomy only when the person's actions harm palpable interests of others; in particular, there is no appropriate ethical ground for interfering with personal autonomy on the paternalistic ground of advancing the interests of the actor alone. The background of Mill's argument is, of course, Victorian moralism which Mill perceived as, without any reasonable ethical justification, interfering in people's personal lives, in effect, enforcing a tyranny of majoritarian convention which Mill believed to erode the foundations of autonomous personhood. Mill's argument against any legitimate ethical interference on paternalistic grounds is overstated; his own argument shows that he believed in a just scope for paternalism in the cases of children and "backward states of society" (1947, p. 10) and even in certain cases of imminent harm to any unwary adult (pp. 97–98). Clearly, a principle of paternalism, limited to cases of extreme irrationality or nonrationality likely to harm serious human interests (for example, life) irreparably, is ethically justified (Richards 1971, pp. 192–95). Mill refused to formulate any such general principle, though he has invoked several specific applications of it, because he took seriously the extreme abuses of paternalistic (applied, for example, to women) as well as moralistic arguments of his period (Mill 1970). Many forms of majoritarian incursion into people's personal lives could not, Mill believed, be justified by any ethical principle (including paternalism) which treats persons as equals. Accordingly, Mill formulated a simply and not easily abused principle which roughly articulates that, outside the scope of principles which treat persons as equals, there is a general right to personal autonomy. Because paternalistic arguments may have appeared to him intrinsically prone to abuse, he formulated his principle of noninterference overbroadly but with dramatic and cogent simplicity: the *only* warrant for interference with an agent is that the agent's actions harm the palpable interests of others (1947, p. 6).

The general thrust of Mill's argument is clarified by the autonomy-based interpretation of treating persons as equals. A certain class of background ethical principles (namely, the principles of obligation and duty), which express the idea of treating persons as equals, does limit the scope of the right of personal autonomy. These principles, as earlier suggested, define minimal moral rights of social decency, which are the necessary moral conditions for the proper application of the criminal sanction. Accordingly, these principles limit personal autonomy wherever countervailing rights are involved; but, once such rights are not in issue, persons have a general right of personal autonomy. The right of personal autonomy grounds a general prohibition on forms of coercive interference with this right, for, as Mill has clearly suggested (1947, chap. 3), only by allowing people themselves to assume final normative responsibility in making these choices can one secure the desired respect for the basic higher-order capacities of the person as a free and rational being.

Autonomy is a natural capacity which may be encouraged or frustrated in various ways depending on one's purposes. An autonomy-based ethics takes the normative attitude that the capacity is not only to be encouraged, but to be affirmatively defended—on the ground that in this way people better realize their capacities for free and dignified personhood. Mill's argument is that constitutional democracy, committed to the liberal interpretation of treating persons as equals, must affirmatively extend such a right in defense of those persons whose moral freedom is illegitimately denied by forms of social convention which are not grounded in the ethical imperative of treating persons as equals. Mill is acutely sensitive, unlike Kant, to the degree to which social convention blinds people to the moral freedom they possesss, disfiguring and distorting their capacity to take an attitude toward their lives which Mill likens to that of the creative artist with a willingness to explore, to try experiments in living, to take risks with one's talents, to be open and vulnerable to the impulses of creative design (Mill 1947, pp. 56, 59). Accordingly, an autonomy-based theory of ethics *requires* an affirmative moral right that people be protected from social conventions that are not grounded in treating persons as equals, so that people are encouraged to realize their moral freedom. For Mill, the gravamen of tyrannous convention was Victorian moralism, which he took systematically to violate the right to personal autonomy by its excessive criminalization and social condemnation of acts which do not violate the moral rights of others; Mill took women to be a central example of persons whose moral freedom had, by unjust social convention, been disfigured.

This account illuminates the general nature of arguments for decriminalization in a way efficiency-based arguments cannot. The crucial arguments for decriminalization are that the acts in question, on critical examination, are not immoral, and that those acts do not, in principle, fail to treat persons as equals in the ethically fundamental sense. There is no defensible criterion for the immorality of acts or persons other than treating persons as equals. Consensual homosexuality or prostitution, for example, do not violate this imperative; the criminal and social condemnation of them clearly do. Accordingly, criminal statutes such as those that prohibit consensual homosexual relations unethically distort the moral freedom people in fact possess and can be justly condemned as violations of the right to personal autonomy.

B. Punishment and Proportionality

On the model of just punishment proposed above, punishment and the criminal justice institutions which express it are based on the symbolic vindication of basic moral principles of obligation and duty, defining minimum conditions of social decency, within the constraints of principles of justice. The role of the criminal law and its institutions is to afford an appropriate dramaturgy expressive of the forms of moral condemnation resting on these principles, namely, the denunciation of failures of responsible people to give due weight, in the exercise of their personal autonomy, to the rights of others. The whole force of punishment depends on its expressing the appropriate attitude to its natural object, personal responsibility. The prevalent utilitarian punishment institutions are inconsistent with this aim.

The considerations of just punishment earlier advanced suggested two aspects of proportionality rooted in treating persons as equals: first, that the gradations among criminal sanctions reflect the relative gravities of underlying moral wrongs; and second, that upper limits be placed on the kind of sanctions in general (for example, death for a quite trivial offense).

The present theory explains the moral basis for these principles (rooted, as they are, in the expression of underlying ideas of human rights) in a way which utilitarianism cannot. As Stephen observed (1967, pp. 152–54), for a utilitarian rationale of punishment, it would make no sense to impose a lesser sanction on a person who committed a theft out of great temptation from realistic privation and need than on a wealthy person who committed the same crime but "for kicks," for greater deterrent effectiveness would be secured by imposing a higher sanction on the former than on the latter since more of a sanction would be required to overcome the temptation. But, one could argue that the poor man, who appears less culpable, should receive a lesser sentence than the other. Rights theories, which ground such proportionality concerns in the reflection of underlying perceptions of culpability and gravity of moral wrongs, explain and support such judgments, which may, in a particular case, call for higher or lower punishments as the case may be.

Recent critics of the criminal justice system, like Norval Morris (1974), focus not merely on the failure of rehabilitative programs but on their immorality, their failure to respect human rights (pp. 26–27). Critics like Frankel (1973), Morris (1974), and von Hirsch (1976) argue, in consequence, that discretion in sentencing, probation, and parole must be radically limited, if not eliminated altogether.

The moral analysis here proposed supports both the criticisms and the general line of recommendations of such writers. On the view here proposed, the central aim of criminal justice is to express and vindicate underlying moral principles of obligation and duty consistent with principles of justice. A salient mark of this approach is one aspect of the principle of proportionality, namely, that criminal sanctions must reflect and express underlying gradations both of the seriousness of moral wrongs and of the moral culpability of agents. The methods of utilitarianism wreak havoc with this objective, indeed, are not able to account for it and, in their focus on rehabilitation, fundamentally violate it, leading to the unjust American patterns of sentencing and probation and parole that are unjustified by proportionality considerations of any kind. In contrast, theorists of human rights, like Kant, have been centrally absorbed in giving expression, in their theories of punishment, to equality and fair dealing among criminals. Kant's mode of so doing, by his qualitative and in-kind equivalences, cannot be justified, but his concern—treating like cases alike—must be given expression by any conception of punishment that claims to respect human rights.

In order to do so, a just theory of punishment must, at a minimum, insist on some articulation of standards which determine the gravity of offenses and the culpability of offenders, and some standards for weighing these considerations, at least in paradigmatic cases of conflict, and, of course, some form of appellate review which ensures patterns of consistency in the application of such standards. Such standards would govern clearly at the sentencing stage, and probably would require concomitant reforms in the plea bargaining process; probation practices, accordingly, would be rationalized; and parole policies radically circumscribed, if not eliminated. Such reforms, in addition to being intrinsically more just on grounds of proportionality, would discourage the manipulative ethos that present parole policies encourage, clearly communicating to criminals the moral discriminations which their conduct culpably violated.

VI. Natural Rights and Utilitarianism Reassessed

I earlier identified four focal differences between natural rights and utilitarian theories in the context of my examination of Kant and Bentham: first, decriminalization (Kant's defense of the traditional scope of the criminal law, Bentham's and later Mill's attack thereon); second, structural principles of criminal justice (Kant grounding them in autonomy, Bentham, in a specious argument, on general deterrence); third, the role of general deterrence (Kant ignoring it altogether, Bentham giving it fundamental weight); and fourth, discretion (Kant's attack thereon, Bentham's implicit celebration thereof). In view of the discussion above, we are now in a position to transcend these sterile divisions. The recent rebirth of serious deontological moral theory and the consequent jurisprudence of rights enable us to reassess these antagonisms and to construct a theory and practice of just punishment which gives full expression to the complex of considerations which should govern these matters.

To summarize, first, issues of decriminalization should not be conducted exclusively in efficiency-based utilitarian terms. On examination in light of recent theories of human rights, arguments for decriminalization are, in fact, most reasonably conducted in terms of human rights, which the overextension of the criminal law (for example, into consensual adult sexuality) egregiously violates.

Second, the place of structural principles of just punishment in the criminal law cannot be explained on utilitarian grounds but can be given solid foundations in human rights considerations of respect for personal autonomy.

Third, there is no reason why considerations of general deterrence cannot play a fundamental role in the concept of just punishments required by a human rights perspective. Kant's rejection of general deterrence is rooted in his metaphysical theory of moral freedom as acausal indeterminism, but Rawls and his followers have shown that there is no necessary connection between the explication and elaboration of the Kantian autonomy-based interpretation of treating persons as equals and causal indeterminism. Indeed, in recent work, Rawls has insisted that the full understanding of his construction and the fundamental level of social choice at which it operates requires taking very seriously indeed the causal role of social and economic institutions in shaping our lives (Rawls 1978, pp. 47–71). Once human rights theory is disencumbered from causal indeterminism, general deterrence takes a role in determining just punishment which Kant, wedded to metaphysical notions of absolute freedom, could not give it. In short, the traditional utilitarian concerns for assessing the propriety of sanctions in terms of effectiveness (for example, emphasizing certainty, over severity, of sanctions) have a place in the human rights assessment of criminal justice.

Fourth, the utilitarian rationale for reform and discretion violates human rights. In order to justify this judgment, we do not have to accept Kantian equivalences (which probably rest on his theory of absolute freedom), but we do have to take seriously the deeper values of human rights which Kant was trying to articulate, namely, respect for the personal responsibility of criminals.

The results of our inquiry may surprise. On the one hand, human rights arguments can be deployed against standard moralistic arguments for overcriminalization. On the other hand, human rights arguments support standard utilitarian positions for decriminalization and the central normative role of general deterrence but critically attack the discretion-centered utilitarian prescriptions for punishment and the role of discretion in criminal practice. That is my point. Correctly understood, the burgeoning jurisprudence of rights enables us to transcend the sterile traditional antagonism between natural rights and utilitarianism—to acknowledge the moral foundations of the criminal law and yet, consistent with the best traditions of humane liberal reform, to develop and deploy sharper tools of ethical criticism in terms of the values under which we realize and express, on fair terms to all, our moral and rational dignity.

REFERENCES

Ackerman, Bruce. 1977. *Private Property and the Constitution*. New Haven: Yale University Press.
Baier, Kurt. 1958. *The Moral Point of View*. Ithaca, N.Y.: Cornell University Press.
Barry, Brian. 1973. *The Liberal Theory of Justice*. Oxford: Clarendon Press.
Bazelon, David L. 1976. "The Morality of the Criminal Law," *Southern California Law Review* 49:385–405.
Beccaria, Cesare. 1963. *On Crimes and Punishments*. Translated by Henry Paolucci. Indianapolis: Bobbs-Merrill. Originally published 1764.
Bentham, Jeremy. 1817. *Papers Relative to Codification and Public Instruction*. London: Payne and Foss.
———. 1843. *Works*. Edited by John Bowring. London: Simpkin Marshall.
———. 1853. "Anarchical Fallacies, Being an Examination of the Declaration of Rights, Issued during the French Revolution," *Works of Jeremy Bentham* 2:488–526.
———. 1864. *Theory of Legislation*. Edited by R. Hildreth, London: Trubner.
———. 1948. *Principles of Morals and Legislation*. New York: Hafner.
———. 1978. "Offences against One's Self: Paederasty," Parts I, II, *Journal of Homosexuality* 3:389–405; 4:91–107.
Bickel, Alexander M. 1962. *The Least Dangerous Branch*. Indianapolis: Bobbs-Merrill.
———. 1970. *The Supreme Court and the Idea of Progress*. New York: Harper and Row.
———. 1975. *The Morality of Consent*. New Haven: Yale University Press.
Bradley, F. H. 1962. *Ethical Studies*. 2d ed. Oxford: Clarendon Press.
Daniels, Norman. 1975. *Reading Rawls*. New York: Basic Books.

Donagan, Alan. 1977. *The Theory of Morality*. Chicago: University of Chicago Press.
Dworkin, Ronald. 1978a. *Taking Rights Seriously*. Cambridge, Mass.: Harvard University Press.
———. 1978b. "Liberalism." In *Public and Private Morality*, ed. Stuart Hampshire. New York: Cambridge University Press.
Epstein, Richard. 1973. "A Theory of Strict Liability," *Journal of Legal Studies* 2:151–204.
———. 1974. "Defenses and Subsequent Pleas in a System of Strict Liability," *Journal of Legal Studies* 3:165–215.
———. 1975. "Intentional Harms," *Journal of Legal Studies* 4:391–442.
Feinberg, Joel. 1970. *Doing and Deserving: Essays in the Theory of Responsibility*. Princeton: Princeton University Press.
Fletcher, George P. 1972. "Fairness and Utility in Tort Theory," *Harvard Law Review* 85:537–73.
———. 1978. *Rethinking Criminal Law*. Boston: Little, Brown.
Foucault, Michel. 1977. *Discipline and Punish*. Translated by Alan Sheridan. New York: Pantheon.
Frankel, Marvin E. 1973. *Criminal Sentences*. New York: Hill and Wang.
Fried, Charles. 1970. *An Anatomy of Values*. Cambridge, Mass.: Harvard University Press.
———. 1978. *Right and Wrong*. Cambridge, Mass.: Harvard University Press.
Gauthier, David P. 1963. *Practical Reasoning*. Oxford: Clarendon Press.
Gewirth, Alan. 1978. *Reason and Morality*. Chicago: University of Chicago Press.
Grice, Geoffrey R. 1967. *The Grounds of Moral Judgment*. Cambridge: Cambridge University Press.
Halevy, E. 1955. *The Growth of Philosophical Radicalism*. Translated by Mary Morris. London: Faber and Guyer.
Hand, Learned. 1958. *The Bill of Rights*. Cambridge, Mass.: Harvard University Press.
Hare, R. M. 1952. *The Language of Morals*. New York: Oxford University Press.
———. 1963. *Freedom and Reason*. Oxford: Clarendon Press.
Hart, H. L. A. 1961a. "Are There Any Natural Rights?" In *Society, Law, and Morality*, ed. F. Olafson. Englewood Cliffs, N.J.: Prentice-Hall.
———. 1961b. *The Concept of Law*. Oxford: Clarendon Press.
———. 1963. *Law, Liberty, and Morality*. Stanford, Calif.: Stanford University Press.

————. 1968. *Punishment and Responsibility*. London: Oxford University Press.

————. 1979. "Between Utility and Rights." In *The Idea of Freedom*, ed. A. Ryan. London: Oxford University Press.

Hart, Henry. 1958. "The Aims of the Criminal Law," *Law and Contemporary Problems* 23:401–41.

Hart, Henry M., and Albert M. Sacks. 1958. *The Legal Process*. Tentative ed. New York: Columbia University Law School.

Holmes, Oliver Wendell. 1952. *Collected Legal Papers*. New York: Harcourt, Brace and Howe.

————. 1881. *The Common Law*. Boston: Little, Brown.

Home Office, Scottish Home Department. 1957. *Report of the Committee on Homosexual Offenses and Prostitution*. No. 247. London: H.M. Stationery Office.

Hume, David. 1961. "A Treatise of Human Nature, Book III, part II, section II." In *Society, Law, and Morality*, ed. F. Olafson. Englewood Cliffs, N.J.: Prentice-Hall.

Jacobsohn, Gary J. 1977. *Pragmatism, Statesmanship, and the Supreme Court*. Ithaca, N.Y.: Cornell University Press.

Junker, John. 1972. "Criminalization and Criminogenesis," U.C.L.A. Law Review 19:697–714.

Kadish, Sanford H. 1967. "The Crisis of Overcriminalization," *Annals of the American Academy of Political and Social Science* 374:154–70.

————. 1972. "More on Overcriminalization: A Reply to Professor Junker," *U.C.L.A. Law Review* 19:719–22.

Kant, Immanuel. 1959. *Foundations of the Metaphysics of Morals*. Translated by L. W. Beck. Indianapolis: Bobbs-Merrill.

————. 1961. "Concerning the Common Saying: This May Be True in Theory, But Does Not Apply in Practice." In *Society, Law, and Morality*, ed. F. Olafson. Englewood Cliffs, N.J.: Prentice-Hall.

————. 1963. *Lectures on Ethics*. Translated by Louis Infield. London: Methuen.

————. 1964. *The Metaphysical Principles of Virtue*. Translated by James Ellington. Indianapolis: Bobbs-Merrill.

————. 1965. *The Metaphysical Elements of Justice*. Translated by John Ladd. Indianapolis: Bobbs-Merrill.

Kaplan, Louise. 1978. *Oneness and Separateness*. New York: Simon and Schuster.

Locke, John. 1960. *Second Treatise of Government*. In *Locke's Two Treatises of Government*, ed. P. Laslett. Cambridge: Cambridge University Press. Originally published 1689.

Mahler, M., F. Pine, and A. Bergman. 1975. *The Psychological Birth of the Human Infant*. New York: Basic Books.

Michelman, Frank I. 1967. "Property, Utility, and Fairness: Comments on the Ethical Foundations of 'Just Compensation' Law," *Harvard Law Review* 80:1165–1258.

———. 1973. "In Pursuit of Constitutional Welfare Rights: One View of Rawls' Theory of Justice," *University of Pennsylvania Law Review* 121:962–1019.

Mill, John Stuart. 1947. *On Liberty.* Edited by Alburey Castell. New York: F. S. Crofts. Originally published 1869.

———. 1957. *Utilitarianism.* Edited by Oskar Piest. Indianapolis: Bobbs-Merrill.

———. 1970. "The Subjection of Women." In *Essays on Sex Equality,* ed. A. S. Rossi. Chicago: University of Chicago Press.

Moore, G. E. 1960. *Principia Ethica.* Cambridge: Cambridge University Press.

Morris, Norval. 1974. *The Future of Imprisonment.* Chicago: University of Chicago Press.

Morris, Norval, and Gordon Hawkins. 1970. *The Honest Politician's Guide to Crime Control.* Chicago: University of Chicago Press.

Morse, Stephen J. 1976. "The Twilight of Welfare Criminology: A Reply to Judge Bazelon," *Southern California Law Review* 49:1247–68.

Nozick, Robert. 1974. *Anarchy, State, and Utopia.* New York: Basic Books.

Packer, Herbert L. 1968. *The Limits of the Criminal Sanction.* Stanford, Calif.: Stanford Univerdity Press.

Posner, Richard. 1979. "Utilitarianism, Economics, and Legal Theory," *Journal of Legal Studies* 8:103–40.

Rawls, John. 1971. *A Theory of Justice.* Cambridge, Mass.: Harvard University Press.

———. 1978. "The Basic Structure as Subject." In *Values and Morals,* ed. A. I. Goldman and J. Kim. Dordecht, Holland: D. Reidel.

———. 1980. "Kantian Constructivism," *Journal of Philosophy* 77:515–35.

Reiman, Jeffrey H. 1976. "Privacy, Intimacy, and Personhood," *Philosophy and Public Affairs* 6:26–44.

Reiss, Hans S. 1970. *Kant's Political Writings.* Cambridge: Cambridge University Press.

Richards, David A. J. 1971. *A Theory of Reasons for Action.* Oxford: Clarendon Press.

———. 1973. "Equal Opportunity and School Financing: Toward a Moral Theory of Constitutional Adjudication," *University of Chicago Law Review* 41:32–71.

———. 1974. "Free Speech and Obscenity Law: Towards a Moral

Theory of the First Amendment," *University of Pennsylvania Law Review* 123:45–91.

——. 1977a. *The Moral Criticism of the Law*. Encino, Calif.: Dickenson.

——. 1977b. "Rules, Policies, and Neutral Principles: The Search for Legitimacy in Common Law and Constitutional Adjudication," *Georgia Law Review* 11:1069–1114.

——. 1977c. "Unnatural Acts and the Constitutional Right to Privacy: A Moral Theory," *Fordham Law Review* 45:1281–1348.

——. 1979a. "Commercial Sex and the Rights of the Person: A Moral Argument for the Decriminalization of Prostitution," *University of Pennsylvania Law Review* 127:1195–1287.

——. 1979b. "Sexual Autonomy and the Constitutional Right to Privacy: A Case Study in Human Rights and the Unwritten Constitution," *Hastings Law Journal* 30:957–1018.

——. 1979c. "Human Rights and the Moral Foundation of the Substantive Criminal Law," *Georgia Law Review* 13:1395–1446.

——. 1979d. "The Theory of Adjudication and the Task of the Great Judge," *Cardozo Law Review* 1:171–218.

——. 1980a. "Human Rights and Moral Ideals: An Essay in the Moral Theory of Liberalism," *Social Theory and Practice* 5:461–88.

Ross, W. D. 1930. *The Right and the Good*. Oxford: Clarendon Press.

Rothman, David J. 1971. *The Discovery of the Asylum: Social Order and Disorder in the New Republic*. Boston: Little, Brown.

——. 1980. *Conscience and Convenience: The Asylum and Its Alternatives in Progressive America*. Boston: Little, Brown.

Rousseau, Jean Jacques. 1950. "The Social Contract or Principles of Political Right." In *The Social Contract and Discourses*, trans. G. Cole. London: J. M. Dent.

Shue, Henry. 1978. "Torture," *Philosophy and Public Affairs* 7:124–43.

Skolnick, Jerome H. 1966. *Justice without Trial*. New York: Wiley.

Smart, J., and B. Williams. 1973. *Utilitarianism For and Against*. Cambridge: Cambridge University Press.

Stephen, James Fitzjames. 1885. *A History of the Criminal Law of England*. Vol. 2. London: Macmillan.

——. 1967. *Liberty, Equality, and Fraternity*. Edited by R. J. White. Cambridge: Cambridge University Press. Originally published 1873.

Thayer, James B. 1893. "The Origin and Scope of the American Doctrine of Constitutional Law," *Harvard Law Review* 7:129–56.

Twining, William L. 1973. *Karl Llewellyn and the Realist Movement*. London: Weidenfeld and Nicolson.

von Hirsch, Andrew. 1976. *Doing Justice: The Choice of Punishments*.

New York: Hill and Wang.

Wolff, Robert Paul. 1977. *Understanding Rawls.* Princeton: Princeton University Press.

Wootton, Barbara. 1959. *Social Science and Social Pathology.* New York: Macmillan.

————. 1963. *Crime and the Criminal Law.* London: Stevens.

Ted Robert Gurr

Historical Trends in Violent Crime: A Critical Review of the Evidence

ABSTRACT

Recent historical scholarship suggests that the post-1960 increase in violent crime in most Western societies was preceded by a much longer period of decline. In Britain the incidence of homicide has fallen by a factor of at least ten to one since the thirteenth century and the recent tripling of the rate is small by comparison. Evidence of long-term trends in the United States is obscured by the occurrence of three great surges of violent crime which began ca. 1850, 1900, and 1960. The last two upsurges are largely attributable to sharply rising homicide rates among blacks. A number of other Western societies show evidence of nineteenth-century declines in violent crime. The long-term declining trend evidently is a manifestation of cultural change in Western society, especially the growing sensitization to violence and the development of increased internal and external controls on aggressive behavior. Empirical studies of the correlates of violent crime point toward several general factors which help account for the historically temporary deviations from the downward trend in interpersonal violence: warfare, which evidently tends to legitimate individual violence; the stresses of the initial phases of rapid urbanization and industrialization; economic prosperity and decline; and changes in the demographic structure.

It is generally accepted by criminologists and other social scientists that the real incidence of serious crimes against persons and property increased substantially in the United States and most Western European societies during the 1960s and 1970s,

Ted Robert Gurr is Payson S. Wild Professor of Political Science, Northwestern University. Roger Lane, Eric H. Monkkonen, and Michael Tonry provided helpful comments on an earlier draft.

though skepticism remains about the accuracy of official data on the precise magnitude of change. What is less widely recognized is a growing body of historical evidence, some of it examined by Lane in a previous volume in this series (1980), that the incidence of serious crime has traced an irregular downward trend for a much longer period of time, in some places for a century or more. When the historical and contemporary evidence are joined together, they depict a distended U-shaped curve.

The thesis that rates of serious crime in Western societies have traced a reversing U-shaped curve is a simplification of a much more complex reality. It characterizes some but not all offenses. The evidence for it is substantial in some societies, especially the English-speaking and Scandinavian countries, but either lacking or contradictory in others. There are severe problems in the interpretation of official data on crime compiled in different eras. Even where a reversing trend is clearly present, as in England and Wales during the past 150 years, there are substantial short-term deviations around it. For these and other reasons, the U-shaped curve is used here as a hypothesis, not received wisdom, against which to evaluate diverse evidence on trends in violent crime. The first question is whether the evidence from a particular jurisdiction and era is consistent with, qualifies, or contradicts the general model. The subsidiary question is what the evidence suggests about the social dynamics of the long-term trend in violent crime, and of substantial deviations from it.

This essay is limited mainly to evidence about trends in homicide and assault, with occasional reference to robbery. In terms of social importance these offenses are less common than burglary and larceny, but are of greater concern to most people: offenses which inflict bodily harm are and probably have always been more threatening to most people than has property crime. From the perspective of the social and cultural historian, the distribution of these offenses across time, space, and social groups is of particular interest because of what it tells us about interpersonal aggression and the complex of social attitudes toward it. And from a methodological viewpoint, when dealing with data on homicide in particular we can be more confident that trends reflect real changes in social behavior rather than changes in the practices of criminal justice systems.

The first part of this essay comments briefly on what can and cannot be inferred from data on violent crime. The next four parts summarize the statistical evidence on trends in violent crime, both in single jurisdictions and comparatively, for Britain, the United States, and some other Western societies. These parts also refer to evidence and speculation on the social forces responsible for changes over time in the incidence of violent crime, which are then summarized in the final part of the essay.

Some kinds of trend studies are ruled out of close consideration here:

1. Those which examine trends in total or property offenses but not offenses against persons, for example historical analyses by Monkkonen (1981) and Tilly et al. (n.d.).

2. Studies which describe the changing character or incidence of crime over time or among jurisdictions without making use of time-series data, for example Greenberg (1976) and Hay et al. (1975).

3. Microstudies of the characteristics of offenses and offenders in a limited period in a single jurisdiction, for example Baldwin and Bottoms on Sheffield, England (1976), Block on Chicago (1977), Lundsgaarde on Houston (1977), and Stanciu on Paris (1968).

4. Studies of crime trends in third-world societies.

5. Studies of "trends," however statistical, which span less than a decade (of which there are a great many examples).

6. Official reports which table but do not analyze data on crime trends.

To keep the essay within manageable proportions I have also excluded studies of the ways in which the law, police, or courts treat violent offenses and offenders. Finally, I have avoided detailed criticism of the techniques used in trend and correlational analyses, offering only cautionary notes when there are methodological reasons to question a study's findings about trends.

I. Official Data on Interpersonal Violence

This essay begins with the premise that there is some discernible correspondence between trends in some kinds of official data on crimes against persons and real changes in the incidence of interpersonal violence in society. The validity of many of the criticisms of crime statistics is accepted. It is clear, for example, that the reported incidence of many kinds of offenses can be affected by changing degrees of public concern and by changes in the level and foci of police activity. But I contend that it is possible to overcome these limitations of official data by focusing on the most serious offenses and by obtaining converging or parallel evidence on trends in different types of offenses and from different jurisdictions.[1]

Official data on crime pose many threats to the validity of inferences about trends in interpersonal violence. One is the inherent slippage between the occurrence of an offense and the chain of events by which it does or does not enter official records. The closest approximation in official data to information on violent crime is provided by police data on "offenses known." Victimization surveys show that the more serious the offense, the more closely citizen reports correspond with police data (Skogan 1976), which supports the commonly held view that murder is the most accurately recorded violent crime. But offenses known to police have been recorded for only a relatively brief period in most Western societies, and rarely do the records antedate the establishment of modern police forces in the mid to late nineteenth century.

---

[1] The limitations of contemporary American crime data have been widely discussed, for example by Bloch and Geis (1962, pt. 3); Mulvilhill and Tumin (1969, chap. 2); and Skogan (1975). Detailed discussions of the interpretation of American historical statistics on crime are to be found in Monkkonen's work (1975, 1980, 1981). On the reliability of British historical statistics see Gatrell and Hadden (1972) and Gatrell (1980). My views about what can be inferred from official crime data are spelled out in Gurr, Grabosky, and Hula (1977, chap. I.2).

The alternative sources of information about violent offenses in criminal justice statistics are arrest data and records of indictments or committals to trial, convictions, and sentences. Most studies of nineteenth-century crime, and virtually all earlier ones, use data on indictments/committals or convictions. The slippage between the commission of a felony and the success of private citizens or officials in getting the accused to trial is considerable, and probably was greater before modern police forces were established than since. But because homicide usually has been committed by people known to the victim (as evinced by many microstudies) and in Western societies usually has attracted close official attention, the slippage between act and court record is probably less for homicide than other crimes against persons.

Coroners' records of homicides and death registration data are alternatives to police and court records which have been examined in a number of historical studies (e.g. Brearley 1932; Given 1977; Lane 1979). In principle, data from these sources should be closer to the "true" incidence of homicide than any other, but in fact, as Lane found in his study of nineteenth-century Philadelphia, there may be serious, systematic sources of error in recording the cause of death. And of course death records are of no help in assessing the incidence of other kinds of interpersonal violence.

Official records thus are in varying degrees inadequate for assessing the true incidence of violent offenses, but closer to the mark for homicide than for others. This inadequacy is less a threat to the validity of comparisons across time within jurisdictions than comparisons across jurisdictions, because it is sometimes plausible to assume that the slippage within a given jurisdiction is more or less constant over time. But not always, and there's the rub. Official categories of an offense may change, for example by changes in the inclusion of involuntary manslaughter, infanticide, or attempted murder. This is usually detectable from the sources. More problematic are the results of changes in underlying legal definitions, for example the distinction between murder per se and manslaughter. No distinction was drawn between these two forms of violent death in English criminal procedure until the sixteenth century (see Kaye 1967). Most difficult of all to detect are slow changes in police and prosecutorial procedures. Gatrell observes that English coroners and police became better able to identify death from unnatural causes during the nineteenth century and offers other evidence that homicides were increasingly likely to come to police attention as the century progressed (1980, pp. 247–48). Lane reports on nineteenth-century Philadelphia that "late in the century a number of [manslaughter] cases were prosecuted that earlier would have been tolerated or overlooked" (1979, p. 76).

Lane's observation about lessened tolerance of manslaughter in nineteenth-century Philadelphia is a manifestation of what Soman calls the "sensitization to violence" in Western societies, a process under way for five centuries which was manifest in the gradual "exclusion of most violence from ordinary daily life, and a heightened sensitivity to some of the residual violence" (1980, p. 22). One likely consequence of this shift in values was a growing disposition of private citizens to seek redress for lesser acts of violence, with a parallel increase in officials' disposition to prosecute such cases. The implication for trend analysis is that official data on such offenses as assault and attempted murder could be expected to increase over time (especially before the twentieth century) even if the true incidence of offenses stayed constant.

Because of increased sensitization to interpersonal violence, any long-term upward trend in assault, especially prior to the twentieth century, is prima facie suspect as an indicator of change in social behavior. This is especially so if the trend in assaults runs counter to the trend in homicide. Homicides usually are the result of particularly successful (or unlucky) assaults and it is implausible that the real incidence of serious assaults could increase without a parallel increase in homicide. On the other hand, evidence of long-term statistical *decline* in the incidence of assault has prima facie plausibility because it runs counter to increased public sensitization and official attention. These comments apply to trends observed over a number of decades, not to sharp upward and downward waves in the incidence of assault of a few years' or a decade's duration. Such waves are too brief to be a product of slow change in social values, and, unless they coincide with the creation of modern police forces, are not likely to be an artifact of fluctuating police attention. The same general comment applies also to homicide.

One other artifactual source of long-term variation in assault rates, in the opposite direction from that due to "sensitization," is the shift of cases from higher to lower courts, as happened in early twentieth-century London for example (see Gurr, Grabosky, and Hula 1977, pp. 144–45). I suspect that the following sequence occurred in a number of nineteenth-century jurisdictions: increased public and police attention to minor episodes of violence caused large increases in the numbers of assault cases brought to trial; these soon overloaded the capacity of the higher courts in which most such cases had previously been tried; this overloading led to a shift of most cases, either gradually or abruptly, from higher to lower courts. Gatrell suggests, contrary to my argument about sensitization to violence, that assault rates in England may have declined as drastically as they did between the 1850s and 1914 because of "greater tolerance of petty violence" by the public and police (1980, pp. 289–91). This hypothesis is contrary to most other evidence but warrants attention in future historical research.

The two other main categories of violent crime are sexual assault and robbery. No attempt is made here to assess long-term trends in sexual assault, first because time-series data are sparse, second because it is an offense much more often concealed than reported by the victim: the "dark figure" of reported offenses prior to the use of victimization surveys is unknowably large. Robbery trends, though, may be more reliably estimated and used as a supplemental indicator of changes in interpersonal violence. I regard them as second in reliability only to homicide rates per se, though subject to many of the same questions about validity. Robbery—theft accompanied by the threat or use of force against the victim—has always been regarded as a particularly serious crime in Western societies and usually leaves victims who are more than willing to complain to authorities. I have the impression that robbery's legal definition has not changed appreciably over time in Britain or the United States, and so records of cases brought to official attention should be relatively consistent over time. Robbery is a felony and a relatively uncommon offense and is usually tried before higher courts; it is not likely that any appreciable historical shift of robbery cases from higher to lower courts occurred, although I am prepared to be corrected on both these points by scholars who have done more detailed studies. The most substantial slippage to affect robbery arises from the fact that the offender is usually unknown to the victim, so that court cases (and arrest and clearance rates) are usually much less numerous than offenses, but are likely to have increased—relative to the number of offenses—after the development of modern police systems during the past century. Thus one might expect some artifactual nineteenth-century increase in the number of robbery cases brought to trial, relative to their true or "known to police" incidence. In evidence thereof, the gap between robberies known to police and convictions in London narrowed appreciably between the 1880s and 1930 (see Gurr, Grabosky, and Hula 1977, p. 120). Gatrell asserts that the same principle applies to nineteenth-century English data on indictable crime generally: "the rate of recorded crime crept ever closer to the rate of actual crime" (1980, pp. 250–51).

In summary, I suggest these general guidelines for interpreting long-term trends in violent crime, with special reference to the putative period of decline that ended in the mid-twentieth century. (1) The declining historical trend in *homicide* probably is understated somewhat, because of closer official attention and a stretching of definitions to include more cases of manslaughter. Since the establishment of modern, centralized systems for recording crime and death data, official homicide data are the most accurate of all data on interpersonal violence. A cautionary note: since homicide is a relatively rare offense, it is highly variable over the short run and in smaller localities. Thus homicide rates are best used as an indicator of middle-

and long-run trends in interpersonal violence (see Zehr 1976, pp. 85–86). (2) Data on robberies known are second, albeit a rather distant second, to homicide data in reliability. Long-term trends in trial and conviction data are probably unreliable across those periods in which modern police systems were being established but should be internally comparable before and after that transition. (3) Long-run trends which show increases in assault are suspect because of increasing concern about these offenses. Long-run declining trends in assault are convincing if based on "offenses known," or on trial data for all courts, higher and lower.

Finally, we can be more confident about the underlying trends in interpersonal violence to the extent that there is converging evidence from different studies and different indicators. Conclusions about the directions and magnitude of change in violence are convincing to the extent that they are supported by any of the following kinds of parallel evidence: (1) Similarity in trends of indicators of an offense obtained from two different sources, for example police and coroner's records of homicides. (2) Similarity in trends of indicators of an offense registered at different stages in the criminal justice process, for example offenses known versus committals to trial or convictions. (3) Similarity in trends of indicators of an offense from different cities or regions. (4) Similarity in trends of different offenses, for example homicide and assault, or assault and robbery. Divergence among indicators, especially of types (3) and (4), is not necessarily a threat to validity because the social dynamics of interpersonal violence may vary from region to region, for example, or from one type of offense to another. If they do vary, plausible and testable explanations for the differences must be provided. If this is impossible, then inferences about the social reality underlying the diverging indicators are suspect.

II. Violent Crime in Medieval and Contemporary England

Our knowledge about the general decline of serious offenses against the person in English-speaking countries during the nineteenth century rests first on an analysis of police and court records, which officials collected and aggregated with increasing precision and consistency during the century. Equally necessary to the analysis of trends are accurate population data, without which no reliable estimates can be made of the relative incidence of offenses. Regular population censuses also were largely a nineteenth-century innovation; the first national census in the United States was taken in 1790, in Britain in 1801.

Thus it is difficult to ascertain whether the rates of serious offenses against persons were as high in the eighteenth century and earlier. This question is not entirely a matter of antiquarian curiosity because an unambiguous answer would help us to interpret the nineteenth-century decline and, possibly, the late twentieth-century rise in violent crimes. There are two general possibilities, one developmental, the other cyclical. The developmental possibility is that the nineteenth-century decline in violent crime continued an earlier trend. This would suggest that the decline was due to some fundamental, very long-term social dynamics in the evolution of Western society: perhaps the transition from subsistence agrarian lifeways to town and urban life, or the emergence of more civilized values and nonaggressive modes of personal interaction. The cyclical alternative is that the high level of interpersonal violence of the early nineteenth century was an aberration, the result of a cresting wave that might be analogous to contemporary experience. This would suggest a search for explanation that focuses on such historically discrete processes as the onset of rapid urbanization and industrialization or the impact of war. The two interpretations are not necessarily mutually exclusive: it is possible that violent crime has tended to decline over the long run, subject to short-term reversals, in other words a cyclical pattern of variation around a declining trend.

A. Homicide in Medieval and Early Modern England

Evidence from a handful of historical studies of homicides (and other felonies) in medieval and early modern England helps us choose among these possibilities. A brief characterization of the studies is needed before abstracting their results. First, none is national. Rather they are all based on painstaking analyses of surviving coroners' rolls and court records for specific years in specific jurisdictions, either counties or cities. Second, they are concerned mainly with describing the characteristics of violent crimes: absolute numbers, circumstances in which the crimes occurred, traits of offenders and victims, outcomes of trials, and their relative incidence in different jurisdictions. They are not primarily concerned with estimating rates. Third, the estimates of rates of offenses, or indictments, are subject to substantial error because population data for pre-modern English towns and counties were considerably less accurate than records of violent deaths. One author chooses "to avoid all discussion of rates of crime until, if ever, there is more reliable demographic information for the fourteenth century" (Hanawalt 1979, p. 287). Fourth, all the studies combine data on murder and manslaughter. Finally, few of these studies provide trend information in and of themselves because most are necessarily limited to scattered years by the availability of records (an exception is Beattie 1974). It is only when we juxtapose the results of a number of different studies in different eras that evidence about long-term trends in homicide begins to emerge.

The first systematic records of English homicide are to be found in the thirteenth-century records of the eyre courts, panels of royal justices which visited each county every few years. They had the exclusive prerogative of judging all cases of homicide. Coroners and juries were required to report independently to the court on all violent deaths that had occurred since the previous visit of the court and were penalized for inconsistencies and omissions revealed by comparing their reports. The transcribed records, where they have survived, "portray violent conflict in medieval England with a completeness that is unmatched by the records of any other country in northern Europe in the Middle Ages" (Given 1977, p. 13). Given's study of a wide sample of the eyre rolls shows convincingly that murderous brawls and violent death at the hands of robbers were everyday occurrences in medieval England.

The average annual homicide rates for five rural counties, based in each instance on eyre rolls covering three to five years at scattered points between 1202 and 1276, are: Bedford, 22 per 100,000 population; Kent, 23; Norfolk, 9; Oxfordshire, 17; Warwickshire, 19 (Given 1977, p. 36). (The comparable rate for England and Wales in 1974 was 1.97 per 100,000). Analysis of the episodes which resulted in violent death shows that most resulted from fights among neighbors, while between 10 and 20 percent were attributed to thieves or bandits—a percentage which increased during the second half of the century. Knives, axes, cudgels, and other implements found in every agricultural community were the typical instruments of death. Usually several assailants were charged in each homicide, another item of evidence that most deaths resulted from brawling among small groups rather than one-on-one attacks.

The medieval English population was more than 90 percent rural and cities were small. Fourteenth-century London had 35,000–50,000 people, Oxford about 7,000, for example. Estimates of urban homicide rates for this period vary enormously. Given (1977, p. 36) reports thirteenth-century rates for London of 12 per 100,000 and for Bristol of 4 per 100,000, considerably lower than the rural rates. On the other hand Hanawalt (1976, pp. 301–2) estimates that London in the first half of the fourteenth century had homicide rates of 36 to 52 per 100,000 per annum (depending on which population figures and which year's homicides are used). Hammer's very thorough study of Oxford for the 1340s shows an extraordinarily high rate of ca. 110 homicides per 100,000, a rate to which scholars contributed no more (as victims or assailants) than might be expected from their proportions in the population. Analysis of the details of cases for Oxford shows that virtually all victims and assailants were males, and except for scholars were almost always of low status. Scarcely any homicides were intra-familial and at least one-third of them involved "strangers," i.e. people having no fixed residence in Oxford (Hammer 1978, pp. 9–19). Unlike the rural pattern, however, very few homicides in Oxford resulted from robbery or burglary.

These early estimates of homicide rates and their contemporary descriptions all sketch a portrait of a society in which men (but rarely women) were easily provoked to violent anger and were unrestrained in the brutality with which they attacked their opponents. Interpersonal violence was a recurring fact of rural and urban life. Had medieval Englishmen been equipped with firearms rather than knives and rustic tools, one can only assume that they would have killed one another with even greater frequency.

The eyre courts largely ceased to function during the fourteenth century and it was not until the late sixteenth century, during the reign of Elizabeth I, that county assize courts left records of indictments in sufficient detail to permit statistical study of serious offenses. These records refer to persons charged with crimes rather than records of offenses per se. Cockburn ventures the opinion that "indictments for homicide probably bear a closer relationship to the actual incidence of violent death than is correspondingly the case with other crimes." He offers these estimates of homicide indictment rates for the period 1559–1603 for three counties, the first two close to London and the other more remote: Essex, 7 per 100,000; Hertfordshire, 16; and Sussex, 14 (Cockburn 1977, pp. 55–56). These figures are noticeably lower than those for the thirteenth and fourteenth centuries.

The difficulties of estimating reliable homicide rates from court records are illustrated by comparing Cockburn's data on homicides in Essex with the results of a more detailed analysis by Samaha (1974). The two authors offer different estimates of homicides and total population. Samaha (1974, p. 20) finds significantly more homicide cases (murder, manslaughter, infanticide) from 1559 to 1603, 215 versus 157 in Cockburn (1977, p. 55), presumably because Samaha uses records from coroners' inquests and lower courts as well as assize records. He also notes that some assize court records are missing, especially for the 1560s (1974, p. 14), hence his numbers of offenses, though higher than Cockburn's, are still underestimated. With respect to population, Cockburn estimates that Essex had 52,000 people but says it is impossible to estimate population changes (1977, pp. 53, 311 n.34). Samaha, citing the same basic source (the Elizabethan muster rolls), estimates that the population increased from 60,000 to 80,000 during the period (1974, p. 33). Despite these considerable discrepancies, the rates calculated from these data for the 45-year period are nearly identical: from Cockburn's data, 6.7 homicides per 100,000 population per annum; and from Samaha's data, 6.8 per 100,000.[2] One other observation from Samaha's study should be noted: the trend in recorded violent crime—especially property offenses—was upward during this period, considerably more so than can be attributed to incomplete early records or to population growth (Samaha 1974, pp. 19–22, 115–16).

There is much other evidence that the interpersonal violence of medieval England had lessened only somewhat in Elizabethan England. To quote Cockburn again (1977, p. 57), few of the killings investigated at assizes during this period resulted from calculated violence. "Rather, they occurred during acts of sudden, unpremeditated aggression and resulted from attacks with a variety of knives and blunt instruments. Fatal quarrels could originate in almost any context—at work, in drink or at play." Handguns, known as "pocket dags," had also come into limited use by this time, and about 7 percent of the violent deaths involved firearms (Cockburn 1977, pp. 58–59). One can also examine the relative proportions of crimes against persons versus property offenses in this period. Of 5,980 indictments in three counties between 1559 and 1603, 12 percent were for offenses against the person (homicide, infanticide, assault, rape, robbery) and 69 percent for offenses against property (other than robbery). This differs from the prevailing twentieth-century pattern, in which more than 90 percent of reported felonies are against property. Moreover the sixteenth-century indictments for homicide were more numerous than those for assault (280 versus 133), not because assault was less

---

[2] Rates calculated by the author of this essay from data reported by Cockburn and Samaha, using 70,000 as the mean population figure for Essex when calculating rates from Samaha's homicide data.

common, one suspects, but because it was not often thought serious enough to bring to the assize courts (calculated from data in Cockburn 1977, p. 55). Samaha excludes assaults entirely from his Essex study because the assault indictments he examined usually state that the defendant put the plaintiff out of possession of his land. He concludes that they were not assaults in the ordinary meaning of the term but rather that plaintiffs were using the criminal law to try civil property disputes (1974, p. 17).

For seventeenth- and eighteenth-century England we can report the results of a study by Beattie, who analyzed statistically the indictments brought in the higher courts of Surrey and Sussex for a sample of years between 1662 and 1802. The first of these counties includes London south of the Thames, whereas Sussex was predominantly rural. Although Beattie does not report fully his calculations of rates for each county and period, he does give the following rates of murder and manslaughter indictments per 100,000 population for Surrey (Beattie 1974, p. 61):

1663–65	6.1
1690–94	5.3
1722–24	2.3
1780–84 ⎫ 1795–1802 ⎭	less than 1

A decline was found in both urban and rural parishes of Surrey, and "confirmed in Sussex, where there were on average between two and three indictments for murder every year in the seventeenth century and rarely more than one in the eighteenth" (Beattie 1974, p. 61). Beattie concludes, not surprisingly, that these absolute numbers almost surely reflect a real decline in killing, not changes in public attitudes or judicial efficiency. They also bear comparison against trends in the rate of indictments for assault, which exhibited a pronouncedly different pattern. In both urban and rural Surrey assault rates traced a wavelike pattern, rising to a very high peak in the 1720s and 1730s, with lesser peaks in the 1760s, 1780s, and at the beginning of the nineteenth century. In rural Sussex, however, the assault rates were lower, the peaks of lesser amplitude, and the long-run trend was generally downward, as it was for homicide (pp. 66–69). Beattie attributes the peaks in assault rates to an increased inclination of injured parties to bring cases to court; to the apprehensiveness of authorities about threats to public order, especially in the 1720s; and to real increases in assault (and much greater ones in property offenses) by disbanded soldiers and seamen who periodically flooded London and its environs at the conclusion of wars (of which England was involved in six between 1690 and 1802). There is nothing in Beattie's descriptions of typical assault cases (pp. 62–63) to suggest that any of them were really civil property cases, as Samaha suggests they were in Elizabethan Essex (see above).

B. Violent Crime in the Nineteenth and Twentieth Centuries

Beginning in 1805 there are national data on committals to trial for indictable (serious) offenses. At first these were reported only by type of offense, after 1834 by county as well. Generally the data were reported with increasing reliability and detail as the century progressed (see Gatrell and Hadden 1972). The returns provide the basis for a true time-series analysis of English crime rates. The rate of all offenses against persons tried in upper courts was 12.3 per 100,000 in 1836–40, falling to 9.0 in 1896–1900 and 7.7 in 1906–10. Beginning in the 1850s there are series on homicides known to the police, which trace a similar decline from 1.4 per 100,000 in 1856–60 to 0.8 in 1906–10. Common assaults known to police were 408 per 100,000 in the first period, 135 per 100,000 in the last. Gatrell, whose recent study is the source of these estimates, argues trenchantly that the trends cannot be explained away by changes in public attitudes or official practices: they reflect a real decline in interpersonal violence (1980, pp. 282–93). Their cause, he suggests, was not deterrence because impulsively violent offenders are not likely to be deterred by the threat of arrest or punishment. The explanation must be sought in "heavy generalizations about the 'civilizing' effects of religion, education, and environmental reform" (p. 300).

The national trends are paralleled by the evidence from a study of London beginning in the 1820s. Trends in committals to trial for homicide have been analyzed from 1820 to 1873 for Middlesex County, which included London north of the Thames. Committals for murder varied irregularly throughout the period. In the 1830s, for example, committals ranged from 15 to 35 per year in a county whose population was about 1.4 million. The committals rate for the 1820s and 1830s was about 2 per 100,000, declining irregularly to less than 1 per 100,000 in the 1850s, with temporary upswings in the late 1840s and in the 1860s. Conviction rates were consistently about half the committal rates. Committals to trial for assault declined more sharply during the period. When first recorded in the 1830s and 1840s they ranged from 15 to 25 per 100,000 annually but had declined by 1870 to an average rate of 6 per 100,000 (Peirce, Grabosky, and Gurr 1977, pp. 166–67).

From 1869 through 1931 there are data for all of London (specifically the Metropolitan Police District), which trace a continued irregular decline in rates of homicide. For this period the trend study focuses on convictions. The annual conviction rate for murder and manslaughter gradually declined from about 0.5 per 100,000 in the 1870s to half of that in 1930, while convictions for assault and attempted murder fell from ca. 5 per 100,000 to ca. 1.5 per 100,000 (Peirce, Grabosky, and Gurr 1977, pp. 116–17). Since the 1940s, however, both London and all of England and Wales have experienced increasing rates of violent crime. In London the incidence of homicides known to police has increased from about 0.7 per 100,000 in the 1950s to more than 2.0 in the 1970s. In absolute numbers, the police reported 18 murders and 22 cases of manslaughter in 1950 in London compared with 127 murders and 15 cases of manslaughter in 1974. Indictable assaults increased much more dramatically, from ca. 10 per 100,000 in 1950 to 120 per 100,000 in 1974 (Peirce, Grabosky, and Gurr 1977, pp. 162–64).

The rates of violent crime generally in London since the 1940s have not been substantially higher than those in all of England and Wales. In fact other large English cities tended to have higher rates of indictable crimes against the person in the 1950s than did London. The national trends in violent crime generally parallel the London experience, but as McClintock has noted, the upward trend in these offenses began in London ca. 1950, about ten years later than it became evident in the national statistics (McClintock 1963, chap. 1; see also McClintock and Avison 1968, chaps. 2, 3).

C. Summary: The Long-Term Trend in English Homicide

The comparability of English homicide rates over time is impaired by the fact that only the earliest and most recent studies use data on offenses known to the authorities (the eyre courts in the first instance, the police in the most recent). For the intervening centuries the data refer mainly to committals to trial, which are only roughly comparable. Comparability is further impaired by the lack of reliable population data before 1800 and by the fact that early estimates of rates are available only for a handful of jurisdictions scattered across time and the social landscape. The general trend which emerges from the evidence is nonetheless unmistakable: rates of violent crime were far higher in medieval and early modern England than in the twentieth century—probably ten and possibly twenty or more times higher. The estimates discussed above are displayed graphically in figure 1. Each estimate for a county and city prior to 1800 is represented by a dot, even though the estimate may represent a period of several decades. A speculative trend curve is fitted to these data points. Elizabethan Essex and the period 1820 to 1975 are represented by five-year moving averages.

There are two problematic features of the trends traced in figure 1. One is the extraordinarily high incidence of homicide in fourteenth-century cities by comparison with the preceding century. If the handful of estimates are not grossly in error, there evidently was a tremendous upsurge in violent crime in England (or at least its cities) during the early fourteenth century. Hanawalt suggests as much (1979, p. 260). In general the fourteenth century was more disorderly than the thirteenth. The Hundred Years War, which began in 1337, and the Black

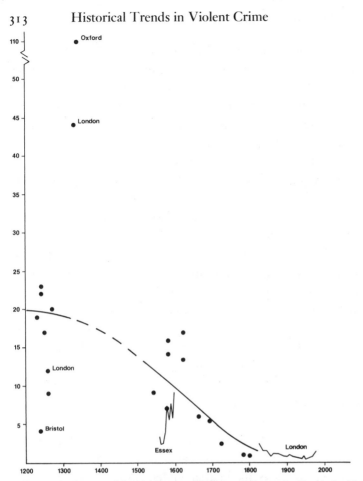

Fig. 1. Indicators of homicides per 100,000 population in England, thirteenth to twentieth centuries. Each dot represents the estimated homicide rate for a city or county for periods ranging from several years to several decades. The sources of the data are referred to in the text, with two exceptions. The estimate of 20 for ca. 1270 is the mean of high and low figures for Bedfordshire, as calculated by Hair (1971, p. 18) using minimum and maximum estimates of population. The estimate for ca. 1550 is the mean of high and low figures for Nottinghamshire for 1530–58, also calculated by Hair (1971, p. 17). Hair's estimates of London homicide rates for the seventeenth through nineteenth centuries, based on the London bills of mortality, are not shown because the source is highly suspect.

Death, which killed perhaps one-third of the population, precipitated social and economic crises of major proportions.[3]

[3] The high urban homicide rates reported by Hanawalt (1979) cannot be attributed to the social disorder which followed the onset of the Black Death because her London and Oxford estimates are for the first half of the fourteenth century whereas the plague arrived in England late in 1348 (see McNeill 1976, p. 166).

The other question is whether homicidal violence remained more or less steadily high until the decline which set in during the late seventeenth century. The evidence ca. 1600 consists of estimates for three different counties which use questionable population data. Neither question can be definitively answered until substantially more research is done by historians who are willing to risk calculating homicide rates which have a substantial margin of possible error. The more estimates that are available for different periods and places, the more certain we can be of the shape of long-term trends, even if not about the precise rates prevailing at a given time.

The evidence thus clearly favors the possibility, raised at the outset of this section, that the nineteenth- and early twentieth-century decline in violent crime in England was the latest phase in a substantially longer trend. The seemingly high rates of homicide in early nineteenth- and late twentieth-century London were actually very low when contrasted with the more distant historical experience. The possibility of cyclical or wavelike movements away from the underlying trend is not ruled out, however. There probably was a surge in violent crime in fourteenth-century England. Violent crime also evidently increased in Elizabethan times. More certainly, Beattie offers evidence of several such waves during the period from 1660 to 1802, and it is likely that violent crime rates were unusually high in early nineteenth-century London.

Most of the evidence surveyed here relates only to homicide. Did assaults also decline over the long run? For the medieval and early modern period we simply cannot say because the court data on assaults are either nonexistent or unreliable. In Elizabethan times they appear in court records less often than homicide, but a century later assaults were much more numerous. Since most homicides of this period resulted from violent altercations, the real incidence of assault was presumably much higher. The infrequency of assaults in early court records almost surely reflects the fact that it ordinarily was not thought serious enough to warrant indictments unless someone died as a consequence of the assault. The higher assault rates of the period studied by Beattie, from 1660 to 1802, very likely reflect increased concern by victims and courts, not a real long-term increase in assault. During the last 150 years, however, trends and peaks in official data on assault in London and all of England have closely paralleled those for murder and manslaughter. Thus for this period we can be reasonably confident that the incidence of assault, like murder, declined for most of the period but increased after ca. 1950.

III. Trends in Violent Crime in the United States

It would be instructive to be able to compare long-term trends in British homicide with those in North America from seventeenth-century settlement to the present. Unfortunately reliable data and detailed historical studies are largely lacking. The handful of studies which analyze colonial and early republican court records are concerned mainly with the characteristics of offenses, not their incidence. Greenberg (1976), for example, compiled data on all surviving criminal records of New York courts between 1691 and 1775, a total of 5,297 cases, but his analysis focuses on the relative frequency of different kinds of cases, characteristics of the accused, and the distribution of outcomes for the accused. Interestingly, the most common of all categories of offense was crimes of violence against persons which did not result in death, i.e. assaults. These offenses constituted 21.5 percent of the cases; second most frequent were thefts, 13.7 percent.

A. Violent Crime in Nineteenth-Century America

Something about the changing incidence of crime in America up to the Civil War period can be inferred from Hindus's recent study of criminal prosecutions in late eighteenth- and nineteenth-century Massachusetts and South Carolina. Without complete court data for the earlier period, only internal comparisons are possible: for example, that crimes against persons made up 11 to 18 percent of all prosecutions in eighteenth- and nineteenth-century Massachusetts, but over 50 percent—mainly assaults—in South Carolina (1980, pp. 63–65). For Massachusetts he reports time-series data from 1836 to 1873 which show that total number of committals for crimes against persons increased fourfold from 1836 to 1855, declined by half until 1865, and then increases again. Property crime moved up simultaneously and stayed high, except for the Civil War years (1980, p. 72). His data on committals to trial in Suffolk County (Boston) show murder committal rates increasing from 2.1 per 100,000 in 1839–41 to 3.1 twenty years later and then a jump to 7.0 in 1869–70.[4] Assault committals increased from 78 to 293 per 100,000 over the same period (1980, p. 74). This increasing trend is the opposite of England's experience in the same period, but it is based on a study of only two jurisdictions.

A different result is evident in Lane's careful study of homicide in Philadelphia from 1838 to 1901.[5] He begins by diagnosing some of the difficulties of inferring homicide rates from nineteenth-century records. Police arrest statistics in Philadelphia date only from 1857 and even then were a "poor barometer" because some homicides were followed by numerous indiscriminate arrests. Health office figures for homicide also are unreliable because of a "legal-bureaucratic quirk" whereby coroners often failed to indicate that a death was due to homicide. Lane concludes that homicide indictments prepared for grand juries are the best records for Philadelphia but notes that these too pose problems of comparability over time. Such difficulties are particularly true of manslaughter cases: "late in the century a number of cases were prosecuted that earlier would have been tolerated or overlooked" (Lane 1979, chap. 4, quotations from pp. 56, 76). Presumably these or equivalent problems affect the homicide records of other

[4] Comparison of Hindus's graphed annual data (1980, p. 72) with tabled data (p. 74) gives rise to the suspicion that the latter may represent two- or three-year rates rather than annual ones. If so, then the rates given in the text are inflated but the *trends* are valid.

[5] An earlier study of Philadelphia examines lower court records from 1791 to 1810 and tabulates, *inter alia*, annual numbers of persons charged with offenses against persons (Hobbs 1943, p. 8). The trend was upward, but, lacking either population data or information on serious offenses against persons, no firm conclusions about changes in rates can be drawn.

American cities, though few of the authors relying on them have examined alternative statistics in Lane's painstaking way.

Homicide indictment rates in Philadelphia declined irregularly during the nineteenth century, from ca. 3.3 indictments per 100,000 population during the two decades before the Civil War to 2.1 per 100,000 after 1880. The trend was not steadily downward, however: there were peaks during the 1850s and again during the fifteen years which followed the Civil War, analogous to the peaks in Suffolk County. Concealable handguns, which came into use in the 1850s, evidently provided an upward push against the declining trend but did not reverse it. Lane excludes from these rates "incidents in which no assault, aggression, or harm was intended." The data understate the real decline because study of individual indictments over time "reveal a further stretching of definitions" of murder over time (Lane 1979, pp. 70–71). Examination of the races of victims specified in indictments shows that homicide rates among blacks in nineteenth-century Philadelphia were considerably higher than the white rate, 7.5 versus 2.8 per 100,000. In the twentieth century this gap widened. In the years from 1948 to 1952 the white victimization rate had declined still further, to 1.8 per 100,000, while the black rate had increased to 24.6. In the early 1970s the white rate was back to its mean nineteenth-century rate of 2.8 while the black rate was an incredible 64.2. "As demographic change has made Philadelphia an increasingly black city, the black homicide rate in itself is enough to account for the differences between the overall official rates" between the nineteenth and the late twentieth century (Lane 1979, pp. 112–13). Lane offers the same general explanation for the nineteenth-century decline in white homicide rates and the growing discrepancy between black and white homicide rates: "while the effect of urban-industrial discipline was increasingly felt among whites, the absence of the same discipline was increasingly evident among blacks" (1979, p. 135).

That homicide rates declined in nineteenth-century Philadelphia is as firmly established as any historical generalization can be which relies on official American records of offenses. In

Boston (Suffolk County), by contrast, we have seen from Hindus's data that the trend in the shorter run was upward. Trials for all categories of crimes against persons, property, morality, and order in Boston (Suffolk County) began increasing in the 1840s—a period of heavy Irish immigration—and continued upward into the late 1850s (1980, p. 72). Parallel evidence comes from Ferdinand's study of Boston's arrest rates for major offenses from 1849 to 1951: arrests increased sharply during the 1850s for most categories of offenses (1967).

Boston continued to be a violent and disorderly place for a decade after the Civil War. Robbery, burglary, and larceny arrest rates increased in the aftermath of war. Murder arrests (Ferdinand 1967) and trials (Hindus 1980) reached their highest peak in 1869–71. Thereafter, however, the trends turned downward. Table 1 shows the average arrest rates in Boston per 100,000 population for offenses against persons in twenty-year intervals. Overall, murder arrests in 1854–74 averaged 4.7 per 100,000 yearly but declined to about half that rate in 1895–1915. Manslaughter arrests are excluded from these figures: they averaged about 1.5 yearly per 100,000 with no evident trend until ca. 1910, when the inclusion of automotive manslaughter evidently pushed them upward. Thus the nineteenth-century arrest rates for murder plus manslaughter fell from ca. 6 to 4 per 100,000 persons, rates that are generally consistent in magnitude and trend with homicide indictments in

TABLE 1

Boston: Average Annual Arrests per 100,000 for Offenses against Persons*

Offense	1854–74	1875–94	1895–1915	1916–36
Murder†	4.7	3.0	2.5	2.7
Assault	720	710	460	290
Forcible rape	3.6	3.1	5.4	7.1
Robbery	32	26	24	32

*Estimated from data presented graphically by Ferdinand (1967, pp. 89–95).
†Excluding manslaughter.

Philadelphia.[6] The incidence of assault arrests in Boston follows the same downward trend as murder, with some similarity in fluctuations around the trend. Robbery arrests also show a slight downward trend in the nineteenth century, followed by a sharp wave that peaked ca. 1918 and another in the early 1930s. (Other studies of crime in Boston during this era are Harrison 1934 and Warner 1934.)

Two other studies provide converging evidence about Boston's trends in violent crime in the late nineteenth century. Lane, using statewide data on court and grand jury cases, and imprisonments, reports that total commitments for homicide, rape, armed robbery, and arson declined from 6.8 per 100,000 population in 1860–62 to 2.9 by 1900 (1968). Ferdinand has analyzed arrests in Salem, Massachusetts, from 1853 to 1966. Murder and manslaughter were too rare in this smaller city to permit any analysis of trends, but arrests for simple assault during the nineteenth and early twentieth centuries were very similar in incidence, trends, and variations within the trend to those of nearby Boston (Ferdinand 1972, pp. 579–80).

Powell's study of Buffalo, New York, is also relevant for our purposes. He traces the trends in arrests from 1854 to 1956, categorized by type of offense. Arrests for offenses against persons rose very sharply between 1854 and 1874, from about 90 to 1,300 per 100,000 population, in a pattern generally similar to that in Boston. Most were assaults; in absolute numbers murders increased from 2 in the former year (or 2.7 per 100,000) to 13 in the latter (or 9.7 per 100,000). Arrests for all offenses against persons declined steadily thereafter, reaching a level of 355 per 100,000 in 1893. The decline continued until about 1905, when a sharp increase began which peaked about 1920 and did not ebb until the 1930s (rates calculated from data in Powell 1966, pp. 163–64). Powell's general explanation of this wavelike pattern is to attribute it to anomie, conceived as

[6] A study of murder and manslaughter indictments in predominantly rural New Hampshire, 1873–1903, yields a substantially lower rate of 1.0 indictments per 100,000 population, with no clear trend discernible over the period (calculated from data in Nutt 1905, pp. 224–25).

the temporary disintegration of the institutional order (Powell 1966, pp. 168–69; 1970, chap. 8).

The broadest evidence for a U-shaped trend in American homicide rates is provided by Monkkonen's study of arrest trends in 23 cities between 1860 and 1920. His main interest is in diagnosing changes in the activities and effectiveness of police. His findings about trends are ancillary to that purpose but highly instructive for ours. The data base includes virtually all cities whose population exceeded 50,000 in the late nineteenth century. The method is to aggregate police data on arrests and population figures for all cities and calculate from them composite arrest rates per 100,000. The aggregate homicide arrest rate had a peak of about 9 per 100,000 during the Civil War years, after which it declined to about 5 during the 1880s. Then there was an upward swing which reached 13 by 1920 (Monkkonen 1981, pp. 76–77). The trend in arrests for drunk and disorderly conduct, estimated in the same way, was different: it moved continuously downward, with only slight deviations, from the 1860s to the 1940s. This was the aggregate pattern; some cities had different trends, notably increases in alcohol-related arrests between 1900 and the onset of Prohibition (Monkkonen 1979). The U-shaped pattern recurs in the trend of total arrests for crimes with victims, a composite in which property offenses bulked large. There was a peak between 1865 and 1876, a decline thereafter, and an irregular movement upward after 1900 (Monkkonen 1981, pp. 74–76). In general Monkkonen regards all these trends as reflections of real changes in social behavior.[7]

B. Violent Crime in Twentieth-Century America

Zahn (1980) has recently made a careful survey of evidence on twentieth-century homicide rates in the United States using both local and national studies. The gist of the evidence is that

[7] Other studies of nineteenth and early twentieth-century trends in property crime, all felonies, and various kinds of petty offenses are synopsized by Monkkonen (1981, app. E).

homicide (excluding auto homicide) tended to increase after 1900 to a peak in the early 1930s. After 1933 the Uniform Crime Reports (UCR) compiled by the FBI show that homicides known to police declined irregularly until the early 1960s, followed by a doubling of the rate in the next fifteen years. The following discussion focuses specifically on the evidence for trends.

Trends in national and urban homicide rates in the early part of the twentieth century were the subject of careful studies by Hoffman (1925, 1928), Sutherland (1925), and Brearley (1932). They relied mainly on death registration data compiled by the federal government from reports of local registrars, but this system was only gradually extended from the New England states to others, which impairs the reliability of trend estimates. Sutherland, using only those states in the "registration area" from 1905 to 1922, found that their annual homicide rates varied little, from 2.22 per 100,000 population in 1905–9 to 2.86 in 1920–22 (summarized in Brearley 1932, pp. 16–17). Hoffman, on the other hand, compiled the death registration records of twenty-eight large cities for 1900–1924 and found that their aggregate homicide rate increased steadily from 5.1 in 1900 to 10.3 in 1924 (summarized in Brearley 1932, p. 16). Brearley, working with data from the entire registration area, reports national rates of 7.5 in 1919 (excluding nine states, three of them southern) and 8.5 in 1929 (excluding only Georgia).

Of equal interest to the aggregate trends are the differences between white and black homicide rates. The former remained virtually constant over the decade at 5.3 per 100,000 in both 1919 and 1927. The rate for blacks, however, increased from 30.5 to 43.8. Moreover, separate figures by states show that every southern state in the registration area experienced an increase over the decade in black homicide rates (Brearley 1932, pp. 19–20). This is consistent with Lane's (1979) observations about an increasing black-white difference in Philadelphia's homicide rates over a much longer time span. A more recent study of homicide arrests in Washington, D.C., from 1890 to 1970, pro-

322   Ted Robert Gurr

vides documentation of the same trend.[8] These are the homicide arrest rates for whites and nonwhites in selected decades, calculated from annual data in Count–van Manen (1977, pp. 200–201):

	Whites	Nonwhites
1890–99	2.9	9.1
1910–19	5.1	20.0
1930–39	6.3	36.1
1960–70	5.0	25.4

Evidence about trends in other kinds of offenses against persons during the first third of the century comes from studies of city arrest data. Sutherland and Gehlke (1933, p. 1127), using arrest data for Baltimore, Buffalo, Chicago, and Cleveland combined, find that robbery declined from 1900 until ca. 1910, then doubled in the next decade and remained at roughly that level through 1931. Wilbach, studying arrest rates for males over 15 in New York City from 1916 to 1936, finds that offenses against the person (mainly assaults) declined from a 1916–18 average of 602 per 100,000 to a 1934–36 average of 289. There was a slight upward trend in robbery arrests, however (Willbach 1938, pp. 69–70, 73). In a parallel study of Chicago from 1919 to 1939 he finds a somewhat different pattern. The rate of arrests for offenses against persons increased by more than half between 1919 and 1927, then declined steadily to 1939, when it was far below the 1919 level. Robbery arrests traced a similar pattern of moderate increase, then substantial decline (Willbach 1941, p. 722). Ferdinand's long-term trend study of arrest rates in Boston, summarized above, shows a sharp increase in robbery arrests from 1900 to ca. 1920, fol-

[8] Homicide *mortality* rates by race can be expected to correlate closely with homicide *arrest* rates by race because murder in the United States has always been almost entirely intraracial. In the 1970s there was an increase in big-city robbery homicides in which the assailant was black and the victim was white, but even so, Block's study of criminal homicide in Chicago from 1965 to 1974 shows that victim and offenders were of the same race in 88 percent of cases (Block 1977, p. 40).

lowed by a decline and another peak in the mid-1930s (1967, p. 93). With the exception of New York these studies are generally consistent with the national homicide trends: violent crime tended to increase in the first three decades of the century, then declined.

The UCR national homicide data on offenses known to the police show a decline in rates from about 6.5 in the mid-1930s to a low of 4.8 in the 1950s, interrupted by a temporary increase after World War II. Most scholarly research on homicide in this period consists of microanalyses of characteristics of homicides and their victims in particular cities, both northern and southern. Only Boudouris's (1970) study of Detroit from 1926 to 1968 spans more than a decade. The studies provide a composite picture of homicide that arose mainly out of quarrels between family members, lovers, or two males who knew one another. Murders during robbery were rare. Homicide death rates for black males were much higher than for other groups. Representative figures for Philadelphia, 1948–52 (Wolfgang 1958) and Cleveland, 1946–53 (Hirsch et al. 1973), are: black males, 22.5, 72; black females, 9.6, 16; white males, 2.9, 4; white females, 1, 1.

The increase in violent crime—and property crime—since the 1960s has been so pronounced and so well documented that most scholars have accepted it as a given and focused their attention on explaining rather than debunking it. The national homicide rate was at 4.5 in the early 1960s, increasing to 9.0 in 1978. Increases in a number of cities were higher. In Chicago, for example, the 1960 rate was 10.3, the 1975 rate 25.0 (Block 1977, p. 2). From 1960 to 1978 the UCR rate of aggravated assaults known to police tripled (from 85 to 256 per 100,000) and so did robbery (from 60 to 191 per 100,000) and forcible rape (from 9.4 to 30.8 per 100,000). There was some evidence that rates were peaking out by the late 1970s, however (see Skogan 1979).

The characteristics of homicides which contributed to the increase also are well documented. Block's Chicago study shows that "altercation homicides" between people who know one

324 Ted Robert Gurr

another have increased relatively little compared to the increase in robbery-related homicides in which offender and victim are strangers. In northern cities generally, Zahn concludes, a consistent picture emerges of "an increasing homicide rate in the late 1960s and into the 1970s; an increase in homicides by gun; and an increase in homicides with unknown assailants" (Zahn 1980, p. 123). The only appreciable difference in southern and southwestern cities is that family and acquaintance homicides there remain a major category.

C. Summary: The Long-Term Trend in American Homicide

The composite picture of violent crime in nineteenth-century America is a stable or declining trend with a pronounced upward swing which began shortly before the Civil War and persisted into the 1870s. The evidence is summarized graphically in figure 2. It is limited to cities, mainly on the eastern seaboard and in the Midwest, which may not be representative of what was happening in towns or on the frontier. The trends in violent crime before the Civil War are especially problematic because only Philadelphia and Boston have been studied prior to 1850. After 1900 there was a sustained rise in violent crime to the early 1930s, a thirty-year subsidence, and another increase since 1965. Current national homicide rates are higher than any recorded previously, though only slightly greater than those of the 1920s. They are also greater than any indicated by the fragmentary nineteenth-century evidence.

There is also evidence, summarized graphically in figure 3, that the two waves in twentieth-century homicide rates may be attributable mainly to increases in killings among blacks. White homicide rates have varied much less. The trends in black homicide arrests in Washington, D.C., are especially suggestive in this regard. There is need for careful long-term trend studies on this question which use both homicide and arrest data, distinguished by race, for cities and the nation.

In conclusion, we may ask to what extent the American evidence is consistent with the reversing U-shaped curve proposed at the outset of this essay. The dominant feature of crime

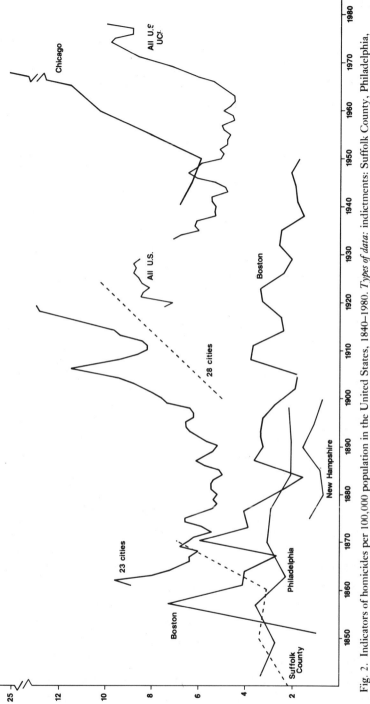

Fig. 2. Indicators of homicides per 100,000 population in the United States, 1840–1980. *Types of data:* indictments: Suffolk County, Philadelphia, New Hampshire; arrests: Boston, 23 cities; homicide registrations: 28 cities, all U.S. 1919–29; offenses known: all U.S. 1933–77, Chicago 1940–75. Sources are given in the text.

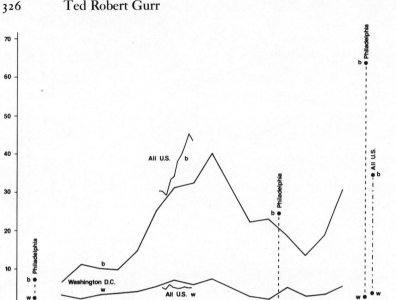

Fig. 3. Differences in homicides per 100,000 by race in the United States, nineteenth century to 1980. *Types and sources of data:* Philadelphia: race of victims in homicide indictments in 1838–1901 (mean), 1948–52, and 1972–74 (Lane 1979); Washington, D.C.: arrests for homicide by race (Count–van Manen 1977); all U.S., 1918–27: homicide mortality rates by race (Brearley 1932); all U.S., 1976: calculated by the author from UCR data on arrests for murder and nonnegligent manslaughter.

trends in the United States is the occurrence of three pronounced upsurges of interpersonal violence which began
roughly fifty years apart: ca. 1860, 1900, and 1960. These
waves or cycles are of such amplitude that we cannot say con-
clusively whether the cycles are superimposed on a longer-run
decline. To the extent that North America from settlement to
industrialization was an extension of British culture and society,
I suspect that the underlying trend was downward. At least it
was for Anglo-Americans. But as Lane points out (personal
communication), non-English immigrants have unquestionably
added to the violence of American cities: the Irish, especially
from the 1840s through the 1860s; possibly the Italians, in the
early twentieth century; and in-migrating blacks throughout. In
culturally heterogenous societies the aggregate trends and cycles
of interpersonal violence are instructive only about how disorderly society is, not about the social behavior of its con-

stituent groups. The trends-and-cycles problem of understanding homicide in America calls out for social-historical studies which trace the social characteristics of murderers and their
victims over long periods of time.

IV. Correlates of Crime Trends in Britain and the United States

A number of studies, including some of those cited above, have
used time-series crime data to test hypotheses about the causes
of temporal variation in violent crime. This section reviews the
findings of some representative English and American studies.
Correlates of crime trends in other societies are examined in the
following section.

A. Psychocultural Variables

Some studies examine the impact of psychocultural variables
on the changing incidence of violent crime. It has long been
observed, for example, that rates of violent crime are higher in
the American South than in the North, and Hackney (1969) has
shown that the differences are only partly accounted for by
differences in socioeconomic and racial characteristics. The
prevailing interpretation is that a distinctive southern subculture sanctions interpersonal violence (Hackney 1969; Gastil
1971; for reviews and reanalyses see Loftin and Hill 1974 and
Jacobson 1975). Jacobson uses a series of cross-sectional comparisons of UCR crime rates between southern and nonsouthern cities between 1951 and 1970 to demonstrate that "the historically observed pattern of higher crime rates in the South
remains today only in vestigial form" (1975, p. 239). The differences remain significant for murder and assault, however:
southern cities continue to have higher rates. Unfortunately
Jacobson does not control for the racial composition of the
urban population. Another test of a psychocultural explanation
is an unpublished time-series study by Dunham and Kiyak
(1975) which correlates "anomie," inferred from national public
opinion poll data, with homicide rates in thirteen cities from
1940 to 1973. Very strong relationships are reported (sum-

marized in Count–van Manen 1977, p. 40). But which way . does causation flow? Does anomie breed violent crime or does rising urban violence provoke anger and disorientation among the polled public?

B. Economic Variables

Other time-series studies have focused on the economic correlates of trends in offense rates. Some emphasize the stressful effects of economic decline, which is assumed to motivate people, especially those living near the subsistence level, to crime either from frustration or necessity (see Bonger 1967 for a review). The method typical of historical work is to compare graphs of economic conditions and crime. Hanawalt does so for fourteenth-century England, for example, and finds strong evidence that the total number of cases brought to trial "rose and fell with the price of grain" (1979, pp. 238–60). A similar pattern is observed between trials and price indexes in Elizabethan Essex (Samaha 1974, pp. 31–37, 168–69) and, specifically for property crime, in eighteenth-century Surrey and Sussex (Beattie 1974, pp. 85–95).

As a rough generalization, property offenses are more closely related to fluctuating economic conditions than are crimes against persons. Thomas, using data on all England and Wales from 1857 to 1913, concludes from time-series analysis that offenses against property with violence (including robbery) have rather strong inverse correlations with the business cycle (when conditions are good, crime goes down), whereas offenses against persons are unrelated to changing economic conditions (1925, pp. 138–41). Studies using twentieth-century American data, however, detect significant relations between some aspects of economic conditions and violent crime.

For example, Henry and Short (1954) have correlated twenty-three time-series of violent crimes against persons known to police ca. 1929 to 1949 (murder and aggravated assault separately, for various aggregations of city data) with the business cycle. All but four of the series correlate positively with economic conditions. Closer examination leads the authors to conclude not that prosperity causes increased violence but rather that "downward movement of the economic cycle brings with it downward movement of these crimes" (p. 47). They also correlate national data on white and nonwhite homicide rates separately with the business cycle, 1900 to 1940, and find sharply divergent results. White homicide rates increased when the business cycle was low, nonwhite rates decreased when the cycle was low (p. 50). Their interpretation is that blacks, locked into the bottom of the status hierarchy, feel more frustrated and are hence more likely to commit violent acts during good times, when they become increasingly aware of their low status and lack of mobility (pp. 59–62). This is also a plausible explanation for the soaring rate of black homicides during the prosperous 1960s and early 1970s.

As another example, Glaser and Rice (1959) examined the impact of national levels of unemployment on arrest rates for males from 1932 to 1950 nationally and in Boston, Chicago, and Cincinnati. Whereas previous research generally showed little relationship between unemployment and arrest rates in the United States, they argued that the effects should be different for different age groups. And in fact they found that high un-employment was consistently related to high arrest rates for both property offenses and violent crimes for males in their twenties and thirties, but negatively related to juvenile arrest rates.

The most substantial comparative study of the relationship between economic conditions and crime, by Brenner (1976), examines the impact of growth, unemployment, and inflation on national crime statistics ca. 1900 to 1970 in the United States, England and Wales, Scotland, and Canada. Measures of age composition and urbanization also are used. Generally, both growth *and* economic adversity are related to changes in the incidence of property and personal crimes in all four political units, although the relationships vary from one period to another within the larger seventy-year span. Before World War II, cyclical economic fluctuations were the dominant fac-tors, analogous to the more remote historical evidence cited above. Since then the effects of economic growth and inflation are stronger, and—combined with unemployment—account for 90 percent or more of the variation in trends in many offense categories. (Growth and adversity as measured in this study are only weakly related. Brenner argues that long-term economic growth is criminogenic because it causes *comparative* decline in the socioeconomic status of the lowest income and occupational groups.) Most important for this essay are findings concerning changes in violent offenses, estimated by using data on mortality and criminal justice separately:

crimes of violence are more strongly related to economic growth and adversity after World War II than before;

the size of the population under age 30 and the gap between their incomes and that of others are strongly related to changing homicide rates since World War II;

in the period 1920–40 the Great Depression affected the homicide rate somewhat differently than it affected other offenses in that it tended to move upward as employment increased, rather than vice versa, but since World War II "the patterns for both the homicidal and property crimes are identical: they increase sharply during periods of short-term reductions in employment and income" (Brenner 1976, p. 37).[9]

C. Opportunity Theory

Whereas the above studies focus on the stressful effects of economic change, others attribute increases in property and other crimes to changes in the opportunities to commit them. Gould (1969, 1971) uses national data for 1933 to 1965 to show that the availability of property in the United States has been curvilinearly related over time to the incidence of property crime. More exactly, in the 1930s and early 1940s greater abundance was associated with decreasing property crime, but thereafter the relationship was positive. The explanation offered is that the more abundant and less well protected property is,

[9] These results are abstracted from a summary paper which does not report any specific trend or correlation data. The full study has not yet been published.

the easier it is to steal, whether the motives are fun or necessity. A more recent time-series analysis by Cohen, Felson, and Land (1980) of property crime rates in the United States from 1947 to 1977 provides a strong and persuasive test of this "opportunity" theory. A parallel analysis by Cohen and Felson (1979) shows that measures of increased vulnerability of targets (a household activity ratio and the proportion of persons aged 15–24) explain much of the variance over time in homicide and assault rates (R^2 = .68 and .74, respectively).

D. Correlates of Diverging Crime Trends

The studies cited thus far examine the correlates of crime changes over time in single entities (countries; cities singly or in the aggregate). There are also empirical studies of American cities which try to ascertain why their crime trends differ from one another. Skogan (1977) has examined the differential rates of increase in serious offenses known to police in 32 cities between 1948 and 1970, finding that cities with the greatest levels and rates of suburbanization had the greatest increases in crime. His interpretation is that high suburbanization means the concentration of criminogenic forces in the central city. The most substantial studies of this genre are being carried out as part of the "Reactions to Crime" project at Northwestern University. An initial paper by Jacob and Lineberry (1980) reports an analysis of differential rates of change in crime in 395 cities from 1948 to 1978. They find, for example, that the upward trend in violent crime rates—but not property crime—was considerably higher in cities with declining population than others. With respect to race and crime, the proportion of black population is strongly related to rates of violent crime in 1978 (r = .65), but *changes* in the black population from 1950 to 1970 are only weakly related to *changes* in the rate of violent crime (r = .33). They also report that changes in the size of the youthful population had very little effect on crime rates over time. Nor did changes in inequality of income over time have any significant effect on crime rates. Finally, in an intensive study of a sample of ten cities, they tested for evidence of police or political manipulation of official crime data, and while there was evidence of such manipulation in a few cities (especially Newark), a general pattern of manipulation could not be detected.[10] Other papers report on the ways in which trends in crime rates in the ten-city sample are affected by policing, news media coverage, and demographic, economic, racial, and lifestyle variables (e.g. Jacob and Rich 1980; Jacob and Lineberry, forthcoming).

The correlational studies of twentieth-century crime trends suggest that socioeconomic change is an underlying but indirect source of variation in violent crime. The dynamics differ so greatly from one period, place, and social group to another, however, that we must conclude that contextual and intervening variables determine the specific effects of change. For example, Henry and Short (1954) distinguished between the correlates of crime (more exactly, homicide victimization) for blacks and whites. They found that economic conditions affected black and white homicide rates in different ways. It is also evident from Count–van Manen's study of determinants of crime in Washington, D.C. (1977) that the time-series correlates of homicide mortality and murder arrest rates for blacks are quite different from those of whites.[11] And Lane's Philadelphia study shows that the suicide rates for blacks and whites also have diverged over time, implying that all manifestations of violence in the two groups are different (Lane 1980, p. 137; and personal communication). This suggests that quantitative studies of determinants of crime trends in the United States

---

[10] Seidman and Couzens (1974) demonstrate the impact of political pressures in selected American cities on police crime reporting practices using monthly data from 1967 to 1971.

[11] The study is so badly flawed that none of its specific correlation results are worth mentioning here. A large grab bag of independent variables is used; they are correlated with the crime-rate data using stepwise regression, so that a different assortment of variables is to be found in each equation; the data are not de-trended nor are coefficients corrected for auto-correlation; indeed, no regression coefficients or levels of significance are reported; and the discussion of results is fuddled. Tables of simple correlations nonetheless show that the correlates of black and white homicide rates are quite different one from another, and also differ by time-period (Count–van Manen 1977, pp. 139, 141).

ought to be disaggregated along racial lines. Separate models should be estimated for blacks and whites (using arrest or victimization data) and explanations sought for the observed differences. This follows the suggestion, offered above, that there is much to be learned from examining differential trends in violent crime rates among other kinds of social and economic groups, in the United States and elsewhere. The suggestion is a contemporary twist to an enduring concern among social historians of crime, namely the changing characteristics of offenders and their treatment over time (for example Given 1977; Hanawalt 1979, chap. 4; Lane 1979, pp. 100–14).

V. Violent Crime Trends and their Correlates in Other Western Societies

Here we review the evidence from other European and European-settled societies on long-term trends in violent crime, testing each country's evidence against the U-shaped curve.

A. The Nineteenth and Early Twentieth Centuries

I first suggested that there might be a long-term decline in serious crime common to all Western societies on the basis of a comparative study of London, Stockholm and New South Wales. The incidence of murder and assault in the early history of New South Wales (including Sydney) was very high, not surprising in view of the fact that the majority of its male inhabitants through 1840 were convicts and emancipists. Committals to trial for murder between 1819 and 1824 averaged 35 per 100,000 population per annum, for example, compared with ca. 2 per 100,000 in Middlesex County (London) in the same period. The rate dropped sharply after 1830, however: a composite measure of Supreme Court convictions for murder and assault in the colony shows a decline from ca. 45 per 100,000 in the 1830s to ca. 10 in the 1850s and less than 5 in the 1890s. A variety of indicators of serious and lesser offenses against persons show that the decline in interpersonal violence persisted until 1940 (see Grabosky 1976; Gurr, Grabosky, and Hula 1977, pp. 622–25). (Also see Addendum at p. 353.)

Since New South Wales imported most of its population and crime problems, as well as its institutions of criminal justice, from Britain, it is not surprising that its trends in violent crime paralleled those of the mother country. The most consequential difference is that the decline in New South Wales was considerably more precipitous once the convict era come to an end. It is somewhat more surprising to find Scandinavian evidence of a similar long-term trend. In Stockholm convictions for murder, manslaughter, and attempted murder combined were ca. 3.5 per 100,000 population in the 1830s, ca. 1.5 in the 1850s, and less than 1.0 by the turn of the century—although there was a temporary doubling of the rate in the 1880s. Data on offenses known to police from 1841 on trace a similar irregular decline. The rate of known homicides and attempts never exceeded 1 per 100,000 per annum (or five cases annually) from 1920 to 1940 (see Gurr, Grabosky, and Hula 1977, pp. 237–320, 622–24).

France offers the best and most thoroughly studied nineteenth-century crime statistics of any continental country, thanks to the publication of annual reports of criminal justice beginning in 1826. There are several English-language studies which make use of these data on numbers of persons tried for various kinds of offenses (Lodhi and Tilly 1973; MacDonald 1910; Zehr 1975, 1976). Zehr's studies are the most thorough, providing detailed descriptions and time-series analyses of trends in homicide and serious assault from 1826 to 1913, nationally and in a sample of eight departments. Homicide trials declined from ca. 3.5 per 100,000 adults in the 1830s to ca. 2 in the 1860s, then increased and varied between 2.5 and 3 during the remainder of the century (Zehr 1976, pp. 115–16). The incidence of serious assaults tried before the high courts fell precipitously (MacDonald 1910, p. 66), but this may simply reflect a shift of lesser cases to the lower courts. The trend in lower-court cases of assault and battery was positive: the rates doubled from the 1830s to the first decade of the twentieth century and were closely correlated over time with per capita wine consumption but negatively correlated with price indexes (Zehr 1976, pp. 87–110).

Zehr's analysis of the timing of changes in assault rates, and their variable distribution among departments, leads him to the more general conclusion that "most major upswings in violence appear to be relatable to urban-industrial growth or more precisely, to the initial and/or most disruptive stages of the process" (1975, p. 128). In contrast, Lodhi and Tilly make a series of cross-sectional correlation analyses for the 1840s and 1850s, using data on crime rates in departments, and find virtually no relationship between measures of urbanization or industrialization and crimes against persons (1973, p. 311). (They do, however, find strong relationships between the proportion of population urban and property crime.) Since Zehr uses time-series analysis, which is appropriate to testing dynamic arguments, his findings about the economic and other correlates of assault rates carry more weight.[12]

Crime trends in Germany have also been carefully studied from ca. 1882, when the first national data were compiled, to the outbreak of World War I in 1914. Studies by McHale and Johnson (1976, 1977) and by Zehr (1975, 1976) deal particularly with the connections between urbanization, industrialization, and crime in this era. They are less concerned with national trends than with differences in trends, and rates, among regions at different levels of urban and industrial growth. The overall trend in offenses against persons (using court data on persons tried and convictions) shows a 50 percent rise from the early 1880s to the late 1890s followed by a more gradual decline (McHale and Johnson 1977, p. 215; Zehr 1976, pp. 91–94).

---

[12] Alternatively, the difference in findings may be due to Lodhi and Tilly's use of Assize Court data (1973, p. 300), which includes only the most serious offenses against persons, while Zehr uses data from the lower correctional tribunals on simple assault and battery. Data tabled in MacDonald (1910, p. 66) show that numbers of persons tried for the former averaged about 600 per year compared with 25,000 annually for the latter. Oddly, the rates of serious crimes against persons reported and used by Lodhi and Tilly bear no discernible relationship to rates I have calculated using the data on numbers of persons tried from MacDonald. If nothing else, Tilly and Lodhi are cryptically casual in describing their index. There is no problem reconciling Zehr's index with MacDonald's data.

But, as in France, the trend was due to changes in the incidence of assault, and as I suggested in an earlier section, upward trends in assaults during the nineteenth century are prima facie suspect because they are more likely a reflection of growing sensitization and closer official attention to assaults than evidence for real increases in interpersonal violence. Indeed, the trend in homicide trials in Germany was downward, declining from an initial rate of about 1.0 trials per 100,000 to 0.76 after 1900 (Zehr 1976, pp. 115–16).[13] Zehr's general observation about France and Germany is that "during the nineteenth century violence became more frequent but possibly less severe" (1976, p. 115). He briefly considers but tentatively rejects the argument that the increase in assault may have been due to more thorough reporting (1976, pp. 88–89).

What of the correlates of trends in crimes against persons in Germany? McHale and Johnson (1977, p. 227) find, as Zehr did for France, that personal crime rates were rather stable in their geographical distribution across time—evidence, in other words, for persisting regional subcultures of interpersonal violence, especially in poorer districts. But levels of personal crime appeared to be unrelated, in any and all cross-sectional comparisons of districts, to urban industrial development (1977, pp. 235–42). This requires modification in light of Zehr's time-series analysis of assault trends in thirteen towns and cities. Though the evidence is mixed, it fits his general thesis that rising assault rates coincided with the initial, not the later stages of urbanization. Once industrial growth and urbanization were well under way, social adjustment set in and interpersonal violence tended to decline (Zehr 1976, pp. 94, 107–14). This fits well with McHale and Johnson's general interpretation of their results, that the incidence of all categories of crime in Germany was highest in regions where social stress was greatest, owing

---

[13] Zehr also reports graphically earlier homicide data for Prussia alone which show a U-shaped curve with a downslope in the 1850s and a sharp increase in the 1870s (associated with the Franco-Prussian War of 1870–71). Still earlier data for Bavaria from 1835 to 1860 show, at most, a slight upward trend (Zehr 1976, pp. 115–16).

either to depopulation (in rural areas) or to very rapid population growth (in the swollen urban-industrial centers). As stress increased, then lessened in a particular district, so did crime rise and ebb (1977, pp. 243–44).[14] For a general theoretical analysis of the effects of industrialization and urbanization on crime see Shelley (1981).

B. *From World War I to the 1970s*

World War I had profound effects on crime in Germany and Austria. The incidence of most kinds of property and personal offenses declined during the war, a pattern widely observed during wartime in other Western societies and readily explained by the fact that the most crime-prone demographic group, young males, were in military service. Immediately after the war, most categories of offenses against persons rose sharply, though more so in Germany (Liepman 1930, pp. 35, 39, 58–59, 77) than in Austria (Exner 1927, p. 24).

The evidence from Germany and Austria is consistent with Sellin's study of postwar murder trends in nine European nations (1926) and with a much broader comparative study by Archer and Gartner (1976) on the impact on homicide rates of a country's participation in war. Archer and Gartner's general procedure is to compare average homicide rates during the five years before the outbreak of war with rates during the first five postwar years. Their comparisons for fourteen of the combatant nations in World War I show postwar increases greater than 10 percent (and averaging 40 percent) in eight of the fourteen; unchanged rates in two; and substantial declines in three. They find even stronger evidence for homicide increases after World War II. Among fifteen combatant nations homicide rates in-

[14] These conclusions about the relation of modernization to assault rates are not necessarily invalidated by my suggestion that the upward trend in nineteenth-century assault rates was probably spurious. It is plausible that rapid industrialization and urban growth could cause substantial short-term increases in assault rates in particular jurisdictions, increases superimposed on a longer run decline. It is the upward surge and then subsidence of rates at the onset of modernization that is the essential evidence for arguments advanced by Zehr and McHale and Johnson, not the underlying trend.

creased substantially in eleven, by an average of 89 percent.[15] Rates were unchanged in one and lower in three others (Archer and Gartner 1976, p. 947). The data on these and other nations which participated in twentieth-century wars are used to test alternative hypotheses about why war leads so often to increases in homicide. Explanations which focus on social disorganization, economic stress, and the violence of war veterans are found insufficient to account for homicide increases, and the authors conclude, without direct test, that the most plausible explanation is "that wars . . . tend to legitimate the general use of violence in domestic society" (1976, p. 958).

Aside from studies of the impact of war on crime, not much attention has been given to crime trends in Europe from the 1920s through the 1950s.[16] Reference was made above to studies of Stockholm and New South Wales (Sydney) showing low and stable rates of offenses against persons for most of this period (Gurr, Grabosky, and Hula 1977, pp. 282–85, 438–43). What is strikingly absent from these studies, and those of British and American crime trends reviewed above, is evidence of increases in personal crime during the Great Depression of the 1930s. *Property* offenses evidently increased, especially in Britain (see Gurr, Grabosky, and Hula 1977, pp. 118–24), but homicide and assault were at or near their lowest recorded levels in virtually all countries and jurisdictions. In the United States, homicide rates *declined* substantially during the depression era (see fig. 2, above).[17]

The "crime waves" in the European countries most affected by World War II had largely subsided by 1950. The most re-

---

[15] A study of trends in violent crimes known to police in Japan during and after World War II provides detailed evidence of these dynamics. Homicides declined sharply from ca. 2,500 in 1935 to about 1,000 per annum in the early 1940s, then soared above 3,000 in the early 1950s before beginning a long, gradual decline, falling below 2,000 by the early 1970s. Robbery, an uncommon offense in prewar Japan (less than 2,000 cases annually) increased by 700 percent immediately after the war, and then declined to 2,000 by the early 1970s (Lunden 1976).

[16] My bibliographic search for trend studies has been confined largely to those published in English. Undoubtedly there are crime-trend studies of continental countries in other languages which escaped my attention.

[17] This decline may be attributable to the end of Prohibition in 1933. The high homicide rates of the 1920s were partly the result of conflict over the control of illegal alcohol (see Zahn 1980, pp. 115–17).

markable subsequent phenomenon is the near universality of rising crime during the period of unprecedented prosperity of the 1960s and early 1970s. The British and North American experience was by no means unique. The late 1940s and early 1950s marked the low ebb of crimes against persons in virtually every English-speaking country. Thereafter the trends were consistently upwards. The same was true of Scandinavia. In Stockholm after 1950 virtually every category of offense against persons and property skyrocketed. Some twenty-year increases in rates of offenses known to police are: murder and attempts, 600 percent; assault and battery, more than 300 percent; rape and attempted rape, 300 percent; robberies, 1000 percent. Stockholm experienced in more serious form a malaise that affected all the Scandinavian countries beginning somewhat later, in the 1960s rather than the 1950s. Elsewhere in continental Europe the trends in personal crimes were somewhat different. The model pattern, evident in convictions data from West Germany, Austria, and France, was one in which offense rates declined from postwar peaks through the 1950s and 1960s but turned sharply upward after 1970. Switzerland is the only European country whose rates of offenses against persons remained steady throughout this period (see Gurr 1977, 1979).

One factor which may help account for the differential timing of increases in personal crimes among Western countries is the shape and timing of the "baby boom" which followed World War II. All records of crime in Western societies, past and present, show that young males are disproportionately represented among offenders. The coming of age of the postwar generation of youths is closely linked to the onset of major increases in personal and property crime in the United States and Britain, as is evident from Ferdinand's study of demographic and crime changes in the United States from 1950 to 1965 (1970) and from the graphs which relate the changing size of the youthful population with offense rates in these two countries in my recent essay (Gurr 1979, pp. 368–69). But the shape and timing of the "age bulge" differ among Western societies. In Britain and the United States, the proportion of the population aged 15 to 29 increased by roughly 50 percent between the mid-1950s and the mid-1970s. Germany and Austria, by contrast, had baby "boomlets" which were smaller than those of the United States and Britain and which began after economic recovery set in during the 1950s. The precise nature of this relationship needs to be specified more precisely and studied longitudinally using demographic and crime data for each Western country. For an exemplary study see Zimring (1979).

The upward trend in violent crime since the 1960s thus seems most pronounced in the English-speaking and Scandinavian countries but it is by no means universal. Among Western democracies it is notably absent in Switzerland, perhaps because of the sociocultural factors specified by Clinard (1978), in Italy, and in Israel (see Gurr 1977, pp. 69–70). Japan has had a steady decline in serious offenses against persons and property since the mid-1950s (see Lunden 1976; Gurr 1977, pp. 69–73), which Bayley (1976) attributes both to policing practices and cultural traits. Last but far from least, the statistical evidence from Eastern European countries, recently summarized by Redo (1980), shows little change in the incidence of violent crime between 1964 and 1977 despite significant increases in the population aged 15–24 in most of these countries.[18]

VI. Some Observations

How well does the U-shaped curve of declining, then rising violent crime fit the evidence reviewed here? The English evidence on homicide covers the longest timespan and is the most convincing in documenting a sustained decline of substantial magnitude. By the same token it makes the post-1960 upturn appear to be a minor perturbation, proportionally no greater than upward swings in homicide rates in Elizabethan times and during the Napoleonic wars—swings which proved to be temporary. In the United States the occurrence of three great surges in violent crime, beginning ca. 1850, 1900, and 1960,

[18] Redo, a Polish scholar, implicitly accepts the accuracy of the official data. There is no prima facie why the homicide and assault data should be misreported for the sake of gilding the official portrait of socialist reality, and even if they are systematically underreported, that should not invalidate the assessment of their trends.

makes it impossible to say whether these increases are superimposed on a long-term decline. My reading of the evidence is that the long-term trend in homicide rates among whites has been generally downward until recently, whereas homicide rates among blacks not only have been higher and more variable but have moved generally upward since the beginning of the twentieth century, perhaps earlier. Declines in homicidal violence also are established for nineteenth-century Stockholm, New South Wales, France, and—beginning late in the century—Germany. In general we have not seen any evidence from any country or jurisdiction that there was a sustained increase in homicides during the nineteenth century—with the important codicil that most of the time-series studies span only the second half of the century. An increase in homicide rates since the 1960s is also a common though not universal phenomenon in Western societies. The exceptions are some continental democracies which began later or avoided the trend entirely. Moreover the increase is specific to Western democracies: Eastern European states and Japan have had steady or declining homicide rates.

The evidence on assault and robbery is more limited but in general parallels the trends in homicide. That is strikingly evident in countries which experienced the post-1960 increase in crime: robbery and assault rates usually increased much more than homicide. In the nineteenth century, however, assault rates moved contrary to homicides in France, Germany, and some American jurisdictions. There is reason to attribute this to increased official attention to minor offenses, not to real and sustained increases in assault.

The discussion of trend evidence has touched on a number of explanations for trends and variations around them. There are two separate questions for which explanation is needed. One is, What social dynamics underlie the long-term decline in violent crime? The other is, What accounts for the big deviations of crime above this trend, especially those sustained upwellings of violence that persist for ten or twenty or more years before subsiding again? I think that there is a simple and singular answer to the first question, but multiple and complex answers to the second. I also think that no special, *sui generis* explanation is needed for the late increase in violent crime. Its explanation should follow from an understanding of the dynamics of the long-term decline and of the deviations from it. In other words I propose to regard the upturn of the U-shaped curve as simply the latest, and best-documented, deviation from the underlying trend.

A plausible explanation for the long-term decline in interpersonal violence is what Norbert Elias calls "the civilizing process" (1978) and all that it implies about the restraint of aggressive impulses and the acceptance of humanistic values.[19] By their own accounts, medieval Europeans were easily angered to the point of violence and enmeshed in a culture which accepted, even glorified, many forms of brutality and aggressive behavior (see Given 1977, chap. 1 for a summary; also Elias 1978, pp. 191–205). The progress of Western civilization has been marked by increasing internal and external controls on the show of violence. People are socialized to control and displace anger. Norms of conduct in almost all organized activity stress nonviolent means of accomplishing goals. Interpersonal violence within the community and nation is prohibited and subject to sanction in almost all circumstances. The process is in essence a cultural one and like most cultural change had its origins in the changing values of social and intellectual elites. The process, so far as it pertains to violence, contributed not only to the decline in homicide and assault but also to the humanization and rationalization of social policy. It led, for example, to the decline and ultimate abandonment of executions in most Western nations, the end of slavery and the brutalization of wage labor, the passing of corporal punishment in schools and prisons, and many other humane features of contemporary life that are often taken for granted (on the effects of humanitarian thought on criminal justice policies see Gurr, Grabosky, and Hula 1977, chap. V.5).

[19] The following discussion is drawn largely from the conclusion to my 1979 essay on the same topic (Gurr 1979, pp. 365–71).

The cultural process of sensitization to violence, to use So-man's phrase (1980, pp. 20–23), has not been uniform. It took root first among the urban upper and middle classes and only gradually and selectively was promulgated among rural people and the lower classes. It has been suggested, for example, that one significant social function of the new nineteenth-century police forces was to serve as missionaries of upper and middle class values to the theretofore dangerous lower classes (see for example Silver 1967 and Monkkonen 1975). Be that as it may, the thesis that sensitization to violence spread from the social center to the periphery and from upper to lower classes is intrinsically plausible as an explanation of some basic features of nineteenth-century and contemporary criminality. Interpersonal violence historically may have been higher in rural than urban areas—the evidence is mixed—because of the persistence there of traditional patterns of interpersonal behavior. It tended to increase in cities during the early stages of urbanization and industrialization because new immigrants from the countryside, or from overseas, only gradually assimilated the lifeways of the city. Violence declined overall during the nineteenth century and the first half of the twentieth because Western societies became increasingly urban and formal education became universal. The further down the class and status ladder, past and present, the more common is interpersonal violence, because the lower classes did not assimilate and still have not wholly assimilated the aggression-inhibiting values of the middle and upper classes. And the black minority in the United States has far higher rates of interpersonal violence than the white majority because the barriers of discrimination and segregation have fostered a subculture which encourages aggressive behavior.

There is one other group that may become *de*sensitized to violence: youth. The historical process of sensitization to violence must be replicated in the socialization of each new generation of children in each Western society. To the extent that socialization fails, or is incomplete because it is not reinforced

Ted Robert Gurr

by other social institutions, youth are susceptible to other kinds of values, including those which celebrate violence. This is a potential factor in the generation of violent behavior which stands independently of, but is reinforced by, the social fact that young males are in general more likely to be caught up in interpersonal violence, as offenders and victims, than any other demographic category.

The long-run downslope of interpersonal violence is irregular and some of the irregularities take the form of sharp and sustained increases. I referred above to the evidence, mainly from studies of France and Germany, that violent crime tends to rise in the early stages of industrialization and urbanization, though there is little evid'nce that the pace of urban growth in general has affected rates of violent crime. Modernization may have been one of the sources of high rates of violent crime in early nineteenth-century England and in the United States in the 1860s and 1870s. But urbanization and industrialization usually are gradual processes, not likely of themselves to create a single tidal wave of disorder except in regions and cities experiencing very rapid change.

The connection between warfare and waves of violent crime is more precise. In fact, war is the single most obvious correlate of the great historical waves of violent crime in England and the United States. Civil and foreign war contributed to the crime peak of the 1340s (Hanawalt 1979, pp. 228–39). A mid-eighteenth-century wave of crime coincided with Britain's involvement in a succession of wars from 1739 (war with Spain) to 1763 (the end of the Seven Years' War). The upsurge of crime at the onset of the nineteenth century began while Britain was enmeshed in the Napoleonic wars, from 1793 to 1815, and continued through the severe economic depression which followed their end. In the United States the peak of urban crime in the 1860s and 1870s coincides with the social and political upheavals of the Civil War. The disproportionate fondness for dueling and less genteel forms of violence among white southerners may not have originated with the Civil War (see

Hackney 1969; Gastil 1971), but surely it was reinforced by it. The second high wave of violent American crime crested during the decade after World War I. The third began near the onset of the Vietnam war. Lesser increases in violent crime coincided with or followed both world wars in Britain, the United States, and most continental democracies. We also noted the great increase in violent crime which followed Germany and Austria's defeat in World War I.

War may lead to increased violent crime for a number of reasons, reviewed and tested by Archer and Gartner (1976). I opt for the interpretation, consistent with their evidence, that it does so mainly because war legitimizes violence. It does so directly for young men who become habituated to violence in military service; it does so indirectly for others who find in the patriotic gore of wartime a license to act out their own feelings of anger. The interpretation is difficult to prove. But it is consistent both with the evidence on crime trends and with the social dynamics proposed for the long-run decline in interpersonal violence: if the civilizing process has been accompanied by sensitization to violence, then war, including internal war, temporarily desensitizes people to violence. If there is such an effect it is probably greatest among youth who are at the most impressionable age during wartime. This suggests that the argument could be tested indirectly by careful study of changes in age-specific rates of arrests for violent offenses during periods following war.

Another basic factor that influences the extent of personal crime is the size of the youthful population. If their relative numbers are high in a particular city or era, its crime rates are likely to be higher than in times and places where the population is older. Hanawalt, for example, suggests that some of medieval England's high incidence of homicide may have been due to the fact that it had a relatively youthful population (1979, p. 127). It is also the case that if the relative number of young males increases substantially in a short time, so will crime against both person and property. Such changes have occurred periodically in Western societies, often as a consequence of socioeconomic change or war. A population boom was underway in England during the first half of the nineteenth century, thanks to better nutrition and higher birth rates. As one result there was a remarkably high proportion of young males in London's population. Over the long run, 1801 to 1971, the changing proportions of males aged 15 to 29 in London's population trace a time-path very similar to, though of much lower amplitude than, the time-path of felonies (Gurr, Grabosky, and Hula 1977, p. 43). The explosion in youth crime in the 1960s and 1970s also is closely linked to substantial changes in the age structures of the United States, Britain, and most other Western societies, as noted in the preceding section.

The strands of this speculative discussion can be brought together by concluding that each great upsurge of violent crime in the histories of the societies under study has been caused by a distinctive combination of altered social forces. Some crime waves have followed from fundamental social dislocation, as a result of which significant segments of a population have been separated from the civilizing institutions which instill and reinforce the basic Western injunctions against interpersonal violence. They may be migrants, demobilized veterans, a growing population of disillusioned young people for whom there is no social or economic niche, or badly educated young black men locked in the decaying ghettoes of an affluent society. The most devastating episodes of public disorder, however, seem to occur when social dislocation coincides with changes in values which legitimate violence that was once thought to be illegitimate. Historically, wars seem to have had this effect. There is also the possibility that other factors, such as the content of popular culture or the values articulated in segmented groups, may have the same consequences.

These conclusions are speculative and imprecise. I will conclude simply by expressing the hope that the next generation of research on trends in violent crimes will be as much concerned with testing these and competing kinds of general explanations as with description.

REFERENCES

Abbott, Edith. 1922. "Recent Statistics Relating to Crime in Chicago," *Journal of Criminal Law, Criminology, and Police Science* 13:329–58.

Archer, Dane, and Rosemary Gartner. 1976. "Violent Acts and Violent Times: A Comparative Approach to Postwar Homicide Rates," *American Sociological Review* 41:937–63.

Baldwin, John, and A. E. Bottoms. 1976. *The Urban Criminal: A Study in Sheffield.* London: Tavistock.

Bayley, David. 1976. *Forces of Order; Police Behavior in Japan and the United States.* Berkeley: University of California Press.

Beattie, J. M. 1974. "The Pattern of Crime in England, 1660–1800," *Past & Present* 62 (February): 47–95.

Block, Richard. 1977. *Violent Crime: Environment, Interaction, and Death.* Lexington, Mass.: Lexington Books.

Bloch, Herbert A., and Gilbert Geis. 1962. *Man, Crime, and Society: The Forms of Criminal Behavior.* New York: Random House.

Bonger, William. 1967. *Criminality and Economic Conditions,* trans. Henry P. Horton. New York: Agathon Press.

Boudouris, James. 1970. "Trends in Homicide, Detroit, 1926–1968." Ph.D. dissertation, Wayne State University.

Brearley, H. C. 1932. *Homicide in the United States.* Chapel Hill: University of North Carolina Press.

Brenner, M. Harvey. 1976. *Effects of the Economy on Criminal Behaviour and the Administration of Criminal Justice in the United States, Canada, England and Wales and Scotland.* Rome: United Nations Social Defence Research Institute.

Clinard, Marshall B. 1978. *Cities with Little Crime.* New York: Cambridge University Press.

Cockburn, J. S. 1977. "The Nature and Incidence of Crime in England, 1559–1625: A Preliminary Survey." In *Crime in England 1550–1800,* ed. J. S. Cockburn. Princeton: Princeton University Press.

Cohen, Lawrence E., and Marcus Felson. 1979. "Social Change and Crime Rate Trends: A Routine Activity Approach," *American Sociological Review* 44:588–607.

Cohen, Lawrence E., Marcus Felson, and Kenneth C. Land. 1980. "Property Crime in the United States: A Macrodynamic Analysis, 1947–1977; with Ex Ante Forecasts for the Mid-1980s," *American Journal of Sociology* 86:90–118.

Count–van Manen, Gloria. 1977. *Crime and Suicide in the Nation's Capital: Toward Macro-Historical Perspectives.* New York: Praeger.

Dunham, H. Warren, and Asuman Kiyak. 1975. "Cultural Change and Homicide: An Interrelationship." Unpublished paper summarized in Count–van Manen 1977, p. 40.

Elias, Norbert. 1978. *The Civilizing Process: The History of Manners.* New York: Urizen. (Originally published 1939.)

Ellwood, Charles A. 1910. "Has Crime Increased in the United States Since 1880?" *Journal of Criminal Law and Criminology* 1:378–85.

Exner, Franz. 1927. *Krieg und Kriminalität in Österreich.* Vienna: Hölder-Pichler-Tempsky; New Haven: Yale University Press.

Ferdinand, Theodore N. 1967. "The Criminal Patterns of Boston since 1869," *American Journal of Sociology* 73:688–98.

———. 1970. "Demographic Shifts and Criminality: An Inquiry," *British Journal of Criminology* 10:169–75.

———. 1972. "Politics, the Police, and Arresting Policies in Salem, Massachusetts since the Civil War," *Social Problems* 19:572–88.

Gastil, Raymond D. 1971. "Homicide and a Regional Culture of Violence," *American Sociological Review* 36:412–26.

Gatrell, V. A. C. 1980. "The Decline of Theft and Violence in Victorian and Edwardian England." In *Crime and the Law since 1850*, ed. V. A. C. Gatrell, B. P. Lenman, and G. Parker. London: Europa.

Gatrell, V. A. C., and T. B. Hadden. 1972. "Criminal Statistics and Their Interpretation." In *Nineteenth Century Society: Essays in the Use of Quantitative Methods for the Study of Social Data*, ed. E. A. Wrigley. Cambridge: Cambridge University Press.

Giffen, P. J. 1965. "Rates of Crime and Delinquency." In *Crime and Its Treatment in Canada*, ed. W. T. McGrath. New York: St. Martin's Press.

Given, James Buchanan. 1977. *Society and Homicide in Thirteenth-Century England.* Stanford: Stanford University Press.

Glaser, Daniel, and Kent Rice. 1959. "Crime, Age, and Employment," *American Sociological Review* 24:679–86.

Gould, Leroy C. 1969. "The Changing Structure of Property Crime in an Affluent Society," *Social Forces* 48:50–60.

———. 1971. "Crime and its Impact in an Affluent Society." In *Crime and Justice in American Society*, ed. Jack D. Douglas. Indianapolis: Bobbs-Merrill.

Grabosky, Peter N. 1976. *Sydney in Ferment: Crime, Dissent, and Official Reaction, 1788–1973.* Canberra: Australian National University Press.

Greenberg, Douglas. 1976. *Crime and Law Enforcement in the Colony of New York, 1691–1776.* Ithaca: Cornell University Press.

Gurr, Ted Robert. 1977. "Crime Trends in Modern Democracies since 1945," *International Annals of Criminology* 16:41–85.

———. 1979. "On the History of Violent Crime in Europe and America." In *Violence in America: Historical and Comparative Perspectives*, ed. Hugh David Graham and Ted Robert Gurr. 2d ed. Beverly Hills: Sage Publications.

———. 1980. "Development and Decay: Their Impact on Public Order in Western History." In *History and Crime: Implications for Criminal Justice Policy*, ed. James A. Inciardi and Charles E. Faupel. Beverly Hills: Sage Publications.

Gurr, Ted Robert, Peter N. Grabosky, and Richard C. Hula. 1977. *The Politics of Crime and Conflict: A Comparative History of Four Cities.* Beverly Hills: Sage Publications.

Hackney, Sheldon. 1969. "Southern Violence," *American Historical Review* 76:906–25.

Hair, P. E. H. 1971. "Deaths from Violence in Britain: A Tentative Secular Survey," *Population Studies* 25:5–24.

Hammer, Carl I., Jr. 1978. "Patterns of Homicide in a Medieval University Town: Fourteenth-Century Oxford," *Past & Present* 78 (February): 3–23.

Hanawalt, Barbara A. 1976. "Violent Death in Fourteenth- and Early Fifteenth-Century England," *Comparative Studies in Society and History* 18:297–320.

———. 1979. *Crime and Conflict in English Communities, 1300–1348.* Cambridge, Mass.: Harvard University Press.

Harrison, Leonard V. 1934. *Police Administration in Boston.* Cambridge, Mass: Harvard University Press.

Hay, Douglas, Peter Linebaugh, John G. Rule, E. P. Thompson, and Cal Winslow. 1975. *Albion's Fatal Tree: Crime and Society in Eighteenth-Century England.* New York: Pantheon Books.

Henry, Andrew F., and James F. Short, Jr. 1954. *Suicide and Homicide: Some Economic, Sociological, and Psychological Aspects of Aggression.* New York: Free Press of Glencoe.

Hindus, Michael Stephen. 1980. *Prison and Plantation: Crime, Justice, and Authority in Massachusetts and South Carolina, 1767–1878.* Chapel Hill: University of North Carolina Press.

Hirsch, Charles S., Norman B. Rushforth, Amasa B. Ford, and Lester Adelson. 1973. "Homicide and Suicide in a Metropolitan County. I. Long-Term Trends," *Journal of the American Medical Association* 223:900–905.

Hobbs, A. H. 1943. "Relationship between Criminality and Economic Conditions," *Journal of Criminal Law, Criminology, and Police Science* 34:5–10.

Hoffman, F. L. 1925. *The Homicide Problem.* Newark: Prudential Press.

————. 1928. "Murder and the Death Penalty," *Current History* 28:408–10.

Jacob, Herbert, and Robert L. Lineberry. 1980. "Cities and Crime." Paper read at the 1980 meeting of the Social Science History Association, Rochester, N.Y.

————. Forthcoming. *Governmental Responses to Crime.*

Jacob, Herbert, and Michael J. Rich. 1980. "The Effects of the Police on Crime: A Second Look." Paper read at the 1980 meeting of the Law and Society Association, San Francisco.

Jacobson, Alvin L. 1975. "Crime Rates in Southern and Nonsouthern Cities: A Twenty-Year Perspective," *Social Forces* 54:226–42.

Kaye, J. M. 1967. "The Early History of Murder and Manslaughter," *Law Quarterly Review* 83:365–95.

Lane, Roger. 1968. "Crime and Criminal Statistics in Nineteenth Century Massachusetts," *Journal of Social History* 2:156–63.

————. 1979. *Violent Death in the City: Suicide, Accident, and Murder in Nineteenth-Century Philadelphia.* Cambridge, Mass.: Harvard University Press.

————. 1980. "Urban Police and Crime in Nineteenth-Century America," *Crime and Justice* 2:1–44.

Liepmann, Moritz. 1930. *Krieg und Kriminalität in Deutschland.* Stuttgart, Berlin, and Leipzig: Deutsche Verlags-Anstalt; New Haven: Yale University Press.

Lodhi, Abdul Qaiyum, and Charles Tilly. 1973. "Urbanization, Crime, and Collective Violence in 19th-Century France," *American Journal of Sociology* 79:296–318.

Loftin, Colin, and Robert H. Hill. 1974. "Regional Subculture and Homicide: An Examination of the Gastil-Hackney Thesis," *American Sociological Review* 39:714–724.

Lunden, Walter A. 1976. "Violent Crimes in Japan in War and Peace, 1933–74," *International Journal of Criminology and Penology* 4:349–63.

Lundsgaarde, Henry P. 1977. *Murder in Space City: A Cultural Analysis of Houston Homicide Patterns.* New York: Oxford University Press.

McClintock, F. H. 1963. *Crimes of Violence: An Enquiry by the Cambridge Institute of Criminology into Crimes of Violence against the Person in London.* London: Macmillan.

McClintock, F. H., and N. Howard Avison with G. N. G. Rose. 1968. *Crime in England and Wales.* London: Heinemann.

MacDonald, Arthur. 1910. "Criminal Statistics in Germany, France and England," *Journal of Criminal Law and Criminology* 1:59–70.

McHale, Vincent E., and Eric A. Johnson. 1976. "Urbanization, Industrialization, and Crime in Imperial Germany: Part I," *Social Science History* 1:45–78.

————. 1977. "Urbanization, Industrialization, and Crime in Imperial

Germany: Part II," *Social Science History* 1:210–47.

McNeill, William H. 1976. *Plagues and Peoples.* New York: Double-day, Anchor Books.

Monkkonen, Eric. 1975. *The Dangerous Class: Crime and Poverty in Columbus, Ohio, 1860–1885.* Cambridge, Mass.: Harvard University Press.

———. 1979. "A Disorderly People? Urban Order in the Nineteenth and Twentieth Centuries." Paper read at the 1979 meetings of the American Studies Association, Minneapolis.

———. 1980. "The Quantitative Historical Study of Crime and Criminal Justice." In *History and Crime: Implications for Criminal Justice Policy,* ed. James A. Inciardi and Charles E. Faupel. Beverly Hills: Sage Publications.

———. 1981. *Police in Urban America, 1860–1920.* New York: Cambridge University Press.

Mulvilhill, Donald, and Melvin Tumin. 1969. *Crimes of Violence, Report to the National Commission on the Causes and Prevention of Violence.* Vol. 11. Washington, D.C.: Government Printing Office.

Nutt, Harry G. 1905. "Homicide in New Hampshire," *Journal of the American Statistical Association* 9:220–30.

Peirce, David, Peter N. Grabosky, and Ted Robert Gurr. 1977. "London: The Politics of Crime and Conflict, 1800 to the 1970's." In *The Politics of Crime and Conflict: A Comparative History of Four Cities,* by Ted Robert Gurr, Peter N. Grabosky, and Richard C. Hula. Beverly Hills: Sage Publications.

Powell, Elwin H. 1966. "Crime as a Function of Anomie," *Journal of Criminal Law, Criminology, and Police Science* 57:161–71.

———. 1970. *The Design of Discord: Studies of Anomie: Suicide, Urban Society, War.* New York: Oxford University Press.

Redo, Slawomir M. 1980. "Crime Trends and Crime Prevention Strategies in Eastern Europe." Paper read to the Sixth United Nations Congress on the Prevention of Crime and the Treatment of Offenders, Caracas.

Samaha, Joel. 1974. *Law and Order in Historical Perspective: The Case of Elizabethan Essex.* New York and London: Academic Press.

Seidman, David, and Michael Couzens. 1974. "Getting the Crime Rate Down: Political Pressure and Crime Reporting," *Law and Society* 10:457–93.

Sellin, Thorsten. 1926. "Is Murder Increasing in Europe?" *Annals of the American Academy of Political and Social Science* 126:29–34.

Shelley, Louise I. 1981. *Crime and Modernization: The Impact of Industrialization and Urbanization on Crime.* Carbondale: Southern Illinois University Press.

Silver, Allan. 1967. "The Demand for Order in Civil Society: A Review of Some Themes in the History of Urban Crime, Police, and Riot." In *The Police: Six Sociological Essays*, ed. David J. Bordua. New York: John Wiley and Sons.

Skogan, Wesley G. 1975. "Measurement Problems in Official and Survey Crime Rates," *Journal of Criminal Justice* 3:17–32.

———. 1976. "Citizen Reporting of Crime: Some National Panel Data," *Criminology* 13:535–49.

———. 1977. "The Changing Distribution of Big-City Crime: A Multi-City Time Series Analysis," *Urban Affairs Quarterly* 13:33–47.

———. 1979. "Crime in Contemporary America." In *Violence in America: Historical and Comparative Perspectives*, ed. Hugh Davis Graham and Ted Robert Gurr. 2d ed. Beverly Hills: Sage Publications.

Soman, Alfred. 1980. "Deviance and Criminal Justice in Western Europe, 1300–1800: An Essay in Structure," *Criminal Justice History: An International Annual* 1:1–28.

Stanciu, V. V. 1968. *La Criminalité à Paris*. Paris: Centre National de la Recherche Scientifique.

Sutherland, E. H. 1925. "Murder and the Death Penalty," *Journal of the American Institute of Criminal Law and Criminology* 15:522–29.

Sutherland, E. H., and C. E. Gehlke. 1933. "Crime and Punishment." In *Recent Social Trends in the United States*, Report of the President's Research Committee on Social Trends. New York: McGraw-Hill.

Thomas, Dorothy Swaine. 1925. *Social Aspects of the Business Cycle*. New York: E. P. Dutton.

Thorner, Thomas. 1979. "The Incidence of Crime in Southern Alberta, 1878–1905." In *Law and Society in Canada in Historical Perspective*, ed. D. J. Bercuson and L. A. Knafla. Calgary: University of Calgary.

Tilly, Charles, Allan Levett, A. Q. Lodhi, and Frank Munger. n.d. [ca. 1974]. "How Policing Affected the Visibility of Crime in Nineteenth-Century Europe and America." Unpublished paper.

Warner, Sam Bass. 1934. *Crime and Criminal Statistics in Boston*. Cambridge, Mass.: Harvard University Press.

Watts, Reginald E. 1931. "The Influence of Population Density on Crime," *Journal of the American Statistical Association* 26:11–20.

Willbach, Harry. 1938. "The Trend of Crime in New York City," *Journal of Criminal Law and Criminology* 29:62–75.

———. 1941. "The Trend of Crime in Chicago," *Journal of Criminal Law and Criminology* 31:720–27.

Wolfgang, Marvin E. 1958. *Patterns in Criminal Homicide*. Oxford: Oxford University Press.

Zahn, Margaret A. 1980. "Homicide in the Twentieth Century United States." In *History and Crime: Implications for Criminal Justice Policy*, ed. James A. Inciardi and Charles E. Faupel. Beverly Hills: Sage Publications.

Zehr, Howard. 1975. "The Modernization of Crime in Germany and France, 1830–1913," *Journal of Social History* 8:117–41.

———. 1976. *Crime and the Development of Modern Society: Patterns of Criminality in Nineteenth Century Germany and France*. Totowa, N.J.: Rowan and Littlefield.

Zimring, Franklin E. 1979. "American Youth Violence: Issues and Trends," *Crime and Justice* 1:67–108.

ADDENDUM

After this essay was in proof an exhaustive new study of Australian crime trends came to my attention: Satyanshu K. Mukherjee, *Crime Trends in Twentieth Century Australia* (Sydney: Allen and Unwin, forthcoming in 1981). Using newly compiled data on cases charged before magistrates' courts, the charging rates of various offenses are traced nationally and for each of six states. Offenses against persons, consisting mainly of petty assaults, show a distinctive U or dish-shaped curve from 1900 to 1976, nationally and in most states. The national rate declined from ca. 300 offenses charged per 100,000 population aged 10 years and over at the beginning of the century to a low of ca. 110 in the late 1930s, followed by an increase to ca. 300 again in the mid-1970s. Separate analyses for assaults and rape show the same general reversing trend. Homicides trace a less pronounced, more irregular trend whose increase since the 1950s is due at least in part to automotive manslaughters. Robberies charged had no clear trend until the 1960s, when they began a threefold increase. Time-series correlation analysis shows that offenses against persons in Australia tend to vary positively both with size of the police force (because of proactive policing?) and with economic productivity.